INTERSECTIONS

SUNY Series, The Margins of Literature
Mihai I. Spariosu, editor

INTERSECTIONS

Nineteenth-Century Philosophy and Contemporary Theory

Edited with a Critical Introduction by
Tilottama Rajan and David L. Clark

STATE UNIVERSITY OF NEW YORK PRESS

Published by
State University of New York Press, Albany

© 1995 State University of New York

For information, address the State University of New York Press,
State University Plaza, Albany, NY 12246

Production by Bernadine Dawes • Marketing by Fran Keneston

Library of Congress Cataloging-in-Publication Data

Intersections : nineteenth-century philosophy and contemporary theory
    / edited by Tilottama Rajan and David L. Clark.
        p.   cm. — (SUNY series, the margins of literature)
    Includes index.
    ISBN 0-7914-2257-7 (hdbk.) — ISBN 0-7914-2258-5 (pbk.)
    1. Philosophy, Modern—19th century. 2. Literature—Philosophy.
3. Criticism. I. Rajan, Tilottama. II. Clark, David L.
III. Series.
B803.I55   1995
190'.9'034—dc20   94-15204
                                                       CIP

Table of Contents

■ Acknowledgments

Our warm thanks go first to Stanley Corngold, who has generously supported this project from its inception. At State University of New York Press, we would especially like to thank Carola Sautter, whose faith in the merits of the book never wavered during its long gestation. We are also grateful to Bernadine Dawes, who expertly shepherded the book into print; to Phil Martin, who designed the book; to Wyatt Benner, who edited and typeset the manuscript; and to the readers for SUNY Press, from whom we received acute criticism. Our thanks also go to Stephen Barber, who helped prepare the book for publication.

Partial funding for this book has been provided by the Arts Research Board of McMaster University, the Social Sciences and Humanities Research Council of Canada, and the Smallman Fund at the University of Western Ontario.

For permission to reprint a chapter from Christopher Norris's *The Deconstructive Turn*, we are grateful to Routledge, Chapman & Hall, Ltd.

We are grateful to the Curt Marcus Gallery, New York, for permission to reproduce Mark Tansey's *Utopic* (1987; oil on canvas; 68 x 70 inches; private collection; © Mark Tansey).

Finally, we would like to thank our contributors, for whom this book provided the occasion for an extraordinarily wide-ranging and fruitful discussion about the theory and practice of philosophical history.

Introduction: Idealism and its Rem(a)inders

Tilottama Rajan and David L. Clark

I

Although there is now a long tradition of connecting current critical theory and nineteenth-century (especially romantic) literature, there is still relatively little sustained discussion of the relationship between contemporary and post-Enlightenment *theory*. This volume seeks to address that gap in the writing of intellectual history, and more generally to explore the reasons why it has come to exist in the first place. Certainly there are now studies (by Butler, Rajan, and Dews, among others)[1] that read figures from the past with and against certain contemporary counterparts, but these studies deal only with individual theorists or traditions and do not as yet construct "post-Enlightenment theory" as a discursive field in its own right. Moreover, revisionary discussions of these earlier writings frequently follow one of two patterns: they either examine them in relative isolation, or treat them teleologically as pre-texts for recent critical theory. Thus while Marshall Brown and Andrew Bowie[2] deal with earlier theory in ways that would have been impossible two decades ago, neither has as his principal aim the drawing of connections with the current theoretical scene. On the other hand, the works of Derrida and de Man (or of followers like Henry Sussman and Andrzej Warminski)[3] translate the thought of nineteenth-century philosophers—Nietzsche, Hegel, and, more recently, Schelling being the prominent examples—into terms that are largely those of contemporary theory.

The connection between recent theory and Nietzsche has been well developed, in no small part due to his wholesale appropriation by post-structuralism as its uncanny philosophical precursor. The nature and limits of that appropriation are the subject of Tilottama Rajan's essay in this volume. Current interpretations of Hegel and Schelling differ in that they exemplify the teleological revisioning of nineteenth-century philosophy through contemporary theory that characterizes practices of reading "against the grain." Hegel is treated as a systematizer whose philosophy of absolute knowledge is drawn vertiginously into problems that his system can neither contain nor evade, and that await the twentieth century for their fullest articulation. These problems include his theorization of desire, which, as reinterpreted by Kojève and Hyppolite in their discussions of the master-slave relationship in the *Phenomenology*, is widely recognized as seminal for Lacan. Likewise, recent deconstructive readings of Schelling recuperate him for contemporary theory by challenging the two roles that intellectual histories have attributed to him: either as the author of a comprehensive (if Protean) *Naturphilosophie* written in Hegel's shadow; or (as is certainly the case in the English-speaking world) as the philosophical source of the organicist aesthetic that underwrites an earlier phase in twentieth-century literary theory. But the essays collected in this volume do not simply use current critical models to colonize an earlier discourse. Rather we are interested in the *intersections* between two areas of theory, and with the ways in which each might cause us to reconsider the philosophical investments and discursive shape of the other.

The period that begins with the late eighteenth century is seminal in two ways. It not only marks a major site in the genealogy of "theory" as we now conceive it, but also initiates a rethinking of concepts like reading, influence, and tradition, and thus encourages theoretical intersections or "reframings" of one theory by another. Friedrich Schleiermacher, for instance, distinguishes between historical and divinatory readings of the intellectual tradition: that is, between a reading that treats a past text as a finished product, and one that is also concerned with its catalytic role in an ongoing process that requires an imaginative leap on the part of a reader to discern its direction. Godwin similarly opposes the "moral" or authorial intention of a text to its "tendency," characterizing the latter as the sum of the text's possible interpretations once it has been inserted into the discursive space of its present and future readers. These interpretive models[4] provide a justification for reconceiving nineteenth-century

philosophy in the light of the contemporary "theory" to whose development it has contributed. Nevertheless, one of the guiding assumptions of
this volume is that it would be misleading merely to superimpose the
distinctions by which theory is presently constituted—for instance, the
distinction between phenomenology and deconstruction—onto post-
Enlightenment theoretical discourse. Thus some of the essays included
here (those by Bowie and Sallis, for instance) define an "intersection"
between present and past in which difference is as important as connection. But several contributors explore relationships of a more intertextual
nature. They are interested not simply in how an earlier theorist might
differ from or might provide an "embryonic" version of a later approach,
but also in how the present might be reread through a past that remains
its condition of possibility.

Such reading, we need hardly emphasize, does not presume a meta-
cultural synthesis of present and past. Nor does it imply a "return to the
romantic" through a corrective privileging of the earlier at the expense of
the later. Rather it creates a space in which we can continue to think
through issues that are sometimes closed off by the more unilinear analyses generated by models of "origin" and "influence" or of "intersection."
Thus an intertextual reading that explores the multiple lines of influence
or critical genealogies joining earlier theories to more than one contemporary approach can lead us to reconceive the relationships between
those approaches. The fact that Hegel has been an important (if contested)
presence in Marxist theory from Lukács to Althusser, combined with the
fact that he also develops a phenomenology of modes in the *Aesthetics*,
can lead us to ask whether phenomenology and cultural criticism are as
antithetical as they are often thought to be.[5] Moreover, in exploring how
positions that have now become hypostatized as schools intertwine in
the more fluid context of the past, we also have another aim. If conventional history of ideas criticism reads the present as developing from the
past, the practice of reading against the grain is no less committed to a
genetic logic, in that it makes contemporary theory the teleological
completion of nineteenth-century philosophy. We hope to complicate
and to contest this logic by supplementing these genetic models with
other ways of writing intellectual history. "Intertextuality" and "genealogy" are but two ways of rethinking intellectual history in such a way as
to qualify the more classical models of "continuity" and "revolution."

In refiguring the relationship between contemporary and post-
Enlightenment theory as intertextual *and* genetic, our intention is to

bring out ambivalences and complexities in both areas that might otherwise remain undiscussed. We begin with the assumption that what we presently call "theory," as opposed to criticism or *literary* theory, emerges at the end of the eighteenth century partly as a response to Kant. Kant decisively transforms philosophy into a philosophy of the subject, and recasts the metaphysical preoccupations of his age into a critique of the conditions of the possibility of knowledge. Refocusing the terms and object of philosophy in this way, Kant argues that mental categories are regulative rather than constitutive: an argument that points forward to the contemporary awareness of the purely constructed nature of reality. But the German philosopher remains in some respects pretheoretical inasmuch as he neither historicizes the categories nor places them in a context attuned to the relationship between the apprehension of knowledge and what we now term "language" or "writing." The tension, elided by Kant, between a sense of "reality" as constructed and a naturalizing emphasis on the knowing subject has powerful implications for the discursive shape of much of nineteenth-century philosophy, in which concepts like the subjective universal and absolute knowledge are exposed to the force of processes that are homologous to what is now called *écriture*. We can cite only two examples. For Hegel, history conceived as the medium of the disclosure of "Spirit" must negotiate with the emerging notion of a "language" of events. This negotiation is played out in the *Aesthetics* as a constant difference between "theme" and "execution," a deferral of the "Idea" by its outward "shape" or expression. Similarly, for Schopenhauer the will conceived as the psychological and biological subversion of consciousness puts under erasure the distinction between reason and the realm of material automatism. This distinction had made possible Kant's idealistic insistence on the assertion of mental categories against the world of necessity. Its deconstruction structurally anticipates the contemporary emphasis on the subversion of the subject by writing and the unconscious, even as Schopenhauer's resistance to this deconstruction intimates a survival of idealism that is not without its ramifications for contemporary theory.

The discourses that result from these conflicting pressures have several implications for unpacking the relationship of post-Enlightenment to twentieth-century theory. Very briefly, we suggest that the two areas may be most similar at the points at which they seem most unlike. With the notable exceptions of Nietzsche and perhaps Kierkegaard, post-Kantian philosophers seem to want to protect metaphysics from semiotics and psychology, but find ultimately that they are unable or unwilling to sustain this discrimination. Current theory serves to bring out that self-division both by separating out from the nineteenth century that which resembles or portends the twentieth, and by mounting a massive critique of the idealistic assumptions of its earlier counterpart. Indeed, contemporary theory could be said to have been constituted by a rigorous turn *away* from what it has characterized as the unreflective principles of nineteenth-century philosophy, especially German idealist thought. The materialist objectives of structuralism and, to a certain extent, poststructuralism displace the totalizing nineteenth-century attempts at developing what Schelling called "a system of transcendental idealism." After Nietzsche, the subject conceived as a tissue of conflicting forces permanently supplants Hegel's dream of a purely transparent self-consciousness. Affirmations of absolute knowledge give way to the negative knowledge of the mind's derealization by figure. Yet the implicit historiographical notion that philosophical thought has thus moved from idealism to irony and from a philosophy of the subject to a philosophy of language should probably be recognized as a hermeneutical construction designed to authenticate the sophistication and originality of contemporary thought. Our contention is that by positioning itself as the demystified aftermath of the nineteenth century, current theory may simply have suppressed its covert connections to the philosophies it is said to supersede. Each period may, in fact, be the other's uncanny double.

To begin with, there is a curious resemblance between the encyclopedic claims of both periods. Post-Kantian theory is overtly encyclopedic in attempting to totalize knowledge by encompassing areas as diverse as history, mythology, and aesthetics, not to mention precursive versions of psychoanalysis and semiotics. At the same time its inclusion of these various discourses means that it is constantly "reframing" and rereading itself. Indeed, it is the way in which Hegel's *Logic* is reframed by his *Aesthetics*, and the way in which metaphysics for Schopenhauer is contaminated by psychology, that leads us to describe the period in question as one in which philosophy gives way to "theory."

On the other hand, contemporary theory, with its replacement of Boeckh's encyclopedia by Foucault's archive, would seem to question all attempts at totalization. Yet despite an interdisciplinarity in which discourses are used to reframe each other, recent theory seems to make semiotics into a Saussurean *langue* that underlies and unifies the various disciplinary formations. Correspondingly, its confident pronouncements about the death of the subject and the end of history may well reinscribe the absolute subject of nineteenth-century theory as the "heroically" meta-critical subject of the twentieth. Our project of rereading current theory through its covert links to an ambivalently idealistic past that it seeks to displace may thus have as a final consequence the exploration of how theory is involved in what Paul de Man calls "the resistance to theory." If post-Kantian thought resists the reflexiveness of being "theoretical," its encyclopedic claims are resisted by its own heteroglossia. On the other hand, if contemporary theory has such reflexiveness as its starting point, its totalizing pretensions (as Lacoue-Labarthe and Nancy have pointed out)[6] mark its own complicity in the resistance to theory. In recovering the philosophical idealism that contemporary theory rejects, but that is nevertheless dialogically present within it, we can begin to articulate both the desires and the evasions that inhabit that resistance.

II

BETWEEN IDEALISM AND DECONSTRUCTION

The essays in this volume are concerned with connections between specific philosophers or theories. The fact that earlier thinkers regularly surface as "figures" in the work of recent theory—Kant and Nietzsche in Deleuze, Schelling in Benjamin, Rousseau in de Man, to name only a few—represents the most obvious sign of the importance of these connections in the history of ideas from Kant to the present day. The essays forming the first section of this book demonstrate that these connections are also worth investigating in the context of larger issues, such as the limits and pretensions of contemporary theory, and the (in)compatibility (or, as Arkady Plotnitsky puts it, the "complementarity") of idealism and deconstruction. Understood from this somewhat broader perspective—which is really the *intersection* of two perspectives—the idealistic remainder within deconstruction becomes as significant as the deconstructive pressures that trouble idealism. If "deconstruction"—read as a figure for the rupture with classical rationalism—brings out "the hidden articulations and fragmentations"[7] inhabiting nineteenth-century philosophy, the same philosophy is capable of casting a light on structurally homologous divisions within contemporary theory, now seen as equivocally—rather than fearlessly— committed to pursuing the end of the logocentric epoch. In other words, the "space" between idealism and deconstruction is not only *historical*, marking the dialectically evolving and revisionary path of thinking joining the nineteenth to the twentieth century, but also *conceptual* and *discursive*, an interior distance that displaces idealism and deconstruction respectively from themselves.

Here we might recall Barbara Johnson's useful deconstructive axiom: "[T]he differences *between* entities . . . are . . . based on a repression of differences *within* entities, ways in which an entity differs from itself."[8] For the purposes of this volume, the task of mapping the crossings and self-displacements of idealism and deconstruction begins by recognizing that the movement from Kant to Kierkegaard marks the process in which "philosophy" unfolds into "theory." For it is Kierkegaard who, in his self-conscious use of both "aesthetic" and "religious" discourses as ways of reframing each other, most explicitly exemplifies our sense of what distinguishes "theory" from other forms of abstract discourse. Appropriately, he is the figure with which this volume begins. As Christopher Norris's essay on Kierkegaard and de Man suggests, Kierkegaard's entire pseudonymous production, with its shifting narrative strategies and voices, deconstitutes itself at every turn, as if to anticipate any "deconstructive" reading that contemporary readers might bring to it. But this process of self-transgression has a limit: as Norris points out, the ultimate goal of Kierkegaard's quasi-fictional writings is to force an ethical decision on the part of the reader to turn from the vain graces of the aesthetic to the religious order of experience. Kierkegaard represents himself as exemplary in this regard, but it is there, in those representations, that Norris discerns displacements of sense that Kierkegaard can neither evade nor control. On the one hand, Kierkegaard assumes a panoptic mastery over his life, retrospectively describing it in *The Point of View for My Work as an Author* as always already anchored in a spiritual inwardness and knowledge. Norris maintains that Kierkegaard is Nietzschean insofar as he derides Hegel's faith in system, but remains in the shadow of idealism for continuing to treat ethical truths as available to the properly disciplined thinker. On the other hand, Kierkegaard openly concedes that he is a "reader" of his own texts, and thus fully exposed to their rhetorical effects, duplicitous ironies, and conflicting points of view. Norris analyzes how Kierkegaard's textual strategies of repetition and reduplication threaten his presumed mastery over their ethical intent. For example, Kierkegaard finds that he must rely on the support of illustrative metaphors at the precise moment that rhetorical indirection is decreed to be an impediment in the path of "true seriousness." Nowhere is the trouble-some work of the supplement of figurality more evident, not to say more overdetermined, than in the case of the metaphor of "woman": as Norris brings out, the "material" presence of Kierkegaard's abandoned fiancée, Regine Olsen, returns to de-idealize the contrived reconstructions of his "ethical" treatment of her. Under the critical pressure of Norris's herme-neutics of suspicion, Kierkegaard's apologetic discourse shades indeter-minately into fiction, as if the exhibitionist pleasures of excusing himself had contaminated his confessional desire simply to "come clean."

The intelligibility of Kierkegaard's project rests to a large degree on maintaining the distinction between the "aesthetic" and the "religious" orders of experience, yet this distinction proves almost impossible to maintain. Texts like *The Point of View for My Work as an Author* may well be cleft by what Norris calls—citing de Man—"the radical estrangement between the meaning and the performance of any text,"[9] but what is more compelling is that they do not therefore unravel into a mobile army of metaphors: notwithstanding the "self-deconstructive" pressures within Kierkegaard's work, Norris concludes his essay by observing that he remains "the strongest, most resourceful challenge to" the "powers of textual demystification." In other words, Kierkegaard demonstrates that "the end of the [philosophical/theological] book" is not the same thing as "the beginning of writing."[10] This strategic refusal has complex implica-tions for how we understand what Norris calls "the belated encounter" between Kierkegaard and de Man, idealism and deconstruction, for Kierke-gaard remains one of the nineteenth century's most vivid examples of how the rigorous questioning of metaphysics can be conducted without necessarily adopting the "discontinuous and irruptive" strategies that Derrida identifies with Nietzschean deconstruction. Rather, as Tilottama Rajan has also argued, Kierkegaard performs his critique from *within* a discernible hermeneutical tradition that it expands and challenges to the very limit.[11] Kierkegaard's pseudonymous works frankly announce the death of the *author*, but precisely in order to reclaim a productive—if unavoidably unstable—place for the *reader*, whose negotiation with the text is unpredictable to the precise degree that it is made in earnest of apprehending meaningfulness of some kind—of making interpretive *choices*. Whether these choices have the sanction of a providential au-thority is precisely the challenge of "hermeneutic faith"—as Norris aptly puts it—that Kierkegaard's writings frankly put to their readers. His "ethics of reading" therefore stands in direct contradiction to thinkers like de Man, for whom no god is available to rescue us from our ironies. In Norris's hands, Kierkegaard is complexly ethical—self-subverting to be sure—yet capable of marshaling a moral idealism whose tenacity is all the more resourceful in the face of that subversion.

Beyond Norris's essay, we might observe that Kierkegaard illuminates how de Man's work is itself preoccupied with the question of ethics, even if the locus of this concern has been transposed—in theory—from the realm of the subject to that of language. J. Hillis Miller has in fact argued that far from being "nihilistic" and "irresponsible," de Man's later work is everywhere ethically motivated, insisting as it does that readers "*must* take responsibility for [their readings] and for [the] consequences [of their readings] in the personal, social, and political world."[12] Kierkegaard could not help but agree. De Man would of course further contend that any "ethics of reading" is a structural effect of language rather than something willed by the "existential" subject; yet it is curious to note that Miller's own reading of de Man, although scrupulously observant of de Man's strict renunciation of the subject, remains residually "humanistic" in tone and rhetoric: even in Miller's hands, a mild "hermeneutic faith" springs up to haunt the barren heath of de Man's posthumanist project.[13] Under what circumstances, we might then ask, would reading *not* invoke not only the expectation of readability but also the possibility of an interpreting subject capable of making interpretive decisions? Reading Kierkegaard *after* de Man, "hermeneutic faith" can only be an expression of a deeply rooted aesthetic ideology that erroneously promises a truth beyond the unreliability of signs. But Miller's meliorism suggests that we might just as productively read de Man through Kierkegaard. From this reversed perspective, the "inhuman" imperatives and "radical estrangements" that de Man attributes to language are displaced figures for an irreducibly humanistic and existential predicament, the predicament of the reader reading.

In Hegel, Kierkegaard thought he saw the worst implications of German idealism, especially its reduction of existence to the bloodless logic of necessity. Hegel "was in the German sense a professor of philosophy on a large scale," Kierkegaard wryly remarks in *The Concept of Anxiety*, "because he at any price must explain all things."[14] As an extravagant figure of totalizing understanding against which Kierkegaard pits the perilous life of the wayfaring Christian, "Hegel" serves Kierkegaard's purposes all too well; but his is not the only, nor even the most complex, negotiation with the great "professor" that the nineteenth century witnessed, and that our own age continues to witness. It is therefore no accident that Hegel is discussed by five contributors to this volume, and that in the process he too gets placed on both sides of the great divide between idealism and its deconstruction. If one were to attempt a psychotropology of the narratives used to construct and empower the current theoretical canon, Nietzsche would emerge as the "figure" most crucial to the self-legitimation of a contemporary theory that paradoxically craves a historical foundation for a variety of antifoundationalisms from Derrida and de Man to Deleuze and Foucault. Schelling would function more straightforwardly: as a philosopher once linked to Coleridge and now reread through Derrida, he serves as a paradigm for a relegitimation of the romantic that thereby recontains it within the contemporary. Hegel, however, focuses for us the highly overdetermined nature of the transition from past to present. If he is represented as a classical and totalizing thinker, there remain in his corpus areas that exceed that representation. Why one should wish to repress these intellectual surpluses (or to claim that Hegel repressed them), so as to write the past into a position of naïveté becomes a legitimate question. Alternatively, one can speculate that Hegel conceived of completion as an excuse to think its romantic deferral. But why one should wish to privilege only the subversive elements in Hegel then becomes an equally valid question. Reflecting on Hegel, but doing so reflexively, raises the symmetrical issue of whether we now theorize deferral precisely in order to think totality in the mode of nostalgia.

Hegel's position as a figure for the openings created by the very closure of theory's past is the subject of John Sallis's essay on the role of mimesis in the (re)thinking of metaphysics. Mimesis is inevitably implicated in the question of metaphysics because it is concerned with the relation between image and original, and more particularly because the concept itself is the site of a slippage between the image as a disclosure of truth and the image as the absence of the original. Indeed this slippage, this difference between image and original, is the very condition for thinking the concept of imitation, which therefore turns out to have been from the beginning a folding in of Platonic mimesis and Derridean representation towards each other. Focusing on this slippage, Sallis traces two "axiomatics" unstably at work within the concept of mimesis: the positive power of the image to bring truth to presence and thus to complete metaphysics (by bringing it to its end or completion), and a negative value deriving from the inability of the copy to be its original, so that art as the image or phantasm of truth is also the end (or undoing) of the metaphysical project. By thinking both values together, Hegel, he argues, surmounts the apparent polysemy of this end "in the direction of unity."

By emphasizing that the tension between art as a completion of metaphysics and as its impossibility is paradoxically (re)covered in the notion of an "end," Sallis reads Hegel as bringing to an end (or completion) the metaphysical tradition that begins with Plato. Pointing briefly to what is opened up by the Hegelian closure, Sallis nevertheless implies a narrative in which we move "beyond" Hegel to the rethinking of art by Nietzsche and Heidegger. It is possible, however, to position Hegel somewhat differently on the border we have been tracing, by reading the end of the *Aesthetics* not as *Aufhebung* but as overdetermination. The telescoping of two radically different "axiomatics" into one signifier would then figure the difficulty of choosing between idealism and its deconstruction. This difficulty, which is not an obstacle (as in Derrida) but an opening, also opens up the overdetermination of the contemporary scene by a different but equally powerful double axiomatic. The intellectual economies of idealism and poststructuralism, in the term employed by Arkady Plotnitsky, become complementary rather than contradictory: each one functions as the unconscious of the other.

If Sallis's essay closes by opening onto a space between idealism and deconstruction, that space is precisely the subject of the essays by Rajan and Clark. Clark's paper traces the conflicting strata of awareness and self-contesting rhetoric characterizing Friedrich Schelling's last major published work, *Philosophical Inquiries into the Nature of Human Freedom*. The *Freedom* essay marks an ambivalently signaled turn for its author, after which he will harshly criticize Hegelian philosophy, including his own Hegelianism, for confining itself only to questions of form, essence, and idea. Anticipating Kierkegaard, Schelling insists instead on considering reality more complexly as "existence," as the encounter with the irreducible there-ness of things, even evil and accidental things. The paradox is that precisely this turn to a *positive* philosophy—as he eventually characterized it—leads him to confront the complicity of existence with all forms of the inconceivable and the unforeseen, with chance, contingency, and irrationality: in short, to facing that which resists and *negates* performatively all pretensions to systematic—not to say idealistic—thought.

Ironically, as Clark points out, Schelling addresses the pervasiveness of the irrational (or of the other-than-rational), while at the same time seeking to establish a *rational* ground for human freedom. Simply put, human freedom is real—uncaptured by necessity—because it has its origin in a more primordial act of freedom, namely God's self-originating struggle to become a determinate being out of his darkly elemental ground. For Schelling, as for Jacob Böhme (to whom he silently adverts at crucial moments in the essay), humankind's difference from God, and thus its exposure to the contingent, reproduces God's primordial difference from himself. As Clark observes, the fact that the origin is characterized by a root duplicity leads Schelling to a deeper and a more troubling question: how is that the "light" and the "dark," God's freedom and his necessity, can come to be opposed *in the first place?* To think the infrastructure of the origin, Schelling evokes Böhme's obscure notion of the *Ungrund* or non-ground, not to abandon rationality for mysticism but to reframe his own idealistic discourse in order to obtain an "ir-rational" point of leverage on the negative foundations of the Absolute.

The sudden influx of an apophatic rhetoric—more usually associated with negative theology—into Schelling's otherwise scrupulously dialectical thinking opens up two radically opposed possibilities for this "tropic of negativity."[15] Like the Platonic *khora*, as Derrida describes it in his account of the intersections between deconstruction and negative theology, the *Ungrund* is "immediately" and inevitably subject to onto-theological appropriation: the *beyond*-being of the *Ungrund* translates into a *being*-beyond, which is partly what happens in Heidegger's lectures on the *Freedom* essay.[16] On the other hand, the *Ungrund* augurs a wholly Other "place," though one about which Derrida would say "nothing, or almost nothing, can be said."[17] For Schelling, the *Ungrund* is closely related to a "Longing," co-original with the "Word" or "*Logos*" of that longing: following Schelling's own linguistic philosophemes, Clark argues that the *Ungrund* is comparable to the *saying* of that which is said by God, a pure linguistic act or archperformative, utterly meaningless in itself. Contemporary articulations of Schelling's *Ungrund* would thus include quasi-transcendentals like Derrida's *différance* and de Man's concept of the "positional power of language," which is to say, the blank, insignificant or in-determinate opening of signification. Where God "starts," he can—before deflecting attention from this beginning—be understood as an act of positing, linguistic positing. This archperformative is not derived; it is a sudden, catachrestic imposition whose senselessness *marks*—de Man will say *disfigures*—in advance all subsequent figurations and representations .

For the Word to be spoken, it must be possible to speak. Here language, or, at least, the trace of language, "has started without us, in us, and before us." "This," Derrida writes, "is what theology calls God."[18] For Schelling, similarly, the opening of the Word occurs, and the Word means, but no dialectical power will ever enable us to hear this Word occurring or to comprehend its emergence from the radical nothingness of the *Ungrund*, since by becoming audible the Word performs the erasure of its having taken place. This root quality of "thrownness" or of "not Being-the-basis-for-itself" Manfred Frank usefully identifies with "post-Hegelian philosophy in its entirety," and it marks a point of intersection between neostructuralism and German idealism's self-critique in the texts of Fichte, Schleiermacher, and, of course, Schelling.[19] Schelling's self-contested idealism might well be used as a way to bring out the *differences* between de Man's and Derrida's treatment of the asymmetrical and aporetic structure that binds and promises us to the trace. Derrida readily concedes that the trace is "radically non-human and atheological," and that even to say that it "gives something" already "too vividly announces or recalls the dispensation of God, of man, or even that of the Being of which certain texts by Heidegger speak."[20] Yet Derrida would seem much closer to Heidegger insofar as he insists that the inescapable tardiness of the subject vis-à-vis language "presents no limit to its freedom." If the existent cannot come "back behind its own thrownness," as Frank points out, this does not mean that "it is not the basis for the possibilities through which it relates to its thrownness and to its future."[21] De Man also evokes the fundamentally nonhuman character of language whose in-determinate nature forces us to read—which is to say, to seek *shelter from self-erasure* within the humane space of legible language. Yet the self's not-Being-the-basis-for-itself is felt to be somewhat different than in Derrida: like Wordsworth's mountain climbers in the *Prelude*, the knowledge of the subject's structural anachronism is not only always in arrears vis-à-vis the inhuman event of language, as it is in Derrida, but, more important, it is consistently *felt* or luridly described as a rectification, a reproach, or, as is often the case, as the threat of extinction and dismemberment at the hands of the monstrous.

For both Derrida and de Man, it could be argued, the theoretical task turns on the difficulty of thinking the "play" of language as something truly serious and in any case inevitable in a genuinely historical, future-oriented way. Yet human freedom as the contingent exposure to this absolute risk remains figured in revealingly divergent terms. Whereas

Derrida positively affirms *différance* for its liberatory power to unsettle the metaphysics of presence, de Man attends to the formal materiality of the sign, stressing the hidden threat that its radical senselessness inescapably poses for reading and for cognition. For Derrida, as Spivak points out, the trace figures the "lure of the abyss as freedom."[22] Thus when he calls for a "rediscovery of the trace, still unique, in . . . other languages, bodies, negativities,"[23] there is a sense that German idealism's operative distinction between necessity and freedom has been strangely repeated in contemporary theory in terms of an opposition between the abiding closure of Western metaphysics and the thinker who claims to possess the freedom to make it tremble: for Schelling, as for Derrida, philosophical speculation is itself taken to be an exemplary performance of this freedom. Whether or to what degree the same could be said for de Man is unclear, since for him inquiries into the nature of human freedom more consistently point to the subject's entrapment in the determined indeterminacy of a "language machine" that demands meaningfulness to the precise extent that it exposes "the exigent contingency"[24] of its functioning. Knowledge of this madness does not make you sane, de Man suggests, since in disfiguring the figuration *whose error we are* only reinscribes the same error. If this vertiginous spiral is the mark and movement of human freedom, it has attached to it a mood of absurdity that is overstated in de Man even as it is understated in Derrida.

Whereas Clark's essay uses Schelling to articulate an overlap between de Man and Derrida, Tilottama Rajan's essay attempts an intertextual reading of deconstruction through Nietzsche, who provides an "origin" both for the poststructuralism of de Man and the very different "semiotic materialism" of Kristeva. In doing so, Rajan presses for a new philosophical history of post-Enlightenment thought that would disentangle "deconstruction" from a "poststructuralism" committed to an almost ascetic emphasis on language. As she has argued elsewhere, "[T]he existence of nineteenth-century ancestors for deconstruction reminds us that poststructuralism is simply one form taken by the deconstructive impulse, and that deconstruction itself is a historically more extensive movement: one that may still be in the process of evolving."[25] Among those ancestors, arguably no one is more significant than Nietzsche, whose critique of being and representation seems to lay the basis for recent theory's dismantling of the metaphysics of presence. But the critical power that contemporary theory has invested in Nietzsche is partly the result of a certain *Nachträglichkeit:* as Rajan points out, "Nietzsche" is to some extent a figure that Derrida and de Man have constructed, a nineteenth-century mirror in which they (re)cognize recent theory's "newest insights" as "those we always already possessed." As such, this recognition is also necessarily a *mis*recognition, whose "asymmetrical" features Rajan brings out by exploring the ways in which Nietzsche's work resists rather than simply prefigures and facilitates the work of poststructuralism. Thus while Derrida locates *différance* in the nonmaterial processes of "writing" and the "trace," Nietzsche finds it in music, and then, more complexly, in the body, which he treats as a figure for a heterogeneity in excess of linguistic or conceptual representation.

The differences between Nietzschean deconstruction and its poststructuralist legacy bring out analogous divergences *within* that legacy. Returning to Nietzsche as a way of distinguishing Kristeva from Derrida and Lacan, Rajan suggests that he provides a pre-text for Kristeva's work by locating *différance* in the organic and nonlinguistic media of music and the body, while disaffiliating these figures from any association with unity and presence. Crucial to both Nietzsche and Kristeva is the permeability of the bounded ego, constructed within the Apollonian order of the Symbolic, to the inchoate play of differences generated within the Dionysian chorus: a space analogous to Kristeva's semiotic *chora*, which Nietzsche represents through figures linked less to language than to mat(t)er. As important is the centrality accorded to art in a theoretical discourse that is not so much aestheticist as, in David Carroll's words, "paraesthetic." Rajan's contribution, however, is not just a tracing of Nietzsche's "influence" on Kristeva. Rather this influence causes us to rethink the relationship that exists in contemporary theory between deconstruction and a phenomenology seen as part of the idealist succession. Where Derrida has made the opposition between these two discourses virtually canonical, Kristeva's intersection with Nietzsche becomes a space in which we can explore their possible complementarity. Complementarity, however, should not become a way of totalizing the differing conceptual investments of these discourses. Moving beyond Rajan's essay, which deals only with their theoretical symbiosis in *Revolution in Poetic Language,* we can suggest that Kristeva's later work constitutes a nontotalizable practice in which the reader can experience (in the gaps between philosophy, art, and psychoanalysis) the ways in which the theoretical drives of deconstruction and phenomenology differ from and defer each other.

As Rajan demonstrates, Nietzsche's presence in the texts of Kristeva must also cause us to rethink contemporary theory's curiously Hegelian promotion of a linguistic absolute. For the semiotic, linked as it is to nontextual categories like "body" and "voice," is a sub-version of Derridean *écriture* that compels poststructuralism to reflect upon its own absent body. The figure of the body reinscribes a concern with the subject, though the body—for both Nietzsche and Kristeva—is the site of the subject's (dis)embodiment rather than of a naïve, prereflective immediacy. In other words, the notion of a semiotic materialism allows Kristeva to locate the infrastructure of *différance* in the experience of the subject-in-process, an experience that poststructuralism had elided in opposing itself to phenomenological thinking. Recovering a phenomenological resistance to poststructuralist theory, then, Kristeva's work throws into relief the ways in which this critical elision is never complete: for instance, the "body" stubbornly remains in de Man's anxiously visceral rhetoric of "disfiguration" and "defacement," haunting his "ultra textualism"[26] much as de Man himself says Shelley's corpse haunts romantic criticism.

RETHINKING THE SUBJECT

Among the most influential paragraphs of *The Phenomenology of Spirit,* those describing the dialectic of master and slave stand out, not only for arguing that the subject's true liberation lies in suffering the vicissitudes of servitude, but also for placing work at the center of self-realization. As Charles Taylor has suggested, however, Marxist appropriations of the "Lordship and Bondage" section of Hegel's text have tended to ignore "the role of the fear of death" in the emergence of the subject at the conclusion of this section and in the subsequent account of the "unhappy consciousness."[27] Judith Butler's essay returns us to this evocative transition in Hegel's text, rereading it not positively as a phenomenology of spirit, but critically as a genealogy of morals in which the subject shelters itself from existential dread through the reflexive application of ethical principles and religious ideals.

Butler's account of the salient features of this "logic of subjection" is worth briefly rehearsing here. As Hegel describes them at the end of his discussion of lordship and bondage, the origins of the unhappy consciousness lie in what he calls sheer "stubbornness" *[Eigensinnigkeit],* the slave's blind attachment to itself as it recoils defensively from the threat of annihilation at the hands of the "Absolute Master," namely death. From this flinching and self-preserving *reflex*, as it were, the first glimmerings of reflexivity in the servile consciousness are born, and the difficult path toward authentic freedom begun. Through a kind of psychic mitosis, the "subject" anxiously divides from itself, or, more precisely, emerges as the phantasmic effect of this splitting: the self simultaneously denies death and fearfully stakes its claim to "freedom" from physical negation by becoming lord and master over that which seems most mortal about itself—the body. If the slave's coming-into-awareness of his determinate thingness is the inaugural moment of his liberation from his master, however, it is also his initiation into increasingly subtle strategies of self-enslavement predicated on the refusal of bodily life. Kojève's evocative term for these strategies of subjection is "slave ideologies":[28] read from Butler's Foucauldian perspective, these "ideologies" in effect describe the simultaneous creation and regulation of the subject through successive (self-)disciplinary regimes.

Perhaps it is no accident, therefore, that Sir James Baillie translates Hegel's term for the formative influence that a culture has on the production of the subject—i.e., *Bildung*—as "the *discipline of culture*" (emphasis ours).[29] Paradoxically, as Butler observes, the particular discipline of the renunciation of bodily experience serves only to mark the irreducibility of that subject's connection to the body it renounces. The subject's freedom is thereby constrained by the very process by which that freedom is achieved: to put it another way, there is no overcoming the subject's resistance to itself, because the subject is itself this resistance. Butler demonstrates, however, that Hegel avoids the most radical implications of his critique of the subject's (dis)embodiment, and treats the section on the unhappy consciousness not as a deconstruction of the self but as a transitional moment in the movement from insufficiently rational forms of self-consciousness towards the rule of Reason and true autonomy. Powerful in its insistence that the subject cannot fully renounce life *while it remains within life,* Hegel's text nevertheless finds itself practically pursuing the fleshless freedom of Reason that it has had to renounce theoretically. The disruptive significance of Hegel's work thus awaits both Nietzsche's critique of the origins of Christian virtue and the will-to-nothingness in ressentiment, and Freud's retheorization of the logic of subjection in terms of the psyche's libidinal economy. Butler describes how the unhappy consciousness's uncontrolled attachment to the bodily life that it seeks to control strikingly prefigures Freud's conclusion that the repression of libido is itself libidinally invested, and that the prohibition of desire is therefore also a displaced site of that desire's reassertion. (The abyssal nature of this self-perpetuating economy, in which the renunciation of desire becomes the object of desire, is a subject that Ned Lukacher addresses in his essay on the history of conscience in Freud and Nietzsche.)

In *The Phenomenology of Spirit*, the attachment of the subject to itself is originally *stubborn*, a minimal autonomy born of sheer wilfulness, as Hegel's pun on *Eigensinnigkeit* suggests. But what is for Hegel a tenacious impediment/stepping-stone to the realization of *full* self-consciousness is for Foucault the condition of the possibility of resistance. For Foucault, subjection not only produces desire, as Freud had argued, but also reproduces "bodies," vigorously multiplying the sites at which subjects may be formed and regulated. If Foucault's work can be said to contain any liberationist promise, Butler suggests, it lies in the crowded midst of this propagation of bodies, whose very unpredictability exposes regulatory regimes to (potential) disruption. Like a breeder reactor generating fissionable material, the carceral operates in a tense condition of barely controlled uncontrollability. Reading beyond Foucault, Butler speculates that this proliferation may be possible because of the very excess or surplus that troubled Hegel at the end of the "Lordship and Bondage" section, the stubborn desire to desire that, as desire, necessarily exceeds all possible disciplinary regimes because it forms their structural unconscious.

The irreducible and implicitly disruptive presence of the desiring body that underwrites the logic of subjection from Hegel to Foucault throws into relief the curious tendency of other contemporary theories (also written in the shadow of *The Phenomenology of Spirit*) that either refuse the body or reintroduce it in anxiously revealing ways. Paul de Man's early work, for example, affirms the ascetic denial of desire as the sign of authenticity, as Stanley Corngold's essay points out, while his later work, evoking as it does luridly threatening images of dismemberment, disfiguration, and self-erasure, negatively reinscribes the body as a visceral figure for cognition's absolute vulnerability to "the uncontrollable power of the letter as inscription."[30] Hegel's slave faced with the shattering recognition of his own potential destruction here prefigures de Man's "reader," always and everywhere exposed to the radically inhuman "materiality of language," "whose power, like the power of death, is due to the randomness of its occurrence."[31] Derridean poststructuralism could also be said suffer a certain disembodying tendency, replacing the putative materiality of lived experience with a highly attenuated world of traces of traces. Seen from the critical perspective that Hegel provides in "The Unhappy Consciousness," poststructuralism's claim that nothing lies outside of the text would then amount to the last expression of the slave ideology: as the triumph of a certain "intellectualism" (to cite a recent description by Drew Leder),[32] Saussurian characterizations of the sign as "both material thing and self transcending intention"[33] effectively renounce bodily experience by absorbing it into a deathless world of language.

Schelling's speculative work on knowledge's inability to grasp its own origin and on the irreducibility of the irrational leads him not only to recognize the intrinsic place of otherness within reality, but also, more consequently for the twentieth century, to affirm the subject's unsublatable indebtedness to that otherness. Heidegger, who declared that he found in Schelling "a new beginning" for philosophy,[34] will famously identify this obligation to the unhidden with the "call of conscience."[35] But what can conscientiousness mean in such a context? To what and in what way are we *ultimately* responsible? For Heidegger, conscience is strictly the concern of *Dasein*, at once near to hand but quite beyond the residual anthropomorphisms of the philosophical subject. For Nietzsche and Freud, on the other hand, the recognition of human obligation to an absolute Other, though Heideggerian in its implications, is more closely tied to a revaluation of conscience as it articulates the psychological subject. As Ned Lukacher argues in his essay on the history of conscience, Nietzsche and Freud conduct their projects in surprisingly similar ways: both attempt to write a history (or perhaps an archaeology) of the Judeo-Christian conscience and its secular derivations, de-idealizing human dutifulness by pointing to its instinctual origins; both imagine primal scenes, not unlike the one Butler discusses in Hegel, in which the subject's coming-into-consciousness coincides with its coming-into-conscientiousness under the force of moral law; and both seek to alleviate the ravages of "bad conscience" by reinventing the subject's relationship to the "interior" Other. Yet as Lukacher points out, the two projects do not remain entirely aligned: at the end of Freud's life, on the eve of European civilization's most horrendous abrogations of conscience, Freud will swerve from his otherwise "Nietzschean" critique of self-beratement by characterizing the momentous advent of Mosaic law not as the catastrophic error that violated the authentic "promise" of human being, but as the triumph of intellectuality over sensuality, culture over nature. At this overdetermined point of intersection between the two projects, Judaism functions like a *pharmakon*, for what is *poison* for Nietzsche must be, in the final (psycho)analysis, *cure* for Freud.

Notwithstanding this important difference, however, the two thinkers remain committed to the task of radically divesting consciousness of its self-certainty. In this regard, Gadamer is helpful: "The self that we are," he writes, "does not possess itself; one could say that it 'happens'."[36] *That* the subject "happens" at all, in addition to the anonymous logic of this strange "occurrence," is perhaps the deepest source of astonishment driving the work of Freud and Nietzsche. In probing the interminably peculiar fact that "spirit is the life that itself cuts into life,"[37] they evoke a deeper incision, one marking the trace of the inorganic other as it withdraws from life in order to set life on its perilous way. The critique of conscience, Lukacher argues, thereby becomes a means by which Nietzsche and Freud open the question of the fate of the subject out on to the largest possible vistas: Why is there life, much less "human" life and freedom, rather than endlessly recurring subjectless inorganicity? It is a question that absorbed German idealism before the "Freudo-Nietzschean" critique of the subject, even as it engaged Heidegger, and then Derrida after him. For Lukacher, these thinkers persistently summon us to the knowledge that human beings are ineluctably promised to and derivative of something Other than themselves, whether we call that Other "materiality," "the trace," "Being," "the unconscious," or "the will to power." Though this lifeless Other leaves barely anything of itself in life, it calls us to the same fundamental question: what is "our *ethos* or dwelling-place as human beings?"[38]

If Lukacher addresses the notion of conscience in a radicalized psychoanalytic and finally ontological context, showing how that context dictates the limits of the philosophy of the (rational) subject, Thomas Pfau approaches a similar problematic from a quite different perspective, one that points to the survival (or perhaps revival) of a certain Enlightenment commitment to providing a rational framework for human conduct. For him, the focus is not the subject's "not-Being-the-basis-for-itself" (i.e., its "thrownness"),[39] but the theoretical and historical links joining nineteenth-century reflection on the subject's ineluctably social, ethical life to more recent forms of cultural criticism, historicism, pragmatism, and contextualism. To borrow Jürgen Habermas's language, Pfau implies that "subject-centered reason" is not simply to be displaced by reason's Other(s), but reconceived as fundamentally "communicative" and discursive in nature.[40] Hegel's work is once again the conceptual benchmark against which contemporary theories are critically compared and assessed, especially insofar it summons these theories to reproblematize the question of moral agency. *The Phenomenology of Spirit* is of course centrally concerned with this question, though not everyone, including those favorably disposed to Hegel, has recognized that fact. Herbert Marcuse, for example, complains about the brevity of Hegel's treatment of morality, but must concede that "Hegel's moral philosophy is absorbed in his political philosophy. . . . [T]he submersion of ethics in politics conforms to his interpretation and valuation of civil society."[41] Pfau's essay focuses on the densely argued and highly suggestive paragraphs that Marcuse found to be disconcertingly undeveloped, emphasizing that it is there, precisely, that Hegel demonstrates how the social and the political unavoidably converge with the moral. Pfau points out that Hegel's reflection on the condition of the possibility of true *Sittlichkeit* goes beyond arguing that the recognition of the subject's moral integrity by others is fundamental to the existence of that subject as a moral being. Rather than adducing a morality claimed to exist as an innate substance within or beyond the subject, Hegel demonstrates that morality is "performed" in and by the communicative action of language itself. In other words, the subject comes into its ethical life at the exact moment that it makes a "declaration" *[Aussprechen]* of its conscientiousness in the public space that is articulated by language.

Hegel would seem here to anticipate Habermas, who resists contemporary theory's irrationalisms and logics of disintegration by asserting that "anyone acting communicatively must, in performing any speech action, raise universal validity claims and suppose that they can be vindicated."[42] Firmly rooted in the ideals of the Enlightenment, these "validity claims" would be perfectly recognizable to the author of *The Phenomenology of Spirit:* justice, rationality, social harmony, and the free pursuit of understanding and accord. For Pfau's purposes, however, J. L. Austin (to whose work Habermas has also had recourse) proves more immediately provocative: read through speech-act theory, Hegel's moral meaning is an illocutionary force, intelligible and socially efficient within a specifically linguistic context by activating, quoting, and reiterating features of that context. For moral "declaration" to function as a declaration, it must be recognizable as such by others; in other words, as a performance, this declaration cannot succeed without being "identifiable as *conforming* to an iterable model" and "identifiable therefore in a way as a citation."[43] Meaningful performances are therefore *structurally* predisposed towards a certain "propriety" and "responsibility," an archmorality, as it were, since their meaningfulness—their "uptake" by the "listener"— is entirely a matter of "successfully" or "unsuccessfully" *conforming* to the shifting social context in which they occur and have their sole being.

Pfau's essay thus evokes a kind of Hegelian-Austinian *Ereignis*, the eventful appropriation/constitution of the subject by its social context, whose shared language, precisely because it *is* shared, is the signal means by which individual speakers recognize in the other what they understand themselves to be. In this regard, Hegel and Austin provide a useful philosophical-linguistic framework for rereading Michael Oakeshott's neopragmatist work on the nature of "human conduct." As Oakeshott succinctly argues, the subject "comes to consciousness in a world illuminated by a moral practise and as a relatively helpless subject of it."[44] Reading relevant passages from *Of Human Conduct* against rather than with Hegel, however, Pfau reminds us that Oakeshott is not simply analyzing the languages of moral agency but deploying an ideologically restricted—and insufficiently reflective—conception of what comprises human conduct. For Pfau, Oakeshott's theorizing is characterized by a problem that is in fact constitutive of "Theory" as such, but never more vividly so than in theories that structure themselves around the notion of a reflection on the modes of cultural production—"the return to the particularities of history." But from *where*, and in *whose* present interests is this "return" to the past made? In making legible the sociolinguistic conditions in which historical phenomena occur, conditions that are assumed to be mostly illegible to those subjects who are the "immediate" effects of this production, contemporary cultural criticism inhabits an explicitly normative and ultimately "moral" stance vis-à-vis its critical object: the present felicitously accounts for the past's more or less infelicitous performances, proffering insight where once there was mostly blindness. As Pfau suggests, we have good reason to be suspicious of this historicism, not least for its sometimes barely palpable social efficiency. Alan Liu has argued more sharply that "high" postmodern cultural criticism "appropriates the world from the masses of the less articulate and literate. It is a statement of privilege."[45] Pfau's point is that in the wake of Hegel's *Sollenkritik*, "Theory" in general "performs" these sorts of regularizing exclusions, having come to embody "the infrastructure of a postmodern, dis-individuated morality."

In the final contribution to this section, Andrew Bowie approaches the problem of the subject from a somewhat different perspective. His concern is Adorno's critique of Hegel for an idealism that subordinates being to the concept, thus privileging the subject over the object. Like Peter Dews, who argues that Derrida's deconstruction of the subject is limited by his inability to think beyond a subject reflexively constituted in its relationship to an object, Bowie suggests that Adorno's correction of post-Kantian idealism is limited by his neglect of a "romantic position" far more complex than Hegel's notion of the absolute subject. Privileging the objective as a resistance to this absolute subject, a site of something indigestible in things, Adorno does no more than invert Hegel so as to perpetuate his assumption of a subject (de)constructed by its (non)identity with a confirming object. By contrast, Schelling speaks of a "thinking that carries on independently of the thinking that reflects upon it," and thus distinguishes a prereflective subject quite distinct from the self-present cogito, a being that cannot be grasped in reflection. If the cogito is aligned with Hegel's choice of philosophy as a means to the absolute, the prereflective subject is aligned with the Jena Circle's sense that the absolute can only be grasped allegorically through art, as a way of thinking that constantly defers itself. Moving beyond Bowie's triangulation of Adorno, Hegel and Schelling, we can speculate that this subject (so different from the one deconstructed by Derrida and de Man) is in fact the concern of the deconstructive phenomenology that emerges in the prewar work of Sartre and Blanchot and that recurs in Kristeva's category of the semiotic, as discussed in Rajan's essay.

REINSCRIBING HISTORY

Although we are now inclined to be skeptical about mapping one area onto another, it seems that we still find it useful to think in terms of metaphoric transfers between the question of the subject and that of history. Thus if post-Kantian idealism conceived history in anthropomorphic terms as the history of a (collective) subject, poststructuralism rethinks the cogito according to theories of history that make consciousness a process without a subject. The recurring affinity between models of the subject and models of history within each period suggest that more complex intersections in theories of the subject across periods will be repeated in a similar rethinking of the problem of history. Not only is the shape of history inextricable from the (de)construction of the subject. The relationship between nineteenth-century theory and contemporary theory also provides a unique space for unraveling the implications of this entanglement.

Arkady Plotnitsky's essay poses precisely this question of what constitutes "history" in the age of theory. For him, as for another contributor, Eric Meyer, this question is inseparable from a question about the place of Hegel in the history of ideas. Plotnitsky's Hegel remains a figure for a logocentric history whose differences are forgotten in the closure of what Georges Bataille calls a restricted economy. Without denying that the totalizing and teleological form of Hegel's phenomenologies (whether of spirit, history, or art) might be contradicted by excesses in their content, Plotnitsky nevertheless sees this heterogeneity as bracketed by a system that equates history with the history of *Geist* and thus with consciousness itself, conceived as (Absolute) Knowledge emancipated from its unconscious. Turning from Hegel to Nietzsche and Freud, he argues for a history more archaic than history: one that can be reached only by rethinking, through his radicalization of the concept of "memory," a "history" that remains traditional even in Freud. The relation between these two histories is therefore very different from the one envisioned in Jameson's *Political Unconscious*, which constructs an external rather than internal relation in which history as narrative is posited and tested against the limit it finds in the unconscious. In order to describe this relation, Plotnitsky employs Niels Bohr's term "complementarity," which he reads through Derrida so as to make clear that complementarity does not exist as such, but is apparent only as a network of textual effects. The complementarity between Hegelian history and the forgetting that is a condition of possibility for historical memory necessitates, in turn, a new kind of historical description that is written across the differences between the two registers of "knowledge" and the "unconscious." While such a project remains within the boundaries of philosophical rather than material history, it is a "philosophy" already contaminated by psychology. Such a contamination is similarly present in Nietzsche but not, curiously enough, in Foucault's still positivist concentration on the concept of genealogy rather than that of the will.

In the next essay, Eric Meyer uses Habermas's notion of a crisis of legitimation as a context to think through theories of history that are often seen as a prelude to the rise of imperialism in the nineteenth century. While Plotnitsky is concerned with the philosophy rather than the politics of "history," his Hegel is implicitly conservative. Meyer, by contrast, characterizes the tradition culminating in Hegel as a "speculative" rather than programmatic historicism, and thus locates it in the space between the modernity theorized by Habermas and a (post)modernity whose prefix marks its "aporetic relation" to a past that it "both climaxes and brings to a close." This complex relationship is evident first of all in the continued presence of Hegelian phenomenology at the very heart of what Meyer broadly terms postmodernism: an *episteme* that encompasses both poststructuralist theory and the artistic and cultural practices more narrowly referred to as "postmodern." Correcting and subl(im)ating Hegel's *grand récit*, postmodernism repeats the form if not the content of Hegel's vision in its own totalizing commitment to a decentered world of texts and simulacra. As importantly, its very emphasis on the absence of what Lukács calls "totality" functions as a phantasmic rem(a)inder of the romanticism that still constitutes its political unconscious.

The relationship between the postmodern and the nineteenth-century cultural text is, however, more complex than these remarks by themselves suggest. For Meyer reminds us that romantic historicism emerges in the aftermath of the French Revolution, as a response to an earlier legitimation crisis with which it remains in speculative dialogue. Reading Hegel through his Jena precursor's *Letters on Aesthetic Education*, Meyer suggests that the Hegelian narrative is best approached as a form of historical play. He thus restores to Hegelian historiography an awareness of figurality absent from more totalizing appropriations of the Hegelian system. In effect he sees the cultural narratives constructed by Schiller and Hegel not as descriptions of fact or impositions of desire, but as what Jameson calls "symbolic resolutions" that we can use heuristically in addressing the legitimation crisis. What is important in these narratives is therefore not their *parole* but their *langue* or grammar: a grammar of historical positions and possible structures that allow subjects to experiment with inserting themselves into the network of culture. Insofar as these structures, inverted and displaced, persist in contemporary theory, Hegel continues to have an important intertextual role in postmodern culture. It is a role that is both admonitory and enabling, warning us against the dangers of intellectual totalitarianism, but also providing us with a way of reinscribing Habermasian rationality as what Meyer calls "aesthetic rationality."

Like Meyer, Paul Hamilton questions the view that the romantics were precritical, and takes issue in this case with the claim that they were massively invested in a "romantic ideology." Instead, the self-critical shift we identify with Marxist and Althusserian conceptions of ideology is located by him as much earlier, as in the period after the Enlightenment. The three principal texts in his genealogy are the treatises on love by Destutt de Tracy and his younger friend Stendhal, and Sade's perversion of this tradition into a pornography whose scandalous intrusion into the history of ideas paves the way for the similarly excessive writings of Bataille. Tracy remains the figure par excellence for the Enlightenment: his theorizing of belief assumes a universalist (almost Kantian) sense of "ideology" as the study of invariant structures, and bases itself on assumptions about language developed by the Port Royal grammarians. Stendhal, by contrast, does not so much *tell* us as *show* us despite himself that ideologies are historically relative, immanently produced by their subject-matter, and linguistically constructed expressions of a society's imaginary relation to the real. Stendhal's text is not only a treatise on love but also a performance of "the power of love . . . to turn anything to its object." As we move from Tracy to Stendhal the theory of ideology is rewritten by its practice in such a way as to make the history of "ideology" itself an instance of Hamilton's contention that ideology after Tracy is immanent, (de)constructed in and by its practice. Sade would seem to complete the trajectory. Perversely parodying love, he demystifies his subject in a way that we might consider paradigmatic of ideological critique: by the reduction of superstructural idealisms to their base materiality. But Sade is also scandalously self-impugning. Stendhal's text defamiliarizes its romantic ideology, but Sade's text reveals the ways in which materialisms are also ideologies. Sade of course means to parody his own parody, but the barbarity of his writing calls in question a further ideology: that of an excess that makes critique seem as naïvely humanist as faith. Because Sade's offensiveness, despite itself, "keeps questionable the postmodern use of perversity as a trope for sophistication," he resensitizes us to the value of romantic ideologies. In other words, as they perform in Hamilton's argument, the figures of Stendhal and Sade complement each other so as to create a space in which the reader must rethink the relation between romanticism, materialism, and ideology.

The essays by Hamilton and Meyer are both unusual in challenging the assumption made by other contributors to this volume that the major site for theory before the twentieth century is philosophy. While Meyer's texts are philosophical, he sees them as continuous with a social or cultural text: a continuity signaled by his refusal to draw a line between poststructuralism and postmodernism. For his part, Hamilton conspicuously locates the "theory" of ideology not in Feuerbach or Marx, but in two writers who work on both sides of the border between fictional and nonfictional prose. This border allows Stendhal's ideology of love, for instance, to draw metonymically on the force of its performance (as both desire and critique) in Stendhal's novels. Clearly the questioning of the boundary between theory and literature is dependent precisely on drawing the boundary. But this questioning has at least two consequences that are worth unpacking for the project initiated by this volume. To begin with, artistic practices can be seen as genotextual or precursive manifestations of what theory later works out in a metalanguage. Secondly, the origins and functioning of theory as practice also challenge this subsequent claim to metalinguistic status. In other words, Hamilton's approach has the heuristic value of reminding us that theory, like the version of ideology he describes, is an immanent rather than a transcendental analytic.

THE END(S) OF THEORY

Questions about the boundaries and thus the nature of "theory" are explicitly taken up in the last section of this volume. These "border disputes," as Mark Cheetham calls them, function as episodes in theory's immanent self-critique, and occur not only between disciplines but also between periods whose identities do not remain cleanly separate. Thus Jean-Pierre Mileur reflects on the ends of theory by returning to one of its possible beginnings in the work of the Jena romantics. It is here, at what we might better see as a genealogical beginning than as a point of absolute origin, that Lacoue-Labarthe and Nancy locate the inception of theory in the syncretizing of literature and philosophy within texts that contain their own self-doubling commentary. This doubling may take the form of a "symphilosophy" in which speculation offers itself as fiction (as in Kierkegaard), or of a "sympoetry" in which literary mimesis is interrupted by its own self-commenting specul(ariz)ation (as in Schlegel's *Lucinde*). Regardless of which form it takes, Jena romanticism responds to the Kantian challenge to reconcile the Idea with its sensible presentation by replacing the philosophical or theological absolute with a literary absolute: a philosophy-in-practice whose conjoining of speculation and textuality has strong affinities with what we now call "theory." By writing itself as an allegory of its reading, Jena romanticism paradoxically achieves the absolute as the (im)possibility of reconciling Idea and presentation. It thus grasps the Idea not as something transcendent, but as the very process of its self-reflexive production.

Lacoue-Labarthe's and Nancy's aim in writing *The Literary Absolute* is not celebratory. Rather they revisit the beginnings of theory in order to correct what is now repeated at and as its end. In other words they find in the Jena romantics (and potentially in theory today) an *Aufhebung* of reflexiveness masked by the substitution of a literary for a philosophical absolute. Mileur sees much to agree with in their analysis. But his return to a genealogical site that he conceives more complexly than they do has a further aim: that of questioning whether the authors of *The Literary Absolute* have really left behind Jena romanticism's use of literature as an excuse to reinstall philosophy in the guise of "theory." Focusing on what Lacoue-Labarthe and Nancy do rather than on what they say, he reframes the internationalism of "Theory" within a more old-fashioned comparative literature aware of the need to discriminate among romanticisms. Lacoue-Labarthe and Nancy suggest that German idealism continues to infiltrate French theory, co-opting self-criticism within the absolute of theory. But for Mileur this use of Jena as a paradigm for "romanticism" contains its own fallacies. For by identifying romanticism with a tradition rich in philosophy and poor in literature, Lacoue-Labarthe and Nancy are able to ignore the ways in which (English) romanticism stages its own autocritique through its literature, and are able in the process to marginalize the theoretical importance of literary practices. Theory thus becomes the culmination of the disciplinary structure characteristic of Western metaphysics, which from Plato onwards constructs art as the handmaiden of philosophy.

Arguing for a "heterogenealogy" of theory in differing romanticisms, Mileur suggests (with reference to analyses of Wordsworth and Nietzsche) that romanticism's contribution is not the literary absolute, but rather theory as a reconfigured relationship between practice and concept. Ironically, while we have grasped this reconfiguration in theory, we have yet to grasp it in practice. Or more accurately we have grasped it as literary critics but not within the discipline of a theory that excludes criticism. This is not to argue for a positivism that would identify theory with practices (whether artistic or cultural). For it is worth repeating again that the questioning of boundaries is predicated on drawing and not on dissolving them. But it is to argue that "theory" is intertextually constituted across its borders, and that a "border" marks both a limit and an opening.

Mark Cheetham's essay complements Mileur's in taking up not only a specific border dispute between art and philosophy, but also the way in which the figure of the border can help us to think through the question of the resistance to theory. Mileur locates this resistance in theory's failure to read between the lines of the border it shares with criticism. Approaching the same problem from a somewhat different angle, Cheetham finds in Derrida's analysis of frames and *parerga* in *The Truth in Painting* a way of utilizing this resistance constructively by recognizing that discourses and disciplines are *constituted* by the borders they share with each other. Frames do not simply exclude what is outside them, like Foucauldian discourses. In David Carroll's words, the frame "permits, and even encourages, a complicated movement or passage across it both from inside-out and outside-in."[46] Approaching Derrida's conjunction of the *parergon* and the sublime as an intertextual continuation of Kant, Cheetham reads in the latter's analysis of the sublime a rethinking of the correlative disciplinary boundaries that we normally associate with the Kantian subject. In other words, if we commonly associate Kant with the drawing of boundaries between disciplines and faculties, the analytic of the sublime is the place where he rethinks the very nature of the boundary. While Kant's concern is with spatial boundaries, Derrida returns to Kant as part of a larger reflection on the borders between art and philosophy: their competitive and supplementary relationship in the field of "aesthetics." Derrida thus allows Cheetham to deploy the Kantian sublime within an argument about theory as interdisciplinarity. Following Derrida, Cheetham argues that the sublime is neither a mind-expanding experience of boundlessness, nor is it a failure in representation that deconstructs the bounded ego. The sublime reaffirms boundaries by making us aware of what exceeds them. It constructs what is inside the frame self-critically, by recognizing it as a resistance to what is outside it.

The "sublime" is clearly part of the post-Kantian problem of the "absolute"—an intersection that creates fruitful resonances between the essays by Mileur and Cheetham. Arising in the gap between the Idea and its sensible presentation, the sublime communicates the Idea as the inadequacy of its presentation. Both concepts are involved in an analysis of boundaries. The Kantian sublime deals with spatial boundaries, while from Kant onwards the "absolute" becomes the scene of a contest between faculties and disciplines. As figures for an exceeding of boundaries, however, the sublime and the absolute function as partially reversed mirror images of each other, and generate two very different narratives about the contest of disciplines in post-Enlightenment theory. The literary absolute is the sublimation of an aporia: it describes itself as autocritique, but performs self-criticism as self-overcoming. It brings together philosophy and literature, but sometimes seems to turn philosophy into literature only to colonize the latter. The sublime, on the other hand, involves an experience of anxiety as well as exhilaration. A discipline is drawn towards its sublime as towards an other that is "at once feared and desired." Nowhere is the oscillation between these two figures more evident than in the conflicted relationship of art and philosophy in the Hegelian corpus. On the one hand, Hegel is the "prime offender" in the attempt of philosophy to master art; but on the other hand, art "is the sublime for philosophy, that which it is fascinated by . . . but which remains supplemental and defines a border."

The "absolute" and the "sublime" are not the only figures of excess by which theory reflects upon its own ends. As "the possibility of the impossibility of existence in general"[47] *death* has also proven to be crucially important to the articulation of theory precisely because it marks the unconditional limit of its powers. Death plays a pivotal role in Bataille and Blanchot, and in Heidegger's account of the structure of *Dasein* as being-for-the-end. As Stanley Corngold's essay suggests, the work of Paul de Man demonstrates how the post-Nietzschean critique that we associate with contemporary theory is entwined with a distinctly Schopenhauerian pathos—a certain "nihilism" and valorization of death—which in turn helps us reframe that theory in the context of nineteenth-century philosophy. In an age often enamored by the "playfulness" of the sign and the "pleasure of the text," de Man's work stands out for its stringently self-denying and conspicuously ethical character; this critical ethos of renunciation, Corngold argues, is the chief sign of Schopenhauer's legacy to de Man. For both thinkers, the empirical subject existing in inauthentic desire is sacrificed at the altar of art: the aesthetic experience properly embarrasses the subject into the painful negative knowledge of the contingency and fatality of human being. Like Schopenhauer, de Man affirms the aesthetic observer as one who outfaces the contingent world precisely through a form of ascetic concentration: the authentic human project is not an escape from the deathliness of existence but a courageous confrontation with its dissipating force.

Schopenhauer is himself divided on the nature and goal of aesthetic representation, at once affirming art as a metaphysically independent category, a triumph over life, *and* demystifying art as a sublimatory fiction projected upon the abyss. The cleft nature of his project accounts for his complex influence on the twentieth century, which includes strands of both nihilism and idealism. In inheriting Schopenhauer's aesthetic, de Man would seem to have absorbed this division into his own work. For example, Schopenhauer's work led to the Symbolists' quest for pure representation, and the curiously utopian conclusion to de Man's essay entitled "The Intentional Structure of the Romantic Image" demonstrates that he was attracted to this sort of Mallarméan poetics, even while he was pressing for an "authentic" recognition of the ontological priority of the natural object over the delusions of consciousness. Moreover, de Man's early privileging of literature over other forms of discourse would seem to reproduce Schopenhauer's typology of art forms, a typology that orders and values these forms according to their proximity to the deathliness of life.

If de Man models his authentic critic on Schopenhauer's artist, however, he does so with one crucial difference: whereas the author of *The World as Will and Representation* imagines a "pure knowing subject" intermittently inhabiting the ideal time of Platonic contemplation, de Man is sufficiently Heideggerian to insist that acts of understanding, including even the ascesis of the aesthetic, are themselves fully caught in the flux they would repudiate. De Man's more demanding ascesis, which in effect renounces the temptation to renounce the temporality of understanding, leads him not only to refuse the kind of "pure" knowledge that Schopenhauer attributes to the artist, but also, more radically, in the later essays, to forsake the notion of the "knowing subject" as such. Throughout his career, however, de Man retains a Schopenhauerian emphasis on the ethical power of renunciation and sacrifice, even if the strategies and indeed the target of this ascesis change. In *Blindness and Insight*, death is all dispersion and contingency, the chaos of the desiring subject that the aesthetic consciousness dutifully holds away from itself; in the essays published after "Shelley Disfigured," death is reconfigured as hardness and opacity, the radical perdurability of the *texte brut* [48] whose unfailing indifference to all forms of philosophy and theory turns the tables on the ascetic understanding—and *renounces human beings.* To experience this renunciation at the hands of language, de Man argues, one needs more than the mind of winter: only the hyperascesis of *Augenschein*, the *dead calm* of an impossibly stony gaze, provides us with a glimpse of what language "might look like in our own absence."[49]

George Steiner once said that de Man's work was "instinct with sadness,"[50] a phrase that reminds us that its antimetaphysical character is no defense against the incursion of pathos, even Schopenhauerian pathos. Corngold concludes his essay by suggesting that far from compromising de Man's project, Schopenhauer's austere legacy brings out its most pertinent features for the ends of theory. Corngold sees in de Man's work a salutary instance of ascetic concentration in a postmodern world otherwise too much given over to contingency. In calling for criticism to return to this kind of steadfastness, he concedes that the devaluation of the empirical subject as a source of value and meaning under the aegis of an ethos of renunciation is not intrinsically benign, Heidegger's political life being a notorious case in point. As Ned Lukacher points out, "Heidegger's sacrifice on behalf of the Other lends itself too readily to a calculated sacrifice of the others who do not appear to share the experience of essential thinking."[51] As a young man, de Man himself may once have unreflectively embraced what Adorno smartly dismisses as the dehumanizing "cult of *Geist*,"[52] and with similarly dreadful implications, though it may surprise readers of this volume to see that this is precisely *not* a charge that Corngold makes. Instead, his essay opens up the possibility that the ubiquity of death in de Man, and, by implication, in the larger arena of contemporary theory, points to an ongoing desire for something beyond language and beyond contingency: a "nineteenth-century" desire, perhaps, that we can characterize as "metaphysical," though since Schopenhauer only in a negative mode. The valorization of death in the final book of Schopenhauer's *World as Will and Representation* can be seen as a displaced effect of his inability to posit the in-itself except as that which cannot be represented. Reading de Man through Schopenhauer, the identification of death with the "materiality" of language constitutes a site of resistance *within* language to the antimetaphysical claim that there is nothing outside language. Nietzsche criticizes Schopenhauer for his stoicism, his residually humanistic refusal totally to immerse himself in the flux. Corngold finds traces of the same melioristic quality in de Man's Schopenhauerism, not to pronounce the end of theory but to return it to a certain "attitude of ascetic concentration on texts." The stakes can be no greater, he suggests, since in a pervasively Nietzschean "world of signs without fault, without truth, and without origin,"[53] this "adversion may be the last, the only resource of the human."

Notes

1. Judith Butler, *Subjects of Desire: Hegelian Reflections in Twentieth-Century France* (New York: Columbia University Press, 1987); Tilottama Rajan, *Dark Interpreter: The Discourse of Romanticism* (Ithaca: Cornell University Press, 1980), 27–57; Rajan, *The Supplement of Reading: Figures of Understanding in Romantic Theory and Practice* (Ithaca: Cornell University Press, 1990), 15–100; Peter Dews, *Logics of Disintegration: Post-Structuralist Thought and the Claims of Critical Theory* (London: Verso, 1987), 11–44. See also Manfred Frank, *What is Neostructuralism?* trans. Sabine Wilke and Richard T. Gray (Minnesota: University of Minnesota Press, 1989), 183–214, 295–314.

2. Marshall Brown, *The Shape of German Romanticism* (Ithaca: Cornell University Press, 1979); Andrew Bowie, *Aesthetics and Subjectivity: From Kant to Nietzsche* (Manchester: Manchester University Press, 1990).

3. Henry Sussman, *The Hegelian Aftermath: Readings in Hegel, Kierkegaard, Freud, Proust* (Baltimore: Johns Hopkins University Press, 1982); Andrzej Warminski, *Readings in Interpretation: Hölderlin, Hegel, Heidegger* (Minneapolis: University of Minnesota Press, 1987).

4. For further discussion of such models, see Rajan, *The Supplement of Reading*, particularly 41–43, 168–70, 293–97.

5. For further discussion of this problem, see Rajan, "Phenomenology and Romantic Criticism: Hegel and the Sub-Version of Aesthetics," in *The Question of Romantic Criticism*, ed. John Beer (forthcoming, Johns Hopkins University Press).

6. Philippe Lacoue-Labarthe and Jean-Luc Nancy, *The Literary Absolute: The Theory of Literature in German Romanticism*, trans. Philip Barnard and Cheryl Lester (Albany: State University of New York Press, 1988), 1–17.

7. Paul de Man, *Allegories of Reading: Figural Language in Rousseau, Nietzsche, Rilke, and Proust* (New Haven: Yale University Press, 1979), 249.

8. Barbara Johnson, *The Critical Difference: Essays in the Contemporary Rhetoric of Reading* (Baltimore: Johns Hopkins University Press, 1980), x–xi.

9. De Man, *Allegories of Reading*, 298.

10. Here we evoke the title of the opening chapter of Derrida's *Of Grammatology*, trans. Gayatri Spivak (Baltimore: Johns Hopkins University Press, 1974), 6.

11. See also Rajan, *The Supplement of Reading*, 62–98.

12. J. Hillis Miller, *The Ethics of Reading: Kant, de Man, Eliot, Trollope, James, and Benjamin* (New York: Columbia University Press, 1987), 59.

13. Marc W. Redfield makes a similar point in "Humanizing de Man," *diacritics* 19, no. 2 (Summer 1989): 50.

14. Edited and translated by R. Thomte and A. B. Anderson (Princeton: Princeton University Press, 1980), 20.

15. Jacques Derrida, "How to Avoid Speaking: Denials," in *Languages of the Unsayable: The Play of Negativity in Literature and Literary Theory*, ed. Sanford Budick and Wolfgang Iser (New York: Columbia University Press, 1989), 10.

16. Martin Heidegger, *Schelling's Treatise on the Essence of Human Freedom*, trans. Joan Stambaugh (Athens: Ohio University Press, 1985).

17. Derrida, "How to Avoid Speaking: Denials," 24.

18. Ibid., 29.

19. Frank, *What is Neostructuralism?*, 87.

20. Derrida, "How to Avoid Speaking: Denials," 36.

21. Frank, *What is Neostructuralism?*, 88.

22. Translator's preface to Derrida, *Of Grammatology*, trans. Gayatri Spivak (Baltimore: Johns Hopkins University Press, 1974), xxvii.

23. "How to Avoid Speaking: Denials," 38.

24. Marc Redfield, "De Man, Schiller, and the Politics of Reception," *diacritics* 20, no. 3 (1990): 63

25. "The Future of Deconstruction in Romantic Studies," *Nineteenth-Century Contexts* 11, no. 2 (Fall 1987): 132.

26. Rajan cites David Carroll's phrase, from *The Subject in Question: The Language of Theory and the Strategies of Fiction* (Chicago: University of Chicago Press, 1982), 7.

27. Charles Taylor, *Hegel* (Cambridge: Cambridge University Press, 1975), 155.

28. Alexandre Kojève, *Introduction to the Reading of Hegel*, trans. James H. Nichols, Jr., ed. Allan Bloom (New York: Basic Books, 1969), 53.

29. G. W. F. Hegel, *The Phenomenology of Mind*, trans. Sir James Baillie (New York: Humanities Press, 1949), 507.

30. Paul de Man, "Hypogram and Inscription," in *The Resistance to Theory* (Minneapolis: University of Minnesota Press, 1986), 37.

31. Paul de Man, "Shelley Disfigured, " in *The Rhetoric of Romanticism* (New York: Columbia University Press, 1984), 123.

32. Drew Leder, *The Absent Body* (Chicago: University of Chicago Press, 1990), 194.

33. Julia Kristeva, *Language—The Unknown: An Initiation into Linguistics* (New York: Columbia University Press, 1989), 121–22.

34. Martin Heidegger, *Schelling's Treatise on "The Essence of Human Freedom,"* trans. Joan Stambaugh (Athens: Ohio University Press, 1985), 3.

35. See, for example, *Being and Time*, trans. John Macquarrie and Edward Robinson (New York: Harper & Row, 1962), 318.

36. "On the Problem of Self-Understanding," in *Philosophical Hermeneutics*, trans. and ed. David Linge (Berkeley: University of California Press, 1976), 55.

37. Lukacher cites Nietzsche, *Thus Spake Zarathustra*, in *The Portable Nietzsche*, ed. Walter Kaufmann(New York: Penguin, 1976), 363.

38. Ned Lukacher, "Mourning Becomes Telepathy," introduction to Jacques Derrida, *Cinders* (Lincoln: University of Nebraska Press, 1991), 18.

39. Martin Heidegger, *Being and Time*, 329–40.

40. See, for example, *The Philosophical Discourse of Modernity*, trans. Thomas McCarthy (Cambridge: MIT Press, 1987).

41. Herbert Marcuse, *Reason and Revolution* (Boston: Beacon Press, 1968), 200.

42. Jürgen Habermas, "What is Universal Pragmatics?" in *Communication and the Evolution of Society*, trans. Thomas McCarthy (Boston: Beacon Press, 1979), 2.

43. Jacques Derrida, *Margins of Philosophy*, trans. Alan Bass (Chicago: University of Chicago Press,1982), 326. As Pfau also suggests, the irreducibly iterative nature of the performative necessarily introduces other questions, questions that Hegel and Austin alike feel to be a kind of threat to the intelligibility of their projects: for any performative (moral declarative or otherwise) to be recognizable as a repetition or iteration necessarily

introduces the possibility that it could be reenacted in quite other contexts, both "serious" and "non-serious."

44. Michael Oakeshott, *Of Human Conduct* (Oxford: Clarendon Press, 1975), 63.

45. "The Power of Formalism: The New Historicism," *ELH* 56 (1989): 755.

46. David Carroll, *Paraesthetics: Foucault, Lyotard, Derrida* (London: Methuen, 1987), 136.

47. Giorgio Agamben, *Language and Death: The Place of Negativity* (Minneapolis: University of Minnesota Press, 1991), 1.

48. Rodolphe Gasché, "In-difference to Philosophy: de Man on Kant, Hegel, and Nietzsche," in *Reading de Man Reading* (Minneapolis: University of Minnesota Press, 1989), 265.

49. In a discussion of de Man, Fredric Jameson recalls "Stanley Cavell's great insight" that "the philosophical meaning of film . . . is to show us what the world might look like in our own absence." See *Postmodernism; or, the Cultural Logic of Late Capitalism* (Durham, N.C.: Duke University Press, 1991), 248.

50. George Steiner, *Real Presences* (Chicago: University of Chicago Press, 1989), 122.

51. Lukacher, "Mourning Becomes Telepathy," 18

52. Corngold cites Adorno from "On the Question: 'What is German?'" trans. Thomas Y. Levin, *New German Critique* 36 (Fall 1985): 127.

53. Jacques Derrida, "Structure, Sign, and Play in the Human Sciences," in *Writing and Difference*, ed. and trans. Alan Bass (Chicago: University of Chicago Press, 1978), 292.

1

Between Idealism
and Deconstruction

Fictions of Authority:
Kierkegaard, de Man, and
the Ethics of Reading

Christopher Norris

I

What might it mean to "deconstruct" Kierkegaard? From one point of view it would produce a reading not only allowed for but actively *pre-empted* by much of what Kierkegaard wrote. His entire pseudonymous production—the "aesthetic" as opposed to the "religious" writing—can be seen to deconstruct itself at every turn, remaining always one jump ahead of the *hypocrite lecteur* who thinks to have fathomed its meaning. According to his own retrospective account (in *The Point of View for My Work as an Author*), Kierkegaard was wholly in command of this process from the outset. His "aesthetic" production was a means of ensnaring the reader in fictions and speculative arguments that would ultimately self-deconstruct, so to speak, at the point of transition to a higher, ethical plane of understanding. The reader would thus be brought to comprehend the inherent limitations and self-imposed deceits of a purely aesthetic attitude to life. This "ethical" stage would in turn be transcended by a recognition of its own insufficiency in the face of authentic religious experience. Such is the threefold dialectical process as Kierkegaard strives to reveal it. From the standpoint thus gained atop all the shifting perspectives of Kierkegaard's authorship, the reader will achieve that inwardness of self-understanding that alone constitutes religious faith.

This is how Kierkegaard defends his duplicitous strategies in a key passage from *The Point of View:*

> Teleological suspension in relation to the communication of truth (i.e., to suppress something for the time being that the truth may become truer) is a plain duty to the truth and is comprised in the responsibility a man has before God for the reflection bestowed upon him.[1]

The uses of deception are justified strictly by the interests of a higher, self-authenticating truth. "Reflection" is a highly ambiguous virtue in Kierkegaard's usage of the term. On the one hand, it can lead to those fashionable forms of romantic irony—the endless relativization of meaning and value—that Kierkegaard attacked in the writers of his age. Such was the "aesthetic" attitude pressed to a dangerous and ethically disabling extreme. On the other hand it provides Kierkegaard with a means of "teleological suspension," a strategy for conducting the reader through and beyond the perils of ironic self-evasion. He defends himself in advance against the criticisms of those who would condemn such tactics in the name of a straightforward truth-telling imperative. Things being what they are in the present age, the choice must fall between absolute silence and the use of "indirect communication." And, given that choice, a timorous silence is scarcely to be regarded as "a higher form of religiousness."

The purposes of edification are therefore served indirectly by the detour that leads through various stages of "aesthetic" reflection. Kierkegaard is at pains to demonstrate that this was all along his guiding purpose, and not just an attitude adopted in the wisdom of hindsight with a view to redeeming his early aberrations. He points to the fact that both kinds of production were carried on simultaneously at every stage of his authorship, rather than forming a linear progression that might be equated with the gradual maturing of Kierkegaard's soul. Thus the first ("aesthetic") volume of *Either/Or* was written during the period that also produced the first pair of *Edifying Discourses.* Likewise, toward the end of his authorship, when Kierkegaard's energies were mainly devoted to religious productions, he nevertheless wrote a "little article" *(The Crisis and A Crisis in the Life of an Actress)* that belonged to the "aesthetic" dimension. "The Religious is present from the beginning. Conversely, the aesthetic is present again at the last moment" *(PV,* 12).

This reversal of normal expectation is repeated in what Kierkegaard records of his experience in writing *Either/Or.* The first volume (including the famous "Diary of a Seducer") presents an exploration of the aesthetic outlook in all its manifold guises and disguises. The second volume—with Judge William's "ethical" reflections on the sanctity of marriage—seems to offer itself, in private-confessional terms, as the outcome of the first. Yet in fact, as Kierkegaard reveals, the second volume was the first to be composed, and already bore the marks of his limiting judgment on the "ethical" as an ultimate philosophy of life. The author at this stage, he assures us, was "very far from wishing to summon the course of existence to return comfortingly to the situation of marriage" (*PV*, 18). The implied reference is to Kierkegaard's agonized courtship and final rejection of Regine Olsen, an episode that he saw as confirmation of the need to pass from an ethical to a religious order of existence. So far from implicitly endorsing Judge William's sentiments on marriage, the second volume was written from the viewpoint of an author "who religiously was already in the cloister—a thought that lies concealed in the pseudonym Victor Eremita" (*PV*, 18).

The ethical stage is thereby deprived of the culminating weight and authority that it might appear to claim if one reads *Either/Or* in terms of a straightforward narrative-confessional logic. Its arguments are already subject to the same kind of qualifying irony, or "teleological suspension," that works retroactively to frame and disavow the aesthetic attitude. *Either/Or* became a kind of "poetical catharsis," one that was yet unable to "go farther than the ethical." Kierkegaard can therefore return to his work as a reader in much the same position as any other, compelled to reenact its dialectical structure in terms that define his own (past and present) relationship to it. This attitude becomes quite explicit in the closing pages of *The Point of View*. "That I was without authority I have from the first moment asserted clearly. . . . I regarded myself preferably as a *reader* of the books, not as the *author*" (155). By adopting this viewpoint Kierkegaard can thus claim to enact a nonprivileged but fully "existential" encounter with his own previous productions.

It should be obvious by now that Kierkegaard carries deconstruction only to the point where its strategies supposedly come up against an undeconstructible bedrock of authenticated truth. His techniques of "indirect communication" have a strictly prelusive function, designed as they are to confront the fit reader with the absolute necessity of passing decisively beyond them. Self-consciousness and irony exert such a hold on "the present age" that truth cannot emerge except by exploiting such ambiguous means. "Immediate pathos is of no avail—even if in immediate pathos one were to sacrifice his life. The age has at its disposal too much reflection and shrewdness not to be able to reduce his significance to zero" (*PV*, 90). It is almost as if Kierkegaard treated the claims of authentic, truth-telling discourse as a form of bad faith or pious pretense in an age so much given over to "reflection." He repeatedly fends off moral objections voiced in the name of what he calls "a scrupulous and pusillanimous notion of the duty of telling the truth" (*PV*, 90). Only by adopting its own forms of cunning indirection can thought regain the authentic inwardness lost to an age of aesthetic self-reflection.

This is of course the point at which Kierkegaard parts company with the present-day avatars of deconstruction. They would deny what Kierkegaard so strenuously asserts: the existence of a grounding authenticity that can call a halt to the mazy indirections of language and motive. For a rigorous deconstructor like Paul de Man, such beliefs are always delusory, a product of the "normative pathos" that leads us to assume that language should ideally mean what it says, or say what it means.[2] Kierkegaard's project depends on his adopting this skeptical attitude only up to a point, in order to perplex and finally confound the unbelieving reader. One can certainly find many passages, in *The Point of View* and elsewhere, that anticipate de Man by calling into doubt the normative relations of language, truth, and subjectivity. Such are Kierkegaard's remarks on the powerlessness of "immediate pathos" (or appeals to self-authenticating belief) in the face of a "reflective" culture at large. Deconstruction turns on a similar claim: that thought should no longer be beguiled into accepting the delusive "immediacy" of language once the instruments are at its disposal for dismantling the covert metaphysics at work behind all such presumptions. For Kierkegaard, however, this work of demystification is always at the service of a higher imperative, ethical or religious. Deconstruction as practiced by conceptual rhetoricians like de Man would surely have figured for Kierkegaard as a warning example of "aesthetic" reflection lost in the abysmal regressions of its own creating.

To read Kierkegaard in the knowledge of modern deconstructionist criticism is therefore to face very squarely the choices that his authorship seeks to impose on the reader. The internal dialectics of *Either/Or* are reproduced at every stage of Kierkegaard's writing, the design being always to implicate the reader in questions of interpretative choice that simultaneously force an ethical decision.[3] The unreconstructed aesthete (or purist deconstructor) will read *Either/Or* as a fascinating instance of textual strategies engaged in a shuttling exchange of "undecidable" priorities. He or she will be impressed by the text's unresolved contradictions of viewpoint, its power to suspend or defer any final, authoritative reading. Its title would in this case be taken to signify the holding together of two possibilities ("aesthetic" and "ethical"), without the least need or justification for choosing between them. Yet this response would of course be "aesthetic" insofar as it refused the absolute choice of priority envisaged by Kierkegaard's authorial design. The either/or of ethical decision is intended precisely to transcend or discredit that supposedly facile interpretation. Such a text confronts the "implied reader" with problems of interpretative grasp more momentous than those usually entertained by current narrative theory. Kierkegaard—to put it crudely— will see you damned if you fail to divine the innermost, self-redeeming aspect of his authorship.

For Kierkegaard, there is always a decisive moment of advance from "indirect communication" to truth directly apprehended and thus no longer subject to the ruses and dangers of reflection. To ignore this moment, or willfully repress it, is to prove oneself lacking in the "serious" powers of mind prerequisite to higher understanding. Kierkegaard's reader is constantly on trial, required to give evidence of his or her capacity for taking this decisive leap into faith. But Kierkegaard's authorship is equally put to the test, since its very reliance on deceptive techniques might actually mislead and pervert the understanding of a well-intentioned reader. Kierkegaard counters this likely objection by making it the reader's duty to approach his texts with sufficient "seriousness" of purpose. Otherwise, he admits, understanding can only be perplexed and undone by the effects of "dialectical reduplication" everywhere present in his writing. This is the pivotal point of encounter between truth and its indirect means of reflective presentation. The burden now rests with the reader to prove that Kierkegaard's intentions are not simply lost on his or her capacities for inward self-knowledge.

Kierkegaard is at pains to justify his position on this crucial point. His indirect proceedings have to be defended as absolutely necessary if the reader is to grasp the requisite stages of spiritual progress. On the other hand, that same dialectical grasp can only come about on condition that the reader is *already* endowed with an adequate depth of understanding. As Kierkegaard explains, it is "the mark of a dialectical reduplication" that "the ambiguity is maintained." The unfit reader (one assumes) may seize on this ambiguity and rest content with its fascinating play. The elect reader, on the other hand, will respond as Kierkegaard wishes. "As soon as the requisite seriousness grasps it, it is able to release it, but always in such a way that seriousness itself vouches for the fact of it" (*PV*, 17). Again, one could extrapolate something in the nature of an ethical riposte to the claims of current deconstruction. Harold Bloom has already pointed to what he sees as the "serene linguistic nihilism" manifest among certain of his deconstructing colleagues at Yale.[4] Bloom's way of coping with this threat—his wholesale rewriting of poetic tradition in terms of psychic defense and aggression—is perhaps not an earnest of "seriousness" in Kierkegaard's sense. But it does partake of the same desire to save the authentic individual—Christian or poet—from the otherwise endless fabrications of "unauthorized" language.

Kierkegaard therefore stands in a highly ambiguous relation to certain current theories of reading and textuality. His authorship presents a double and contradictory challenge to the claims of deconstruction. It anticipates those claims to a remarkable degree, making Kierkegaard appear at times a kind of uncanny elective precursor. But it also—and with far greater "seriousness"—promises the reader a viewpoint that would render deconstruction at best redundant, and at worst a species of mischievous "aesthetic" distraction. The remainder of my essay will examine some of the issues raised by this belated encounter.

II

The deconstructor might ask, to begin with, why it is that Kierkegaard is so often constrained to fall back on distinctly "aesthetic" parables and metaphors when arguing the case for a higher, non-aesthetic truth. Some striking examples have to do with female sexuality, such as the image of woman as endlessly seductive, developed in relation to the Don Juan theme in *Either/Or*. Kierkegaard reverts to this metaphor in a passage from *The Point of View* purporting to explain the approach to truth by means of indirection or "dialectical reduplication": "For as a woman's coyness has a reference to the true lover and yields when he appears, but only then, so, too, dialectical reduplication has a reference to true seriousness" (*PV*, 17). The sexual image retains its hold, not only on Kierkegaard's "aesthetic" imagination but on the very process of argument by means of which that stage is supposedly transcended. *The Point of View* was written, after all, from the standpoint of one who claimed to reread and comprehend the entire dialectical progress inscribed in his authorship to date. "That I understand the truth which I deliver to others, of that I am eternally certain" (*PV*, 8). Yet this truth appears still incapable of finding adequate expression without the aid of those "aesthetic" parables and devices that characterize the earlier, pseudonymous writing.

The "question of woman" cannot be confined to that single, decisive episode of courtship and rejection in Kierkegaard's past. That the episode figures in his writing only by indirect allusion—that it belongs, so to speak, to the *vita ante acta* of his authorship—does not prevent it from obtruding metaphorically into the progress of Kierkegaard's arguments. Woman comes to signify, however obliquely, that aspect of dissimulating metaphor and fiction that alone points the way to truth in an age of universal deceit. One is put in mind of Derrida's remarkable pages on the imagery of womanhood in Nietzsche. There emerges a strange articulation of philosophic themes and sexualized metaphor, such that the idea of woman becomes textually intertwined with a deconstruction of "truth" and its forms of masculine conceptual mastery. Derrida quotes Nietzsche: "Progress of the idea: it becomes more subtle, insidious, incomprehensible—*it becomes female.* . . ." And he offers the following gloss, drawing on Nietzsche's own metaphorical suggestions:

> [A]ll the emblems, all the shafts and allurements that Nietzsche found in woman, her seductive distance, her captivating inaccessibility, the ever-veiled promise of her provocative transcendence . . . these all belong properly to the history of truth by way of the history of an error.[5]

Kierkegaard's uses of "aesthetic" indirection—especially where the detour passes by way of woman—are likewise subject to a certain ambivalence that questions his assumed dialectical mastery.

One could press the parallel further. Kierkegaard constructs an entire dialectics of disguised confessional intent, designed to vindicate his treatment of Regine Olsen by viewing it from the standpoint of a higher, self-achieved religious wisdom. In *Either/Or* the "question of woman" is dealt with successively by two powerful ruses of dialectical cunning. The seductress—ever-changing and tantalizing object of "aesthetic" desire— is mastered by the ethical precepts of Christian marriage, as enunciated by Judge William in volume 2. This provisional ideal is in turn rejected from the "higher" religious plane of understanding that Kierkegaard claims as his own in *The Point of View* (and that, moreover, he finds implicit in volume 2 of *Either/Or*). Woman is thus thematized in retrospect as the dark side of man's self-knowledge, the source of an illusion that blinds him to the need for transcendence, first to the ethical, then to the religious spheres of value. Kierkegaard's writings enable him to perform an act of self-vindication so complete that it reverses the roles of innocent and guilty, sinned-against and sinning. Whatever the feelings of guilt that may have attached to the memory of Regine Olsen, Kierkegaard's strategy is designed to convert them into causes of his own deepening estrangement from commonplace human affection, and hence his attainment of a true religious inwardness. The confessional motives of Kierkegaard's authorship can thus be represented under the guise of a spiritual progress from stage to stage of predestined self-edification.

Yet this process cannot entirely conceal the marks of that original repression upon which Kierkegaard's edifying narrative depends. The fact of his self-inflicted break with Regine is everywhere present in *The Point of View*, for all that Kierkegaard strives to consign it to the remote prehistory of his misspent youth. At the figurative level, as we have seen, these reminders take the form of a recourse to sexual-aesthetic metaphors in order to communicate religious truth. Derrida points to a similar emergence of disruptive "feminized" imagery in Nietzsche's apparently misogynistic writing. Woman, it seems,

> is recognized and affirmed as an affirmative power, a dissimulatress, an artist, a dionysian. And no longer is it man who affirms her. She affirms herself, in and of herself, in man . . . and antifeminism, which condemned woman only so long as she was, so long as she answered to man . . . is in its turn overthrown.[6]

Whatever its provision of sustaining alibis, Kierkegaard's narrative still falls victim to the "dissimulating" power of womanly aesthetic imagery.

Similar complications surface to vex the idealized projection of his "authorship" in its self-professed form of a religious education-into-truth. The Regine episode is cryptically alluded to as a "factum" that Kierkegaard refuses to elaborate, except by stressing its decisive importance and its complex role in the threshold experience that led to his becoming an author. Kierkegaard expressly denies that this experience was directly religious. "I can only beg the reader not to think of revelations or anything of that sort, for with me everything is dialectical" (*PV*, 83). This disclaimer can be seen as consistent with Kierkegaard's reiterated stress on the element of "reflection" prerequisite to any vouchsafing of religious truth. But it also serves the more devious *narrative* function of presenting the youthful Kierkegaard as one "dialectically" removed from the commonplace sphere of human obligation:

> However much I had lived and experienced in another sense, I had, in a human sense, leapt over the stages of childhood and youth; and this lack, I suppose, must be somehow made up for: instead of having been young, I became a poet, which is a second youth. (*PV*, 83)

The "aesthetic" stage thus becomes the pretext—by a kind of narrative doubling—for Kierkegaard's suspension of ethical judgment as regards his treatment of Regine. As a "second youth" it effectively stands in for what the narrative cannot directly face without threatening to undermine its own self-approving moral stance. The broken engagement is represented as a crisis, but one that both begins and ends (it would seem) within a kind of "aesthetic" parenthesis. Only thus can *The Point of View* maintain its precarious narrative coherence and the author's claim to ethical and religious self-vindication.

Kierkegaard's text therefore works to exclude the possibility of any guilt that might attach to episodes beyond its dialectical control. For all its decisive significance, the event in question is banished to a realm of "aesthetic" exteriority where it cannot interfere with the author's growth toward spiritual inwardness and grace. But the price of this exclusion is a certain persistent ambivalence as to the motives and status of Kierkegaard's self-revelation. *The Point of View* supposedly belongs to the religious and inwardly authenticated portion of Kierkegaard's authorship. It stands alongside such works as the *Edifying Discourses*, where the author speaks (we are meant to assume) *in propria persona* and without the aid of aesthetic ploys and devices. To read it as a species of fiction would surely represent a perverse disregard of the author's very plain intentions. Yet its handling of the Regine episode—displaced and deployed as it is in the interests of "dialectical" coherence—suggests the presence of an overriding narrative concern. *The Point of View* has this much in common with the typical nineteenth-century novel. The quotidian sequence of mere "events" is reordered and adjusted to suit the requirements of a well-formed "plot." Different viewpoints within the narrative are placed and judged according to the dominant authorial voice. Ideally there should take place a final convergence of interpretative views between "implied author" and "implied reader." The narrative works to ensure this convergence, provided always that the reader proves fit to share its commanding perspective.[7]

Kierkegaard offers precisely such a narrative in *The Point of View*. Yet might it not occur to a different kind of reader—one, say, who questioned Kierkegaard's absolute religious assurance—to detect even here the distinctive signs of fictional representation? Kierkegaard refers to the "duplex" character of the event that signaled his religious awakening (*PV*, 83). In this lay its power of dialectical development and hence the spur to Kierkegaard's incipient authorship. But not all "duplicities" are capable of thus being channeled into the path of a secure self-knowledge and spiritual vocation. *The Point of View* lies open to a reading that would question the supposedly decidable choice between "aesthetic" and "religious" modes of understanding. As a self-professed record of Kierkegaard's motives and intentions, it demands that one read in good faith and accept its full authenticity. But to read it as a narrative—and one, moreover, that bears distinct marks of its own very deliberate contriving—is to doubt the very grounds of Kierkegaard's crucial distinction. By devising such a perfect sequence of pretexts for his spiritual life-history, Kierkegaard risks the collapse of his own founding categories. Fact can no longer be separated from fiction, or "aesthetic" motivation from ethical choice. The system of distinctions becomes strictly undecidable.

Paul de Man has described a similar subversive logic at work in the text of Rousseau's *Confessions*. The danger of confessional narratives is that they tend to build up a self-exonerating case for the accused that leaves him paradoxically with nothing to confess. Excuses generate a logic of their own that finally evades the need for "honest" self-reckoning. "The only thing one has to fear from the excuse is that it will indeed exculpate the confessor, thus making the confession (and the confessional text) redundant as it originates" (*AR*, 280). The narrative form permits any number of face-saving strategies, thus providing Rousseau (or Kierkegaard) with a means of transforming guilt into a pretext for displays of redemptive self-approval. At its most extreme this process can substitute the pleasure of a tale well told for the ethical imperative that supposedly prompted the confession in the first place. Thus, as de Man reads it, "Rousseau's own text, against its author's interests, prefers being suspected of lie and slander rather than of innocently lacking sense" (*AR*, 293). In Kierkegaard's terms, there must always be a risk that the "aesthetic" will return to recapture and distort the deliverance of authentic truth. De Man describes Rousseau's textual predicament in words that might just as well be applied to Kierkegaard. It is always possible, he writes, "to face up to any experience (to excuse any guilt), because the experience always exists simultaneously as fictional discourse and as empirical event." Furthermore, from the reader's point of view, "it is never possible to decide which one of the two possibilities is the right one" (*AR*, 293).

De Man's reading of Rousseau is detailed and compelling, for all its seeming perversity. The central premise is that texts cannot always effectively *perform* what they manifestly set out to mean. There is a frequent disjunction between ethical purposes (like the will to confess) and the business of working them out in narrative-textual form. More specifically, there occurs a shift of priorities, such that the reckoning with private guilt becomes subdued to the need for demonstrable public veracity. To confess, as de Man puts it, "is to overcome guilt and shame in the name of truth: it is an epistemological use of language in which ethical values of good and evil are superseded by values of truth and falsehood. . . ." (*AR*, 279). And these latter "epistemological" values are compromised in turn by the inherent tendency of confessional narratives to construct a self-accusing penitential stance by way of exhibiting the penitent's remarkable candor. Confessions of guilt thus become self-exonerating, but also seem to be intensified by the very tactics that serve to excuse them. In short, "there can never be enough guilt around to match the text-machine's infinite power to excuse" (*AR*, 299).

Kierkegaard's text is not unaware of this irony lying in wait for its own good intentions. At one point the question is explicitly raised as to whether his entire "literary production" might not be viewed as self-deluded and belonging to the "aesthetic" sphere (*PV*, 17). Kierkegaard's defense is curiously unconvincing. Let the reader indeed imagine by way of experiment (he suggests) that all his works were composed from the aesthetic point of view. This hypothesis would soon break down when it met with texts (like *The Point of View*) that claimed an edifying purpose. On the other hand, by adopting the contrary hypothesis—that Kierkegaard's entire authorship, including the "aesthetic" texts, was governed by motives of edification—the reader can see how everything ultimately fits into place. It need scarcely be remarked that this argument rests on a foregone assumption that the reader will accept Kierkegaard's categorical distinctions absolutely at face value. She or he will accept, that is, the progression from "aesthetic," via "ethical" to "religious" self-knowledge, precisely as described (at the manifest level) in *The Point of View*. Again, it is the fit (or "serious") reader who thus falls in with Kierkegaard's purposes. But if one reads his text against its manifest intentions—alerted to its blind spots of metaphor and narrative indirection—one may come to entertain a very different understanding.

Had de Man's deconstructionist arguments been applied to Kierkegaard rather than Rousseau, his conclusions would be yet more disturbing. For Kierkegaard stakes his entire religious project on the assumption that his writings can effectually convince and convert the reader to a state of inward grace commensurate with his own. Rousseau is at least intermittently aware of the pleasure to be had from shocking the reader by ever more scandalous examples of his "honest" self-accounting. The air of a "performance," of frank theatricality, is very much a part of Rousseau's confessional style. For Kierkegaard also, but in a more crucial sense, writing must exert a "performative" force if it is ever to serve the purpose of communicating truth. It must function both to authenticate the author's meaning—his "inward" commitment to stand by his words —and to produce a correspondingly inward acceptance on the reader's part. Such performative effects (nowadays the province of "speech act" philosophy)[8] are omnipresent in normal language, but they assume a critical dimension of faith to an author like Kierkegaard. His writing cannot entertain any doubt as to its own capacity for winning the reader to an answering state of hard-earned inward commitment.

It is precisely this faith that de Man so disconcertingly calls into doubt. His reading of Rousseau dissociates "the cognition from the act," denying that there can possibly exist any genuine, assured correspondence between linguistic meaning and performative intent. "If we are right in saying that 'qui s'accuse s'excuse,' then the relation between confession and excuse is rhetorical prior to being intentional" (*AR*, 282). And again: "[A]ny speech act produces an excess of cognition, but it can never hope to know the process of its own production (the only thing worth knowing)" (*AR*, 300). De Man's argument turns, as we have seen, on the element of undecidability that often prevents any clear-cut distinction between ethics and epistemology, issues of "right and wrong," on the one hand, and questions of "true and false," on the other. And this would be enough radically to suspend the entire existential project of faith upon which Kierkegaard's authority stands or falls.

III

It is Nietzsche who provides de Man with a model and exemplary practice for the strategy of deconstruction. Nietzsche's awareness of the figural dimensions of language, the ways in which rhetoric both asserts and undermines its own performance, forms the topic of de Man's most compelling chapters in his book *Allegories of Reading*. Nietzsche deconstructs the claims of philosophy by showing how they rest on an unacknowledged basis of metaphor and figural representation. The most rigorous effort to exclude such devices from the text of philosophy always at some point fails to recognize their buried or covert metaphorical workings. Nietzsche determined to press this insight to the point where it produced an ultimate aporia or "undecidability" with regard to all texts, his own included.

Arguments must always be "rhetorical" in the sense of aiming to persuade one of their truth, even where that truth is proposed as a matter of straightforward (logical or factual) self-evidence. Yet rhetoric also has another, self-critical aspect, exploited by Nietzsche in his relentless uncovering of the tropes and devices that philosophers refused to acknowledge in their own discourse. Rhetoric in this sense is the ceaseless undoing of rhetorically persuasive effects. De Man makes the point with elegant concision. "Considered as persuasion, rhetoric is performative but when considered as a system of tropes, it deconstructs its own performance" (*AR*, 131). The upshot of a Nietzschean critique of language is to break down the system of decidable oppositions that assign a proper place to ethical judgments on the one hand and analytic concepts on the other. Nietzsche's "genealogy of morals" negates every system of ethical values—religious and secular alike—by claiming to derive their precepts from those various emanations of the will-to-power that prevail from one epoch to the next. On a world-historical scale, this repeats the undoing of "performative" language by that power of rhetorical disarticulation vested in its own constitutive tropes and devices. At the same time it admits that any such critique, however "demystified," must always acknowledge its own persuasive (or rhetorical) character. What is so difficult to accept, as de Man writes, is that "this allegory of errors" (or undecidability) is the "very model of philosophical rigour."

Kierkegaard and Nietzsche are often classed together as textbook "existentialists," thinkers who rejected the great systematic philosophies of their time in order to assert the freedom of individual choice and values. Certainly they shared an aversion toward Hegel, expressed by Kierkegaard in a famous image: that of the philosopher who erects a magnificent edifice of theory, while dwelling himself in a wretched hovel beneath its shadow.[9] Nietzsche likewise saw nothing but grandiose delusion in the claims of Hegelian dialectic. But the two had very different reasons for adopting this negative attitude to Hegel. Nietzsche's objections took rise from a thoroughgoing epistemological skepticism, a belief that Hegel's entire dialectical system was founded on nothing more than a series of metaphors, or figural constructions, disguised as genuine concepts. In Hegel the will-to-power within language achieved its most spectacular and self-deluded form. For Kierkegaard, the case was to be argued on ethical and religious rather than epistemological grounds. The danger of Hegel's all-embracing dialectic was that it left no room for the "authentic" individual, the agent of choice and locus of existential freedom. Subject and object, experience and history, were all taken up into a massive unfolding of Absolute Knowledge that no human act—no motion of will—had the power to resist or decisively push forward. Dialectics in this guise was a form of "aesthetic" aberration, a means of evading responsible choice by setting up a fine philosophical system that the mind could contemplate at leisure.

Nietzsche is decidedly not an "existentialist" in anything like the Kierkegaardian sense. His critique of systematic philosophy goes along with an ethical skepticism more sweeping and corrosive than anything Kierkegaard could possibly entertain. The Nietzschean "transvaluation of values" is finally a matter—as de Man makes clear—of deconstructing ethics by way of an epistemological reduction. Nietzsche stands to Kierkegaard as a false ally, one whose undermining of conventional ideas is in the service of a radically nihilistic outlook. Such skepticism is the enemy of true Kierkegaardian inwardness, as becomes all the more evident when a critic like de Man draws out the full deconstructive implications of Nietzsche's thought. Their effect on his reading of Rousseau's *Confessions* is a measure of their power to subvert every last vestige of "authentic," truth-telling language. It scarcely makes sense any longer to speak of Nietzsche as an "existentialist" in the company of Kierkegaard and his latter-day disciples.

Yet to treat this antagonism as a matter of straightforward divergence is to ignore the many complicating factors at work in Kierkegaard's authorship. These take the form—as I have argued—of "aesthetic" and fictional devices that work to suspend the dialectical progress that

Kierkegaard equates with the inward coming-to-truth. The duplicity of language is always in excess of the elaborate strategies that Kierkegaard adopts to explain and justify his authorial conduct. Thus *The Point of View*, by its complex "dialectical" reordering of memories and motives, creates a text that partakes as much of fiction as of spiritual self-revelation. De Man describes this alienating logic of narrative contrivance as it affects the writing of Rousseau's *Confessions*. It is a process that "threatens the autobiographical subject not as the loss of something that was once present and that it once possessed, but as a radical estrangement between the meaning and the performance of any text" (*AR*, 298). It is equally impossible to decide just how much in *The Point of View* is dictated by a logic of narrative self-vindication basically at odds with Kierkegaard's idea of existential good faith.

De Man's prime example is the case of "the purloined ribbon," an episode in which (according to the *Confessions*) a servant girl was blamed for a theft that Rousseau had himself committed.[10] The enduring shame that resulted from his silent acquiescence is supposedly the spur and motive of Rousseau's confession. But the incident becomes—as de Man reads it—a pretext for narrative "revelations" far in excess of what mere honesty entailed. The plot is further enhanced by the idea that Rousseau (on his own admission) was prompted to betray the girl partly out of motives of obscure sexual attraction and jealousy. But this does not so much acknowledge guilt as generate a further excuse for the excessive display of it. "What Rousseau *really* wanted," de Man suggests, "is neither the ribbon nor Marion, but the public scene of exposure he actually gets" (*AR*, 285). The narrative produces guilt to order and profits in turn from the additional interest thus created.

Kierkegaard is far from wishing to impress by guiltily exhibiting his treatment of Regine. Yet his very reticence on the subject is presented as a form of strategic indirection, a means of bringing the reader to appreciate its crucial significance. Like Rousseau, but more subtly, he stages a withholding of vital information the better to guarantee its ultimate effect. What de Man writes of Rousseau could equally apply to Kierkegaard:

> The more there is to expose, the more there is to be ashamed of; the more resistance to exposure, the more satisfying the scene, and, especially, the more satisfying and eloquent the belated revelation, in the later narrative, of the inability to reveal. (*AR*, 285)

The difference between Rousseau and Kierkegaard thus is one of narrative tactics rather than of demonstrable truth-telling probity. Rousseau "reveals" his self-incriminating secrets, projecting them back into a past that inhabits the ambiguous zone between truth and fiction. Kierkegaard, on the other hand, constructs an exemplary self-justifying narrative that works both to repress and "dialectically" to display its deep-laid motivating secret.

IV

Kierkegaard thus stands in a highly ambiguous relationship to Nietzsche. The working out of his standpoint as a religious author necessitates a detour through dangerous regions of thought that bring him close to a Nietzschean position of all-consuming skeptical doubt. This "maieutic" strategy—as Kierkegaard terms it—holds out a means of awakening his reader from a state of unreflective slumber. But there is always a risk that the method will get out of hand, that the "aesthetic" production will be found to reappear at a stage where its preliminary services are definitely not required. The uses of reflection may not be so easily held within tight dialectical bounds.

Take the following passage from Kierkegaard's early (pseudonymous) text *Johannes Climacus; or, De Omnibus Dubitandum Est:*

> Reality I cannot express in language, for to indicate it, I must use ideality, which is a contradiction, an untruth. But how is immediacy annulled? By mediacy, which annuls immediacy by presupposing it. What, then, is immediacy? It is reality. What is mediacy? It is the word. How does the word annul actuality? By talking about it. . . . Consciousness is opposition and contradiction.[11]

The argument has obvious Hegelian overtones, placing subject and object (language and reality) in a constant dialectic of reciprocal negation. It is also much akin to what Derrida or de Man might have to say about the delusions engendered by naïve ontologies of language. Deconstruction sets out to demonstrate that meaning can never coincide with its object in a moment of pure, unimpeded union, and that language always intervenes to deflect, defer, or differentially complicate the relation between manifest sense and expressive intent. Meaning can be neither straightforwardly referential nor ultimately grounded in the speaker's (or author's) will-to-express. Mediation—or "reflection" in Kierkegaard's terminology—is the inescapable predicament of language, whatever those pretenses to the contrary maintained by poets, philosophers, or the normal run of commonsense metaphysicians.

Kierkegaard, of course, entertains this outlook under cover of a pseudonym ("Johannes Climacus") intended to mark it as a strictly "aesthetic" and hence inauthentic standpoint. But this tactic again begs the question of an author's power to bracket certain portions or aspects of his work simply by issuing a magisterial fiat in the name of authority and truth. Here, as in *The Point of View*, the issue is undecidable since Kierkegaard's intentions are not unambiguously there to be consulted. What necessity compels us to acknowledge just one of his implied narrators (the "religious" or authentic), thus consigning the others to a subordinate realm of merely fictive existence? As de Man remarks of Rousseau, "[T]he presence of a fictional narrator is a rhetorical necessity in any discourse that puts the truth or falsehood of its own statement in question" (*AR*, 294). This applies as much to ethical or philosophic texts as to those that openly or implicitly acknowledge their fictional status. It thus becomes impossible to separate Kierkegaard's authentic authorship from the various surrogate identities deployed in the course of its allegorical unfolding. Such supposedly clear-cut distinctions are the basis for our normal habit of categorizing "literary" as opposed to (say) "historical" or "philosophical" texts. Our readings of the latter are thereby deprived—de Man argues—of "elementary refinements that are taken for granted in literary interpretation" (*AR*, 130).

Kierkegaard's writing is peculiarly susceptible to such treatment. It provides all the materials for its own deconstruction in the form of those fictions, "aesthetic" devices and allegories of reading that make up the larger part of his literary production. Or perhaps, indeed, that production in its entirety? Kierkegaard undoubtedly labors to interpellate a reader who will find herself obliged to choose once and for all between alternative (aesthetic or ethico-religious) positions. But his text is unable to impose that choice—or even to state its necessity—without in the process seeming to render it impossible. The edifying logic of "either/or" deconstructs into the always available option of removing the disjunctive bar and deciding that any ultimate decision is beyond reach. In a passage from *The Point of View*, Kierkegaard reflects on the ironies of public misrecognition suffered in the course of his authorship. "I held out *Either/Or* to the world in my left hand, and in my right the *Two Edifying Discourses;* but all, or as good as all, grasped with their right what I held in my left" (*PV,* 20). To deconstruct Kierkegaard's text is knowingly and consistently to exploit that ever-present chance of interpretative crossed purposes. At the same time it is only to read Kierkegaard in accordance with those self-deconstructive gambits—those modes of rhetorical or narrative *mise-en-abyme*—that characterize his authorship.

Nietzsche's deconstructionist interpreters often cite a passage from his essay-fragment "On truth and falsehood in an ultramoral sense." What is truth? Nietzsche asks, and—unlike jesting Pilate—stays to provide an answer to his own question. Truth is

> a mobile army of metaphors, metonymies, anthropomorphisms, . . . truths are illusions of which one has forgotten that they are illusions, . . . coins which have their obverse effaced and now are no longer of account as coins but merely as metal. . . .[12]

The passage nicely exemplifies Nietzsche's epistemological skepticism, his reduction of knowledge and values alike to the status of arbitrary fictions, incidental products of the figurative play within language.

One could set alongside it a strikingly similar reflection from Kierkegaard's Journals, written during the final few years of his authorship. Here, if anywhere, Kierkegaard must be taken as speaking in propria persona, with the authentic voice of achieved inwardness. The passage needs quoting at some length:

> What money is in the finite world, concepts are in the world of spirit. It is in them that all transactions take place.
> Now when things go on from generation to generation in such a way that everyone takes over the concepts . . . then it happens only too easily that the concepts are gradually changed, . . . they become like false coinage—while all the time all transactions happily continue to be carried out in them. . . . Yet no one has any desire to undertake the business of revising the concepts.[13]

Up to a point, the metaphors work to similar effect. Nietzsche and Kierkegaard each perceive a process of conceptual devaluation at work within the handing down of knowledge and truth. They both attribute this process to the way in which meanings are routinely accredited as tokens of a currency subject to no kind of validating issue or control. But where

Kierkegaard treats this as a symptom of latter-day cultural malaise—a measure of spiritual inanition—Nietzsche regards it as inevitable, given that all truths and values are arbitrary constructs from the outset. Kierkegaard is still able to imagine a decisive "revision" of values, a task allotted to the few elect individuals whom Providence singles out for that purpose. No such intervention is possible for Nietzsche, since the concepts of truth and falsehood are so closely intertwined that thought must be deluded if it hopes to reestablish them on a proper, authentic basis.

This is to state Kierkegaard's difference with Nietzsche as it would strike a convert or implicitly believing reader. But again, his argument seems obliged to pass through a detour of strategic indirection that leaves itself open to further deconstructive reading. Under present conditions the Christian "reviser" cannot assume the self-evident truth vouchsafed to an "apostle." His way must necessarily partake of duplicity and fiction:

> If the apostle's personal character is one of noble and pure simplicity (which is the condition for being the instrument of the Holy Spirit), that of the reviser is his ambiguous knowledge. If the apostle is in a unique and good sense entirely in the power of Providence, the reviser is in the same power in an ambiguous sense.[14]

Again the question presents itself: how can limits be set to the dissimulating power of this "ambiguous" knowledge? What is to vouch for these roundabout and duplicitous tactics being ultimately on the side of inwardness and truth? The passage provides an answer in the form of that Providence that everywhere governs Kierkegaard's design and underwrites his authorial good faith even when it suffers the necessary swerve into conscious double-dealing. Yet Providence itself appears unable to distinguish such religiously motivated tactics from the general run of deceit and delusion. In the place of true "apostles" there nowadays come only "connoisseurs in dishonesty," and they—since they are a part of the "general dishonesty"—are treated alike by Providence as "ambiguous creatures."[15]

Kierkegaard's text thus goes to quite extraordinary lengths to make trial of its own most crucial assumption. By the end of his journal entry the argument has come round to the point of implicitly endorsing *Nietzsche's*, rather than Kierkegaard's own, deployment of the monetary image. Or—what amounts to the same thing—it has effectively denied the possibility of deciding between them. Any restoration of authentic truth achieved by the Christian "reviser" can only appear under the worldly guise of dissimulating "ambiguity." If genuine inwardness exists, its credentials are self-evident only to the true believer, and are not to be vouchsafed by way of communicable argument. Nietzsche's contention—that the coinage of truth is always already a devalued and fraudulent currency—seems to infect the very logic of Kierkegaard's argument.

Deconstruction is indeed the devil's work when applied to an author like Kierkegaard. It seeks to undermine conventions of interpretative tact that authority would have us believe are more than just "conventions," providing as they do the very basis of truth-seeking utterance or good-faith dialogic exchange. Kierkegaard's commentators may disagree as to the best or most fruitful way of interpreting his work. While some declare in favor of a largely biographical approach, others argue that the writings are more complex and elusive than any meaning—any narrative or thematic pattern—supposedly conferred on them by reference to the life. There are likewise far-reaching differences of opinion as regards the relative importance of Kierkegaard's pseudonymous works, or their place and dialectical function within his authorship as a whole.[16] Nevertheless, there is a powerful normative assumption that underlies and unites these otherwise divergent views. This principle holds that it is always the commentator's duty to expound an author's texts in obedience to the deep-lying purposive intent that serves to justify both his work and theirs. Kierkegaard's appeal to "Providence"—his trust in an end to the duplicities of language—is thus taken up and applied by his interpreters as a matter of hermeneutic faith. But deconstruction breaks with this providential ethics of reading. It affirms the irreducibility of writing to any preconceived idea of authorial design or truth at the end of enquiry. In Kierkegaard it meets perhaps the strongest, most resourceful, and hard-pressed challenge to its powers of textual demystification.

Notes

1. Kierkegaard, *The Point of View for My Work as an Author*, trans. Walter Lowrie (London: Oxford University Press, 1939), 91. Subsequent references to this text *(PV)* will be provided in parentheses.

2. See Paul de Man, *Allegories of Reading: Figural Language in Rousseau, Nietzsche, Rilke and Proust* (New Haven: Yale University Press, 1979). Subsequent references to this text *(AR)* will be provided in parentheses.

3. Kierkegaard, *Either/Or*, vols. 1 and 2, trans. David F. Swenson and Lillian Marvin Swenson (Princeton: Princeton University Press, 1971).

4. See especially his powerfully argued riposte to deconstruction in the closing chapter of Harold Bloom, *Wallace Stevens: The Poems of Our Climate* (Ithaca: Cornell University Press, 1977).

5. Jacques Derrida, *Spurs: Nietzsche's Styles*, trans. Barbara Harlow (Chicago: University of Chicago Press, 1979), 89.

6. Ibid., 97.

7. On the general topic of narrative viewpoint and strategy, see Wayne C. Booth, *The Rhetoric of Fiction* (Chicago: University of Chicago Press, 1961). For a critique of their specific ideological implications, see Colin MacCabe, *James Joyce and the Revolution of the Word* (London: Macmillan, 1978), especially pp. 13-38.

8. See for instance J. L. Austin, *How To Do Things with Words* (London: Oxford University Press, 1963) and John R. Searle, *Speech Acts: An Essay in the Philosophy of Language* (Cambridge: Cambridge University Press, 1972).

9. For much useful comment on Kierkegaard's relationship to Hegel, see Mark C. Taylor, *Kierkegaard's Pseudonymous Authorship* (Princeton: Princeton University Press, 1975).

10. For the passage in question, see Rousseau, *Oeuvres Complètes*, vol. 1: *Les Confessions, et autres textes autobiographiques*, ed. Bernard Gagnebin and Marcel Raymond (Paris: Gallimard, 1959), 85–87. In the most convenient English translation (London: Dent, 1931) it appears on 74–77.

11. Kierkegaard, *Johannes Climacus; or, De Omnibus Dubitandum Est and a Sermon*, trans. T. H. Croxall (Stanford, Calif.: Stanford University Press, 1967), 148–49.

12. As translated by Gayatri Chakravorty Spivak in her preface to Jacques Derrida, *Of Grammatology* (Baltimore: Johns Hopkins University Press, 1977), xxii.

13. Kierkegaard, *The Last Years: Journals 1853–55*, ed. and trans. Ronald Gregor Smith (London: Collins/Fontana, 1968), 198–99.

14. Ibid., 200.

15. Ibid., 201.

16. For a detailed and informative discussion of these differences, see Taylor, *Kierkegaard's Pseudonymous Authorship*, 11–37.

Mimesis and the
End of Art

John Sallis

The Greek view of art as essentially mimetic remained effective throughout much of the history of metaphysics. Yet, at least by the time of Kant, of romanticism, and of German idealism, this classical concept seems to have lost much of its force and to have given way to an approach that focuses on the creativity of the artist, on the natural poetic genius, rather than on the talent for fashioning mimetic reproductions of nature. Thus Kant draws the contrast in the *Critique of Judgment:* "Everyone is agreed that genius is to be wholly opposed to the spirit of mimesis [thus I translate, back in the direction of Greek, Kant's word *Nachahmungsgeist*]."[1] In romanticism the corresponding contrast between genius and talent becomes virtually a commonplace.[2]

And yet, along with this devaluation of mimesis, there is also a doubling by which another, superior form of mimesis is both opposed to the devalued form and put forth as essential to art. Thus, with Kant, despite the opposition of genius to the spirit of mimesis, there occurs a certain reinstatement of mimesis: "[A]rt can only be called beautiful if we are conscious of it as art while yet it looks like nature *[als Natur aussieht]*."[3] Similarly, in discussing the role of classical models in art, Kant notes that they are to serve as models not to be copied but to be imitated [thus I translate, in the spirit of English romanticism: *Muster nicht der Nachmachung, sondern der Nachahmung*]."[4] Coleridge is explicit regarding this hierarchical opposition within mimesis, this doubling of

mimesis: "Now an *Imitation* differs from a copy in this, that it of necessity implies and demands *difference*—whereas a copy aims at *identity*."[5]
In Schopenhauer the doubling is even more explicit: a false, concept-
bound mimesis is rejected precisely in order to reinstate mimesis in its
genuine form, as repetition *(Wiederholung)* of the eternal ideas apprehended through pure contemplation.[6]

But with Hegel it would seem to be otherwise. Almost at the beginning of the *Aesthetics* one finds an extended critique of the view of art as
essentially mimetic. This critique one might easily take as definitively
excluding mimesis from the Hegelian view of art, in which case Hegel's
Aesthetics would, in this regard at least, constitute a decisive break with
the history of metaphysics rather than a completion, rather than the
moment in which the metaphysics of art is thought through to the end.

And yet—as I shall undertake to show—there is no such break. Not
only does Hegel's critique of an impoverished form of mimesis come to
be matched by a reinstatement of another, transformed mimesis, one so
transformed that it goes unnamed as mimesis; but also, by reclaiming at
a more profound level the Greek determination of art as essentially
mimetic, Hegel thinks this determination, *the* metaphysical determination of art, through to its end. In the end, thinking the metaphysics of art
through to its end, Hegel announces the end of art.

My concern is, then, with mimesis: with the word, with the concept,
and with the thing itself. With the word—that is, with the Greek word
that has been both transliterated into the modern European languages
and translated into those languages, for instance, as *Nachahmung* and as
imitation. With the concept—that is, with the meaning of the word, or,
rather, the configuration of meaning corresponding to the history of the
transliteration and translation of the word. With mimesis itself, with the
thing itself— if indeed one can speak of the thing itself in the case of the
operation that, reproducing the thing by setting alongside it an image,
opens the very opposition by which the *itself* of the thing itself would be
determined.

First, then, I shall want to consider how the concept of mimesis
comes into play in the Greek determination of the essence of art. In this
determination the word *mimesis* comes to be taken as that which says
what art itself *is*. And yet, at the same time, it comes also to signify a certain
reproduction that almost the entire history of metaphysics denounces as
sham, as a mere phantom of genuine art, if not indeed of truth as such. From
Plato to Nietzsche it will be said again and again: the poets lie.

The determination of mimesis as the essence of art is governed by metaphysics as it opens in the thought of Plato and Aristotle. And yet, it is not as though metaphysics is itself first determined and then simply brought to bear on the determination of mimesis; for the opening of metaphysics is itself inextricably bound up with mimesis, most notably by way of such oppositions as that between image and original. Precisely because a concept of mimesis will already have been in play in the formation of the very means, of the conceptual resources, by which it will then come to be determined, the concept of mimesis will never have been simply determined. It will never have been delimited once and for all beyond all possibility of slippage but will retain a certain indetermination, a certain play, outlining the space in which the reiterated determination of mimesis will be carried out, most notably the doublings in which an inferior mimesis is devalued and opposed to a superior form of mimesis.

It is just such slippage that will prove to be in play when Hegel, having excluded an impoverished concept of mimesis, recovers another mimesis at a more profound level. I shall want to show, then, that through this recovery Hegel thinks the Greek determination of art through to its end and that he does so precisely in thinking through the end of art, in announcing that art is at an end.

In the afterword to "The Origin of the Work of Art" Heidegger discusses a series of passages from Hegel's *Aesthetics* in which the end of art is declared. He refers to the *Aesthetics* as "the most comprehensive reflection on art that the West possesses," explaining that its comprehensiveness derives not (as one might suppose) from the wealth of material discussed, but from the metaphysical basis on which the reflection proceeds. Then Heidegger concludes: "A decision has not yet been made regarding Hegel's declaration, for behind this declaration there stands Western thought since the Greeks."[7] Heidegger's point is that Hegel's declaration of the end of art issues from the completion of the metaphysical determination of art originating with the Greeks. What has not yet been decided is whether Hegel's declaration is to remain in force, or whether there are means by which to rethink art outside the end announced by Hegel. Can mimesis, the essence of art, be reconstituted outside the closure of the metaphysics of art?

I shall deal, thus, with three themes: (1) the Greek determination of art as essentially mimetic; (2) Hegel's recovery of mimesis at a level that allows him to think the Greek determination of art through to that end at which the end of art can be declared; (3) the question of rethinking art outside the metaphysical end.

I

Let me begin by recalling the familiar scene in Book 10 of the *Republic* where Socrates, resuming what he calls "the old quarrel between philosophy and poetry" (607b), poses to Glaucon the question: What is mimesis? Taking the example of a couch, Socrates distinguishes between the couch itself, that is, the εἶδος, and the many couches that are fabricated by craftsmen. Then Socrates mentions another, a different sort of craftsman, one who "is not only able to make all implements but also makes everything that grows naturally from the earth." Socrates continues: "And he produces all animals—the others and himself too—and, in addition to that, produces earth and heaven and gods and everything in heaven and everything in Hades under the earth." Glaucon is amazed at this marvelous craftsman and even more so when told by Socrates that he, Glaucon, could make all these things. Socrates explains: "You could fabricate them quickly in many ways and most quickly, of course, if you were willing to take a mirror and carry it around everywhere." Glaucon answers: "Yes, appearances but not beings in truth" (596c–e).

Such appearances, such images cast in this craftsman's mirror, constitute a third order, the order of mimesis. The ordering is ontological: still further from the couch itself than the couches made by other craftsmen, the image produced by mimesis is an image only of the looks of a couch—of its φαντάσμα, its phantom, if you will—not of its truth. Socrates concludes: "Therefore, mimesis is surely far from the truth" (598b). It is because of this remoteness from the truth and because of the corruptive power of the phantoms produced by mimesis that the poet must be banished from the philosophic city, at least as long as he is not able to give an apology for poetry:

> But as long as it is not able to make its apology, when we listen to it, we shall chant these words to ourselves as a countercharm, taking care against falling back again into this love, which is childish and belongs to the many. We are, at all events, aware that such poetry must not be taken seriously as a serious thing laying hold of truth, but that the man who hears it must be careful, fearing for the regime [πολιτεία] in himself, and must hold what we have said about poetry. (608a)

But then—most remarkably—having banished the poet, having posed in the discourse on mimesis the opposition between philosophy and poetry, having posed it as the opposition between truth and phantom, the *Republic* itself ends in a way that tends to efface in deed that very opposition. Socrates tells a story, that of Er's visit to the underworld. It is a story not unlike those told by the poets, not unlike the story of Odysseus's visit to the dead, to the phantoms in Hades, the story told by Homer in Book 11 of the *Odyssey*. It is as though, in order to complete his struggle against the poets, Socrates had himself to become a kind of poet. It is as though, even after the philosophic denunciation of poetry, even after poetry is set outside the truth and the poet banished from the city—it is as though poetry continued to haunt philosophy, as though philosophy could never quite be done with the phantom of mimesis.

Aristotle's discussion of mimesis is quite different. It is set much more within predetermined limits, within a discourse on poetry as such that does not open so directly upon ontology and politics. Precisely for this reason Aristotle's discussion has been, from the point of view of art, the more effective, and indeed the *Poetics* has served as the paradigmatic statement, the classical formulation, of the mimetic character of art.

Let me review a few points of that formulation, taking it up at the level where the question is that of mimesis as such and not yet specifically of the form assumed by mimesis in tragedy. The first point pertains to a passage in which Aristotle asks about the origin of poetry. How is it, he asks, that there came to be poetry? He answers that it arose from natural causes; hence, what later thought will regard as the opposition between art and nature is thought by Aristotle as an opening within nature. Here is the passage in which he describes the first of the two natural origins of poetry: "Mimesis is natural to man from childhood, one of his advantages over the lower animals being this, that he is the most mimetic and learns at first by mimesis" (1448b2). So, mimesis belongs naturally to man from childhood, and poetry grows out of the naturally mimetic activities. Aristotle notes that especially in childhood one learns by mimesis. But if one can learn by mimesis, then mimesis must have a capacity to disclose things—that is, mimesis of something must serve to bring that thing into view in such a way that one comes to know it, that is, learns about it. One thinks, for example, of the way in which a child learns about things by drawing pictures of them; also of the way in which children learn about doing certain things by playing mimetically at doing them. This connection between mimesis and disclosure is of utmost importance; for it indicates that mimesis is not simply remote from the truth, that it does not merely produce phantoms that would mislead and hence corrupt the regime within the soul but rather that it produces images of the truth, images opening disclosively upon things in such a way that one can, through mimesis, learn of those things.

Let me refer next to the passage in which Aristotle goes on to identify the second cause of poetry:

> And it is also natural for all to delight in works of mimesis. This is shown by experience: Though the things themselves may be painful to see, we take delight in seeing the most perfect images [εἰκόν] of them, the forms for example of obscene beasts and corpses. The reason is this. Learning things gives great pleasure not only to philosophers but also to the rest of mankind, however small their capacity for it. The reason that we enjoy seeing images is that one is at the same time learning and gathering what each thing is. . . . (1448b2–6)

The second cause of poetry is thus the delight, the pleasure, afforded by products of mimesis. Yet, again, it is the connection with learning that is most significant, that is even the cause of the delight in imitation, the cause of the cause: one takes delight in seeing images because one learns by looking at them and learning is naturally a source of pleasure for all men. By looking at works of mimesis, one learns, with delight, about things that, if looked upon directly, would be painful to see. Both the delight and the learning are constituted in the difference between the image and the thing itself: instead of turning away in pain, one looks at the image, with delight, and learns of the thing. The difference, the remoteness of the image from the truth, is no longer just a source of deception but rather is the very condition of the possibility of a certain kind of learning.

Yet only of a certain kind of learning, one subject to a certain precondition. Thus, Aristotle continues: "If one has not happened to see the thing before, one's pleasure is not due to the mimesis as such but to the technique or the color or some other cause" (1048b6). This says: in order to be able to take delight in an image produced by mimesis, in order to be capable of that delight that arises in learning of the thing imaged, one must already have seen the thing itself. Otherwise, whatever delight one may take in the image has a different source, has no connection with learning. For—though Aristotle leaves it unsaid—one can learn through the image *only* if it is recognized *as* an image of the thing itself; and such recognition requires that somehow one has seen the thing itself already, in advance, that one has already caught a glimpse of those obscene beasts and corpses themselves, even if only in turning, in pain, away from them to their images. Poetry, arising in mimesis, would be subordinate to a prior vision of the truth.

The more radical import of this subordination is broached when, a bit further in the *Poetics*, Aristotle focuses on the difference between poet and historian:

> The difference between a historian and a poet is this, that one tells what happened and the other what might happen. Hence poetry is something more philosophic and serious than history, since its statements are of the nature rather of universals, whereas those of history are singulars. (1451a-b)

The differentiation turns on the difference between the things addressed by historian and poet, respectively. Whereas the historian speaks of the singular, of what has happened, the poet refers mimetically to what might happen, to what is possible, to the universal. Unlike those things of which Herodotus tells in his history, the things of which the poet would bring forth images are not things that one can simply see, as the historian may have seen the events of which he tells. But, if these things of which the poet speaks are not to be seen as such, then poetic mimesis, bringing forth an image, would not simply allow one to see better—for instance, with delight rather than with pain—something that could also be seen without the intervention of mimesis. On the contrary, mimesis would make visible something that otherwise could not be seen at all, a thing itself withdrawn as such from sight.

Now the questions begin to accumulate—open questions, left open by Aristotle, opening the very space in which subsequent thinking about art will be played out.

What of the subordination of poetic mimesis to a prior vision of the truth? What of the requirement that one must have seen the thing itself in order to be able to recognize and to learn from the image? How is one to have seen the thing if the thing cannot as such be seen? Is the prior vision to be entrusted, as it were, to the mind's eye? Must art be preceded by an intellectual vision of the universal? Would this not amount to subordinating art to philosophy?—at least in the sense that philosophy would always need to be called upon to give art its ratification, to demonstrate that the images produced by artistic mimesis are not deceptive phantoms but rather open upon the true things themselves? In this case philosophy and not poetry would be called upon to give the apology for poetry and to recall to the city those poets thus ratified.

But even if subordinate to a prior vision and subject thus to such philosophic ratification, poetry remains distinct. For the poet does not tell of what might happen in general, simply translating in his discourse a vision of universality, but rather tells, for example, the story of Odysseus, of Agamemnon, or of Oedipus. In a singular image the poet—somehow—constitutes a mimesis of the universal. Somehow, the poet lets the universal shine forth in the singular images evoked by his words or, in the case of the dramatic poet, brought upon the stage to voice those words and to enact what is bespoken.

For all that is said in the *Republic* about the remoteness of the artistic image from the truth, it is in another Platonic dialogue that this shining forth of truth in the image is named. In the course of the *Phaedrus*, which takes place, not at the limit of the city, but entirely outside, in the countryside, Socrates contrasts τὸ καλόν (the beautiful) with the other εἴδη that, according to the story he has just been telling, are gazed upon when the soul, prior to birth, follows in the train of the gods up through the heavens. Whereas subsequently, after embodiment, none of the other εἴδη can be seen by that sight provided through the body, the beautiful is an exception: "For the beautiful alone this has been ordained, to be the most shining-forth and the most lovely [ἐκφανέστατον εἶναι καὶ ἐρασμιώτατον]" (250d). Τὸ καλόν names, then, the shining forth of being, of what will be called the universal, its way of shining forth amidst the visible and the singular. If art is a matter of beauty, of bringing forth works that are beautiful, it is because the work of art is a privileged site for the shining forth of being amidst the visible and the singular.

Through the Platonic and Aristotelian discussions of mimesis, there is established a certain axiomatics that will remain in force throughout the history of metaphysics. This axiomatics is such as to assign to mimesis contrary values. These values may be taken as corresponding to the two standpoints from which the mimetic relation between the thing itself (i.e., the original) and its image may be considered. If one takes the standpoint of the original, then the image will represent a falling away, a derivativeness, a certain decline—in short, remoteness from truth, as in the discussions in Book 10 of the *Republic*. But if, on the other hand, one takes the standpoint of the image and looks to the original, then the image will have the positive value of being disclosive of the original.

It is an open question—and I shall leave it open—whether and how these two contrary valuations of mimesis come to be thought together in Greek thought. However this may be, they do come eventually, in the history of metaphysics, to be thought together, within a certain unity. Such thinking reaches its culmination in Hegel's *Aesthetics*, where such unity is thought as the end of art.

II

Let me turn now to Hegel's *Aesthetics*, focusing, first of all, on Hegel's extended critique of the view that would identify mimesis as the aim, the end, of art. In Hegel's text *mimesis*, the word, has been translated into *Nachahmung;* and the mimesis in question is oriented to nature. Both the translation and the orientation mark, if they do not indeed produce, such a divergence from the Greek determination that it is little wonder that when Hegel addresses *das Prinzip von der Nachahmung der Natur* his tone is utterly critical. Hegel's formulation of the principle marks the divergence even more clearly: "According to this view, *Nachahmung*, as facility in copying *[nachbilden]* natural forms just as they are, in a way that corresponds to them completely, is supposed to constitute the essential end [or: aim—*Zweck*] of art."[8]

The first of the three criticisms that Hegel offers of this view begins by indicating, still further, how impoverished the concept of mimesis here employed really is. This determination of art as mimetic involves a purely formal end—namely, that whatever exists in the world is to be made a second time, made over again. But such mere repetition, Hegel observes, is superfluous labor, for whatever might be displayed by such mimesis—flowers, natural scenes, animals—we possess already in our gardens or in the countryside beyond. And those originals will always be superior, for mimetic art can only produce one-sided deceptions, the mere *Schein der Wirklichkeit*—that is, the mere "look," a phantom of what truly is, not the reality of life but only a pretense of life. Hegel retells some stories about such deceptive copying: the story of the grapes painted by Zeuxis and declared a triumph of art because living doves pecked at them; and the story of Büttner's monkey, which ate away a picture of a beetle in Rösel's book *Amusements of Insects* but then was pardoned by its master because it had proved how excellent the pictures in the book really were. Hegel summarizes by way of a bizarre comparison: "In sum, however, it must be said that, by mere *Nachahmung*, art cannot stand in competition with nature, and, if it tries, it looks like a worm trying to crawl after an elephant" (52/43).

Despite the exotic examples, none of this is very far from what Socrates said of that marvelous craftsman who could make everything and whom one could imitate by carrying a mirror around everywhere; in particular, it is not far from what Socrates said about the images produced by such a third-order craftsman. And yet, in declaring such images remote from truth, Socrates was attentive to their power, their power to deceive and hence to corrupt; and it was because of this dangerous power of the products of mimesis that the poets had to be expelled from the philosophic city. For Hegel, on the other hand, there is no danger at this level. Hegel's examples illustrate deception exercised not on human beings but on monkeys and doves; and what for Socrates was a deceptive power capable even of corrupting the soul becomes with Hegel a matter of mere conjuring tricks, in which one might take a certain brief pleasure but by which one would not for long be deceived. This difference again indicates the divergence between such *Nachahmung* and mimesis—the impoverishment that mimesis has undergone in the translation. One might thus expect that a certain doubling is to come into play, a return of mimesis at a more profound level, in a more powerful form. But not yet.

Hegel proceeds to the second criticism: since the principle of *Nachahmung* is purely formal, prescribing simply that things be made over again, copied, no place is given in art for objective beauty. For if this principle is made the end of art, then there will be no question of the character of *what* is supposed to be copied, but only a demand for the correctness of the copy. As for the choice of objects and their beauty or ugliness, everything will depend on merely subjective taste; that is, even if art remains oriented to the beautiful, bound to produce copies only of beautiful objects, the decision regarding which objects are beautiful will be purely subjective.

Yet, even aside from the question of objectivity, this principle of *Nachahmung* of nature is not to be accepted, says Hegel, "at least in this general, wholly abstract form" (54/44). For though painting and sculpture represent objects that appear similar to natural ones, such is not at all the case with works of architecture or even with works of poetry insofar as they are not confined to mere description. This is, then, the crux of the third criticism: the principle is not universally applicable, if indeed it is applicable to any of the arts.

Hegel's conclusion, delimiting succinctly the form of mimesis thus brought under criticism, differentiates it decisively from the end of art: "The end [or: aim—*Zweck*] of art must therefore lie in something still other than the merely formal *Nachahmung* of what is present, which in every case can bring to birth only technical tricks but not works of art [*Kunststücke, nicht aber Kunstwerke*]" (55/45).

And yet, despite all the criticism, Hegel's formulations betray that his rejection of mimesis is qualified, is limited to mimesis "in this general, wholly abstract form," to mimesis as formal *Nachahmung* of what is merely present, of particular things in nature. Indeed, in the sentence immediately following the just cited conclusion he broaches the doubling thus prepared, the transition to what, though he will not name it as such, will prove to be another form of mimesis, one that is not a matter of mere form, that is not merely formal, one to which a certain content is essential. Here is the sentence that follows the conclusion: "Certainly it is an essential moment of a work of art to have a natural shape as its basis, because what it presents is presented in the form of an external and therefore also natural appearance." The work of art is thus to be conceived as a natural appearance that presents something else, as a natural appearance through which some content distinct from the work is presented. The word that I am translating as *present*, the word that names the more profound, more powerful form of mimesis is *darstellen*.

The question that arises at once concerns the content presented by the work of art. Hegel discusses various alternatives—for example, that the content is everything that has a place in the human spirit, an alternative whose inclusiveness makes it, in the end, no specification of content at all, only something purely formal; or, again,that it is a matter of a certain spiritual content by which moral improvement would be accomplished, art thus being reduced to a means to an end other than itself. Recalling the need to supersede the rigid oppositions especially characteristic of what he calls the modern moralistic view, Hegel asserts, finally, "that the vocation of art is to unveil the truth in the form of sensuous artistic configuration and to present the reconciled opposition, and so to have its end [*Endzweck*] in itself, in this very presentation and unveiling [*Darstellung und Enthüllen*]" (64/55). Art is sensuous presentation of the truth and as such remains, in a profound sense, mimetic.

Such is, then, in the most general terms, Hegel's redetermination of mimesis.

In order to gauge the profound import of this redetermination, it is necessary to consider the way in which it constitutes a recovery of the Greek determination of art as essentially mimetic; indeed, not only a recovery but a fulfillment of the Greek view, carrying it through to the end. Let me consider, then, three points: first, the way in which Hegel recovers the positive value assigned to mimesis by the axiomatics constituted in Greek thought; second, the way in which, beyond the negativity that led him to reject the impoverished concept of mimesis, he also recovers a negative value for mimesis as redetermined, a negative value that parallels (up to a point, at least) that assigned by the ancient axiomatics; and third, the way in which Hegel thinks both values together, in a unity, precisely by thinking the end of art. In this thinking even the apparent polysemy of *end*—that it would mean aim, also fulfillment of the aim, as well as a certain termination—will be surmounted in the direction of unity.

The positive value is evident in Hegel's formulation of the redetermination. It is a matter of a mimesis that would consist in presenting the truth, unveiling it, disclosing it, just as those images of which Aristotle tells disclose the things themselves in such a way that one learns, with delight, of those things. Also, as with Aristotle, that which art sensuously presents, which it discloses, is the universal, even if thought concretely, not the particular things of nature that would be copied by that form of mimesis which Hegel has rejected.

Though Hegel himself passes quickly over the Platonic idea of the beautiful, criticizing its abstractness, insisting that it must now be thought more concretely (32/22), there is, in fact, a profound affinity between Hegel's discussions of beauty and that discussion that I have recalled from the *Phaedrus* as expressing, in contrast to the *Republic*, the positive value accorded to art. From the very outset Hegel's *Aesthetics* is oriented to the idea of beauty, essentially to the idea of artistic beauty; and the beauty of art is taken to lie in its sensuously presenting (the word is, again, *darstellen*) the most comprehensive truths of spirit (19/7). Hegel addresses an objection that might be raised concerning the worthiness of art, thus determined, to be treated philosophically. The objection is aimed at the character of art as *shining* and as *deception (Schein und Täuschung*—I merely transliterate the German *Schein*, in hopes of retaining something of its broad range of meanings: shine, look, appearance, semblance, illusion). Hegel's response is that the objection would be justified if shining could be considered something that, in principle, ought not to be. But, he continues,

Shining itself is essential to essence. Truth would not be truth if it did not shine and appear *[scheinen und erscheinen]*, if it were not truth *for* someone, *for* itself as well as for spirit in general too. (19/8)

Art presents sensuously the truth, the truth of spirit. But it belongs to the essence of spirit to be for itself, to be not only essence but also actual appearance, to appear to itself. Thus, the appearing, the shining, that is characteristic of art has its justification in the very essence of truth, in the very determination of spirit as for itself. Or, rather, the shining has its full justification in the determination of spirit as in and for itself *(an und für sich)*, for it is as such that the shining has its proper a priori, the prior vision of truth that Aristotle required for mimesis; for as in itself spirit is always already implicitly what it comes to be explicitly, for itself, namely, self-present. Not only does the shining of art have its justification, but indeed it constitutes the very beauty of the work of art: when, later in the *Aesthetics*, Hegel develops a rigorous determination of beauty, he defines it as "the sensuous shining of the idea" (117/111). Virtually a translation of Plato: τὸ καλόν as the shining forth of the ideas, as the idea that most shines forth, τὸ ἐκφανέστατον.

Still further in the *Aesthetics*, when he comes to discuss specifically the beauty of art, Hegel—in a move comparable to the classical form of art—illustrates artistic shining, i.e., beauty, by referring to the human body and to the privilege of the eye. Let me cite some excerpts from this remarkable passage:

> But if we ask in which particular organ the whole soul appears as soul, we will at once name the eye; for in the eye the soul is concentrated and the soul does not merely see through it but is also seen in it. . . . It is to be asserted of art that it has to convert every shape in all points of its visible surface into an eye, which is the seat of the soul and brings the spirit into appearance. . . . So, art makes every one of its productions into a thousand-eyed Argus, whereby the inner soul and spirit is seen at every point. And it is not only the bodily form, the look of the eyes, the countenance and posture, but also actions and events, speech and tones of voice, and the series of their course through all conditions of appearance that art has everywhere to make into an eye, in which the free soul is revealed in its inner infinity. (155f./153f.)

Art would bring spirit to shine forth in pure transparency, in a transparency as pure as that of the eye, or, rather, in as pure a transparency as is possible in a presentation that is sensuous. And yet, one cannot but wonder about this limit, especially since Hegel, having posed the objection that art involves shining *and deception,* has proceeded to vindicate the shining of art but has said nothing directly regarding the charge of deception.

Let me turn, then, to the second point, the negative value of mimesis, which in the ancient axiomatics was constituted primarily by the deceptive and corruptive power of art. For Hegel, on the other hand, the negative value lies in the inadequacy of art with respect to the higher phases of the content to be presented. Hegel outlines this negativity in the following passage near the beginning of the *Aesthetics,* just after the vindication of shining:

> But while, on the one hand, we give this high position to art, it is, on the other hand, just as necessary to remember that neither in content nor in form is art the highest and absolute mode of bringing to consciousness the true interests of the spirit. For precisely on account of its form, art is limited to the specific content. Only one sphere and stage of truth is capable of being presented in the element of art. In order to be a genuine content for art, such truth must in virtue of its own determination be able to go forth into [the sphere of] sense and remain adequate to itself there. This is the case, for example, with the gods of Greece. On the other hand, there is a deeper comprehension of truth which is no longer so akin and friendly to sense as to be capable of being taken up and expressed in this medium. (21/9f.)

That deeper comprehension of truth belongs to those two forms that supersede art, namely, religion, in which the content is linked to the inwardness of the subject; and philosophy, in which the same content comes to have the form, not of representation *(Vorstellung),* as in religion, but of conceptual thought. Hegel is outspoken about the subordination of art to philosophy, about the authority of philosophy, from which art, he says, must receive its genuine ratification.

And yet, that ratification cannot but also declare that art, however much it may let truth shine forth, falls short of the truth as it has now come to be comprehended. The end of art, its aim, falls short of the intrinsically highest end, namely, the self-presentation of spirit in its true form and content. Because art falls short of that end, as it is now comprehended, art is at an end.

Hence the third point: precisely by thinking art in reference to its end, the sensuous presentation of spirit, Hegel thinks together the positive and the negative values to be attributed to art—that is, he thinks the axiomatics of mimesis in its unity. But, in turn, to think thus the end of art is also to be led to declare that art is at an end. Hegel's *Aesthetics* abounds in such declarations.

Art is now at an end. Hegel declares that it "no longer fills our highest needs . . . , no longer affords that satisfaction of spiritual needs that earlier ages and nations sought in it and found in it alone" (21f./10). He continues: "In all these respects art, considered in its highest destination, is and remains for us a thing of the past" (22/11). Not that art will now simply cease to be; not that there will no longer be artists producing works of art. Hegel says: "We may well hope that art will always rise higher and come to perfection." And yet, he continues, "[T]he form of art has ceased to be the supreme need of the spirit. . . . We bow the knee no longer" (110/103). Art is at an end precisely in the sense that it is *aufgehoben;* and the polysemy of ends is submitted to the complex unity of *Aufheben.*

And yet, this *Aufhebung* of art was prepared long ago, prepared by art itself, by the very limitation of its end in comparison with the highest end of spirit. Art is not only now at an end but was already at an end with the end of classical Greek art. For in Greek art, the classical form of art, the human body counts as the natural shape of spirit; the presentation of spirit that is thus given, most notably in Greek sculpture, is the most adequate presentation that art can achieve. In Hegel's words:

> The classical form of art has attained the pinnacle of what illustration *[Versinnlichung]* by art could achieve, and if there is something defective in it, the defect is just art itself and the restrictedness of the sphere of art. (85/79)

When romantic art, attentive to the inwardness of self-consciousness, cancels the undivided unity achieved by classical art, it becomes, Hegel says, "the self-transcendence of art but within its own sphere and in the form of art itself" (87/80).

And yet, if one refers to the individual arts, the self-transcendence will prove not to have waited for the accomplishment of the classical art of the Greeks. For in poetry the very last remaining sensuous element, sound, becomes merely a sign of an idea; and thus poetry is not dependent on external sensuous material for its realization, as are the other arts. Or, rather, poetry is precisely in the movement of passing over from such dependence into freedom from the sensuous—that is, poetry too is as such the self-transcendence of art: "Yet, precisely, at this highest stage, art now transcends itself, in that it forsakes the element of a reconciled embodiment of the spirit in sensuous form and passes over from the poetry of representation to the prose of thought" (89/94). But there has always been poetry, just as there has been, at least for a long time, stern denunciation of art, of its claim to present the truth; Hegel mentions the Jews, the Mohammedans, Plato, and the Reformation (110/103).

Not only now is art at an end. Not only with the end of classical Greek art was it at an end. Art was always already at an end.

III

According to the determination that is in play from Plato to Hegel, mimesis is a matter of imaginal presentation, of presentation in and through an image. In mimesis something is presented, made present, brought to presence, while also remaining to a degree withdrawn, absent, never being quite captured in the image. Through its presence the image makes present an original while also, by its very character as an image, leaving the original withdrawn, keeping open the difference. Mimesis, thus determined, aims at making present; it is governed by a certain demand for presence, even though the very structure of mimesis is such as to preclude the possibility of full presence. Correspondingly, the ancient axiomatics of mimesis is governed by a privileging of presence: the positive value of mimesis lies in its capacity to present, to bring the original to presence; its negative value derives from its incapacity to bring that original fully to presence, from the necessity of leaving the original also withdrawn, to some extent concealed.

The privileging of presence operative in this axiomatics is not merely a gratuitous presupposition; it is not an unmotivated assumption with which one can simply dispense with impunity. On the contrary, the Platonic discussions show unmistakably that the demand for presence, the privileging of it, is linked to a certain need, a need that one might even venture to call ethical, namely, the need for vigilance in the face of the possibility of deception and of the corruption that can be spawned by deception. It is because of the deceptive and corruptive power of the mimetic phantoms that one must safeguard the regime within oneself; it is thus that Socrates and Glaucon require the poets to deliver an apology before the tribunal of philosophy with its demand for presence.

And yet, from the side of the poets, this is a demand that is improper, not to say unjust. For the axiomatics that philosophy brings to bear upon mimesis serves only to disguise an instability within the very concept of mimesis. The instability lies in the conflict between two moments constitutive of the philosophical concept of mimesis: on the one hand, mimesis is subject to the demand for presence, is determined by an orientation to full presence; yet, on the other hand, its very structure, the difference between image and original, precludes the possibility of full presence. A mimetic presentation that succeeded in bringing the original fully to presence would thereby—by an essential, structural necessity— have ceased to be a mimetic presentation. The instability is thus a tendency to self-effacement, self-annulment.

It is precisely this tendency, inherent in the very determination of mimesis, that allows Hegel to reinscribe mimesis within the logic of *Aufhebung*. Passing over that power of deception and corruption that marked the negative value of mimesis in the ancient axiomatics, Hegel regards the negativity of mimetic presentation as merely its incompleteness, its inadequacy for presenting its content; he regards it, in short, as a determinate negation, which, even if harboring deception and the possibility of corruption, is to be overturned into revelation and perfection. Thus, it is by releasing the tendency to self-effacement inherent in the very concept of mimesis that Hegel comes to declare the end of art. Thus it is too that he settles the old quarrel between philosophy and poetry, indeed so decisively that it hardly matters anymore whether the poets remain in exile or return to the city.

Under the reign of the demand for presence, mimesis cannot but be effaced and art declared to be at an end, the very determination of end, the unity of its senses, being governed by the logic of *Aufhebung*.

And yet, one might venture with justification a break with that logic. One might venture to set the demand for presence out of action so as to reconstitute and rethink mimesis within the field thus opened. One might so venture in the interest of justice to art, in behalf of art itself, art proper, which one would then want to distinguish from the improper determination brought to bear upon it in the history of metaphysics. But also one might so venture still in the name of philosophy, justifying the break by appeal to the necessity of *questioning* the privilege of presence. Even though neither the venture nor its justification will be able to escape the continual risk of falling back into the very system that would be suspended.

Traces of such a rethinking of mimesis can be found in the work of Nietzsche and of Heidegger. In *The Birth of Tragedy*, for instance, where with the familiar double gesture Nietzsche dismisses the determination of art as mere imitation of nature only to restore to art a more profound sense of mimesis as supplement. Most notable is Nietzsche's determination of Dionysian art—hence also, of tragedy—as involving a form of mimesis in which no images are operative, a form of mimesis that is thus such as to preclude the demand for presence. With Heidegger, on the other hand, one finds only the negative gesture, the dismissal of mimesis as presentation of natural things or of universals. And yet, despite Heidegger's silence regarding any reconstitution of mimesis beyond these determinations, one could read the entire analysis in "The Origin of the Work of Art" as elaborating a mimetic relation between the work of art and the truth (redetermined as strife of world and earth) that would be set into the work, that would be constituted only in being set into the work, that would thus not precede its mimesis.

If one can gather these traces into a rethinking of mimesis outside the privilege of presence, one will disrupt the unity of end enforced by the Hegelian *Aufhebung*. Then a decision will have been made regarding Hegel's declaration that art is at an end. Then one will have to think differently the end of art, to think it from difference, to think its relation to the limit of presence, to that which, delimiting presence, remains itself withheld, concealed,

And yet, one will need—perhaps more than ever—to recall the Socratic warnings about the deceptive and corruptive power of the phantoms produced by art. One will need to renew—at the limit—the old quarrel between philosophy and poetry. Without reinvoking the demand for presence, one will need nonetheless to resume Socratic vigilance, to learn the vigilance of questioning at the limit, at the end.

Notes

1. Kant, *Kritik der Urteilskraft* (Hamburg: Felix Meiner, 1974), 161.
2. See John Spencer Hill, ed., *Imagination in Coleridge* (Totowa, N.J.: Rowman and Littlefield, 1978), 133f.
3. Kant, *Kritik der Urteilskraft*, 159.
4. Ibid., 163.

5. Hill, *Imagination in Coleridge*, 91.

6. A. Schopenhauer, *Die Welt als Wille und Vorstellung* (Cotta-Verlag/Insel-Verlag), vol. 1, §§36, 52.

7. M. Heidegger, *Holzwege*, vol. 5 of *Gesamtausgabe* (Frankfurt a.M.: Vittorio Klostermann, 1977), 68.

8. G. W. F. Hegel, *Ästhetik*, ed. Friedrich Bassenge (West Berlin: Verlag das Europäische Buch, 1985), 1:51. English translation by T. M. Knox: *Hegel's Aesthetics: Lectures on Fine Art* (Oxford: Oxford University Press, 1975), 1:41. Subsequent references to this work (all to volume 1) will be given by page number within the text, the first number referring to the German edition, the second to the English translation.

"The Necessary Heritage of Darkness": Tropics of Negativity in Schelling, Derrida, and de Man

David L. Clark

> Nothing is easier than to displace oneself into the realm of pure
> thinking; but it is not so easy then to escape that realm. The world
> does not consist of mere categories or pure concepts, . . . but of
> concrete and contingent things, and what must be considered is the
> illogical, the other, which is *not* concept, but its opposite, which only
> unwillingly accepts the concept. It is here that philosophy must take
> its test.
> —Friedrich Schelling, *Zur Grundlegung der Positiven Philosophie*

What was God doing before the creation, before even the creation of himself as the original, determinate being? An impossible question to ask, admittedly, for how could anything be said to have *been*, much less to have been *done*, before the beginning? Even to think the question is to risk a certain transgression and irrationality, for, already, the answer will necessitate contemplating a past that could never have been present as such. An unrepresentable past, then, but for all that perhaps no less undeniable. What, indeed, could be more primordial than the *Logos*, except possibly the inaugural performance of its enunciation, its *saying*, as it were, "spoken" out of a wholly other space that Blanchot will feel compelled to call "the terrifyingly ancient"?[1] A strange thought, risking, Heidegger would say, the "destruction of all thinkability."[2] Schelling thought it. So, in his own skeptical way, did Kant. Although I want to concentrate almost exclusively on Schelling in this essay, I will begin with Kant. On the beginning. "Unconditioned necessity, which we so indispensably require as the last bearer of all things, is for human reason the veritable abyss," Kant warns in the First Critique.

> The thought is as unbearable as it is unavoidable: that of the being that we represent to ourselves as the highest of all possible beings saying to itself, "I am from eternity to eternity, outside of me is nothing except that which is something through my will; *but from where, then, am I?*" Here, everything sinks beneath us, and the greatest perfection, like the least, wavers unsupported for speculative reason which can, without losing anything, allow the one as well as the other, without the least hindrance, to disappear.[3]

The context for this complexly ironic passage is Kant's impatience with the theologians and metaphysicians who seek to mount a "cosmological proof" of the existence of God. Since such proof involves extending knowledge quite beyond the finitude of reason, Kant will have none of it, at least not officially. As he says in another, though related, context, "At bottom we would perhaps do better to rise above and thus spare ourselves research into this matter; since such research is only speculation and since what obliges us (objectively) to act remains the same."[4] Like a man drawn to a dangerous precipice, however, the naïve theologian ignores this warning and moves, as if driven by an inner compulsion, from the ground to the grounds of that ground, beyond which even God cannot see. God asks: from where am I? Such a childish question: Kant infantilizes God, going so far as to ventriloquize and belittle him; he makes him ask this anxious question as a way of mocking the pretensions of the theologians, who will only make the same impertinent and unreasonable inquiry on his behalf. The fact that God raises the question in the first place means that his origins are invisible to his panoptic eye, which claims to see everything—"from eternity to eternity"—*but* this primal abyss. God asks what circumscribes him, but in the asking he is necessarily after the fact, belated with regard to the already there of this mysterious, inchoate place from which he has come. One might even say that insofar as God is delayed, deferred by the *Ungrund* or nonground to which he is answerable, he is *historical*. Preposterous! And if God suffers from a blind spot vis-à-vis his determining grounds (so the logic of Kant's playful irony goes), how much more blind can the theologians and metaphysicians be?

But the passage from the First Critique is not all mockery, for there is a way in which Kant must acknowledge, against the grain of his empiricism, the undeniable attraction of the enigma of the origin. The thought of the absolutely prior, beyond knowledge, is an aporetic thought, not only because it is simply nonrational and nonexperiential, but also because it is *both* "unbearable" *and* "unavoidable": it cannot be reasonably thought, Kant rightly insists, but for all that, *it cannot be avoided either*. Perhaps it is this radical undecidability about the origin, at once attractive and repulsive, that makes it truly abyssal from the perspective of reason. Where Kant's philosophical anthropology leaves off, Schelling begins. His last, major published work, *Philosophical Inquiries into the Nature of Human Freedom [Philosophische Untersuchungen über das Wesen der menschlichen Freiheit und die damit zusammenhängenden Gegenstände]*, takes up the task precisely of asking after the nature of the origin of the origin, and finds, as we shall see, that beyond the primal ground there is only the *Ungrund*, where, even as Kant warns, speculative reason must shatter and disappear.

That the *Freedom* essay was Schelling's final, important public writing is significant, though readers of German idealism disagree on exactly how significant. It could be argued, for example, that the philosopher suffered a terrible anxiety of influence under the imposing shadow of Hegel, whose *Phenomenologie*—published two years before the *Freedom* essay—may or may not contain an implied attack on Schelling's philosophy of identity. The death of Schelling's wife Caroline in 1809 cannot be discounted, though of course the traumatic effects of this terrible loss will be the first thing to be repressed by disembodied histories of ideas (my own included). In a series of luminous lectures delivered at the University of Freiburg in 1936, Heidegger begins by comparing Schelling to Nietzsche and by suggesting that Schelling's "great breakdown"—as he rather melodramatically puts it—is "not a failure and nothing negative at all."

> On the contrary, it is the sign of the advent of something completely different, the heat lightning of a new beginning. Whoever really knew the reason for this breakdown and could conquer it intelligently, would have to become the founder of the new beginning of Western philosophy.[5]

Heidegger's extravagant claims emphasize that inasmuch as Schelling's "closural" essay is ahead of itself, its most radical insights remain unarticulated even to their author. "The something completely different" that inhabits and energizes the *Freedom* essay is paradoxically visible but as yet unheard, even as the heat lightning to which he compares this alterity augurs the approach of a summer storm but not its thunderous presence. In what amounts to a philosophical *Nachträglichkeit*, Heidegger retrospectively figures himself as Schelling's privileged auditor, the very one who will hear, long after the fact, the un-thought that lies concealedly revealed in his predecessor's thinking. What is it, then, that is momentarily illuminated but unvoiced by the *Freedom* essay? What "tropic of negativity"—to borrow a phrase from Derrida[6]—is evoked here without being said directly?

To be sure, Schelling may not be as unaware of its flickering presence as Heidegger makes him out to be. Looking back on his development as a philosopher, Schelling characterizes his own work as the source of a very Heideggerian sounding question: "What if, some day, wholly *new* concepts of philosophy were to be found?"[7] The pressure to unearth these "new concepts" surfaces relatively early on in Schelling's work, but perhaps most decisively in *Philosophical Inquiries into the Nature of Human Freedom*. It should be recalled that the essay marks a crucial turn for Schelling, after which he will not cease to criticize Hegelian philosophy, including the perdurable residue of his own Hegelianism, for its seeming prejudice against the real—its reduction of reality to essence, form, and idea. As Schelling comes increasingly to see, reality is much more than formal intelligibility; it is also an open-ended question of existence and of the brute confrontation with the enigma of the actual. The paradox is that the turn to a *positive* philosophy—as he will eventually characterize this strand of his work—leads him inexorably to recognize the ineluctable operation of the *negative* within existence: accidents, matter, evil acts, the unforeseen, and the irrational, the sheer fact *that* things exist. Like Kierkegaard, who heard his lectures in Berlin in 1841, Schelling resists the temptation, whose most general name is *metaphysics*, to "find an excuse to sneak out of life"[8] in the surreal manner of Hegel. He chooses instead philosophically to embrace "life," insofar as this is possible, and to engage rather than sublate that which *resists* all pretensions to wholly systematic thought. As if in a self-imposed challenge, Schelling's *Freedom* essay, which attacks idealist metaphysics for its failure to accommodate the inchoate nature of the real, is frankly cast in the form of a philosophical argument. In other words, the closest possible engagement with the question of idealism is promised, one that will involve the form of philosophical reasoning itself. The theosophic mysticism of Jacob Böhme proves crucial to Schelling in this regard and provides him with some of the "new concepts"—"new" in the sense of coming from *outside* the discursive regime of philosophy—that he needs to obtain a critical point of leverage on the speculative idealism that he had once vigorously championed, and that, indeed, he never wholly abandoned. As Werner Marx characterizes the *Freedom* essay:

> The irrational, that which cannot be accounted for, that which is essentially alien and unfamiliar in Being, the demonic and the magical that are to be found in reality, the undisclosed, uncanny forces slumbering in everything that is forceful and vital, that which is demonically threatening, and in particular, all the terrifying power and reality of evil—all of these issues were now taken up as problems, problems presented in the special sort of Christian thought in which Böhme . . . related the powers of darkness to the powers of light.[9]

Marx and others have outlined the kinds of questions that forced themselves upon Schelling, once he employed Böhme to read for what he calls the "deficiencies" of "modern European philosophy" (7:356/30):[10]

> How can one conceive of the Christian God of Creation if his creation is permeated by the powers of darkness? How can the struggle between the powers of darkness and the powers of light be compatible with revelation as it is conceived of in Christianity? . . . If evil is real, and if man can choose evil precisely because he is free, then how can one conceive of a theodicy? How can a system of pantheism be conceived in which God's absolute freedom and infinite goodness are consistent with a human freedom that is finite and capable of evil?[11]

These are the questions that preoccupy Schelling in his treatise. After Böhme, Schelling finds that human freedom has its origin in a more primordial act of freedom, namely God's self-originating struggle to become a determinate being out of his dark, elemental ground. In the Stuttgart seminars given to supplement the *Freedom* essay, Schelling is very succinct about his revisionary position and about the curious implications that come of adopting it:

> In short, *God creates Himself*, and just as He creates Himself, He is certainly not immediately present or complete either; for why otherwise create Himself? What, then, is this primordial state in which this primordial Being exists, one that exists entirely in itself and has nothing outside of itself?[12]

Because he is a (self-)constructed entity, God is "from the outset" not punctually present; nor does he possess himself absolutely. We could say that he lags slightly behind himself, like all other existent beings. Here Schelling evokes the negativity of that which exceeds and precedes God as the structuring material of his self-realization; in more contemporary terms, whose intersection with Schelling's rhetoric will take up the better part of this essay, we might say that the origin is always already derivative. If Thomas De Quincey saw in Kant's account of God a murderous violence against the fundamental precepts of Christianity,[13] one wonders what he would have made of this claim, which calmly unravels the integrity and self-sufficiency of the *Logos*. As one of Schelling's best contemporary readers argues, the *Freedom* essay "speculates with surgical skill on the wound that has opened in the very ground of the Christian God."[14]

Needless to say, this is a metaphysical injury that informs and is informed by the intellectual turmoil of early-nineteenth-century philosophy. Schelling's provocative figure of an incompletely present origin surfaces at precisely the point at which, as Manfred Frank argues, "German idealism—as the last great climax of metaphysical interpretation of Being as Being-at-one's-disposal, i.e., as graspable presence—enters into the phase of self-critique."[15] The rest, as it were, is history. Whereas idealism had represented "the unprecedented exultation of reason,"[16] its revision from within triggers the emergence of various philosophies of finitude, each of which illuminates consciousness's temporal character and its inescapable dependence upon unconscious or other-than-conscious structures, whether psychic, linguistic, or social. In a series of important studies, Frank and his students have demonstrated that "post-Hegelian philosophy" shares with "neostructuralism" the presupposition that "the reflection through which we strive to gain absolute clarity about our situation always protrudes with one of its poles into *the unprescribable*, into that which is never totally dissolvable in knowledge."[17] Schelling has increasingly proven to be crucial in this regard, an uncanny precursor not only of Kierkegaard, Marx, and Nietzsche, but also of Heidegger and, more recently, Derrida. Read through Derrida and de Man, as I attempt here, Schelling approaches the thought of the most radical contemporary expressions of "the unprescribable"—*différance*, in the case of Derrida, and "the materiality of the letter," in the case of de Man. But it should also be said that the condition of the possibility of reading contemporary theory back through Schelling is the ability to reverse these perspectives, and to read Derrida and de Man through Schelling. This more difficult hermeneutical maneuver, toward which this essay can only make certain implied gestures, brings out how much of contemporary theory remains preoccupied, like Schelling's "positive" philosophy, with the enigma of the origin and with the "concrete and contingent things . . . which only unwillingly accept the concept."[18] Like de Man after him, Schelling is always interested in theorizing the resistance to theory.

In the case of the *Freedom* essay, idealism's self-critique is not without its difficulties, in part because it sometimes occurs against the grain of Schelling's knowledge. Schelling emphatically points to the calamity of "modern European philosophy," which *"emasculates"* itself (7:357/ 31)—that is his lurid figure of crisis, to which we must return—by failing to take into account the "vital power and fullness of reality" (7:356/31). As the polemical opening pages of the *Freedom* essay make clear, Schelling considers his treatise to be an important first step by which "idealism realizes itself and takes on flesh and blood" (7:356/30). The raison d'être for this essay, however, is that in Schelling's treatise we have what de Man would call "a text that pretends to designate a crisis when it is, in fact, itself the crisis to which it refers."[19] The philosopher seeks to circumvent one predicament, but rapidly finds himself incurring another: in David Farrell Krell's terms, a "crisis of reason, crisis of divinity, crisis of ontotheology."[20] It may even be the case that criticizing one disaster is the only way that Schelling can allow himself to suffer and to acknowledge the other: a case, exactly, of blindness enabling insight. I want to pursue the fault lines of these multiple crises as they (dis)organize the *Freedom* essay, especially as they are disclosed by the behavior of Schelling's narrative and rhetoric. Schelling's text moves inexorably from considering the primal ground (or *Urgrund*) to the abyss of the nonground (or *Ungrund*). The *tropics* of negativity that characterize each stage of this regressive movement, the figural *turns* that determine the exotic *place* of "the unprescribable" in the narrative of Schelling's argument, will henceforth orient my remarks.

THE SUPPLEMENT AT THE SOURCE

I never saw thee till this time. . . .
. . . darkness immingled with light on my furrowed field.
—William Blake, *Jerusalem*

How can one reconcile the contingency of human freedom with the system of divine intelligence? According to Schelling, "This is the point of profoundest difficulty in the whole doctrine of freedom, which has always been felt and which applies not only to this or that system, but, more or less to all" (7:352/26). Schelling insists that freedom can be actual only if its *Grund* inheres in the ontological structure of God's being. In other words, for human freedom to be objectively real, God must contain *within* himself an alterity upon which that autonomy is patterned. God *others* himself, or, to be more precise, he is other than himself from his inception, and in that original disappropriation he opens the space of liberty—the condition of possibility of good and of evil acts. To think God in these bifurcated terms, Schelling draws from his *Naturphilosophie* the distinction between existence and its ground, or between "Being in so far as it exists, and Being in so far as it is the mere basis *[Grund]* of existence" (7:357/31). Schelling had already established that existent beings were structured by this originary difference; it is, in a sense, the primal source of their liveliness, the signature of their ontological status as *becoming*. Since God is a God of the living, fully comprehending the rational and irrational nature of the created world, and since the creatures inhabiting that world could hardly be said to possess an ontological structure wholly different from their genesis in God, Schelling takes as a given that the origin must *itself* be characterized by the ground/existence distinction. The circular logic of this move is telling: although Schelling seeks to explain the nature of God in order to account for the freedom of human beings, he initially goes about this explanation by mapping "back" upon God the distinction that obtains in the creatures. Are the creatures thereby ennobled, because their self-division mimics the ontological design of their maker? Or is God rather em-bodied or in-corporated, made *creature-like* (7:381/58), as Schelling says in another context? This is an indeterminacy that troubles and enriches the rhetoric and the argument of almost every page of the *Freedom* essay, whose complex pantheism (impossibly) seeks to restore the innocence of becoming to God without compromising the integrity of his being.

For Schelling, the freedom of the individual to be what he or she *is* replicates the primordial act of separation and independence, namely God's self-originating disclosure of himself to himself in the otherness of his elemental ground. There is no overcoming of this resistance to God— and thus no means of abrogating the reality of human freedom, as Schelling believed was the case in Hegel—because *God is himself this resistance*. The philosopher frankly acknowledges that his position risks falling back into the theological commonplace that God is *causa sui*, his own beginning. As Robert Brown argues, however, Schelling refuses simply to proclaim God's "a-sei-ty" (7:356/31), since to do so begs the more important question of "*how* God's being is self-derived and the distinctions that must obtain within God if this is to be the case."[21] Böhme provides the *Freedom* essay with a language with which to think God's primordial structure not in terms of purely formal differences—as theology and idealistic philosophy had done—but as the agonistic site of his real struggle to come into being. God makes himself: what is the nature of the material out of which this genesis occurs? "[T]he ground of [God's] existence," Schelling writes, is "inseparable from him, to be sure, but nevertheless distinguishable from him" (7:358/32). The contradictory impulses of Schelling's syntax—"to be sure, but" *[zwar . . . aber]*—at once allows and politely denies an ontological difference to inhabit God. Neither "inseparable" nor "distinguishable," but both at once: this *Grund*, this "irreducible remainder," as Schelling will need to describe it in the next paragraph, shimmers before our gaze, simultaneously *there*, distinct from God, and *not* there, its spectral absence/presence transgressing the law of identity even as it is called upon to play a constitutive role in the formation of the identity of identities, namely God's determinate being. A strange and self-estranged God, this, even before the "main point" of Schelling's investigation is well underway. How can God be divided by a difference that does not differentiate, his determinate identity deferred by the "irreducible remainder" that makes it possible? What is the topography of God's inner life in which the darkness and the light dwell in perpetual habitation? This is no ordinary domicile, where opposites might be said to attract and coexist, for God's "Nature" operates as an excluded outsider that is nevertheless deeply *inside*. Inseparable and distinguishable: "*en-crypted,*" Derrida writes in another context, describing how "an inside heterogeneous to the inside of the Self . . . can only maintain in a state of repetition the mortal conflict it is impotent to resolve."[22] The origin would seem to possess a structure as unimaginable and disconcerting as a so-called Klein bottle, whose interior and exterior are folded one into the other. In its relationship to God's existence, Schelling continues, God's dark ground is "to be thought of neither as precedence in time nor as priority of essence":

> In the cycle whence all things come, it is no contradiction to say that that which gives birth to the one is, in its turn, produced by it. There

is here no first and last, since everything mutually implies everything else, nothing being the "other" and yet no being being without the other. God contains within himself the inner ground of his existence, which, to this extent, precedes him as to his existence, but similarly God is prior to [his] ground [because] this ground, as such, could not be if God did not exist in actuality. (7:358/33)

A great deal could be said about the conceptual difficulties—again, so fully mirrored in Schelling's convoluted syntax—of this pivotally original passage in the *Freedom* essay. Heidegger laconically concedes that "Schelling's thought is . . . in a way still strange to common sense."[23] The distinction that so naturally and unsurprisingly obtained in the creatures is now clearly said to obtain in God. At the primordial origin, no origin emerges, at least not as an origin simply self-contained and present to itself, without always already being complicated by the presence of an absence, an "other" that can be neither evaded nor absorbed. Schelling seems to say: the ground grounds only insofar as it grounds existence, and existence exists only insofar as it articulates the ground. God therefore never punctually *is*, but eternally comes into being—"Thus a *becoming* God! *[Also ein* werdender *Gott!]*," Heidegger exclaims[24]—as the effect of a relational activity or "cycle" in which existence is the cause of its own cause and the ground is the effect of its effect. It would be difficult to find a more lucid example of the impossible logic of the supplement and of the (dis)abling impact that it has on precisely those foundational terms— *logos, prius*—that are conventionally said to possess the qualities of "precedence in time" and "priority of essence."

Heidegger suggests that "although the distinction cited of the ground and existence of a being can be found in the first presentation of [Schelling's] . . . system, still it is not yet expressly worked out" until "the treatise on freedom."[25] When Schelling theorizes or "works out" this "distinction," however, Heidegger finds that he can no longer properly call it by that name, presumably recognizing that what is at stake is precisely the condition of possibility of distinctness itself. Heidegger's word for Schelling's explication of God's self-difference is "the jointure of Being *[die Seynsfuge]*,"[26] an evocative portmanteau that exactly captures Schelling's decision to rethink the origin not as that which distinctly is, the inside inside and the outside outside, but as a kind of fault-line or hinge marking the movement of mutual interchange between, across, and beyond the ontological distinctions it articulates. How else to make sense of Schelling's conception of primordial being, which, as Heidegger is compelled to say, "has gone out of itself and in a certain way is *always outside of itself*"?[27] The uncannily Derridean recognition that there is—"in a certain way"—a *"supplement at the source,"*[28] an outside within the inside, effectively upsets what Rodolphe Gasché has aptly called "German Idealism's pretensions to have deduced the oneness of origin."[29] God's being is primordially a conflictual site—turned inside out, as it were—that is constituted rather than compromised by otherness. The creation in turn repeats the folded structure of its origin: as Schelling argues, "every nature can be revealed only in its opposite—love in hatred, unity in strife" (7:373/50). Crucial to this revaluation of values is Schelling's displacement of the hierarchical opposition of identity as goodness and difference as evil, and its reinscription as an opposition between the "light center" and "dark center" as interdependent contraries. The importation of Böhme's rhetoric of centers is here instrumental to the success of Schelling's attempt to acknowledge the "positive" function of lack and nonbeing, for it enables him to conceptualize the *Logos* as always already bivalent in essence, which is thus more properly described as *Dialogos*.[30] Irrational darkness does not befall the *Logos* in the form of an accident; it is with the *Logos*, and in conversation with it, at the outset. In the context of creation and of human beings, the dark center is the enabling condition of being-free, which means that it is "a vital positive power for good and evil" (7:354/28). But as the essential pole within the ontological structure of God, the dark center is more primordially the necessary medium in which the light of his determinate being eternally comes into appearance.

"Duality must therefore be just as original as unity," Schelling concludes in the Stuttgart seminars.[31] What is interesting and difficult about *Of Human Freedom* is the extent to which Schelling's desire to unearth the dialogical complexity of the origin must contend with rhetorical slippages and conceptual ambiguities that complicate the force of his critique in several ways. As we have seen, Schelling's rhetoric of centers is fundamental to his assertion that God's being is constituted by a purely relational "cycle" where "everything implies everything else" (7:358/33); as "a nexus of living forces" (7:365/41), in which neither center has precedence in time or priority of essence over the other, God's doubled ontological structure is properly beyond or before good and evil. Yet the language of darkness and light that is systematically attached to the discussion of these centers almost irresistibly returns his ontological argument to the orbit of a more familiar theology whose terms are hierarchically rather than differentially opposed. In other words, Schelling appears deconstructive at the level of the letter, while at the level of affect he remains idealistic and imagines cosmic history as the narrative of the triumph of spirit over its elemental ground. "All birth is birth out of darkness into light," he argues, in one of the most obvious examples of this reversion to a value-laden rhetoric. "[T]he seed must be buried in the earth and die in darkness in order that the lovelier creature of light should rise and unfold itself in the rays of the sun" (7:360/35). Schelling's ambivalent revalorization of the light is similarly evident in his discussion of the nature of the dark center in human beings: the resistant otherness of the ground ensures human being's substantial independence from God. Schelling argues: "But just because this very principle is *transfigured* in light *[in Licht verklärt ist]*—without therefore ceasing to be basically dark—something higher, the *spirit*, arises in man" (7:363/39). Here Schelling's parenthetical qualification appears momentarily to introduce a contradiction into the heart of his ontological argument: if the dark principle never ceases being dark, then "something higher, the spirit" is neither light nor dark but the afterimage, as it were, of the irreducibility of the one to the other. And yet this is not what is claimed in the surrounding statement, which more readily values the volatilization of the darkness by identifying spirit with the transfiguring triumph of light over an unilluminated world.

The recuperative notion of an Apollonian "transfiguration" of the darkness into light displaces and palliates the more radical conception of the ground-existence relation in which the light and dark are reciprocally and cooriginally implicated in a jointure of Being. But this idealism is not the only hazard to the *Freedom* essay's ontology, for in reiterating the irreducibility of the darkness to the light, Schelling can come perilously close to emptying the light of any ultimate significance. Properly speaking, God cannot simply be the illuminated translation of his ground; he *is* to the extent that he is both a forming force and an indigenous chaos against which that force is formed. "Following the eternal act of self-revelation," Schelling writes,

> the world as we now behold it, is all rule, order and form; but the unruly *[das Regellose]* lies over the depths as though it might break through, and order and form nowhere appear to have been original, but it seems as though what had initially been unruly had been brought to order.

This is the incomprehensible ground of reality of all things, the *irreducible remainder [der nie aufgehende Rest]* which cannot be resolved into reason by the greatest exertion but always remains in the depths. Out of this which is unreasonable, reason in the true sense is born. Without this preceding gloom, creation would have no reality; *darkness is its necessary heritage.* (7:359–60/34; emphasis mine)

For Schelling, the full knowledge that being is a reasonable surface that ceaselessly remembers its irrational depths is precisely the object of authentic philosophical work: "[W]e can think of nothing better fitted to drive man to strive toward the light with all energy," he writes, "than the consciousness of the deep night" (7:360/34–35). Schelling goes on to scoff at "the faint-hearted" who complain that "the unreasonable is in this way made into the root of reason, night into the beginning of light" (7:360/35): he is not a man like the idealists, who are afraid of the dark. But this defensiveness is itself revealing, because it also projects on an imagined audience a real difficulty inhabiting Schelling's own text. By treating the relationship between "the unruly" and the forms of God's "reason," which are imposed upon it in terms that remember Kant's separation of real and phenomenal worlds, Schelling tacitly limits the forms of reason to a merely compensatory, illusory role. Here Schelling's residually idealistic desire to separate God's light from the darkness of the ground is contested by an admission that the light is merely a displacement of the ground by which it is irreducibly exceeded. Schelling can claim that God's spirit as transfiguring light represents a discrete ontological condition, but his rhetoric of surfaces and depths suggests that the light is a sublimatory fiction whose underside is the dark ground from which it springs. As Heidegger notes, "Schelling's presentation gives the appearance that God exists first only *as ground*;"[32] that is to say, whereas the *matter* of Schelling's argument amounts to a dialogical understanding of the ground-existence relationship, the *manner* mistakenly leaves the impression that the dark ground possesses "precedence in time" and "priority of essence." But I would suggest that the frank concession that there is "an irreducible remainder which cannot be resolved into reason by the greatest exertion but always remains in the depths" is not, or not simply, a slip in the "presentation" of Schelling's argument, but a register of the sheer difficulty in sustaining a dialogical understanding of the origin under the imposing shadow of idealist metaphysics.

PRIMAL ADDICTION

"Addiction" *[Die "Sucht"]*—which has nothing to do with searching [*Suchen*] etymologically—primordially means sickness which strives to spread itself; sickly, disease. Addiction is a striving and desiring, indeed, the addiction of longing, of being concerned with oneself. A double, *contrary*, movement is contained in longing: the striving away from itself to spread itself, and yet precisely back to itself.
—Martin Heidegger, *Schelling's Treatise on the Essence of Human Freedom*

Schelling summarizes his position:

> In order to be separated from God, they [the things of nature] must come to be in a ground that is different from him. But since nothing can be outside God *[außer Gott]*, this contradiction can be resolved only by things having their ground in whatever in God is *not He himself*, i.e., that which is the ground of his existence *[daß die Dinge ihren Grund in dem haben, was in Gott selbst nicht, Er Selbst ist, d.h. in dem was Grund seiner Existenz ist]*. (7:359/33; trans. modified)

In order for the things *[die Dinge]* to be outside of God, who is all in all, there must be an exterior that is *interior* to his divine essence. Schelling's resolution succeeds only in replacing one spatial-ontological contradiction with another. The impossibly invaginated topography required to think the relationship of God to this interiorized outside strains the limits of understanding. Schelling candidly admits as much and searches for an illustration, a metaphor, with which "to bring this essence nearer to us from a human standpoint."

> [W]e may say: It is the longing *[Sehnsucht]* felt by the eternal to give birth to itself. It is not the One itself, but is co-eternal with it. It wants to give birth to God, i.e., to the ungroundable unity *[Sie will Gott, d.h. die unergründliche Einheit gebären]*; but to that extent it has not yet the unity in its self. Therefore, regarded in itself, it is also will: but a will within which there is no understanding, and thus not an independent and complete will, since understanding is the true will in willing. Nevertheless, it is a will of the understanding, namely its longing and desire; it is not a conscious but a prescient will, whose prescience is understanding. We are speaking of the essence of longing regarded in and for itself. . . . (7:359/34; trans. modified)

What was God doing before the creation, before even the birth of himself as a determinate being? Borrowing a complex image from Böhme, Schelling declares that he was doing nothing in particular: *nothing doing*. He was not therefore a void—the philosopher is always very careful to avoid that suggestion—but, rather, inarticulate willing. In the beginning, there is starkly a *doing*, a "longing" without determinate object and thus utterly without understanding. Mute and unconscious, this "originary longing" *[die ursprüngliche Sehnsucht]* nevertheless longs to give birth to God and has precedence over him. Craving the One, it is necessarily distinct from that for which it craves; yet it is also equiprimordial with the One, as if God were simultaneously at both ends of the process by which he comes into being, the product of the mother that he also produces. In deference to the enigmatic character of divine parturition, Schelling shifts the focus and speaks in terms of its likeness to the human scene:

> All birth is a birth from darkness into light: the seed must be buried in the earth and die in darkness in order that the lovelier creature of light should rise and unfold itself in the rays of the sun. Man is formed in his mother's womb; and from the darkness of non-understanding (from feeling, from longing, the lordly mother of knowledge) grow clear thoughts. Thus we must imagine the originary longing in this way—turning towards understanding, indeed, though not yet recognizing it, just as we longingly desire unknown, nameless excellence. This primal longing moves in anticipation like a surging, billowing sea, similar to the "matter" of Plato, following a dark uncertain law, incapable of forming something lasting by itself. . . . (7:360/35; trans. modified)

Carefully to read the play of figure and ground, and of figure and figure, in this and cognate passages in the *Freedom* treatise would take up another essay. It must suffice here to note that Schelling's self-conscious decision to describe the ground of God's existence in anthropomorphizing analogies triggers a cascade of metaphors, and metaphors of metaphors: in addition to the master-tropes of a "longing," "desire," and "will" to give birth to itself, the ground is compared to "the dark fetters of gravity," "the earth," a "mother's womb," "feeling," "the sublime mother of knowledge," "a surging, billowing sea," and Plato's "matter." In a more obscure figure that anticipates Lacan, longing functions as the imaging medium in which God, stirring into life, first catches sight of himself as a discrete entity: neither God nor his reflection, longing can only be the "place" where this "reflexive representation" happens—it is, in other words, the tain of the primal mirror. A few sentences later, a figure of reading overtakes the figure of seeing: the unruly field of longing's resistance to articulation is compared to a logogriph or anagram, out of which a word, *the* Word, is deciphered (or deciphers itself, in the same way that God somehow "reads" and recognizes himself in his originary stirring). We might well ask: what are figures, and what is the dark ground such that it causes them to be unfurled in this densely overlapping fashion? Schelling has seen this kind of protean rhetorical activity before: metaphors rapidly unraveling into other metaphors, all of them figuring forth the anarchic and obscure origins of the universe. In the background, no doubt filtered through Böhme and others, is the theogony and cosmogony of the *Timaeus*, as Schelling's allusion to Plato indicates. (The *Freedom* essay in fact cites Plato's dialogue on several other occasions.) Since arguably no classical text offers as searching or as evocative an examination of the universe's primal conditions as the *Timaeus*, it forms a formidable pretext for Schelling's radical attempt to think the source of divine life (and the life that flows from it). Plato too asks: where does God (the Demiurge) come from? Or to put it in more dualistic terms: what is the enabling condition of the distinction between the two orders of existence: the intelligible forms and their sensible copies? To these questions, Plato responds by evoking an obscure "third species," a place or space that makes room, so to speak, for God and for the things of nature. This primeval "receptacle" he calls, provisionally, and only then after some delay in the narrative of the *Timaeus*, the *khora*.

Like Schelling, Derrida is powerfully attracted to the sheer anteriority of the *khora*, about which he has written provocatively on several occasions. (One of the most conspicuous intersections between nineteenth-century philosophy and contemporary theory is this almost obsessive fascination with tracing what Heidegger calls "the origin . . . *concealed in* the beginning.")[33] Because of its indeterminate conceptual location, at once "within" and "without" "ontology and . . . Platonic dialectic in its most dominant schemas,"[34] the *khora* is an uncannily apposite figure with which to think the enigma of *différance*. As Derrida argues in "How to Avoid Speaking: Denials," the disproportion and heterogeneity of the *khora* instantly results in the production of "two concurrent languages" in the *Timaeus*: in the first instance, the *khora* is represented, both by Plato and by his major interpreters, including Aristotle, "as being *at the interior of philosophy*."[35] For structural reasons, the exorbitant *beyond*-being of the *khora* is easily translated and palliated as a *being*-beyond, a kind of "hypermetaphysical" essence that reinscribes "the grammar and the logic of onto-theology." In the second instance, the *khora* is more radically "postmetaphysical," if by this term we mean not what comes "after" the "end" of metaphysics, but the irreducible remainder or unavoidable fallout *of* metaphysical thinking, whether early or late.[36] On this second view, the *khora* is a disruptive figure for the already-there of *différance*. Its shocking alterity and primacy requires "that we define the origin of the world as a *trace*,"[37] as a primordial absence that haunts and constitutes the metaphysics of presence. My sense is that, in mobilizing the *khora*, Schelling unavoidably reproduces both of these languages. In terms to which we will need to return in detail, longing-as-*khora* operates in the *Freedom* essay as *both* an *Urgrund* or primal ground, the familiar object of speculative idealism, *and* as an *Ungrund*, the abyssal nonground that lies somewhere between idealism and deconstruction.

The *khora* does not owe its existence to the Demiurge, but preexists it, exactly as primal longing is anterior to God: borrowing a curious phrase from Plato, Schelling calls longing "the old nature *[der alten Natur]*" (7:374/51), that is, a nature prior to nature/spirit distinction. As the receptacle, "she"—for, in Schelling and in Plato, we are dealing with something that is conspicuously identified as "feminine"—"is a kind of neutral plastic material on which changing impressions are stamped by things which enter into it." The *khora*, like primal longing, forms the "inchoate" or "disorderly" *[das Regellose]* (7:359/34) background against which everything that is, whether illusory or real, copies or forms, *stands out* (or ex-ists). It does not of itself form anything, but rather functions as the medium in which forming happens. It is the fecund site of *Einbildung* (7:362/37), Schelling's punning term for the "in-forming" process by which God "in-vents" or "imagines" himself as the "One." In the *Timaeus*, the *khora* is the "mother" or "nurse of becoming," just as Schelling's longing is "the lordly mother of knowledge" *[der herrlichen Mutter der Erkenntnis]* (7:360/35).[38] When Schelling compares *Sehnsucht* to "Platonic matter" *[Platonischen Materie]* (7:360/35), it is hard not to hear the name of the *mater*, mother. In some versions of ancient Greek gynecology, the mother appears the mere host of fetal life, providing nourishment and a place for growth, but without herself actively contributing to procreation. In terms with which Schelling might readily identify, the Greek mother is thus "indifferent," sexually speaking, to reproduction: we might say that she is the mother, but not a biological parent.[39]

Something of this strange notion of an immaculate generation, in which the mother provides the "material" means for the Demiurge to give birth to himself, not only informs Schelling's account of the primal scene but also deflects some of his deepest ambivalences regarding its human, all too human features. Maternal longing is that mysterious entity "which though it belongs to him Himself, is, nonetheless, different from him" (7:375/51), just as the *khora* is the nurturing field out of which the Demiurge is born without him being, strictly speaking, *of* it. Needless to say, this notion of the mother *as supplement* had almost no scientific currency in Schelling's day, although James Boswell resorts to it, for obviously misogynous reasons, as late as *The Life of Samuel Johnson* (1791).[40] But the anachronistic status of the figure makes it all the more attractive to Schelling, who is willing to go to great lengths to quell, or at least control, his fastidious fears—so well described by Krell—that in speaking of God in terms of "longing, procreation, fecundation, pregnancy, and birth"[41] he has somehow compromised God's essence, made him altogether too fleshly, too "feminine," for comfort. Of course, Schelling cannot deny that his God is alive—that is his central, and, one might say, *existential* thesis about the nature of divine essence. By borrowing from the *Timaeus*, however, he is able to practice a unique form of sexual hygiene and to recast the genesis of this liveliness *in a certain Hellenic way*. Insofar as feminine *Sehnsucht* is the mother of God, she is his Greek mother, at once proximate and distant vis-à-vis the child she bears.

At the same time, by figuring forth their respective tropics of negativity as "the mother" and as "feminine," Plato and Schelling undoubtedly contest the primacy of the *Logos* and put the self-sufficiency of the "father" into question. This is not simply to reverse the sexed polarities of the universe's root principles, in order, for example, to make creation fundamentally "feminine," if by this term we mean a place of life, death, temporality, finitude, and desire (although, of course, *with some crucial qualifications*, Schelling's "positive philosophy" might well be described as such—as a covert and ambivalently marshaled "feminism," beginning with his radical reassessment of the importance of *Naturphilosophie* over and against the "masculinism" of the "philosophy of spirit"). Neither can it be said that, in characterizing longing as maternal, Schelling seeks to strike a blow for the mother against the spiritualizing excesses of the father (who prefers to think of the self-engendering of the Word without all of the bodily indignities associated with maternity and paternity). Against the grain of Schelling's argument, primal longing instead obliges us to consider that which is always *there*, as the work of the "feminine" within the "masculine" and constitutive of it. A *Logos* indebted to a mother, even a Greek mother—what does that mean? Longing and the *khora* are ways of thinking what must have already withdrawn in order for articulation, including (and especially) the articulation mother/ father, feminine/masculine, to happen at all. What "femininity" and "masculinity" *are* becomes much less self-evident once one attempts, as Schelling certainly does, to imagine a longing, an excitation or stirring, so primordial as to lie *before* existent life and thus before the sexual difference that pervasively characterizes and organizes that life. This *déjà-là* lends itself to the name of the feminine, not for essential or biologistic reasons, but because it more readily communicates with all that is systematically and traditionally devalued by the *Logos* as derivative, secondary, resistant, inarticulate, and exterior—in other words, *effaced* by negative philosophy in order that the *Logos* might come into being. To revalue the valuation of the dark ground, to cast a positive light on its inchoate nature without thereby volatilizing it, spiriting it away, in the manner of Hegel or Hegelianism: that might describe Schelling's difficult task vis-à-vis primal longing, a task he explicitly identifies with a radical rereading of the *Timaeus*. Even after arguing strenuously for the "positivity" of primal longing, he concedes that it is difficult *not* to reproduce "the interpretation of Platonic matter [matter and the *khora* are interchangeable terms in the dialogue][42] according to which it is an essence originally resisting God, and therefore in itself evil." Schelling himself is not entirely innocent of this valuation. He continues:

> As long as this part of Platonic doctrine lies in darkness, as it has thus far, a definitive judgment on this point is indeed impossible. However, from the previous considerations [which is to say, the fundamental argument of the *Freedom* essay] it is clear in what sense it could be said of the irrational principle that it resists the understanding, or unity and order, *without* therefore assuming it to be an *evil* principle. (7:374/50– 51; emphasis mine; translation modified)

We could say that Schelling wishes to save "Plato's text" from "Platonism," to shield it from the doctrines and interpretations, undoubtedly legitimated by a certain "Plato," which would contain, demonize, and repudiate the radical heterogeneity of what resists God, and to do so by identifying it as the root of sin.[43] As Derrida's remarks about the *Timaeus* suggest, these two languages, "positive" and "negative," one acknowledging the alterity of the dark ground and the other instantly reappropriating it to the rule of the concept, run concurrently in the dialogue. Against the negative language, Schelling counters that chthonic longing is indifferent to valuations of either good or evil, precisely because it is the condition of possibility of both. He would rather have us think of "Platonic matter" more fundamentally, beyond good and evil, as simply *the root*, as a desire unattached to an object and to which no theodicy can legitimately attach. Thinking the derivativeness of the *Logos* with respect to this root displaces the propriety and stability of supposedly fundamental terms like "the feminine" and "the masculine," and unsettles the other morally saturated oppositions around which these terms cluster with suspicious alacrity: maternity/paternity, *arche/an-arche*, understanding/will, good/evil, light/dark, light/gravity, God/human, existence/ground. These are the distinctions, of course, that provide the conceptual framework for the *Freedom* essay and are the major source of its intelligibility. Clearly, much is at stake when it comes to bringing out the singular anteriority of longing as *khora*. But by treating *Sehnsucht* as feminine and as maternal, Schelling's text obtains a point of critical leverage on the value-laden distinctions he wishes dearly to transform. "Femininity" and "maternality" therefore play a *paleonymic* role in the *Freedom* essay, because they defamiliarize the philosophical terrain that is thoroughly written over by these distinctions. In Derrida's terms, they correspond "to whatever always has *resisted* the prior organization of forces, always constituted the *remainder* irreducible [here, we might recall Schelling's *der nie aufgehende Rest*] to the dominant force which organized the—to say it quickly—logocentric hierarchy."[44] The "feminine" and the "maternal" are names for the specific mode of anteriority by which originary longing claims the *Logos*.

This duplicity about originary *Sehnsucht* helps to explain the dense rhetorical strategies that Schelling adopts while trying to describe its relation to God's existence, strategies that compulsively translate primal longing into spectacular figures while at the same time asserting that the tenor of those figures—"the essence of longing regarded in and for itself"—remains permanently out of the reach of reason. Is this ineffability the result of a human failing, whose thought cannot penetrate down to the *Urgrund?* Or is this resistance to thought structural in nature, and the primal ground the alibi for a more radical anteriority, an *Ungrund?* Is *Sehnsucht* an *un*-thought or an un-*thought*, a thought that is yet to happen to humankind or a wholly unthinkable thought? Schelling's text broaches these unanswerable, concurrent questions and hovers between them. Like longing, the *khora* resists true, rational comprehension, forcing human eyes to look upon it, as Plato almost seems embarrassed to concede, "as in a dream," or with a form of "spurious" or "bastard reasoning."[45] (Schelling [mis]translates Plato's *logismōi tini nothōi* as *falsche Imagination* [7:390/68].) As the opening of the distinction between the intelligible and the sensible, and thus between the figurative and the literal, the *khora* can only be described through a series of more or less lurid figures: matrix, space, malleable gold, nurse, sieve, receptacle, mother.[46] Some of these metaphors coincide with those employed by Schelling, but all play a similar role: namely, figuring forth what Derrida calls "the aporia of the originary inscription,"[47] that is, the locus or place "where" differentiation "first" happens. Plato's figures are therefore not metaphors in any conventional sense of the term, since the *khora* precedes and, in a sense, produces the concepts of metaphoricity and of analogicism that underwrite figuration. The *khora* is radically (im)proper; it is the condition of possibility of propriety and impropriety, whether rhetorical or otherwise. As such, it *obliges* us to speak in analogies: "The spacing of *khora* introduces a dissociation or a difference in the proper meaning that it renders possible, thereby *compelling* tropic detours which are no longer rhetorical figures."[48] As the "irreducible remainder which cannot be resolved into reason" and as the prearchaic source of articulated existence, originary longing is a tropic of negativity that similarly defies positive predication; and because of that resistance, it is the occasion for an influx of figures that suddenly emerge at the moment that Schelling attempts to probe its fundamentally occult nature. Schelling cannot say, simply, that longing *is* "this"; instead, he must say it is *like* "this" (and "this" and "this"), in a rhetorical unfurling whose lateral motion is perhaps the most subtle recollection of the *Timaeus* in the *Freedom* essay. These metaphors bring longing "nearer to us," although not in the sense of actually reducing the conceptual distance between its darkness and the light of understanding, since Schelling frankly admits that that distance cannot be bridged, "even by the greatest exertion" of reason. Speaking in analogies, which is to say, in his own dreamy form of "bastard reasoning," Schelling can only speak *as if* longing were closer to hand, and *as if* the various names that come to mind—womb, anagram, matter, sea—made longing more humanly accessible. But as Heidegger argues, longing "is 'nameless'; it does not know any name; it is unable to name what it is striving for. It is lacking the *possibility of words.*"[49] The movement from metaphor to metaphor, and the inconclusiveness that characterizes each metaphor as it is occupied, compels the philosopher to review his inability to provide a proper name for the wholly other, outside God *[außer Gott]*.

A LOGOS IN LOGOGRIPHS

> . . . Plato mutters as he transcribes the play of formulas. . . The walled-in voice strikes against the rafter, the words come apart, bits and pieces of sentences are separated, disarticulated parts begin to circulate through the corridors, . . . translate each other, become rejoined, bounce off each other, come back like answers, organize their exchanges, protect each other, institute an internal commerce, take themselves for a dialogue. Full of meaning. A whole story. An entire history. All of philosophy.
> . . . Plato gags his ears.
>
> —Jacques Derrida, "Plato's Pharmacy"

Strange likeness, this: *lacking the possibility of words* is analogous to the nonbeing of primal *Sehnsucht*. In and *as* the womb of longing, God is *infans*, without speech. Heidegger does almost nothing to explain himself, perhaps because this privation brings the inarticulate ground of God too near to what he considered to be the dumbness of animals. Schelling had sought to explain himself better and contain the scandal that there is something in God that is not himself, but the analogy of longing only compounds matters. God longs? He craves and behaves as an addict, dispossessed by a need that articulates him? Schelling opens himself to the criticism that his metaphors only humanize and anthropomorphize God. On Schelling's behalf, Heidegger energetically answers this charge:

> Here the objection can hardly be held back any longer that a human state is transferred to God in this statement. Yes! But it could also be otherwise. Who has ever shown that longing is something merely human? Who has ever completely dismissed the possibility with adequate reasons that what we call "longing" . . . might ultimately be something other than we ourselves? Is there not contained in longing something which we have *no* reason to limit to man, something which rather gives us occasion to understand it as that in which humans are freed *beyond* ourselves? Is not longing precisely the proof for the fact that man is something other than only a man?[50]

To claim that Schelling *humanizes* God through his figures is to assume that we know clearly what being human means. Heidegger is of course infamously unconvinced that such knowledge is as punctually available as it sometimes seems in the history of Being, as if it were one thought amongst many: *Dasein* is precisely a lived project and not an ascertainable fact. Rather than committing an indignity to the metaphysical status of God, Schelling's anthropomorphisms summon humankind to the exorbitant demands of that project and to a scandalous reorientation of thinking about the essence of humankind. Heidegger insists in his lectures that Schelling's originary longing heralds a break with the idealistic rendition of Being as idea and exposes the absolute subject to a fundamentally nonsubjective and nonhuman horizon. As the sub-version of consciousness, dialectic, and reason, primal will dispossesses the subject and dislodges it from the absolutized position that it had come to occupy in German idealism, including the idealism of Schelling's work prior to the *Freedom* essay. In the history of Being, idealism is the point of the maximum subjectification of Being, and thus its maximum occlusion. Longing's wordlessness bespeaks a more radical conception of Being, beyond the confines of the knowing subject. For Heidegger, the figural gesture of anthropomorphism marks a turn, a tropological wheeling around, toward the thought of the "something other" in which humankind dwells and for which it is uniquely situated to respond.

There is something in "Man" that is not he himself: that would be Heidegger's interpretation of the meaning of originary longing, which translates Schelling's humanization of God into a "divinization" of the human, if by that term we mean displacing the philosophically naïve, anthropomorphic thought of "Man" with authentic *Dasein*. In varied ways, Derrida has shown how Heidegger's attempt to overcome the subject-centered philosophies of the nineteenth century unavoidably reinscribes the humanism and subjectivism that he reviled. "We see then that *Dasein*, though *not* man, is nevertheless *nothing other* than man," Derrida concludes. "It is . . . a repetition of the essence of man permitting a return to what is before [on this side of] the metaphysical concepts of *humanitas*."[51] I cannot rehearse the intricacies of Derrida's argument here. What is pertinent are the subtle ways in which Schelling's notion of primal longing *resists* this wholesale reappropriation by Heidegger's "metaphysical humanism."[52] Originary longing is at once less and more than the "something other" that Heidegger imagines—less nobly elevating than *Dasein* but perhaps more deeply disruptive of the thought of the human, including its metaphysical thought. As I have noted, Heidegger claims that "longing is lacking the *possibility of words*." Krell rightly associates this wordlessness with a certain discourse of animality, the stirring of biological life from which Heidegger wishes scrupulously to distinguish the activity of *Dasein*:

> Heidegger is careful not to draw the parallel to the animal, which also lacks the word and all the characters, . . . even though that lack is the salient trait of both desirous divinity and disinhibited animality. Lack of the word is the trait and *retrait* of God. It is the re-mark of divinity *within* animality.[53]

As persuasive as Krell's argument is, however, my sense is that longing's speechlessness also registers another tropic of negativity from which Heidegger might well recoil, not the alterity of animality so much as a prosaic, inhuman (and thus, "animal") alterity within speech itself. Arguably no contemporary thinker has brought out both the ineluctable operation of this otherness and its unsettling implications for the thought of the human more insistently than de Man, whose later work indeed summons readers to the counterintuitive possibility "that it is not at all certain that language is in any sense human."[54] There is something resistant in humankind that is not human itself, and for de Man the names of this otherness are "the play of the letter as inscription," the "materiality of the letter," "the positional power of language"—or, simply, *language*. As de Man is quick to explain, language as sheer inscription is "not some kind of mystery, or some kind of secret [in the manner, say, of Heidegger's occulted Being]; the inhuman . . . [consists of]: linguistic structures, the play of linguistic tensions, linguistic events that occur, possibilities which are inherent in language—independently of any intent or any drive or any wish or any desire we might have."[55] Andrzej Warminski glosses de Man's position by pointing out that language is "divided against itself . . . as the *meaning* of words against the order of words, in short . . . between language as meaning and language as syntax, articulation, non-signifying jointings or cleavings, a system of meaningless differential markings."[56] As the condition of possibility of legible language, these "jointings and cleavings" remain fundamentally illegible: they lack the possibility of words because, paradoxically, they *are* the very possibility of words, in the sense of meaningful articulation. Does Schelling's primal *Sehnsucht* resemble this archperformative aspect to language, speechless because it is the grounds for speech? Is originary longing not precisely the wordless basis for the Word?

Derrida argues that there is a long philosophical tradition of privileging the semantic axis of language over its syntactical one. Aristotle's theory of metaphor is partly responsible for inaugurating the view that meaningful words *(phōnē sēmantikē)* are the signs of being human, whereas the jointings, cleavings, and other nonsignifying elements *(phōnē asēmos)* of speech properly belong to the realm of animality. But as Derrida observes, the boundary dividing the two axes and the two realms is impossible to maintain:

> The semantic system (the order of the *phōnē sēmantikē* with all its connected concepts) is not separated from its other by a simple and continuous line. The limit does not divide the human from the animal. Another division furrows the entirety of "human" language.[57]

The "irreducible excess of the syntactic over the semantic," as Derrida elsewhere describes it,[58] demands attention; de Man's later work, with its hyperascetic concentration on the "play of the letter as inscription," answers this demand as no other in contemporary theory. To unearth the origins of de Man's position, we would need to go back as far as Schelling, whose work compels modern European philosophy, on its own terms, which is to say more or less from within the rhetoric and metaphysic of idealism, to recognize, as if for the first time, the "irreducible remainder" that furrows not just humankind but the entirety of creation, up to and including the Creator. Schelling's "Platonic matter" is the *trait* and *retrait* of spirit, and his "positive philosophy" is his attempt at systematically accounting for its inchoate presence in the nature of things. Is it also, then, the ontological equivalent to de Man's linguistic notion of the "materiality of the letter" as the *trait* and *retrait* of language?

To answer these admittedly large questions, if only in the briefest fashion, we must return to Schelling's text and to its operation of a certain linguistic and "scriptural" tropology. As I have suggested, Schelling moves rapidly through a series of metaphors with which to illustrate the activity of the ground. As if to anticipate the metaphor of legibility that is of primary interest here, Schelling first makes sure that in being born, God can *see* what he is doing:

> However, in accord with the longing which, as the still obscure ground, is the first stirring of divine existence *[Dasein]*, there is generated in

> God himself an inner reflexive representation, through which, because
> it can have no other object than God, God envisages himself in a
> likeness. (7:360/35; trans. modified)

God's identity is at once not yet formed and fully presupposed in this
primal scene, for how could he recognize himself in his "inner reflexive
representation" unless he were already a determinate entity in a position
to do the recognizing? The precise nature of the relationship between
originary longing and God's narcissistic attachment to himself is similarly enigmatic. But we have seen, longing would appear to name the
turn of the reflection itself, the sheer recoil that mobilizes God's self-
consciousness and its unconscious determining condition. The self-
deployment of God requires the erasure of the longing that makes it
possible. Schelling provides an illustration for this figure, an illustration
that draws together longing's speechlessness and language: God's representation is "the understanding—the Word of this longing *[der Verstand—
das Wort jener Sehnsucht]*" (7:361/36). To this cryptic comparison,
Schelling feels compelled to add a supporting analogy in the form of a
footnote: "In the sense that one says: the word of a riddle *[In dem Sinne,
wie man sagt: das Wort des Rätsels]*" (7:361/36). This is a puzzling figure,
an analogy of an analogy of an analogy: the relationship of primal longing to the *Logos* is akin to the relationship of an anagram to its solution;
God's sudden emergence as a determinate entity is comparable to the
moment of deciphering a word in a cryptogram (or, as one of Schelling's
translators puts it, "the Logos in Logogriphs").[59]

Schelling's analogy is startling, but not entirely without precedent in
the *Freedom* essay or its classical pre-texts. The simile obliges us to think
of "Platonic matter" or primal longing as fundamentally linguistic in
nature. This is a comparison that Schelling would certainly have found
in his reading of the *Timaeus*. For example, Timaeus refers to the elemental principles of the universe—fire, water, earth, and air—as "the A
B C of everything," the atomic bits of archaic substance that "ought not
really to be compared even to syllables."[60] In the *Theaetetus*, Socrates also
likens "the A B C of things, the elements of which they are built up," to
the letters out of which "syllables and words" are formed.[61] Only two
paragraphs after the logogriph figure, Schelling similarly describes "the
(real) Word," or *Logos*, as "the unity of light and darkness (vowel and
consonant)" (7:363/39). In the Stuttgart seminars, he expands upon his
inscriptive simile:

The bond [or "nexus" of light and darkness] . . . is called very expressly the *word*, (a) because in and through it alone all possibility of difference arises; (b) because in it there obtains for the first time an organic connection between autonomy *[Selbstseyn]* and dependency *[Nicht-selbstseyn]*, between vowel and consonant (A = vowel, B = consonant; the latter is the inherently mute being that is elevated to intelligibility only by means of the Ideal A).[62]

Schelling could not be more explicit in suggesting that being is struc-tured like a language, and that the *Seynsfuge* is textual and diacritical in nature. Beings ex-ist or stand out as articulated entities in the same way that language distinguishes itself from mere noise—namely, through the productive power of difference. A language without consonants would have no contrasting medium in which to articulate its differences: it would be nonsignifying sound. (Derrida says in another context: "It is the consonant that gives the possibility of a linguistic pertinence to sound, by inscribing within it an opposition.")[63] But a language without vowels would be similarly inarticulate: it would be the deathly quiet of "mute being." The word is distinguished from sheer silence and sheer sonority by what enables language to be, namely the cleaving and joint-ing action of articulation. In short, a language without the diacritical play of vowel and consonant would not be a language. Schelling does not (yet) think of this play in terms of a "third species" analogous to the *khora*, for example, as "C = *différance*," or as the *retrait* of writing that precedes and exceeds the thought of language as the spoken word. Instead, he falls back upon the consolation of a conventional ontotheological distinction between animality and humanity, a distinction that shields legible lan-guage from the specter of its illegible condition of possibility. In ani-mals—and here, we might recall Aristotle's anthropocentric prejudice—the Word is confused because of its disproportionate organization of vowels and consonants. The speechlessness of animals voices their deficient ontological articulation. In the natural world, the *Logos* exists as "a dark, *prophetic* (still incompletely spoken) Word *[ein dunkles, prophetisches (noch nicht völlig ausgesprochen) Wort]*" (7:411/93; emphasis mine): longing is not meaningful, but the mere inarticulate *promise* of meaningfulness that precedes language and marks it in advance as a votive structure. In human-kind, however, "the Word is completely articulate" (7:411/93). The essence of humanity, as distinct from animality, is figured forth as the becoming-legible of language out of the play of letters, "the alphabet of everything." Of course, in making this claim, Schelling serenely posits a dualism whose boundaries are always on the brink of collapsing. At a certain level, the *Freedom* essay is all about demonstrating how the fundamental oppositional terms that are dear to the philosophies of spirit—for example, the animal and the human, the human and the divine, the "mute being" of the dark ground and the luminous sonority of the Word, in short, the real and the ideal—share a relationship that is much finer than one of contrast.

These instances of a metaphorics of the grapheme, to which we could add many other examples, provide a richly suggestive background for Schelling's unusual figure of the primal anagram, a figure that precisely evokes the disproportion of vowels and consonants. We might ask what Ferdinand de Saussure, who had a strange and memorable experience with cryptograms, would have made of it. As Saussure's *cahiers* vividly and anxiously attest, the attempt to theorize logogriphs leads quickly to the most fundamental questions about language: what is a word, and what is language—or, of what inscriptive material is language *made*—such that a word can be encrypted within it?[64] Saussure sees, or thinks he sees, words and names buried in Latin verse. But the more he reads, the less sure he is that what he reads is language. Finally unable to distinguish meaningfully between, on the one hand, the accidental aggregation and dispersal of letters in a given text, and, on the other hand, a genuine system of signification, Saussure comes perilously close to apprehending the exorbitant point at which language divulges the abyss of its own groundlessness. Random aggregations of letters, in the total absence of an intending consciousness, form part of the general background of *noise*, "innocently lacking sense," as de Man characterizes it,[65] which makes language at once possible and impossible, both legible and always exposed to the threat of a profound unintelligibility and illegibility. In Schelling's terms, the materiality of the letter is language's *necessary heritage of darkness*. The capacity for language to conceal words—or any meaningful pattern—therefore raises the theoretical possibility of a bare "language" prior to signification: we might say that Saussure's most troubling insight is that language is not reducible to semiosis. Something always remains, the inhuman residue of senseless linguistic functioning that Derrida calls "the movement of the *sign-function*."[66] Saussure finds the prospect of this tropic of negativity within language to be "monstrous," and there is strong evidence to suggest that he abandoned his anagrammatic research for the consolations of the science of linguistics that would eventually bear his name precisely in order to repress knowledge of its prosaic, inhuman indifference to human desire and thinking.[67]

What does it mean, then, for originary longing to possess an anagrammatical texture, as Schelling's strange figure suggests? Saussure had wanted to unearth an *Urgrund* for language, a semiotic key that would unlock its "hypotext" and bring *les mots sous les mots* into orderly legibility, but what he evoked was something much closer to the disquieting rulelessness of an *Ungrund*. The intersections with Schelling are telling. Lacking the possibility of words, yet subtending the articulation of the Word, primal *Sehnsucht* closely resembles what de Man calls language's capacity for "reference prior to designating the referent":[68] it is the dark, prophetic promise of meaningful language. Like the Platonic *khora*, whose negativity Jonathan Culler has compared to de Man's materiality of language,[69] originary longing constitutes the inscriptive space in which articulation takes place, but which is not itself articulate or articulable. In the instant that the Word articulates *itself*—we cannot say that God pronounces the Word, since the Word is precisely the information (*Ein-bildung*) of his determinate being—by organizing itself out of the play of elemental letters, the latter must have been there, *as the there itself*, before the Word. What is the nature of this already *there*? Ordinarily, of course, solving word-puzzles is a case of *déjà lu*, of recollecting and disinterring a previously written word. Like the virtual logographs with which Saussure wrestles, however, Schelling's primal anagram is far from conventional, precisely because it is pressed into the service of figuring forth the radical anteriority of the *toujours déjà*. By Schelling's own argument, there is no word before the Word, nothing articulate or encoded in the already there to retrieve, read, or hear. Because it is prior to the *Logos*, the primal anagram amounts to a logograph without a key. An unthinkable and troublesome prospect, as Saussure discovers. Before the Word is spoken, it is not cryptically sealed up in this matter, in the manner of a hypotext. Neither can the Word be assigned to a subject, or to a speaker, not even the absolute subject of God, whose subversion the logograph forms. When the *Logos* speaks, nothing is said that existed before its being pronounced, or that existed in a way otherwise than the way that it is spoken. In the primal scene, the *Logos* does not recollect a past that was ever present. In effect, the Word is wholly unmotivated: we could say, starkly, that it *happens* to the senseless *hypotexture* of the primal logograph, or that it is read *into* the linguistic matter of the originary anagram as much as it is spoken *out* of it. This anagram constitutes the dark depth that anonymously promises the Word, but in a way that is otherwise than the transmission of an already constituted meaning by an

108 ■ David L. Clark

already constituted consciousness. If inarticulate longing is the sheer senseless power of the possibility to mean, then in the Word we witness something much more exorbitant and at the limits of philosophical speculation (including the speculation of linguistics): namely, the becoming-language of linguistic matter. And, as Kevin Newmark observes in the context of a discussion about the anagrammatic texture of Blanchot's writing, "[W]e have no language in which to speak of the conditions of language, to speak meaningfully of the moment in which meaningless letters become meaningful words."[70]

What, then, is the relationship between the *Logos* and longing? Not genetic or reproductive, as Schelling's allusions to the Greek mother imply. And not mimetic either, since there is nothing prior to the *Logos* for it to repeat, no meaning beyond the threshold of articulation. Schelling's figures of inscription strongly suggest that the source of the Word's enunciation is *linguistic*, but linguistic in a manner that is otherwise than legible language as such. Signification does not exhaust the thought of language, any more than God's light can illuminate, *without remainder*, the dark matter of his longing. Prior to the *Logos* meaning, the logogriph longs for meaning. The primal anagram functions as a metaphor for the reserve of this linguistic desire, the sheer promise of the Word, which paradoxically withdraws from language so that it might be spoken. Considered as an archperformative, longing is the *saying* of that which is said "by" God, the pure linguistic act, utterly meaningless in itself and never allowed to exist as such or as a discrete origin, even though it is the general condition of all that is *said* in particular. In Hans-Jost Frey's useful formulation:

> All saying is always preoccupied with obscuring itself and being forgotten through its adjustment to what it says. By tending away from itself to what is said, saying itself remains unsaid. . . . The act of saying, which makes possible saying's being said, recedes into an unreachable distance.[71]

For the Word to be spoken, it must be possible to speak. The exorbitant conceptual burden of the primal anagram is to figure forth this inarticulate promise of articulation. Its lettered space reminds us that language, or at least the atomic trace of language, "has started without us, in us, and before us." "This," Derrida writes, "is what theology calls God."[72] The promise of language "approaches from elsewhere" as a "singular anteriority" that undeniably obliges us to speak, mean, be. It holds the subject in a "rigorously asymmetrical manner" that Derrida calls *denegation*: there is no saying of the trace, but there is no denying or not saying it either, since it marks in advance all that is subsequently said. Because longing conditions the articulate Word but is itself without the Word, however, it is only available retrospectively, in the *Logos* we hear and read as the articulate origin of the universe. In terms of Schelling's account of the primal scene, this means that the promise of the Word is made, and the Word means, but no dialectical power will ever enable us to hear the Word promised or to comprehend its emergence from the senselessness of originary longing, since by becoming audible the Word performs the erasure of its having taken place. Under these conditions, the Word must necessarily be spoken, yet remains for structural reasons forever incompletely—or *other* than completely—articulated.

MELANCHOLY TERMINABLE AND INTERMINABLE

> Lift not the painted veil which those who live
> Call Life.
> —P. B. Shelley

Schelling most often treats the composite, self-divided nature of "a humanly suffering God" (7:403/84) affirmatively as the primal source of his everlasting "personality" and "*life*." Life is the fundamental ontological structure of existent beings, whose pattern lies in God. If it were not for their agonistic and, in a sense, contingent struggle with the dark ground, these beings—divine and human alike—would instantly fade into the bloodless abstractions for which Schelling repeatedly castigates negative philosophies. Without the contrasting medium of the ground, without being conditioned by the ground's otherness, nothing could ex-ist or stand out, not even God. Animated and actualized beings are dependent beings: this is the lively equation that Schelling's *Freedom* essay writes and rewrites. But it is an equation that brings attendant risks, threatening as it does to collapse all fundamental distinctions between divine life and the life of the created. Schelling is quick to claim that the crucial ontological *difference* lies in the proximity of "the unruly" to the force of "love" that would subordinate it; in God "the conditioning factor" is more intimately accessible to the rule of reason because it is "*within* himself and not outside of himself" (7:399/79). When Schelling writes that God "is not a system but a life" (7:399/78), *Leben* names the immanence of his purposiveness in the churning process of his self-realization: like an organism, he is indistinguishably agent, medium, and product of himself. This self-immanence is clearly not available to a human individual; "the condition" is "only loaned *[geliehene]* to him independent of him." That is, humankind can never wholly possess itself or live entirely within itself, because it is always in arrears vis-à-vis its determining grounds. Much remains to be said about Schelling's curious metaphor of the "loaned" source of human existence, and about the indeterminate propriety and supplemental nature of this strange "property," never owned outright yet self-evidently human life's single most important possession. If the ground of existence is always otherwise than humankind and lies elsewhere, as Schelling indeed claims, it is also strangely near to hand. According to the logic of the loan figure, humankind has "possessory rights" over the ground—the rights to use and enjoy the ground—but the "proprietary rights" (that is, of ownership) are reserved for God.[73]

Behind Schelling's faintly bourgeois rhetoric lies a more familiar and less humane theological language of indebtedness, that of the "forensic theory of the atonement" for which we have Nietzsche's sarcastic description: "God himself sacrifices himself for the guilt of mankind, God himself makes payment to himself, God as the only being that can redeem man from what has become unredeemable for man himself."[74] Details of this theodicy only survive in residual form in the *Freedom* essay, reconfigured as they are through Böhme. As one might expect, something is lost and gained in the translation; whereas the debtor/creditor trope is useful as a way of describing the nature of the negotiation between existence and its ground, it proves unstable in helping Schelling draw a line between the ontological structure of the human and the divine. For example, we know from elsewhere in the *Freedom* essay, at those points where the pressure to differentiate divine animation from its human equivalent is not so keenly felt, that the conditioning ground is never simply "within" (or, for that matter, "without") God, but more complexly the excluded outside encrypted inside him. As I have already argued, the problematical consequences of this contradictory topology are most evident in the case of the "irreducible remainder," the ontological abject whose radical resistance to God's grasp guarantees that divine liveliness goes right down to the core, as it were, but only at a certain price: preceded and exceeded by the surplus of this perdurable ground, God always already incurs a debt for which he cannot by definition atone. Because Schelling does nothing at this point to clarify precisely how divine obligation differs from its human counterpart, the distinction operates more at the level of desire than philosophically argued fact. What is much more evident is that this debt is *not* of the sort that can be discharged, either by God or humankind, since that would only mean the *end* of life as Schelling describes it. "[W]herever there is no conflict," the philosopher insists, "there is no life" (7:400/80). In other words, the ontological difference, crucial to Schelling's attempt to develop a way of reconciling "divine understanding" to the brute reality of human freedom (and of the evil that that freedom necessarily entails), proves almost impossible to preserve in the face of his parallel insistence that both God and human are *alive*, and thus inescapably dependent upon the alterity of the ground. The implication is hard to resist: the human and the divine realms are not divided as between finite and infinite powers of apprehension, but as differing types of finitude. Does God's finitude conflict with Schelling's claim that the ground is proximate and at God's disposal? As if responding to the pressure of this question, Schelling's argument suddenly takes on an affecting quality, opening itself up to a sea of sorrow that threatens to engulf God and human alike:

> Man never gains control over the condition. . . . This is the sadness which adheres to all finite life, and inasmuch as there is even in God himself a condition at least relatively independent, there is in him, too, a source of sadness *[ein Quell der Traurigkeit]*. . . . From it comes the veil of sadness *[der Schleier der Schwermut]* which is spread over the whole of nature, the deep indestructible melancholy of all life *[die tiefe unzerstörliche Melancholie alles Lebens]*. (7:399/79; translation modified)

What is the nature of this ineradicable pall of despondency that is draped over everything that is, a sadness too deep for tears? What is indestructibility *[Unzerstörbarkeit]*, and what must melancholy be if it can be characterized as indestructible? So much of what is disquieting about this passage, and that could be said to open the way of Schelling's path of thinking *from* idealism *to* deconstruction, lies in how seriously we take his description of this sadness as *unappeasable*. All life, *as* life, is originarily dispossessed insofar as it mourns a loss—this, even though Schelling has just claimed that it is human, not divine, existence that mostly feels the burden of indebtedness to the ground. There is a great loss, Schelling now concedes, one so great that even God feels it, sadly. As is the case at so many moments in his work, Schelling here anticipates

Freud, who writes importantly on the question of *Trauer und Melancho-lia*.[75] For Freud, mourning springs from the anguish caused by the libido's disengagement from the lost object. In his earliest formulations of the problem, the work of mourning is properly undertaken to overcome and to survive this loss, the eventual goal being the renunciation of the libido's attachments to the loved one. The melancholic mourner, on the other hand, negotiates with the loss by refusing it, choosing instead to incorporate the forsaken object directly into the structure of the ego. Neither able to accept or deny the loss, nor in a position to resolve the intensely ambivalent feelings invested in the forsaken one, the melancholic ego sets itself against itself, and in this self-division becomes the site of an interior fold for which there can be no simple unraveling. In short, the melancholic becomes *pre-occupied* with and by the lost loved one. (As Freud will eventually come to see, melancholia describes an activity that is not only necessary to the work of mourning, but also fundamental to the birth of the consciencized ego.)

The connections between Freud's *Trauerarbeit* and Schelling's gloomy vision of a universal melancholy are instructive. What in Freud's hands, at least in 1917, is still considered to be a morbid affliction of the psyche is for Schelling the general condition of life, all life. If melancholy "adheres" to life, it is not because it belongs to life but because life in some way clings to its forsaken object. (Freud: "We see only that libido clings *[klammert]* to its objects and will not renounce those that are lost.")[76] Is this melancholia then evidence of a failed or refused work of mourning, as Freud would use these terms? As Schelling describes it, the loss that is the source of pervasive despondency is deep, so deep as to be insurmountable even by God. Conceived this way, a radically unappeasable sadness in fact disables the distinction between successful or unsuccessful mourning, and instead revalues melancholia as the name for (or symptom of) an *impossible* mourning. Impossible, because in this instance the lost object (as the irreducibly dark ground against which the living stand out) is always already absent, and thus utterly unsalvageable. God himself cannot renounce this loss, ending his interminable "clinging" to his own ground so as to become all in all. In other words, this work of mourning is profoundly melancholic because life, *as* life, must negotiate interminably with a loss for which there can be no complete recompense, no eventual renunciation, not if the living are to remain alive. And arguably nothing is more imperative for the purposes of Schelling's positive philosophy than preserving the life of the living, even and especially if this means introducing a certain deathliness and finitude into the heart of God. Not unlike Freud's melancholic, all life—God's and humankind's—"fails" to overcome its loss because it cannot get entirely behind that which determines and conditions its liveliness. Instead, life in effect divides itself from itself; or, more accurately, it is divided from itself from the beginning: life *is* this division. Life *is* no more and no less than the originary incorporation of its ground, the binding of itself to the absent alterity that sets existent beings on their perilous, mortal way. Ineradicable melancholy names the absolute conditionality of life, the subjectless, structural "recognition" that life has from the start "lost control" over its condition. Thirty years after the publication of the *Freedom* essay, Schelling continues to identify this loss with a constitutive sadness:

> But the subject can never possess itself *as* what it is, for precisely as it addressees itself it *becomes* another; this is the basic contradiction, the misfortune in all being.[77]

To forfeit all possibility of working through the basic contradiction of being, and to learn, so to speak, to live with it: that is melancholy. Tarrying with the negative: for life. As the unthought blankness that conditions and pre-occupies knowing as well as being, this tropic of negativity escapes comprehension. Neither humans nor God can know their condition, Schelling suggests, a condition that is not so much possessed by existent beings as they are possessed by it. The fact that this lack unavoidably adheres to God puts to us that absolute knowledge would be indistinguishable from life degree zero. Under the pall of melancholy, Schelling's God is in and of time, and, as Hans-Georg Gadamer writes, "To exist historically means that knowledge of oneself can never be complete."[78] But as Schelling's choice of such a conspicuously affective trope as *melancholia* implies, existent beings might at least "sense" this incompleteness, which is to say, "know" it in their belatedness; here we might recall Schleiermacher's description of the noncognitive awareness of human finitude as the "feeling of absolute dependence."[79]

Melancholia (as an impossible mourning) describes the lack that casts life into the fullness of time. Heidegger would say that existent beings are thereby *thrown*. Ineradicable melancholy is Schelling's name for the underlying rapport that beings share with what conditions them, but which also forever eludes them. It is the mood of finitude, as it were, that sweeps over idealism, with its disembodied dreams of freedom from natural life, and that compels life to recognize that it lives for death, with death. What then lies beneath or beyond that universal veil of sadness? One could certainly call the question naïve, since Schelling's most radical point is precisely that beyond the veil there is nothing—certainly nothing that exists. The veil does not obscure a happier place where the universe is freed from the pangs of loss; it is not a veil that can be lifted. If God himself is unable to recall his origin, but is more accurately called or summoned into finite existence by it, like all other things, then the loss is absolute, a privation from which there is no recovery. Finitude characterizes every thing that *is*, through and through; needless to say, this is difficult to think, perhaps *the* most difficult thing to think. What Manfred Frank calls the "metaphysical interpretation of Being as Being-at-one's-disposal, i.e., as graspable presence,"[80] proves almost impossible to resist. Kant's God, his head full of the babble of the theologians and the scholastics, feels the tug of it: "*But from where, then, am I?*" he asks, believing that there is an origin that is punctually there to unconceal. And we know from the *Critique of Reason* that what he sees there, in that tropic of negativity, is in fact a terrible oblivion. "Beyond" the *Urgrund* that he had for good reason thought himself to be, God glimpses the irrational obscurity of the primal scene—or *Ungrund*, as Schelling will designate it—not without recoiling from its utter senselessness. Perhaps this is the oblivion that Heidegger evokes in the next century, looking back at Schelling:

> The beginning of Western thought is not the same as its origin. The beginning is, rather, the veil that conceals the origin—indeed an unavoidable veil. If that is the situation, then oblivion shows itself in a different light. The origin keeps itself concealed in the beginning.[81]

What is it about the origin that interminably resists being assimilated to thought? In Schelling's terms, what is the nature of the "remainder" whose irreducibility makes mourning melancholic, interminably and abnormally caught up in the process of detaching from the lost object of metaphysics? If there is always something left over, a residue left unresolved and unassimilated, then Schelling's text could be characterized as "half-mourning" *(demi-deuil)*, which is Derrida's evocative nineteenth-century phrase for the condition of being in the midst of metaphysics and the clôture of metaphysics.[82] This origin that is not a beginning, this trace of the (always already) forsaken object, obliges metaphysics to mourn to the precise extent that it prevents this mourning from ever being fulfilled or completed. By characterizing finitude as melancholic, Schelling appears to register a certain regret and a certain clinging attachment to the notion of a work of mourning, in which existent beings would be able to renounce, once and for all, their belatedness, and to gather themselves up in their own grounds. Is *Schelling* then the one who is the melancholic? Does the *Freedom* essay pretend to designate universal melancholy, when it is, if fact, the melancholy to which it refers? Is the philosopher saddened by his inability (or unwillingness) to write a metaphysics that absolves life from finitude? Does he wish it were otherwise? It might be more fair to the conflicting strata of awareness that characterize Schelling's text, and to the melancholic ambivalence that the philosopher in turn seems to feel for the forsaken ground, to say that he is caught *between* the question of mourning and melancholia, as between idealism and deconstruction. As Ned Lukacher describes it, this is "the dilemma of the modern world, and of the postmodern world as well: to recognize that 'mourning is in error' but be nevertheless condemned to mourn."[83] Working through and working with the destabilizing consequences of an unappeasable melancholy, the *Freedom* essay is emotionally idealistic but theoretically deconstructive about the fate of the lost object of metaphysics: it is, in other words, simultaneously "the work *of* mourning and the work *about* mourning."[84]

IL Y A LÀ CENDRE

> Did not we cast three men bound into the midst of the fire?
> True, O king.
> Lo I see four men loose, walking in the midst of the fire, and they
> have no hurt, and the form of the fourth is like the Son of God.
> —The Book of Daniel

"After all this," Schelling observes, "the question ever remains: does evil end, and how? Has creation a final purpose at all . . . ?" (7:403/84). What is the *end* of life, its objective and its conclusion? Schelling makes clear in the opening movement of the *Freedom* essay that the end cannot reside in the beginning, at least not in any determinate way, for this would render the subsequent agonistic struggle of God and of all existent beings all too intelligible, and therefore fatalistic. It would drain the liveliness out of life. As Schelling says, "Being is only aware of itself in becoming" (7:403/

84): the becoming-God of God and the becoming-creation of creation happen in "real time," as it were, so that whatever conclusion awaits them emerges only gradually and in the labor of their self-realization. This makes Schelling's questions less rhetorical and more genuinely inter- rogative than he would appear to realize, for nothing could be more obscure than the "final purpose" of a universe whose melancholy is frankly described as indestructible—that is, without finality. Under these condi- tions of infinite finitude, I have suggested, God's absolute realization could only mean the absolute cessation of his self-constitutive activity— sudden death. Divine life rather lies in the indeterminate zone between the ongoing resistance and compliance of the dark ground, or, in Freud's terms, between absolute binding (the goal of the secondary processes) and absolute discharge (the goal of the primary processes). As if shrink- ing from this complex prospect—it is the fundamental *différance* of life that Freud evokes in *Beyond the Pleasure Principle*—Schelling imagines the end of God's existence not as death but as another form of life, although he does this initially by taking someone else's Word for it: "Scripture," he offers, "puts that time in a distant future when God will be all in all, that is, when he will be completely realized" (7:404/84). Of course, Scripture says no such thing, unless one is reading it through the dark glass of Böhme. Later in the *Freedom* essay, Schelling will risk more details about the nature of this far-flung apocalypse, life beyond divine life, but these details raise more questions than they answer and obey a contradictory logic that is now familiar to us from Derrida's analyses of the supplement. As Schelling contends, the dark ground resists and fuels the light of God's "life-process" *[Lebensproßess]* (7:408/89) until nothing remains to burn. Would this state of pure enlightenment mean absolute life (and would this life mean absolute death)? At the moment of God's complete realization, would the universe be *fully* irradiated (which is to say, emptied of any contrasting medium and thus effectively in a state of undifferentiated illumination), and under these unthinkable conditions, what eye could distinguish between total darkness and total light, or between life or death? Caught between embracing and evading a phi- losophy of radical finitude, Schelling cannot answer these questions, or answer them in a straightforward way. He is half-mourning, if you will. On the one hand, at the end of the world, "all truth and goodness within longing is raised to luminous consciousness." "Then," Schelling an- nounces, recalling his earlier reference to what his hallucinated scripture had promised, "*all* is subjugated to spirit," and "love . . . is *all in all*"

(7:408/90; emphasis mine). On the other hand, not quite everything is found to be worthy of this transfiguration. At the end of the world, all forms of darkness are equal, but certain forms are more equal than others: something always remains, and because of its impertinent resistance to the light it must be cut off and cast away. But it is not discarded anywhere: "[T]he false and impure . . . is eternally locked in darkness, in order to remain back-behind as the eternally dark ground of selfhood, as the *Caput mortuum* of its life-process, as potential which can never proceed to act" (7:408/89; trans. modified). Apocalypse is this act of ultimate self-laceration, "the final, total division *[endlichen gänzlichen Scheidung]*" (7:408/89), as Schelling emphatically puts it, making it seem as if the jointure of being had prepared existent life not for the reconciliation of its elemental principles (since only something that has been rent can be repaired), but for their utter sundering, one from the other. The radical resistance of the impure remainder is the "cause" of its expulsion, but we should also note that in being expelled this perdurability is not annihilated, but, quite to the contrary, *preserved* forever beyond the point of apocalypse; repudiation is never a simple act: it is always, also, a kind of saving.

What is the nature of this excluded other, relegated to an intra-ontological leper colony? What is its *place*, its role in the nexus of God's existence and its location in the order of things? Schelling is explicit: it is the by-product of the engines of life and it must be hidden from the light of God's "luminous consciousness." It is the telltale signature that God is (was) alive, for which the philosopher perhaps feels a certain embarrassment, even disgust. Knowing that absolute illumination signals the death of God (and of the life of existent beings), however, Schelling retains a residue of the darkness and smuggles it back into his account of apocalypse in the form of pure excrescence. What is indispensable to God's existence is thereby conserved, albeit it in the demonized form of an unnecessary addition whose violent exclusion is the means by which God constitutes and recognizes himself as "all in all." A supplementary logic is at work: the impure remainder is maximally real and composed of material so resistant that it endures even the fires of the apocalypse; at the same time, it is sheer rubbish, nothing, or nearly nothing, and, as such, it is so insignificant that God can confidently declare his complete realization and not contradict himself. It is as if the panoptic eye of God's "luminous consciousness" sees and does not see the gloom into which he has chased the remainder. He is blind to this supplement, but unseeing in the special way in which seeing is blind to the origin of sight. Out of sight, out of mind: "*Blindness to the supplement* is the law," Derrida writes.[85] Put most economically, God's "*Caput mortuum*" is (un)necessary: 1) It is utterly expendable, not just dead but *kaputt mortuum*, resoundingly *dead dead*.[86] 2) It is resolutely non-expendable, precisely what *cannot* be expended, the fallout that remains behind; in that survival, it reminds Schelling that no fire burns hot enough, and that no life-process functions at a level of sufficient efficiency, that it can consume its fuel *without remainder*. Something always remains, and Derrida has a name for this stranger and a phrase that describes both its resistant alterity and its profound indifference to metaphysics: *Il y a là cendre*. Cinders there are.[87] The inefficiency about the life-process is structural in nature; it is the necessarily incombustible condition of possibility of combustion, the trace of the inorganic within life, whose perdurability keeps apocalypse, in the decisively totalizing manner that Schelling describes, from actually happening. The cinder says: No Apocalypse, no "final, total *Scheidung*." Not Now. Naturally, God must hide this disgraceful residue, even from himself, in order to claim his plenitude. Where will he put this dross? "Back behind" *[zurückbleibt]* God's essence, Schelling says—describing and unearthing a cache so secluded that both major English translations of the *Freedom* essay forget to mention it altogether. God's cinders are driven into an outer darkness. But outer *where*? Like the dead, the *Caput mortuum* is hidden; but for that reason, it is *everywhere*. This tropic of negativity is as indeterminately located as its contents are impure. Presumably there is nothing outside of God—*Il n'y a pas de hors-Dieu*—especially a "completely realized" God, yet such a space exists and Schelling fills it with waste. To pursue this involuted topography one step further: if God is "all in all," then there is strictly speaking no room for the *zurückbleibt* except in the form of an outside folded *inside*, where the alterity of the remainder can be simultaneously conserved *and* excluded. Like the melancholic who "incorporates" rather than "introjects" the lost love, God creates a *crypt* within himself, a dead-zone of exclusionary inclusion, that enables him simultaneously to prohibit and admit the supplemental object. Schelling, or a certain side of Schelling, would have us think this reserve as simple exteriority, pure addition, or pure absence; yet the very fact that God realizes himself only through its violent exclusion/inclusion suggests that he was contaminated by a general impurity at the origin: an originary infection and violence, whose effacement is, as Derrida says of the trace, "the opening of the first exteriority in general, the enigmatic relation of the living to its other and of an inside to an outside: spacing."[88]

GOD WITHOUT BEING

Between posing his question about the "final purpose" of creation and answering it with his vivid account of the expulsion of God's *Caput mortuum*, Schelling must traverse stranger territory. Whatever its fate, and whatever evil befalls humankind as the contingent part of that fate, creation as a whole progressively realizes the power of goodness: of that Schelling is confident, although not so confident that he does not feel the need to sketch—for the second time in the *Freedom* essay—the historical stages of its evolving triumph. With each stage in history, God's spirit informs the process by which the powers of darkness are resolved by the powers of light, a process that culminates in the form of Christ's love. To speculate on the nature of this love, however, proves to be very difficult, not least because, in Schelling's mind, creation's complex end always points back to its enigmatic beginning. The philosopher hesitates, as if unsure of himself:

> For not even spirit itself is supreme; it is but spirit, or the breath of love. But love is supreme. It is that which was before the ground and before existing beings (as separated) were, but what was not as love, rather— how shall we designate it? . . . *[Die ist das, was da war, ehe denn der Grund und ehe das Existierende (als getrennte) waren, aber noch nicht war als Liebe, sondern—wie sollen wir es bezeichen . . . ?].* (7:406/86; translation modified)

"Here at last we reach the highest point of the whole inquiry," he adds, making the oddly unstable and obscure introduction of that point all the more conspicuous. What is the nature of this unprecedented "before"? What is this "being *[Wesen] before* all ground and before all existence, that is, before any duality at all?" (7:406/87). Schelling has the answer, an answer, a name at least—*die Liebe*—and then loses it, abandoning his first choice in the same breath, so to speak, that he declares it to be "supreme *[das Höchste]*." Before the sentence that attempts to "place" the name—locating it somewhere prior to the jointure of Being—is completed, Schelling renders it provisional, because insufficiently primordial: it is "love"; no, at the origin, it is "what was not [yet] as love." What is it, then, for which *die Liebe* forms a kind of natural alibi? What Schelling wants to evoke is clearly very ancient, perhaps terrifyingly so. The philosopher must speak of this *arche*, of which "Love" is the telling erasure, in the form of a short sequence of strenuously escalating hyperboles, which is to say, in terms not of what it *is* but of what it lies *before* or beyond: before spirit, before the breath of love, before the ground/ existent distinction, before the time when living beings were divided from themselves as separate entities (not only human from human, human from animal, human from God, but also, more radically, God from himself), before all of this . . . what? A primordial ground or *Urgrund?* Schelling does not say, not just yet, but it is very hard *not* to fill in that answer on the philosopher's behalf and on behalf of philosophy. Within the context of classical rationalism, what else could occupy this primordial space, prior to "all ground" and "all existence"? Whatever it is, it resists positive predication, triggering a rhetoric of negative determination that characterizes and organizes Schelling's argument, both here, in these hesitant sentences, and in the next two crucial paragraphs, both of which will need to be read very slowly.

"—[H]ow shall we designate it?" Schelling's hyperbolic gesturing is pulled up short with this question. Perhaps not surprisingly, he will have recourse to ask the question again in a moment, on a second and more detailed approach to the *arche*, but let us pause with the philosopher and consider what this crisis of designation means. Schelling's inquiry is redoubled, I would argue, and posed with two different answers in mind, or rather, one in mind, the other—how shall I say it?—*out of mind*:

1) On the one hand, the question is quasi-rhetorical. Rhetorical, because Schelling has in fact already made significant inroads precisely in designating "it," insofar as he is humanly able, given its fundamentally archaic nature. In a sense, he has been doing nothing but *designating* [*bezeichnen*, to indicate, to name], signing, or gesturing, linguistically marking and remarking the *arche*, and in this motion frankly acknowledging its absent presence. We could say, then, that what he asks is *en route* to being answered, even if the answer *itself*, as the *arche*'s proper name, is something about which Schelling can only speculate, hazard a guess. In other words, Schelling answers, is answering, his own question: obliquely, to be sure, not unlike a curve asymptotically approaching its axis, but in a manner that is entirely consonant with the rhetorical strategies and hyperessentializing gestures of apophatic thought, especially so-called negative theologies, Christian and Greek, extending through Meister Eckhart and Dionysius the Areopagite (Pseudo-Dionysius), back to a certain Platonic and Neoplatonic tradition and ahead into modernity, in Wittgenstein and in Schelling's closest reader, Heidegger. As Derrida

has recently argued, the common discursive feature of these negative theologies consists in how they "reserve, beyond all positive predication, beyond all negation, even beyond Being, some hyperessentiality, a being beyond Being."[89] "[T]hat ontological wager of hyperessentiality," Derrida remarks,[90] is what distinguishes negative theology (which no doubt shares both more and less with deconstructive discourse than is sometimes suggested) from the thought of *différance*. Schelling could be said to make such a gamble, committing himself at this late point in the *Freedom* essay to voyaging upon strange seas of thought. Driven by what Derrida calls "the passion of the origin,"[91] he deliberately risks the mysticism for which Hegel had dismissed his work. There is the promise of the absolutely prior as the ground of the ground: it is a promise, in truth, that has oriented Schelling's entire protean philosophical career. There is the *desire*—or "passion"—to evoke it, if only apophatically and derivatively: these coordinates orient Schelling's thinking as its primary means and ends, elevating and directing it toward the regulating ideal of the nameless in a manner that is irreducibly metaphysical and ontotheological. Whatever Schelling says by way of naming the nameless, it is more than that; yet even in its apparent ineffability and exorbitance, its evocation is worth chancing in the form of a *philosophical* essay on the nature of freedom. The origin of freedom remains his primary target, and, *as* an origin, this foundation fixes Schelling's hyperboles and negations within the orbit of ontology, even if he strains its limits (as he undoubtedly does in the ensuing paragraphs). *What* the *arche* is, is something about which Schelling is willing to commit all the considerable resources of speculative idealism: *that* it is, must go without saying, must be said by *not* saying. Like the negative theology of the inexpressible whose discourse he partly mimes here, Schelling does not so much "overcome" ontology (whatever that could mean) as attempt to reinscribe the "real and actual" (7:357/31) nature of God's absolute substance in surreal or hyperreal terms.

Schelling, whose entanglement with the philosophical text of the Enlightenment is undeniable, is not suddenly transformed into a negative theologian, although this switching, with its attendant interference effects, is always possible in a text in which the theosophic mysticism of Böhme is so tightly woven into the fabric of German idealism. But the fact remains that beyond Schelling's ken, something "real and actual" "positively" exists and steers his thinking, even if, for the time being, this absolute substance can only be determined in a negative fashion, as a

kind of afterimage of that which is more immediately available to positive predication. Considerable conceptual labor is here invested in an
attempt to express the sheer preeminence of this absolute, whose singular
anteriority compels him to adopt what Derrida calls the "logic of the *sur*, of
the *hyper*, over and beyond, which heralds all the hyper-essentialisms,"
including those "of Christian apophases."[92] Apophatically outlining what
he cannot yet know or name, Schelling posits and then gestures across a
boundary between what *is* ("love") and what lies before; but he does so in
order that what exceeds this boundary may be compared to "love" and to
everything else—the list of positive predicates is theoretically unlimited—that comes "after." The nameless entity negatively determined to
be anterior to "love" is therefore not unlike the idea of the "Good"
"beyond Being or essence" that one finds in the *Republic*. As Derrida
describes it, the surreal "excellence" of Plato's "Good" "is not so alien to
Being . . . that the excess itself cannot be described in terms of what it
exceeds."[93] Schelling's hyperbole similarly ensures that some measure of
ontological continuity is maintained between what is familiarly known
(or treated as if known) and the unknown exorbitance that lies somewhere "before." Under these conditions, what lies before-essence is not
unequivocally nonessence (Schelling will emphasize this point in the
Freedom essay's next paragraph; I will come back to this); nor, to get
slightly ahead of myself, can one say that it is unequivocally *other*-than-
essence, as *différance* more or less "is" for Derrida, or the "positional
power of language" "is" for de Man. Schelling's apophatic thought rather
thinks this *before*-being as a form of *being*-before, an archaic or potential
form of what is ("love"). In the next paragraph, indeed, the philosopher
will designate, but only provisionally, the absolutely prior as such, as a
"being before all ground and before all existence." Something like a
ground of the ground, then, or *Urgrund*, the very name that will intrude
upon Schelling's text in a moment, problematically. "[H]ow shall we
designate it?" In designating the nameless as that which lies out of the
reach of designation, Schelling's denials operate, in a manner analogous
to negative theology, as superaffirmations, effectively positing a supra-
essential reality beyond the ground and beyond existence.

2) On the other hand, the question Schelling asks himself is *not*
rhetorical, or not entirely, but contains within itself the trace of a query,
an opening of thought, that is genuinely and disturbingly interrogative.
"—[H]ow shall we designate it?" What if we are to read this question as
one whose "answer" lies in the asking of it? That is: precisely in resisting,

insofar as this is possible within "the element of logic and of onto-theological grammar,"[94] a definitive answer, whether couched in nega-tive or positive terms? As: The undesignated is *radically* nameless; I am telling you that neither can it nor will it be named, *not even apophatically according to the logic of the sur*. Questionable designations and descrip-tions are all that the philosopher has and can hope to have in the face of its sheer priority. "There is no name for it," writes Derrida.

> [A] proposition to be read in its *platitude*. This unnameable is not an ineffable Being which no name could approach: God, for example. This unnameable is the play which makes possible nominal effects, the relatively unitary and atomic structures that are called names. . . .[95]

This unnameable triggers a crisis of adequation: if everything that *is* is articulated in the form of the *Seynsfuge*, if the distinctness of existent beings comes from the activity of the ground/existence nexus, as Schelling has insisted throughout the *Freedom* essay, then what lies "before" must necessarily be profoundly obscure, indistinct, even abyssal. "God"—or some elemental ground *of* God—may or may not be the already-there that orients these strained sentences that either cannot say enough or say too much. Perhaps Schelling's negations do not (only) affirm and reaf-firm an underlying essence that the philosopher wagers philosophy could name, given sufficient conceptual power, but evoke, as in a dream, quite another tropic of negativity, about which nothing, or hardly anything, can be said. The unnameable may not be freestanding and self-named, the perdurable *that* that remains once all positive and negative predica-tions have been exhausted, after all the answers to the question "What is . . . ?" have been answered. *Not* spirit, *not* love, *not Wesen*, neither the grounded nor the *Grund*: "[I]t is written completely otherwise."[96] In-eradicable namelessness or illegibility, like unappeasable melancholy, evokes an absence that may be of an altogether different order than either the hyperessences of negative theology, or the *Urgrund* or "pri-mordial ground" of classical cataphatic ontotheology. Perhaps a placeless place or primal scene so obscure as to never have *been* as such, without having already withdrawn, like Heidegger's origin, *at the beginning*. What-ever Schelling thinks or says about this surreal, it always comes too late, after the fact. Does this simply make the unnameable in Schelling a new name of God? "This reading will always be possible. Who could prohibit it? In the name of what?"[97] "Unless," as Geoffrey Bennington proffers,

"we displace the philosophical (onto-theological) position of God—
which (nothing excludes this *a priori*) can also be done by theologians."[98]
And by philosophers who sometimes speak in the voice of (negative)
theologians. It is that side of Schelling—let us call it the "postmetaphysical"
shadow of his "hypermetaphysical" philosophical self—that I want to
pursue for a moment here.

If not a more primordial ground, then, what is the nature of the
absolutely first in the order of things? The regressive momentum of
Schelling's philosophical narrative, which moves, as Alan White observes, "from phenomena to their grounds, and then to the grounds of
those grounds, leads . . . [Schelling] unerringly" to this primal scene.[99]
"Unerringly" may not be a precise enough term, for the narrative of the
Freedom essay could also be viewed as a complex series of detours that
after all leaves the most critical and potentially destructive matter—from
the perspective of idealist metaphysics—to the last, until it is too late in
the argument to pursue it in any detail. One could almost say that Schelling
is avoiding speaking about it. In any case, what had been treated as the
fundamental ontological distinction throughout the *Freedom* essay is
now preempted by something "older," and this shifting ground leaves
Schelling with no choice but to reflect upon his working hypothesis
about the nature of essence: "What is to be gained by that initial distinction between being insofar as it is ground, and being insofar as it exists"
(7:406/86)? Schelling wants to know not only what kind of conceptual
leverage the ground-existent nexus obtains on the nature of this hidden
anteriority, but also, self-critically, whether it is possible that all this talk
about the jointure of being has deflected his gaze from a more fundamental object. How is it that the light and the dark can come to be
opposed *in the first place?* What is the nature of essence "before" God's
emergence as an articulated being that struggles with its own elemental
ground? If not God, then what atheological or pretheological "structuring" as such enables God's self-determining struggle to be?

Two answers immediately present themselves to Schelling. *Either*
the light and the dark are to be understood as entirely discrete realms,
sharing no "middle point"; *or* the founding principles are resolvable in a
common identity. Schelling had summarily dismissed the former hypothesis earlier in the *Freedom* essay on the basis of its gross hazard to
intelligibility. Because it inevitably leads to the claim that evil constitutes
a wholly separate reality, and thus an irrational limit to God's power,
absolute dualism instantly results in "a system of the self-tearing [or self-

laceration] and despair of understanding *[ein System der Selbstzerreißung und Verzweiflung der Vernunft]*" (7:354/28). This is a strangely visceral response, a kind of flinching reflex where we might more readily expect a dialectical engagement with the problem at hand, especially since a radical dualism is precisely what Schelling's system veers towards when it evokes the specter of a remainder that is irreducible even to God's reasoning power, a source of melancholy that no work of mourning will palliate. Schelling shudders at the monstrous prospect of having to account systematically for a truly *radical* alterity and moves quickly on; it is as if pausing to consider, even in hypothetical terms, how deeply otherness might cleave into the heart of God's being, risked the disjointing of thinking itself.[100] This is not the only instance in which Schelling resorts to tropes of self-mutilation. Two paragraphs later, he rails against "modern European philosophy as a whole" for its inability to account positively for the otherness of "the real" and for its constitutive role in the production of the "ideal": such indifference to the potency of the ground, Schelling declares, produces "a turbid, wild enthusiasm that irrupts in self-mutilation *[Selbstzerfleischung]* or—as with the priests of the Phrygian goddess—self-emasculation *[Selbstentmannung]*" (7:356–57/31). The anxious, even hysterical, tonality of these cutting passages hints that more is at stake than is immediately apparent: on the one hand, rational system castrates itself by succumbing to the ancient prejudice against the otherness of the real; on the other hand, rational system lacerates itself by embracing that otherness radically in the form of an absolute dualism. The shifting valuations attached to the spectacle of self-inflicted mutilation intimate that, on the question of advancing the cause of the otherness of the ground while keeping the body of reason intact, the philosopher finds himself walking on a razor's edge, or, to change metaphors, finds that he wants to wield a magic scalpel that dissects idealist metaphysics in order to reveal its reliance on the dark ground, but to do so without wounding it fatally, or at least without cutting it to the quick.

But is not the absurd prospect of a self-lacerated system exactly the imminent peril facing the *Freedom* essay as it draws towards its enigmatic conclusion, as Schelling prepares to consider the exorbitant otherness of "that which was before the ground and before existing beings"? Schelling's earlier horror of being dismembered at the hands of an absolute dualism now reads like a premonition of what was to come of his regressive search for the nature of the origin. Given the complex depths that he has probed, Schelling cannot avoid asking himself: does this mean that I am in fact working with an absolute dualism? Strictly speaking, the answer is "no." Even to pose the question in this radicalized context, however, produces revealing resonances with the treatment of that same question earlier in the essay, when it was regarded as "merely" theodical—rather than ontological—in nature. By evoking absolute dualism, only to dismiss it outright, Schelling attempts to preempt and palliate the specter of an irrationalism and of an originary doubling that rises to haunt his text yet once more; in other words, it is though Schelling were trying to inoculate his system from irrationalism by attaching to it a hypothesis that he has already safely rejected on theodical grounds. This time, however, it is not the otherness of evil or even of the real that threatens systematic thinking with dismemberment, but an absolute alterity, an otherness beyond good and evil and beyond even the real and the ideal, as Schelling readily concedes in the next paragraph. Under these conditions, the moment that Schelling asks himself whether "absolute dualism" describes his philosophy amounts to a recoil on the threshold of suffering a tear for which there is no healing touch. Considering and rejecting absolute dualism becomes an alibi for turning away from this primal laceration.

To the question "What is to be gained by that initial distinction between being insofar as it is basis and being insofar as it exists?" Schelling suggests another answer: the duality of the founding principles is an illusion, the terms of that duality being the outward expressions of an inner singularity. To fall back, however, upon the security of "one being in all opposites, an absolute identity of light and darkness, good and evil," Schelling immediately counters, would only reinstate the errors of idealism "that befall every rational system" (7:406/87)—errors, Schelling readily confesses, that troubled his *own* earlier philosophical programme. The place to which Schelling now wants—belatedly—to turn his critical gaze is unusual enough to warrant a certain disengagement from the insights into the nature of the Absolute that his previous work has afforded him. This sort of frankly self-critical concession is quite rare in Schelling's work and rarer still in the *Freedom* essay, which begins with the philosopher insisting that his argument will be an extension and clarification of his system of identity rather than its critique. We already know the chief symptom of what it means to *rationalize* the fundamental ontological distinction, in the sense of "explaining" it "away" in the name of a disembodied identity and in the manner of "modern European philosophy": self-mutilation and self-castration. As it turns out, the grim fate of the philosopher of absolute identity is exactly the same as the fate of the philosopher of absolute dualism: in a move that could only be described as both overdetermined and preemptively defensive, Schelling dismisses both possibilities, and in effect announces that nothing, not the slashing of idealism nor the cuts of irrationalism, will unman him now.

Beginning this critically revisionary moment in his essay by twice telling his readers what the Absolute is *not*, then, Schelling quickly returns to a rhetoric of negative determination whose incrementally accumulating weight demands clause-by-clause attention. To continue: no primal ground in the form of *eine absolute Identität* can be said to lie prior to God's founding distinction, since that would neuter this distinction, leaving it conceptually sterile. Nevertheless, "there must be an essence *[Wesen] before* all ground and *before* all existence, that is, *before* any duality at all" (7:406;87; emphasis mine). Three times Schelling points to the logical priority of this (still) unnamed essence; three times we must puzzle over the nature of this *Vor*. A being before the jointure of being? What would that *be*? The phrase seems to confirm that Schelling is indeed committed to the "wager of hyperessentiality" with which Derrida identifies negative theology. How then does God figure in this primal scene? *Dieu sans l'être?* Does Schelling here question the efficacy of naming God by being, in a manner that brings to mind the work of Jean-Luc Marion?

> God, before all else, has to be. Which means at once and the same time that before other beings, he would have to be, and that before every other initiative, he would have also to take that of being. But does Being relate, more than anything, to God? Does God have anything to gain by being? Can Being—which whatever is, provided that it is, manifests—even accommodate any(thing of) God?[101]

In the case of Schelling, in whom Marion finds a strong precursor,[102] the question is whether a God otherwise than the jointure of being is still God. Schelling has said repeatedly that God is a *life*. To *be* means to be alive. Before that life, beyond the "nexus of forces" that constitute that life, then, what "is" God? Even to cast the question in this form is to beg the most important question, namely the question of (God's) being. "It" will be without life, to be sure, lying as it does beyond the veil of tears. But perhaps not therefore *dead*. What is it? Neither God denominated by (living) being, nor not-God. This being before any duality that is *not* absolute identity could be either: either God before (without) being, or a "being" (without) God. If the former, Schelling flirts with negative theology, not the only time in this text, as I have suggested, which so often ventriloquizes Böhme, not to say his eighteenth-century interpreters, including Franz von Baader and Friedrich Christoph Oetinger. If the latter, something else: not so much something other than negative philosophy (and certainly not a positive philosophy of the kind that has always named God by Being), as the evocation of the trace of an alterity within negative philosophy.

To think—in Heidegger's terms—the origin "beyond" the beginning, Schelling will need once again to evoke Böhme in order to twist away from the consolations of philosophy, evoking his obscure notion of the *Ungrund* or nonground: "[H]ow can we designate it except as 'primal ground' *[Urgrund]*," Schelling asks; "or, rather, as the 'nonground' *[Ungrund]*?" (7:406/87). The philosopher's self-correction, performed in midsentence, calls for pause, coming as it does so quickly after he insists that the *Ungrund* is *not* to be confused with the primal ground of an "absolute identity." In the instant before naming the *Ungrund* as such, in the semantic opening created by the query—"How can we designate it . . . ?"— another name rushes in, and not just any name but, so to speak, the "wrong" name, the name that belongs to the near side, the reassuringly familiar side, of the ontological divide that Schelling is attempting to cross. We could paraphrase and explicate the self-contradictory impulses of Schelling's syntax thus: "The origin is *not* the primal ground. How can I name the origin? Strangely, I find that I have no choice but to name it the primal ground. No; it is the nonground." As Krell astutely points out:

> In Schelling's text . . . the primal, primordial, incipient, or original ground and the nonground are brought as close together as possible: only a single letter distinguishes them, and not even an entire letter inasmuch as it is here merely a matter of prolonging a single stroke of one, of one letter extending the arc of the *r* in *Urgrund* to the *n* of *Ungrund*. The one stroke alters origins to nihilations.[103]

Schelling: "The essence of the ground *[Wesen des Grundes]*, as that of the existent, can be only that which precedes all ground, thus the absolute viewed purely and simply, the nonground" (7407–8/88–89; trans. modified). Scandal of reason, crisis of speculative idealism, this laceration of primal *Wesen* shows that the ground is not grounded, but cleft and supplementally inhabited by a nonground, held to be antecedent to the ground: a perdurable *an-arche* haunts and violates the integrity of the *arche*. The nonground is not only the sub-version of the primal ground; its sheer priority suggests that the ground was never punctually *there* to be subverted, that it was never constituted except reciprocally by a nonground, which thus, impossibly, becomes the origin of the origin.[104]

We might be tempted to disregard the play of the letter in Schelling's prefixes—Ur*grund* for Un*grund*—as a contingency of German spelling, if it were not for the linguistic (or rather, "graphological") metaphorics that surface at critical points elsewhere in the essay: for example, when he speaks of the diacritical play of vowels and consonants making up the *Logos*, and when he compares the primal ground's inexplicable emergence from the nullity of the nonground to puzzling a word out of the scattered letters of a logogriph, or riddle. *Ungrund* and *Urgrund*: Schelling's terms are so close, separated only by the stroke of one small letter, as Krell says. Yet so far, too: between *Ungrund* and *Urgrund* falls a rift that no synthesis or work of mourning can resolve, an original difference that is the condition of possibility of all existent beings—"Reality and ideality, darkness and light," as Schelling subsequently writes (7:407/88)—and of all thinking about existent beings, and is therefore not a difference that can be explained in terms of what is. But how else to explain it *except* in those terms? In point of fact, the "Absolute" can never be "viewed purely and simply," as Schelling imagines; the *Ungrund* rules the homogeneity of the *arche*, and thus the *Augenschein*,[105] or stonily indifferent gaze that it would take to see it and grasp it, is out of bounds. This can be stated otherwise: the *Ungrund* is contaminated *from the start* by the universe it subtends, making the impulse to misrecognize the groundless as the primal ground, and thereby firmly reappropriate it to ontotheology, quite irresistible. The articulated life of existent beings, *instantly* displacing the *Ungrund*, never allows it to exist as such. Schelling's stuttering mispronunciation—*"Urgrund, Ungrund"*—registers that imperative. In the caesura that divides *r* from *n*, the world of existent beings as we know it *happens*.

Schelling proceeds: "As it [the *Ungrund*] precedes all antitheses, these cannot be distinguishable in it or be present in it in any way at all. It cannot then be called the identity of both, but only the absolute *indifference* as to both" (7:406/87). Once again, the philosopher guards against confusing the "groundless" with the essence of an absolute identity—

and well he might, for this is a confusion that his own text has just shown to be harbored very nearby. The *Ungrund* is not the sum of its antitheses, Schelling adds; neither does it contain them. It is unattached to them in every way, a "unique essence" *[geschiedenes Wesen]* and a subontological reef "upon which all distinctions break (up)" *[an dem alle Gegensätze sich brechen]* (7:407/88; trans. modified). Its profoundly indifferent character renders it alien to every dialectic and to every antithesis; from the point of view of all distinctions and differends—and, we might well ask, for the thinker, even a *Denker* as profound as Schelling, what *other* point of view is there?—it is pure nullity, an absolute blankness. "It is nothing else than just their non-being *[Nichtseyn]*, and therefore has no predicates except lack of predicates, without its being nothingness [*Nichts*, or simple emptiness] or an absurdity [nonentity; literally, nonthing] *[ein Nichts oder ein Unding wäre]*" (7:406/87). About the *Ungrund*, Schelling's densely apophatic rhetoric suggests, *nothing* can be said. Or next to nothing, since, remarkably, he strains in the same sentence to make shades of negative discrimination where, strictly speaking, none should be possible. To grasp this "Absolute, purely and simply," one really would need a mind of winter, a mind that "beholds / Nothing that is not there and the nothing that is."[106] A chill falls over Schelling's text: the *Ungrund*'s nonbeing is neither the void of nothingness nor the nonsense of nonentity, but it is almost impossible to discern the differences between these shadings of absence in a night of negation in which all distinctions dissolve and break up. Schelling comes perilously close to speaking in a form of apophatic babble: the *Ungrund* is nothing but nothing, about which nothing can be predicated except nothing, neither nothing nor no-thing. One can imagine Hegel wincing at the thought of these dark shapes melting into a dark background. But Schelling presses on, and, as if engaged in a game of brinkmanship with the discursive asceticism of negative theology, he carefully negotiates between the desire to speak correctly about the nonground and thus to respect its singular anteriority, *and* the knowledge that whatever he says will be imperfect. Utterly careless of every predication, the obscure object of Schelling's denegating rhetoric recalls what Meister Eckhart says about God: "[W]hatever you say God is, that is not true; but whatever you do not say God is, that is true."[107] The question is, then: how to avoid speaking (of the *Ungrund*)? Or: *Comment ne pas dire?* Which means, as Derrida observes, both "how not to speak?" and "how, in speaking, not to say this or that, in this or that manner? In other words: how, in saying and speaking, to avoid this or that discursive, logical, rhetorical mode? How to avoid an inexact, erroneous, aberrant, improper form? How to avoid such a predicate, and even predication itself?"[108] Faced with the absolute anonymity of the *Ungrund*, Schelling is thoroughly caught up in the double bind of these questions, questions that would seem to be confined to the relatively specialized realm of (negative) theology's attempt to name an ineffable God, but which Derrida has shown generally to share something with the asymmetrical relationship that ontotheology—including its "deconstruction"—has with the trace of *différance*. Like *différance*, the *Ungrund* cannot be denied; it is absolutely nearby and irrepressible, neither a transcendental signified nor a "real field *elsewhere, another* assignable *site*,"[109] but the truly irreducible and inescapable remainder that imbues every time and space like so much background radiation, the imprint of an originary "Big Bang" whose traces are discernible only after the fact; or rather, they are discernible *in* facticity, even though, strictly speaking, they are not *of* it. (We have glimpsed the twists of this impossible topography in Schelling.) But at the same time it must be said that the *Ungrund* cannot *not* be denied; it *must* be denied and avoided, because it is absolutely distant, indifferent especially to the "essence and dignity" of the *Seynsfuge* called "man" and to the power of rational speech that is conventionally accorded him.[110] The result is that every predicate that is made of the nonground and every name that is given to it always says too little, or too much; in any case, it will be radically untrue, wholly unlike what was there, always and already, "*before* all ground and before all existence, that is, before any duality at all" (7:406/87). "Concerning that about which one cannot speak, one must remain silent":[111] yet at the instant that one says the *Ungrund* is that which is predicateless, indifferent to speaking, one has already misspoken, said more than enough. How (not) to speak?

One cannot avoid speaking, any more than existent beings can avoid being, and that is the double necessity that flows from the *Ungrund*'s sheer priority—as if it were a vacuum that language and life abhorred and attempted instantly to fill. Like *différance*, the nonground's absolute reserve or withdrawal *[retrait]* paradoxically *obligates* humankind:

[A]t the moment when the question "How to avoid speaking?" arises it is already too late. There was no longer any question of not speaking. Language has started without us, in us and before us. This is what theology calls God, and it is necessary, it will have been necessary, to speak. This "it is necessary" *(il faut)* is *both* the trace of undeniable necessity—which is another way of saying that one cannot avoid denying it, one can only deny it—*and* of a past injunction. Always already past, hence without a past present. Having come from the past, language before language, a past that was never present and yet remains unforgettable—this "it is necessary" thus seems to beckon toward the event of an order or of a promise that does not belong to what one currently calls history, the discourse of history or the history of discourse.[112]

The *Ungrund* has no particular design on creation, in the way that certain theologies imagine God to have. Schelling has all along insisted that, whatever the nature of the Absolute, it cannot abrogate human freedom. The *Ungrund* does not tell us what it wants, and it does not care what we make of it. Yet in its radical indifference, the nonground is uncannily God-*like* (it is what "theology *calls* God") because its already-thereness makes it both unforgettable and unspeakable. No matter what we say or do not say, we are subject to what Derrida describes as "the unavoidable denial of the undeniable provocation."[113] The already-there *provokes* and *obliges*: what does it provoke? To whom is this obligation directed? In the name of what? As long as the *Ungrund* withdraws into its indifference, these questions resist definitive answers, though of course theological and philosophical history proffer many suggestions: "Being, Spirit, History, Man," as John Caputo argues: "*ousia* or *eidos*, *Bewußtsein* or *Wille zur Macht*, God or the gods, *abba* or *Jahweh*, the *logos* of the Dialectic or the all-gathering prophets."[114] Theological and philosophical history may be nothing *but* these fabulous and irresistible attempts to predicate the predicateless, to refashion the primal *an-arche* into a primal *arche*, to mispronounce *Urgrund* as *Ungrund*, and thus to make sense of its obligatory hold on humankind. Schelling asks: "How shall we designate *it?*" Caputo: "We must be prepared, precisely in virtue of its cognitive density, to concede that, when it comes to obligation, we do not know what we are talking about."[115] Schelling is ready to make this concession, at least in theory: this is the stern and almost unthinkable price of the *Ungrund*'s sheer, unmitigated indifference to thought and talk. It calls, so to speak, but asks nothing. We automatically answer, but cannot reply directly. Out of the blue, perhaps even out of a night in which all cows are black, comes a disembodied voice, to which we instantly respond, without thinking:

Abraham!
Here am I.

Admittedly, this Old Testament parable of a radically disruptive summoning by the absolute other risks saying too much.[116] As a luridly overdetermined representation of the undeniable provocation it may not be scandalous enough. The nonground's indifference, its wholly—I do *not* say holy—nonhuman character demands that we be scrupulously careful not to speak, or to speak too quickly, of its incitement in terms that familiarize it and draw it back into the lighted clearing of the human. We must look upon this primal scene with what de Man calls, after Kant, *Augenschein*, the impossibly stony gaze of noncomprehension.[117] For de Man, this work of "true 'mourning'" can only be described in apophatic terms: it is "non-anthropomorphic, non-elegiac, non-celebratory, non-lyrical, non-poetic," and "prosaic[ally]" indifferent to the inhuman spectacle of indifference.[118] How to avoid speaking? Perhaps Schelling says it best, which is to say, says it in the most minimal, prosaic, in-significant terms possible—merely a matter of shortening a single stroke of one letter:

Ungrund!
Urgrund.

Krell writes of the stroke that it "alters origins to nihilations."[119] But the reverse is also true: the same stroke positively transforms nihilations to origins, marking the instantaneous passage from the anarchy of the other to ground/existence distinction. The primordial ground, as the basis of the jointure of being that articulates life, automatically "responds" to the absent presence of the *Ungrund* by denying it. In the "simultaneously negative and hyperaffirmative"[120] language of negative theology, never far from Schelling's lips, the nonground obliges without obligation, provokes without provocation. The *Ungrund* demands assent, a kind of eternal "Yea-saying," in spite of ourselves. Whatever one says, by virtue of being-articulated one has already concurred, countersigned the order of the other. One assents to being without ever having assented as such; one speaks without ever having agreed to speak as such. Does living *in* or *as* this structural passivity—which precedes the distinction between passive and active, as with all other distinctions—abrogate our responsibility? This is of course the most important question to ask in the context of an essay that seeks to unearth the "nature" or the origin of "human freedom." For Derrida,

Order or promise, this injunction commits [me], in a rigorously asymmetrical manner, even before I have been able to say *I*, to sign such a
provocation in order to reappropriate it for myself and restore the sym-
metry. That in no way mitigates my responsibility; on the contrary.
There would be no responsibility without this *prior coming [prévenance]*
of the trace, or if autonomy were first or absolute.[121]

In answering the question "How shall we designate it [the *Ungrund*]?"
Schelling attempts, always too late, to sign the provocation of the
nonground, to give it a name and reappropriate it for himself, if only by
way of acknowledging the indebtedness of all existent beings to it. Does
this absolute indebtedness mean the dissolution of obligation to others?
The imperative of the *Ungrund*'s *prévenance* only "feels" like an oppres-
sive law, until we recognize that this law legislates nothing—except,
perhaps, the twin imperatives, *Be!* and *Speak!* Before freedom or "autonomy," but also, importantly, before necessity and irresponsibility,
there is an archresponsibility, the very opening of responsibility, the
fundamental ability or originary competence to *answer*. The *Ungrund*
creates a deficit in us, and we respond by being and saying; but having
always withdrawn, the nonground also prevents us from ever paying this
debt, absolutely, in a total, final settling of accounts of the sort that
Schelling hallucinates when he imagines God being "all in all." (And, as
we saw, this is not nearly as total as it is made out to be.) And in the
infinitesimal space, as large as creation, between the provocation and the
response, between "Abraham" and "Here I am," between *Urgrund* and
Ungrund, lies the source of human freedom.

The nonground is a nondialectical middle point, the jointure of the
jointure of being, as of every other opposition that it articulates and
distributes: real and ideal, light and dark, inside and outside, mourning
and melancholy, freedom and necessity, responsibility, and carelessness.
Neither conscious nor unconscious, being or nonbeing, the *Ungrund* is
the inchoate dimension that presides over the constitution of the identity
and difference, but is not itself concerned with or answerable to the
apparent. Schelling's enigmatic account draws on Böhme's description
of the *Ungrund* as an inert and profoundly insouciant null-space in which
God comes, instantly, to deploy himself: the "Nothing," as he writes,
which is "nothing but a stillness without stirring, where there is neither
darkness nor light, neither life nor death."[122] How then to explain the
fact of creation, including the creation of God, when the universe might
well have remained an undifferentiated and unidentified stillness? Or, to

recall Schelling's infamous query, which looks back to Leibnitz and ahead to Heidegger, "that ultimate question posed by the vertiginous intellect hovering at the abyss of infinity: 'Why [is] something rather than nothing?'"[123] To this question, understandably enough, Schelling cannot provide a definitive answer. The asking of it must suffice, summoning the thinker as it does to a radical astonishment at the fact that creation, replete with existent beings who are entirely made up of the melancholic stirring of light and darkness, exists at all. Of this universe, all that one can say, as Schelling does, is: "It happens." Schelling: "Out of this neither-nor *[Weder-Noch]*, or out of indifference, duality *immediately* breaks forth" *[Unmittelbar aus dem Weder-Noch oder der Indifferenz bricht also die Dualität hervor]* (7:407/88). Beings—as the principal "effect" of the primary duality, the ground/existence distinction—there are. There are beings. Certainly, here I am. Question: Why something rather than nothing? Answer: Something there is. The anonymous and perfunctorily tautological logic of that account of the primordial breaking forth preserves the indifference of the *Ungrund*, shelters it from being too easily reappropriated by metaphysics, in the name, for example, of "Being, Spirit, History, Man." Concerning the *Ungrund*, we could merely say that *es gibt*: it gives. In the context of discussing the startling indifference similarly exhibited by Plato's *khora*, Derrida warns that even to say that *it gives* risks saying too much. "The *es gibt*, thus translated, too vividly announces or recalls the dispensation of God, of man, or even that of the Being of which certain texts by Heidegger speak (*es gibt Sein*)."[124] The nonground, to which we are promised, gives no promises: it gives nothing. Because Derrida's description of the *khora*'s exorbitant retentiveness vividly remembers all that we have said of Schelling's *Ungrund*, it is worth quoting at length:

> *Khora* is not even *that [ça]*, the *es* or *id* of giving, before all subjectivity. It does not give place as one would give something, whatever it may be; it neither creates nor produces anything, not even an event insofar as it takes place. It gives no order and makes no promise. It is radically ahistorical, because nothing happens through it and nothing happens to it. Plato insists on its necessary indifference; to receive all and allow itself to be marked or affected by what is in it, the *khora* must remain without form and without proper determination. But if it is amorphous, . . . this signifies neither lack nor privation. *Khora* is nothing positive or negative. It is impassive, but it is neither passive nor active.[125]

The reverse view of the *Ungrund*'s sheer restraint and impassivity is the instantaneousness of the irruption of what *is* (given) "by" it. This suddenness—here, we must make the most of what Schelling means by "duality *immediately* breaks forth"—is crucial to understanding the nonground's radically hidden and atheological nature. The *Ungrund* is effaced by the dualisms it makes possible. It is instantly omitted, which is to say, not contingently overlooked; it is an event that happened, and then was lost, but *lost from the start*. Another way of saying this is that the *Ungrund*'s recollection in the world's dualisms is inseparable from its being forgotten. Because difference happens *right away*, because it has always already happened, the nonground never punctually exists, as such, nor is it a past that was ever present. It cannot be recalled; but as the perdurable absence in what is present—like the impure remainder back-behind God's "luminous consciousness"—neither can it be forgotten. At the moment of the emergence of difference—of original difference—the *Ungrund* withdraws; more accurately, it is always withdrawn, so that difference might come into being, and creation be set on its perilous way. In a memorable, and, one might say, strategically *careless* translation of the philosophical meaning of indifference, Schelling characterizes the groundless as "apathetic" or "impassive" *[gleichgültig]* (7:407/88) towards our human, all too human, attempts at bringing it within the orbit of dialectical thinking. Here the quality of apathy functions in strangely contradictory ways. In the first instance, it is an intensifier, underlining and amplifying the *Ungrund*'s alterity and resistance to theory. To say that the nonground is conceptually indifferent is not enough; to say that it is "more" indifferent even than that, Schelling resorts to the extraordinary measure of attributing to the nonground a "psychological" disengagement from the world it also obliges. In *gleichgültig* we can almost read an impassivity and a thoughtlessness that is "older" than the active/passive or solicitude/insolicitude distinctions. Almost. By attributing this emotional detachment to the nonground, Schelling also brings it firmly back into a somewhat less than wholly indifferent relationship with the world, if only in the negative form of a certain *carelessness [Gleich-gültigkeit]*. In other words, the primal scene is made all the more pathetic by its insouciant renunciation of pathos. Does Schelling thereby covertly reproach the *Ungrund* for its disengagement from the nature of things? Perhaps in psychologizing the *Ungrund*'s indifference he projects upon the nonground the eerie impassivity that he cannot bring himself to feel both about it and about what it means for it to "give" duality in an absolutely indifferent fashion, an absolute indifference that, for example, Derrida struggles to describe in the case of the Platonic *khora*. It is a question, once more, of how (not) to speak. To think the *Ungrund* in its radical apathos, beyond all humanisms, would be the most difficult thing to do: we cannot be sure that Schelling does it, certainly not as sure as some of his most recent readers have been.

What is certain is that the nonground's extreme insouciance triggers a certain strategic carelessness in Schelling. "Reality and ideality, darkness and light, or however else we wish to designate the two principles," Schelling argues, "can never be predicated of the nonground *as antitheses*" (7:407/88). To do so would be to identify the *Ungrund* as the absolute identity of these principles, a conclusion that Schelling again insists cannot be the case since the nonground *precedes* identity and difference. How then to characterize the nature of the (non)relationship between, on the one hand, the *Ungrund*, and, on the other, all the differends that undoubtedly exist and bear its trace? It is a question with which Schelling and German idealism had been concerned all along: how does difference begin? What Schelling offers by way of an answer is very strange:

> But nothing prevents their being predicated as non-antitheses, that is, in disjunction and each *for itself;* wherein, however, this duality (the real twofold of principles) is established. There is in the nonground itself nothing to prevent this. For just because its relation towards both is a relation of total indifference, it is careless *[gleichgültig]* towards both.... *[W]ithout* indifference, that is, without the nonground, there would be no twofold of principles. (7:407/88)

If the nonground cannot be said to contain opposed terms as antitheses, neither does it preclude them from being posited independently of each other, as sheer disjunctions. Because the *Ungrund* is indifferent to this position, nothing can stop us *[aber es hindert nichts]* from saying this. So Schelling says, twice, in a conspicuous sleight of hand that makes it seem as if he had suddenly grown indifferent to the demands of philosophical thinking and careless of the need to argue a case dialectically. To think the root of difference, Schelling seems to suggest, we must consider the originary emergence of (what Krell calls) *"pure duality,"*[126] a general, primal "twofoldedness" that subtends all identifiable and specific cases of antitheses: darkness and light, reality and ideality, etc. Schelling argues that thinking twofoldedness requires us to distinguish, for the first time, and perhaps only provisionally, between "duality" and antithetical "opposition."

("We may have used the two as meaning the same thing up to the present" [7:407/88], he observes, somewhat coyly, smoothing over the scandal of trying to discern the trace of an originary duality in the midst of empirical oppositions.) "Before" antithetical terms come into relation, there must be something like pure relationality, never allowed to exist as such. We can at least posit this "of" the *Ungrund;* we can hypothesize that it is the site or opening of this twofoldedness. *Es gibt (Zweiheit).* But this is not something we can grasp explicitly, since knowers can know only knowledge and what Schelling here evokes is the un-*thought* infrastructure, or "structural unconsciousness" of knowledge. Like Keats's Grecian urn, the *Ungrund's* steadfast silence teases Schelling out of thought. I can posit this prearchaic donation of the twofold by the *Ungrund* because there is nothing to prevent me; but in making that claim, which amounts, finally, to saying that there is nothing to substantiate such a claim either, I also concede that I cannot *know* it. There seems to be no other way of saying this except, as it were, *simply by saying it:* "*[W]ithout* indifference, that is, without a nonground, there would be no twofold of principles" (7:407/88; trans. modified). Without one, not the other; only with one comes the other: so much depends upon how it is that twofoldedness follows so naturally and spontaneously from the nonground, yet this association, the mechanism by which twofoldedness emerges from indifference and is profoundly indebted to it, is exactly what Schelling does not explain. How could he? This event, as such, is precisely what goes without saying, and must go without saying: the concept that would explain how it is that with the nonground, *there is also, immediately, twofoldness,* discretely withdraws from knowledge, precisely to facilitate it.

To repeat: while the nonground is indifferent to difference, its indifference is what accounts for its coming into existence *in the first place.* The nonground is completely oblivious to such positing. *It does not prevent us from saying such things.* Curious and outrageous move, this, with at least three overlapping implications that I can only list quickly here:

1) The lack of an interdiction is a negative way of saying something positive, albeit in an absolutely minimal manner, about the *Ungrund:* the groundless permits the philosopher to posit what he wants, not because he can derive this justification or find grounds for his argument in it, but because *it could (not) care less.*

2) However, this license—by default—in turn bears the burden of a troublesome negation, whose abyssal consequences reach ahead to

Nietzsche and beyond: the nonground does not prevent the philosopher from making his hypotheses, but, as I have suggested, neither does it authorize him in any way. What is treated positively as an opening to thought also promises that no position on the nonground can ever be wholly certain. And if, at the highest point of Schelling's argument, the nonground refuses to yield any confirmation for the hypotheses made about it, then what is the fate and the surety of the myriad positions, perhaps philosophy in its totality, that flow from it as naturally as the *Urgrund* follows the *Ungrund*? That which makes knowledge possible also makes it *absolutely* impossible. A liberating prospect, in its own way, perhaps even a sign of the very freedom that is the titular subject of Schelling's essay, but also threatening, since it abandons the philosopher to a kind of epistemological free fall. In its indifference, the nonground declines especially to orient Schelling's thinking, exposing him to the vertiginous prospect of making a series of groundless hypotheses about the groundless, as if stuttering a series of philosophical performatives, pronounced without the consolation of a constative ground and without any definitive sense of where to begin or end. For a moment, Schelling comes very close to Derrida: "We must begin *wherever we are* and the thought of the trace . . . has already taught us that it was impossible to justify a point of departure absolutely. *Wherever we are:* in a text where we already believe ourselves to be."[127] We could say, after Thomas Pfau, that the "'subject' of Schelling's philosophy may thus be characterized as a rethinking of philosophy once the latter . . . has come face to face, so to speak, with the crisis of its own discursive authority."[128] We could say this, except for the fact that Schelling's text here betrays no outward sign of being in crisis. About the impassivity of the nonground, he is curiously impassive. Indeed, he concludes his tortuous and consistently surprising account of the *Ungrund* by pointing to how its putative clarity brings out the profundity of the entire *Freedom* essay: "Far from it being the case that the distinction between ground and existence proves itself at the end to have been merely logical, or to have been summoned as an aid that at the end would prove itself to be nongenuine, it has rather shown itself to be a very real distinction, which was confirmed and fully grasped only from the highest standpoint" (7:407/88).[129]

3) "Nothing can prevent us" also means that the philosopher cannot be stopped, that this positing and positioning proceeds as if in a compulsive fashion, as if he were commanded to speak even before he had said anything at all. Whatever he says in particular—the *Ungrund* is utterly

deaf to these details—the one thing that he cannot stop doing is saying *something*. "How to avoid speaking of it? In this context, the singularity that interests [Schelling] . . . is that the impossibility of speaking of it and of giving it a proper name, far from reducing it to silence, yet dictates an obligation, by its very impossibility: *it is necessary* to speak of it and there is a rule for that."[130]

NOTES

Versions and portions of this paper were presented at the University of Victoria, Queen's University, and at the meeting of the Modern Language Association (San Francisco, 1991). For listening to and commenting upon drafts of this essay, I am very grateful to Ian Balfour, Stephen Barber, Stanley Corngold, Thomas Pfau, and Tilottama Rajan. Thanks also to Jean Wilson, who helped me untangle some of Schelling's German. This paper was prepared for publication with the able assistance of Stephen Barber and with the generous support of the Social Sciences and Humanities Research Council of Canada.

1. Maurice Blanchot, *Le Pas au-delà* (Paris: Gallimard, 1973), 8.

2. Martin Heidegger, *Schelling's Treatise on the Essence of Human Freedom*, trans. Joan Stambaugh (Athens: Ohio University Press, 1985), 112.

3. Immanuel Kant, *Critique of Pure Reason*, trans. Norman Kemp Smith (New York: St. Martin's Press, 1965), 513.

4. Immanuel Kant, "On a Newly Raised Superior Tone in Philosophy," trans. Peter Fenves, in *Raising the Tone of Philosophy: Late Essays by Immanuel Kant, Transformative Critique by Jacques Derrida*, ed. Peter Fenves (Baltimore: Johns Hopkins University Press, 1993), 71.

5. Heidegger, *Schelling's Treatise on the Essence of Human Freedom*, 3.

6. Jacques Derrida, "How to Avoid Speaking: Denials," trans. Ken Frieden, in *Derrida and Negative Theology*, ed. Harold Coward and Toby Foshay (Albany: State University of New York Press, 1992), 101.

7. Friedrich Schelling, *Zur Grundlegung der Positiven Philosophie*, ed. Horst Fuhrmans (Turin: Bottega d'Erasmo, 1976), 222. I cite Alan White's translation in *Schelling: An Introduction to the System of Freedom* (New Haven: Yale University Press, 1983), 158.

8. Søren Kierkegaard, *Fear and Trembling* and *Repetition*, trans. Howard V. Hong and Edna H. Hong (Princeton: Princeton University Press, 1983), 131.

9. Werner Marx, *The Philosophy of F. W. J. Schelling: History, System, and Freedom*, trans. Thomas Nenon (Bloomington: Indiana University Press, 1984), 61–62.

10. Pagination refers first to Schelling's *Sämtliche Werke*, ed. K. F. A. Schelling (Stuttgart: Cotta, 1856–61), 14 vols; and second to F. W. J. Schelling, *Of Human Freedom*, trans. J. Gutman (Chicago: Open Court, 1936). All subsequent references to the *Freedom* essay in English will principally be to this translation. Where necessary, I have modified Gutman's translation, in consultation with the somewhat more precise translation by Priscilla Hayden-Roy, in *The German Library*, vol. 23: *Philosophy of German*

Idealism, ed. Ernst Behler (New York: Continuum, 1987), 217–84. I have also consulted the translations that David Farrell Krell provides in "The Crisis of Reason in the Nineteenth Century: Schelling's Treatise on Human Freedom," in *The Collegium Phaenomenologicum: The First Ten Years,* ed. John C. Sallis, Giuseppina Moneta, and Jacques Taminiaux (Dordrecht: Kluwer, 1988), 13–32.

11. Marx, *The Philosophy of F. W. J. Schelling,* 62.

12. F. W. J. Schelling, *Stuttgart Seminars,* in *Idealism and the Endgame of Theory,* trans. and ed. Thomas Pfau (Albany: State University of New York Press, 1994), 206.

13. See, for example, De Quincey's fiercely critical remarks about Kant in *Recollections of the Lakes and the Lake Poets,* in *The Collected Writings of Thomas De Quincey,* ed. David Masson, 14 vols. (London: A. & C. Black, 1896), 2:155. Daniel O'Quinn brought De Quincey's opinion of Kant to my attention in his "Animalizing the Other: De Quincey, Opium and the Consolidation of Community" (diss., York University, 1993), 153–65.

14. David Farrell Krell, *Intimations of Mortality, Time, Truth, and Finitude in Heidegger's Thinking of Being* (University Park: Pennsylvania State University Press, 1986), 108.

15. Manfred Frank, *What is Neostructuralism?,* trans. Sabine Wilke and Richard Gray (Minneapolis: University of Minnesota Press, 1989), 89.

16. Jean Grondin writes that "The passage from Kant to his followers seems to lead from a dismissal of metaphysics to a kind of apotheosis of metaphysical speculation, from the humiliation of classical rationalism to an unprecedented exultation of reason." See "The A Priori from Kant to Schelling," *Idealistic Studies* 19 (1989): 202.

17. Frank, *What is Neostructuralism?,* 89, emphasis mine. See also Frank's *Der Unendliche Mangel an Sein: Schellings Hegelkritik und die Anfänge der Marxschen Dialektik* (Frankfurt: Suhrkamp, 1975) and *Eine Einführung in Schellings Philosophie* (Frankfurt: Suhrkamp, 1985). Persuasive English-speaking exponents of Frank's position include Andrew Bowie, *Aesthetics and Subjectivity: From Kant to Nietzsche* (Manchester: Manchester University Press, 1990) and Peter Dews, *Logics of Disintegration: Post-Structuralist Thought and the Claims of Critical Theory* (London: Verso, 1987).

18. Schelling, *Zur Grundlegung der Positiven Philosophie,* 222.

19. Paul de Man, *Blindness and Insight: Essays on the Rhetoric of Contemporary Theory,* 2d ed., rev. (Minneapolis: University of Minnesota Press, 1983), 7.

20. David Farrell Krell, "The Crisis of Reason," 17. I should say from the outset that my own essay is wholly indebted to Krell's groundbreaking study of Schelling's ground-breaking.

21. Robert Brown, *The Later Philosophy of Schelling: The Influence of Boehme on the Works of 1808–1815* (Lewisburg, Pa.: Bucknell University Press, 1977), 126 (emphasis mine).

22. Jacques Derrida, "Fors," trans. Barbara Johnson, *Georgia Review* 31 (1977): 70.

23. Heidegger, *Schelling's Treatise on the Essence of Human Freedom,* 113.

24. Ibid., 109. The German is cited from Martin Heidegger, *Schellings Abhandlung über das Wesen der menschlichen Freiheit (1809)* (Tübingen: Max Niemeyer, 1971), 190.

25. Heidegger, *Schelling's Treatise on the Essence of Human Freedom,* 108.

26. Ibid. For the German, see Heidegger, *Schellings Abhandlung,* 188.

27. Heidegger, *Schelling's Treatise on the Essence of Human Freedom,* 109 (emphasis mine).

142 David L. Clark

28. Jacques Derrida, *Of Grammatology,* trans. Gayatri Chakravorti Spivak (Baltimore: Johns Hopkins University Press, 1974), 304.

29. Rodolphe Gasché, *The Tain of the Mirror: Derrida and the Philosophy of Reflection* (Cambridge: Harvard University Press, 1986), 181.

30. The most detailed discussion of Schelling's verbal and conceptual borrowings from Böhme remains Robert Brown's *Later Philosophy of Schelling.* As Brown points out (60, 62, 79, and 126) in his *Signature of All Things* Böhme initially develops the notion that God is essentially composed of a light and dark center .

31. Robert Brown cites Schelling's remark in *The Later Philosophy of Schelling,* 157 n. 12.

32. Heidegger, *Schelling's Treatise on the Essence of Human Freedom,* 122.

33. Martin Heidegger, *What is Called Thinking?* trans. J. Glenn Gray (New York: Harper & Row, 1968), 152.

34. Derrida, "How to Avoid Speaking: Denials," 104.

35. Ibid., 104, 105.

36. I borrow this distinction, if that is what it is, from John Caputo, who compares the "breach of metaphysics in a 'postmetaphysical style,' as in Derrida," to the "more Neoplatonic or 'hypermetaphysical' radicalizing of metaphysics, in the style of Plotinus or Meister Eckhart." See *Against Ethics: Contributions to a Poetics of Obligation with Constant Reference to Deconstruction* (Bloomington and Indianapolis: Indiana University Press, 1993), 252 n. 51.

37. Jacques Derrida, "Plato's Pharmacy," in *Dissemination,* trans. Barbara Johnson (Chicago: University of Chicago Press, 1981), 159.

38. Plato, *Timaeus,* trans. H. D. Lee (Baltimore: Penguin, 1965), 71 (52d).

39. See F. M. Cornford, *Plato's Cosmology* (London: Routledge & Kegan Paul, 1948), 187.

40. James Boswell, *The Life of Samuel Johnson,* ed. R. W. Chapman, rev. J. D. Fleeman (New York: Oxford University Press, 1980), 667 n. 1.

41. Krell, "The Crisis of Reason," 23.

42. So Cornford observes in *Plato's Cosmology,* 187.

43. Another way of saying this would be to suggest that Schelling illuminates something in the *Timaeus* that is hidden from its own author. In his *Philosophie und Religion,* Schelling had in fact proposed that the *Timaeus* be ascribed to any author but Plato, a view that he later recanted. See A. E. Taylor, *A Commentary on Plato's* Timaeus (London: Oxford University Press, 1928), 1.

44. Jacques Derrida, "Signature Event Context," in *Margins of Philosophy,* trans. Alan Bass (Chicago: University of Chicago Press, 1982), 329.

45. Plato, *The Timaeus,* 70 (52b).

46. Ibid., 68–72 (50–53).

47. Derrida, "Plato's Pharmacy," 160.

48. Derrida, "How to Avoid Speaking: Denials," 106 (emphasis mine).

49. Heidegger, *Schelling's Treatise on the Essence of Human Freedom,* 125.

50. Ibid., 124.

51. Derrida, "The Ends of Man," in *Margins of Philosophy,* 127.

52. Ibid., 119.

53. David Farrell Krell, *Daimon Life: Heidegger and Life-Philosophy* (Bloomington and Indianapolis: Indiana University Press, 1992), 297.

54. Paul de Man, "Conclusions: Walter Benjamin's 'The Task of the Translator,'" in *The Resistance to Theory*, ed. Wlad Godzich (Minneapolis: University of Minnesota Press, 1986), 87.

55. Ibid., 96. For a discussion of the inhumanity of "the materiality of the letter" see also my "Illegibility, Monstrosity, Denegation: de Man, Nichol, and the Resistance to Postmodernism," in *Negation, Critical Theory, and Postmodern Textuality*, ed. Daniel Fischlin (Dordrecht: Kluwer, 1994), 274–300.

56. Andrzej Warminski, "Missed Crossing: Wordsworth's Apocalypses," *Modern Language Notes* 99 (1984): 986.

57. Derrida, "White Mythology: Metaphor in the Text of Philosophy," in *Margins of Philosophy*, 240.

58. Derrida, "The Double Session," in *Dissemination*, 221.

59. I refer to Gutman's translation of Schelling's footnote in *Of Human Freedom*, 36.

60. Plato, *The Timaeus*, 66 (48b).

61. The comparison is noted by A. E. Taylor in his *Commentary on Plato's* Timaeus, 306.

62. Schelling, "Stuttgart Seminars," in Thomas Pfau, ed. and trans., *Idealism and the Endgame of Theory*, 213.

63. Derrida, *Of Grammatology*, 353 n. 35.

64. Saussure's notebooks are reproduced in Jean Starobinski's *Words upon Words: The Anagrams of Ferdinand de Saussure*, trans. Olivia Emmet (New Haven: Yale University Press, 1979).

65. Paul de Man, *Allegories of Reading: Figural Language in Rousseau, Nietzsche, Rilke, and Proust* (New Haven: Yale University Press, 1979), 293.

66. Derrida, *Of Grammatology*, 60.

67. Sylvère Lotringer argues that "the *Anagrams* weren't published: linguistics was born of that exclusion." See "The Game of the Name," *Diacritics* 3 (1973): 8. Although de Man cites Lotringer approvingly, he disagrees on how Saussurian linguistics is related to the anagrammatic research. "Rather than a 'mere' repression," de Man argues, "Saussure's retheorization of the question in the *Cours* can more charitably be seen as the insistence of theoretical discourse in the face of the dangers it reveals." See "Hypogram and Inscription," in *The Resistance to Theory*, 37.

68. De Man, "The Resistance to Theory," in *The Resistance to Theory*, 8.

69. Jonathan Culler, "On the Negativity of Modern Poetry: Friedrich, Baudelaire, and the Critical Tradition," in *Languages of the Unsayable: The Play of Negativity in Literature and Literary Theory*, ed. Sanford Budick and Wolfgang Iser (New York: Columbia University Press, 1989), 205.

70. Kevin Newmark, "Resisting, Responding," in *Responses: On Paul de Man's Wartime Journalism*, ed. Werner Hamacher, Neil Hertz, and Thomas Keenan (Lincoln: University of Nebraska Press, 1989), 347.

71. Hans-Jost Frey, "Spume," *Yale French Studies* 74 (1988): 258.

72. Derrida, "How to Avoid Speaking: Denials," 99.

73. I am grateful to Tracy Wynne for providing me with this legal rhetoric.

74. Friedrich Nietzsche, *On the Genealogy of Morals*, trans. W. Kaufmann and R. J. Hollingdale (New York: Vintage, 1968), 92.

75. Sigmund Freud, "Mourning and Melancholia," in *The Standard Edition of the*

Complete Psychological Works of Sigmund Freud, trans. and ed. James Strachey, 24 vols. (London: Hogarth Press and the Institute of Psycho-Analysis, 1957), 14:243–58.

76. Ibid., 256.

77. This passage from Schelling's Munich lectures (1833–34) is cited and translated by Andrew Bowie in *Aesthetics and Subjectivity: From Kant to Nietzsche*, 87.

78. Hans-Georg Gadamer, *Truth and Method* (New York: Crossroads, 1975), 269.

79. Friedrich Schleiermacher, *The Christian Faith*, trans. H . R. Mackintosh and J. S . Stewart (Edinburgh: T. and T. Clark, 1928), 17.

80. Frank, *What is Neostructuralism?* 89.

81. Heidegger, *What is Called Thinking?* 153.

82. Jacques Derrida, "Ja, ou le Faux-bond," *Diagraphe* 11 (1977): 98.

83. Ned Lukacher, *Primal Scenes: Literature, Philosophy, Psychoanalysis* (Ithaca: Cornell University Press, 1986), 11.

84. Jacques Derrida, "Ja, ou le faux-bond," 98. What Geoffrey Bennington has recently said of Derrida would then apply to Schelling: "[T]here would be a certain truth in saying that Derrida has not accomplished his mourning for metaphysics, that he is keen not to do so. Half-mourning, rather." See *Jacques Derrida*, trans. Geoffrey Bennington (Chicago: University of Chicago Press, 1993), 147–48.

85. Derrida, *Of Grammatology*, 149.

86. For this point, I have my colleague Howard Jones to thank.

87. Jacques Derrida, *Cinders*, trans. Ned Lukacher (Lincoln: University of Nebraska Press, 1991). Derrida's *Feu la cendre* could be described as an extended meditation on this phrase.

88. Derrida, *Of Grammatology*, 70.

89. Derrida, "How to Avoid Speaking: Denials," 77.

90. Ibid., 78.

91. Derrida: *"To write is to have the passion of the origin."* See "Ellipsis," in *Writing and Difference*, trans. Alan Bass (Chicago: University of Chicago Press, 1978), 295.

92. Derrida, "How to Avoid Speaking: Denials," 102.

93. Ibid.

94. Ibid., 79.

95. Jacques Derrida, "Différance," in *Margins of Philosophy*, 26.

96. Derrida, "How to Avoid Speaking: Denials," 74.

97. Ibid., 77.

98. Bennington, *Jacques Derrida*, 80.

99. Alan White, *Schelling: An Introduction to the System of Freedom*, 144.

100. Here we might recall the similarly lurid System of *Selbstzerreißung* developed in de Man's later work. In these essays, scrupulous attention to what could be called the "absolute dualism" between the "materiality" and "phenomenality" of language threatens to trigger "the undoing of cognition" and "the *dismemberment* of the aesthetic whole into the unpredictable play of the letter as inscription." See, for example, de Man's remarks in his introduction to Hans Robert Jauss's *Towards an Aesthetics of Reception* (Minneapolis: University of Minnesota Press, 1982), xxv. On the rhetoric of this dismemberment, see Clark, "Monstrosity, Illegibility, Denegation: de Man, Nichol, and the Resistance to Postmodernism," in *Negation, Critical Theory, and Postmodern Textuality*, 274–300.

101. Jean-Luc Marion, *God Without Being*, trans. Thomas A. Carlson (Chicago: University of Chicago Press, 1991), 2.

102. Marion writes: "Under the title *God Without Being* we do not mean to insinuate that God is not, or that God is not truly God. We attempt to mediate upon what F.W. Schelling called 'the freedom of God with regard to his own existence.'" See ibid.

103. Krell, "The Crisis of Reason," 25–26.

104. The "deeper disclosure" (7:334/4) that Schelling cryptically promises at the beginning of the *Freedom* essay is finally revealed to be literally true: beyond the beginning lie unfathomable depths, a "bottomless fund *[fonds sans fond]*" or "store of deep background" that Derrida calls *"the pharmacy."* ("Plato's Pharmacy," 127, 128). In a moment, Schelling will look into this abyss, and look away: on the next page, he evokes a mysterious place described as "back-behind" *[zurückbleibt]* God's essence, where a certain excess is "eternally sealed in darkness" at the end of time. Is the *Ungrund* not precisely such a background, the unruly *parerga* that supplements the ground but is not *of* the ground? Schelling has just said that the nonground is beyond good and evil. But here, it is an embarrassing surplus to God, the *"Caput mortuum* [or industrial waste] of his life-process." No longer a pharmacy dispensing existent beings, then, the *Ungrund* is quickly reconfigured as a slag-heap to capture the waste of becoming.

105. See note 117.

106. I of course recall Wallace Stevens's "The Snow Man," in *The Collected Poems* (New York: Vintage, 1982), 10.

107. Cited by John Caputo in *Against Ethics*, 33. (See my note 36.)

108. Derrida, "How to Avoid Speaking: Denials," 85.

109. Derrida, *Of Grammatology*, 60.

110. Derrida, "The Ends of Man," in *Margins of Philosophy*, 128.

111. So Ludwig Wittgenstein commands in the well-known last line of his *Tractatus Logico Philosophicus*, trans. C. K. Ogden (London: Routledge & Kegan Paul, 1922), 189. Derrida recalls Wittgenstein in "How to Avoid Speaking: Denials," 81.

112. Derrida, "How to Avoid Speaking: Denials," 99.

113. Ibid., 86.

114. Caputo, *Against Ethics*, 70, 222.

115. Ibid., 84.

116. Here I recall Caputo's provocative use of the same moment from the Old Testament narrative. Caputo retells the story of Abraham and Isaac as a way of probing the fate of ethics in a postmodern world. See ibid., 70, 9–16.

117. Paul de Man, "Phenomenality and Materiality in Kant," in *Hermeneutics: Questions and Prospects*, ed. Gary Shapiro and Alan Sica (Amherst: University of Massachusetts Press, 1984), 144.

118. Paul de Man, "Anthropomorphism and Trope in Lyric," in *The Rhetoric of Romanticism* (New York: Columbia University Press, 1984), 262.

119. Krell, "The Crisis of Reason," 25–26.

120. Derrida, "How to Avoid Speaking: Denials," 78.

121. Ibid., 99.

122. Robert Brown cites Böhme's *High and Deep Searching Out of the Threefold Life of Man* in *The Later Philosophy of Schelling*, 48 n. 41.

123. I cite Thomas Pfau's translation of Schelling's *System der gesammten Philosophie und der Natur philosophie insbesondere* (1804). See Pfau, " Critical Introduction," in *Idealism and the Endgame of Theory*, 40.

124. Derrida, "How to Avoid Speaking: Denials," 106.

146 David L. Clark

125. Ibid., 107.

126. Krell, "The Crisis of Reason," 26.

127. Derrida, *Of Grammatology*, 162.

128. Thomas Pfau, "Critical Introduction," *Idealism and the Endgame of Theory*, 5.

129. Alan White similarly points to the fact that "Schelling does not acknowledge that his account of the *Ungrund* as indifference is either unclear, incomplete, or incoherent." See his *Schelling: An Introduction to the System of Freedom*, 133.

130. Derrida, "How to Avoid Speaking: Denials," 107.

Language, Music,
and the Body:
Nietzsche and Deconstruction

Tilottama Rajan

I

For the past two decades Anglo-American representations of Nietzsche
have been strongly influenced by the reading provided by Paul de Man.[1]
Nietzsche has emerged as the first philosopher to recognize that truth,
causality, and consciousness are no more than effects of a grammar that
is itself figural. This deconstruction of an existentialist Nietzsche who
dissolved and dissipated romanticism in order to recreate it in a post-
Hegelian mode has been crucial to the authentication of poststructuralism
itself, as a renunciation of the romanticism that continues to mobilize its
apparent deconstruction by thinkers like Sartre and Heidegger. In other
words, by making Nietzsche the figure of a paradoxical "originality" in
which the newest insights are those we have always already possessed, de
Man can place his immediate precursors and indeed his own earlier
work[2] within the parenthesis of a relapse. He can authorize the deconstruction of phenomenology, by depicting the latter as an error already
corrected by Nietzsche before it reasserted itself in our own time through
that unfortunate tendency of intellectual history to perform what it has
shown to be impossible. Nietzsche, however, is present not only in the
texts of de Man but also in those of very different theorists like Kristeva.
The complexity of his affiliations with the present reflects the complexity of Nietzsche himself, as well as the complexity of "deconstruction." In

what ways is Nietzsche different from de Man's representation of him? Perhaps in being closer to a romanticism exiled both from the French tradition and from our reception of it?[3] And what does this proximity tell us about deconstruction itself, as a practice whose recent asceticism may well be constituted on the trace of romantic desire?

We can approach Nietzsche's difference from classical poststructuralism[4] in terms of three related areas: his critique of language, his desire for immediacy, and his locating of the deconstruction of representation in music and the body rather than in "writing." These differences do not diminish the affinity between Nietzsche and deconstruction. Rather they point to a different set of affinities that help us to articulate a realignment occurring within deconstruction itself. Nietzsche's critique of what he later calls the metaphysics of language is well known and can only briefly be recapitulated here. In *The Birth of Tragedy*, language, as "the organ and symbol" of appearances *(Erscheinungen)*, is contrasted with music, which in referring to "primordial contradiction and primordial pain" symbolizes a sphere "beyond and prior to all phenomena" (*BT*, 55; I, 51).[5] More specifically the deficiency of language derives from its attempt to create the illusion of identity. The structure of language as a system of identities reflects, in turn, the way we construct the world as a series of simple ideas, each self-contained and uncomplicated by diacritical relationships with other ideas. To recognize such ideas would be to recognize that there are no positive terms in language, and correspondingly no essences in the world of phenomena, but only differences between words that analogically replicate the intertextural quality of things:

> Our usual imprecise mode of observation takes a group of phenomena *[Erscheinungen]* as one and calls it a fact; between this fact and another fact it imagines in addition an empty space, it isolates every fact. In reality, however, all our doing and knowing is not a succession *[Folge]* of facts and empty spaces *[Zwischenraumen]* but a continuous flux (*WS*, aphorism 11; II, 546)

Perhaps the most famous description of representation as a Platonism constituted on the trace of difference is the passage in "Truth and Lie":

> Let us especially think about the formation *[Bildung]* of ideas. . . . Every idea originates through equating the unequal *[Gleichsetzen des Nicht-Gleichen]*. As certainly as no one leaf is exactly similar to any other, so certain is it that the idea "leaf" has been formed through an

arbitrary omission of these individual differences ("TF," 507; I, 879–80).

In uncovering the radical figurality of a language that substitutes one thing for another, Nietzsche anticipates in obvious ways the critique of logocentrism. Thus de Man has argued for his priority in the dismantling of metaphysics and of a ground outside language, so as to make the German philosopher into the originator of what David Carroll calls "ultra-textualism."[6] Yet it is no less legitimate to approach Nietzsche's agenda archaeologically, through the empiricist epistemology in which he was steeped,[7] and more particularly through the romanticism that preceded him, than to read him teleologically through poststructuralism. To begin with, the famous passage on truth as a moving army of metaphors is not simply, as de Man says of the essay in general, an equation of "rhetoric with error."[8] It is a statement whose predicative and positive form ("Truth is") encloses a negation, but also represents across that negation the desire to make a claim about truth as its own deconstruction:

> What therefore is truth? A mobile army of metaphors, metonymies, anthropomorphisms: in short a sum of human relations which became poetically and rhetorically intensified, . . . and after long usage seems to a nation fixed, canonic, and binding; truths are illusions of which one has forgotten that they are illusions; . . . coins which have their obverse effaced and now are no longer of account as coins but merely as metal. ("TF," 508; I, 880–81)

At the very least the fact that the passage involves a figure should suggest that it speaks with a double voice irreducible to paraphrase: a voice that is both positive and (self-)critical. Like the essay as a whole, the passage denies that there is such a thing as truth in a conventional sense. But within this denial is the trace of a predication: the suggestion that the kind of language that knows itself to be figural (that of art and myth) is somehow *truer* than a conceptual language that has forgotten its origins in metaphor. To read Nietzsche as collapsing truth into error is precisely to maintain the binary opposition he criticizes, by suggesting that there is such a thing as error (and by implication that there is truth). It is also to substitute another position (that rhetoric is error) for the position Nietzsche will not take in refusing to say that metaphor is truth.

Associationist psychology had already recognized the diacritical complexity that underlies the apparent self-identity of concepts. According to Hugh Blair, "[E]very idea or object carries in its train some other ideas, ... [it] never presents itself to our view isolé."[9] Similarly Blair, like Bishop Warburton, recognizes the role of metaphoric abridgment in the formation of language and the construction of ideas: in order to avoid having a word for each thing, he suggests, men made "one word which they already appropriated to a certain idea or object, stand also for some other idea or object."[10] A trajectory in which words and ideas are formed by a process of reduction facilitated by condensations and substitutions was more or less commonplace by the end of the eighteenth century. Accepting this trajectory, but as a genealogy rather than a positive evolution, Nietzsche deconstructs representation out of a distrust of rational knowledge motivated by a desire for immediacy, by a specifically romantic desire to reverse the attenuation of perception accepted by the Enlightenment as a part of civilization. The immediacy that Nietzsche seeks, as Alan Megill points out, is profoundly unattainable.[11] Yet it is evoked as a criterion by which to judge the inadequacy of representation, even as it is recognized as impossible within a system in which even music is only the appearance of the will. Significantly, Nietzsche does not deny the existence of a material substratum outside language, denying only that it is accessible through language.[12] In short, whereas de Man criticizes representation for entertaining the illusion of presence, Nietzsche criticizes it for its inability to capture difference, the *presence* of difference.

This is not to say that Nietzsche *posits* a presence beyond representation. We feel this presence only by reading the spaces in his text: spaces that leave us uncertain whether what is at issue is an unknowable presence, or the desire for presence. Significantly, for Nietzsche drama is at its most authentic when it is only "chorus" and not yet "drama," and when Dionysos is not "actually present" but "merely imagined *[vorgestellt]* as present." The realism of drama, which substitutes for the phenomenological affect of presence, the physical presence of the hero, is a declination from a more original stage of tragedy. At that stage what the audience sees is not "the awkwardly masked human being but rather a visionary figure, born as it were from their own rapture" (*BT,* 66; I, 63). Thus the immediacy of presence is perhaps the immediacy of this rapture, an immediacy whose basis is phenomenological rather than metaphysical.

The acceptance of language as formed by a reduction of the multiple to the single has profoundly conservative consequences. It sets in place the order of Law through the congealing of metaphor into what Lacan will call the symbolic order.[13] The resistance to this order is located by

Nietzsche in music and later in the body. Nietzsche is under no illusion that music can make fully present the "primordial contradiction" that Kristeva will later call the semiotic. Music is repeatedly described in analogical terms, as "symbol" and "copy *[Abbild]*" (*BT,* 55,100; I, 51, 104). Moreover, it is unclear whether music is a representation of the will or whether the will is a representation of music.[14] This indeterminate shuttling of music between figure and ground is symptomatic of the fact that it is still caught within the sphere of appearance, with the result that any claim to give it a metaphysical status (*BT,* 102; I, 106) is itself metaphoric. Indeed, it seems possible to say that where Schopenhauer collapses the binary opposition between will and representation to reveal how all representation is contaminated by the will, Nietzsche collapses it to concede that all will is complicit in the order of representation, thus preserving only as desire the metaphysical thrust of his precursor's philosophy. Nevertheless Nietzsche, in an intentionally paradoxical statement, describes music as "an immediate copy of the will itself *[unmittelbar Abbild des Willens selbst]*" (*BT,* 100; I, 104). He thus grants it a privilege in degree if not in kind over other modes of representation. This authority conferred on music is necessarily negative and liminal. Music cannot manifest whatever is behind it: it can do no more than intimate this substratum by marking a limit to representation that allows immediacy to be felt only as a desire produced by the inadequacy of mediation.

That the negative intimation of immediacy as that which exceeds its mediation is still more authentic than the various forms of intellectual mediacy that intervene for the preservation of the individual is marked by the special vocabulary Nietzsche uses to distinguish not just music but art in general, from philosophy and science. When he speaks of language in general, his word for the signifier is *Bezeichnung* (I, 877). When he speaks of art, whether Apollonian or Dionysian, the process of signification is described through figures of reflection and mirroring. Thus music is described as a "reflection" without image or idea of original pain—*bild-und begrifflose Wiederschein*—(*BT,* 49; I, 44). Likewise the Olympian mythology is a "clarifying mirror" *(verklärenden Spiegel)* to the Hellenic will (*BT,* 43; I, 36).[15] *Wiederschein,* with its links to Schiller's concept of *Schein,* meaning appearance in the double sense of illusion and of a phenomenological appearing, allows what is being represented to be undecidably within and beyond the signifier. No less equivocal is the figure of the mirror, which suggests an iconic rather than purely arbitrary link between signifier and signified. For mirrors, like photographs and paintings, contain the physical image of that to which they refer, rather than pointing to something substantively different from which they are separated as illusion from reality. That a representation for Nietzsche has a synecdochic character is further confirmed by his frequent use of a vocabulary of emanation in which appearance and reality are not opposed but mutually repeat each other. An example is his description of Raphael's *Transfiguration*, in which there arises from the "reflection" or "appearance" *(Schein)* of a "primal and eternal" suffering "a new visionary world of mere appearance" (*BT*, 45; I, 39). It is important to note that the repetition is mutual, and that the relation between the two elements is undecidable rather than hierarchical: illusion is the appearing of reality, manifesting "reality" as the appearance of reality. Or in other words the synecdochic structure of reflections and emanations involves not only the participation of appearance in reality but also the infiltration of reality by appearance. Thus if the synecdochic character of reflections makes them unlike the self-emptying signs that de Man refers to as "allegory," they are also unlike what he calls "symbol" (following Coleridge and Goethe).[16] The symbol in de Man is a self-mystified mode of language that claims to have surmounted the barrier between presence and representation. Reflections, by contrast, are specular symbols: they have the *appearance* of symbols, constructing across the mediacy of all representation a desire for the immediacy they deconstruct.

If music is Nietzsche's first synecdoche for the representation of difference, and if other forms of art have at least the potential to be mirrors of music, it is in the body that the later Nietzsche locates the working of difference. We will not discuss here the fissure between ethics and epistemology in the later writings: between the body as a figure for the denial of asceticism and thus for the positing of a Zarathustran identity, and the body as a set of drives whose heterogeneity deconstructs identity. Our concern will be with those fragments from the so-called *Will to Power* where the body emerges as a resistance to the synthetic judgments on which identity is founded. Like his emphasis on music, Nietzsche's emphasis on the body develops in the context of a critique of language as the law of "the same" (*WP*, 280; IX, 354) and leads to a distinction between language and the body, or between language as logos and the language of the body, of images. The progressive abstraction that valorizes concept over image is held in place by a chain of being in which soul or intellect is higher than body, and in which "the indistinct idea *[Vorstellung]*" is "a lower kind of idea than the distinct"

(*WP*, 285; IX, 361). Returning to the body as the most authentic form of cognition, Nietzsche turns away from Kant and Hegel, and turns from unity to difference. For to grasp the world through our bodies is to feel rather than know it, to be unable to objectify what is still inside us, and thus to experience the real as excess, as that which exceeds representation. In contrast to the world of the intellect, "The evidence of the body reveals a tremendous multiplicity" (*WP*, 281; IX, 355). The body as the limit of representation is the unknowable. On the one hand, we are inside it, yet as *res extensa* it thwarts the attempt of consciousness to know itself in its interiority. On the other hand, as something outside us it cannot be objectified, made the object of scientific knowledge, because it does not remain safely external to us. Collapsing the boundary between inside and outside, the experience of the body precedes and impedes the separation between subject and object necessary to what Kristeva calls the thetic: the faculty of judgment created by the illusion of using language propositionally. Connected with this emphasis on the body is thus a reorientation towards the psychosomatic basis of language, in which a word is a "nerve stimulus" transformed into an image ("TF," 507; I, 878).

We can only speculate on why Nietzsche increasingly replaces music by the body as a figure for difference. As dance, the body in *The Birth of Tragedy* had formed part of a physiology of the aesthetic, in which it had functioned not simply as the material trace of the unconscious, but had been associated with art, with rapture, and thus with the affect of presence (*BT*, 40; I, 33–34). In the later fragments the association between the body and music is dropped, in what would seem a desublimation of Dionysian presence marked by the erasure of the aesthetic. We are closer here to what Drew Leder, expanding on Merleau-Ponty, calls the absent, chiasmatic body.[17] For as Eric Blondel reminds us, "one's own body" for Nietzsche "is not immediately present to man, but must, within the cultural economy, express itself . . . through the medium of a symptomatic language."[18] The body, like the Lacanian Real, is accessible only as a text, the performative text that Nietzsche calls the will to power. This use of the body as a metaphor for non-identity and for the inaccessibility of that which seems to be most inside us will prove important for a theorist like Kristeva, who draws from the later Nietzsche a concern with the body as the material site of the unconscious (unspiritualized, as it is in Schopenhauer, by any expansion into the negative Hegelianism of the world-as-will). Kristeva, as we shall see, also returns to the early Nietzsche's belief in the body as art, giving poetic language a centrality it does not have in the texts after the axial period. But this return is made by way of a later Nietzsche from whom she inherits a sense of the mediacy of both art and physical experience that remains emotionally, if not logically, muted in *The Birth of Tragedy*. At first sight, therefore, the line of affiliation from Nietzsche to deconstruction would seem to involve an increasing radicalization of the concept of difference in the antimetaphysical and antiromantic direction we associate with poststructuralism. The allegorical mapping of a contemporary vocabulary onto Nietzsche's texts is, however, deceptive, because it ignores the ways in which his terms parallel but also displace those of Derrida and de Man. For one thing, the body is still an organicist figure associated with a certain experiential immediacy: it is the most immediate form of that which does not appear, possessing a physiological if not an intellectual identity. In this emphasis on (im)mediacy generated by a typically romantic argument between nature and culture, Nietzsche differs not only from poststructuralism but also from the Humean skepticism so influential on him. Secondly, as we move back from Derrida to Nietzsche, there is a slippage in the site of *différance* from language, which for Nietzsche is logocentric, to music and then the body. An intertextual reading of Nietzsche with poststructuralism thus requires us to pose a crucial question. If Nietzsche anticipates the deconstruction of presence and self-identity, why does he differ in making music and the body, rather than language, the locus for this deconstruction?

To put the matter briefly, language for Derrida and de Man is a site of differences elided by logic and mathematics. For Nietzsche, by contrast, language is fundamentally metaphysical. Words claim to be more than designations: we imagine that through them we actually grasp "the essence *[das Wesen]*" of things (*WS*, aphorism 11; II, 547). The divergence, to some extent, may be simply semantic and historical. We can argue that what Derrida associates with language, Nietzsche designates by a different term, or alternately that the two do not mean the same thing by "language." Nietzsche conceives of language on the model of mathematics and logic; Derrida refers not to the system but to the process of language, to *écriture*. Or to approach the matter differently, Derrida sees "language" as diacritical, whereas Nietzsche still thinks in terms of the atomism he inherits from earlier linguistic theory, which constructs language as an aggregate of discrete word-atoms each capable of positing an autonomous thing or action. Focusing on nouns and verbs, but not on connectives or particles, atomism considers the relationship between signifier and signified in terms of single words and not diacritically in terms of propositions or groups of words.[19] But such a theory of language violates Nietzsche's sense (which is also that of Hume) that at the level of the perceptions organized by words things are not "indivisible, each existing in and for itself" (*WS*, aphorism 11; II, 547). His disaffection for language thus arises from the inability of language theory to keep up with the more radical discoveries of empiricist epistemology. Music then becomes the metaphor that Nietzsche, writing before Saussure, is historically constrained to use for the signifying process we now call "writing," which in turn is *our* metaphor for all other signifying systems, whether or not they are, strictly speaking, linguistic.

These arguments for a parallelism between Nietzsche and Derrida at the level of deep structure are not without value. For any attempt to connect the two must recognize that the division we now locate within language, between work and text or between speech and writing, is already found in *The Birth of Tragedy* as a division between language and music. Nevertheless there remains the fact that the opposition deconstructed by Derrida between the phenomenological category of voice and the textual category of writing appears in Nietzsche in partly reversed form as an opposition between language and the phenomenological categories of music and the body, both of which (like voice) are sensuous rather than textual media. The asymmetry between Nietzsche and poststructuralism, in other words, is also symptomatic of a profound divergence between the two. For in valorizing *différance* over *logos* but associating it with the body, Nietzsche gives it a materiality it lacks in a critical practice that posits nothing outside the text. This turn in Nietzsche may well survive in classical poststructuralism's anomalous references to the "materiality of the trace," and in de Man's interest in material writing—in inscriptions and epitaphs, with their displaced link to the equation between writing and death made in the much more clearly phenomenological essays of Maurice Blanchot. Our point, however, is that in locating *différance* in something other than language, Nietzsche is not conferring on language a logocentric security that, as the sublimatory figuration of the Dionysian, it cannot have except in appearance. Rather he is conferring on *différance* a materiality, and a reference to experience, to how we experience the world through our bodies.

In deferring the site of difference from language to music and the body, Nietzsche conceives of language phenomenologically, as a state of (non-)identity with which we must come into closer touch because it is the most immediate form of that which does not appear. It must be emphasized that this does not make Nietzsche metaphysical in the sense criticized by poststructuralism. As the appearance of something that cannot appear, the will is not the in-itself but simply a sphere of appearance more primal than the order of representation. It is appearance as force rather than form and representation:

> The world of "phenomena" is the adapted [zurechtgemachte] world that we feel to be real. The "reality" lies in the continual recurrence of identical, familiar, related things in their logicized character. . . .
> . . . The antithesis of this phenomenal world is not "the true world" but the formless unformulable world of the chaos of sensations—another kind of phenomenal world, a kind of "unknowable" for us (WP, 307; IX, 388).

II

Using the asymmetry between Nietzsche and poststructuralism as a basis, I shall attempt in the remaining pages to superimpose upon the teleological reading of Nietzsche through poststructuralism an archaeological rereading of deconstruction through Nietzsche. This rereading has two related consequences. As we have seen, it displaces the opposition between deconstruction and phenomenology articulated by Derrida and left unquestioned even by theorists like Kristeva, who is otherwise critical of him. For Derrida phenomenology is a philosophy of identity as removed from deconstruction as is Platonism. It seeks a moment of pure self-consciousness outside language, a "present and in-different being" that "precedes difference and spacing."[20] For Nietzsche what we now call phenomenology and deconstruction are curiously allied: the questioning of presence as Apollonian illusion occurs through a disclosure of the Dionysian body that reintroduces phenomenology even as it deconstructs the possibility of an in-different being. The Dionysian is a phenomenological category not only in being a state of consciousness, but also in being a revelation of something more profound than the ordinary or than the world of textual simulacra described by poststructuralism. But it is also phenomenological in its deconstruction of the noumenon or in-itself. For the Dionysian is the (dis)closure of being through its appearance: "appearance" in the double sense of "manifestation" and "illusion." Moreover, the phenomenological recognition that truth can be known only as a moving army of appearances is linked in Nietzsche, more so than in Heidegger, to an awareness of the tropological and of negativity. This reinscription of the idealist phenomenology we associate with Hegel, Husserl, and even Heidegger occurs through a transposition of the locus of signification from consciousness to the body. But insofar as we are reading Nietzsche through contemporary theory, we can also describe what he does as a transposition of deconstruction into phenomenology. The symbiosis of what now seem opposed terms has a second consequence. It becomes in Kristeva's continuation of Nietzsche the dialectical ground for a deconstruction that combines linguistics with what she calls "practice" in a kind of semiotic materialism. For pure poststructuralism, as many critics have observed, has a tendency to draw the world into the text. By making the body the place of the semiotic, Kristeva insists upon the materiality of difference, using the term "materiality" in both an affective and a political sense.

My argument is not that Nietzsche and Kristeva can be identified, but that they can be read intertextually. By disclosing those elements in Nietzsche that resist assimilation into an ultratextualist economy, such a reading aims to bring out a difference within deconstruction itself that stems from the complexity of its philosophic parentage: a difference I mark by using the two terms "deconstruction" and "poststructuralism." Crucial to understanding how Kristeva diverges from Derrida and Lacan by returning to Nietzsche is her distinction between the symbolic and the semiotic. Briefly, the symbolic is the order of representation, the entry into language, and thus the stage at which propositions are enunciated and positions taken. But because the symbolic is also the order of law and family, of patriarchy, the "thetic" stage occurs through a language that is necessarily a "social effect of the relation to the other, established through the objective constraints of biological (including sexual) difference, and concrete, historical family structures" (R, 29).[21] In the symbolic order the subject must be re-presented through an image with which she is not identical. Inscribing its images as Law, the symbolic subjects us to a social language that has forgotten its origins in a moving army of metaphors. This language is of course tacitly self-deconstructing. Precisely because the symbolic is the order of representation, its structure is that of the mirror stage that forms the psychological analogue for the separation of subject and object necessary to predication, and reflected in the division of the sentence into subject and predicate. In other words the process of representation requires the subject to "separate from and through his image, from and through his objects" so as to achieve an "always split unification that is produced by a rupture" (R, 43, 49). Although the symbolic requires an act of "identification" that constitutes subject and object as separate entities, thereafter subject and object remain specular, displaced, because they must be "posited in a space that becomes symbolic because it connects the two separated positions" (R, 43).

This specularity, however, is what the symbolic order both discloses and resists. By contrast, the semiotic underlies and precedes "the realm of positions," being a "stage" or "region . . . hidden by the arrival of signification" (R, 43, 40), a stage at which there is as yet no distinction between subject and object. The site of an undifferentiated and prethetic rather than (syn)thetic unity, the semiotic is connected with the mother's body, conceived in de-idealized and nonpersonal terms. It is thus organized in terms of drives and pulsions, of marks made in the body that are graspable only as traces. These traces disclose the symbolic as the body's symptomatic conversion into language. In this sense the semiotic resembles what Schopenhauer calls the will, which reveals the order of representation to be the body's metaphorical displacement in codes and symbols, a nerve stimulus artificially clarified as an image. But unlike the will, the semiotic is not the in-itself. As the very word, meaning "precursory sign . . . trace, figuration" indicates, the body is already a language: its "energy charges" and "psychical marks" are "always already involved in a semiotic process" because they are distributed according to social and familial constraints (R, 25). Where the semiotic differs from the symbolic is in the nature of the language it produces, which is rhythmic rather than propositional, producing "articulations heterogeneous to representation" (R, 36). The semiotic, in other words, does not yield meaning, because it is "not yet a position that represents something for someone (i.e., it is not yet a sign)" (R, 26). If symbolic language is a system of signs that have forgotten their metaphorical basis and become canonical, the semiotic takes form as a *chora* that unsettles the very concept of the sign: a "mobile and extremely provisional articulation constituted by movements and their ephemeral stasis" (R, 25). Producing movements that are too indeterminate to mean anything, the semiotic exceeds and thwarts its own movement towards the symbolic and, as the mainspring of art, it becomes the site of a potential revolution in language.

Kristeva's distinction must be seen as a revision of classical poststructuralism that not only marks her own divergence from it but also tries to articulate its political unconscious. For Lacan the symbolic order, as the site of the subject's displacement in language and the linguistically constructed world of law and patriarchy, is opposed not by the semiotic but by the imaginary order. The symbolic, as in Kristeva, remains a world of representation, substitution and nonidentity. In it the subject must represent herself through an object of desire that stands in place of something else, thus deferring her identity with a desire that always remains symbolic. Likewise she must experience herself through the various codes in which she finds herself inscribed, thus making contact with herself only through the already displaced and symbolic language of the other. The imaginary creates a world of simultaneity and identity in which the ego identifies with its unified image seen in the mirror, transcending its original experience of itself as a fragmented body. Visual rather than linear, the imaginary escapes both the logocentric compulsion exercised by language and its operation as a system of displacements, and it substitutes for the disturbed stasis of the symbolic something that is even more static. The distinction between Kristeva and Lacan can best be approached in terms of the way they distribute the elements of difference and identity in the two orders. Whereas Kristeva counteracts the outwardly logocentric but inwardly displaced world of the symbolic order by opposing to it a more authentic language of non-identity, Lacan, similarly valorizing *différance* over identity, opposes to the symbolic a world of illusory identities impermeable to difference. He thus legitimizes by default the sterile displacements of the symbolic order as the only alternative locus of difference. The distinction between the symbolic and imaginary orders restates Freud's distinction between the reality principle and the pleasure principle, and as such the imaginary becomes a form of private fantasy whose genuine value in the psychic economy is suspended by its specularity.

But the parallel with Freud is also misleading. Insofar as inscription in the symbolic makes us subjects instead of egos, subject to the law in Althusser's sense, its status in the political economy of Lacan's text is different from its status in Freud. The symbolic is not embraced as a necessary stage in the civilizing conquest of the id by the ego, but is accepted with a fatalism that leaves unvoiced a certain desire in Lacan's text. It is this desire that Kristeva tries to articulate. In replacing the imaginary by the semiotic as a site of resistance to the symbolic, she legitimizes resistance as revolutionary rather than purely narcissistic by affiliating it not with identity but with difference. In other words, she constructs a way out of Lacan's binary opposition between equally specular orders. Crucial to Kristeva's revision of Lacan is her de-idealization of the Apollonian order of the imaginary, and her rewriting of its project in terms of the more Dionysian order of the semiotic. For the semiotic, as a protolanguage, cannot be a source of identity. At the same time, as a site of difference it radically reconceives the Lacanian representation of difference as desire. Desire in Lacan is simply empty: it is the unending difference of the subject from a series of objects that are substitutive representations of absence. Hence Kristeva's rejection of the term "desire," and her attempt to represent the semiotic by the terms "negativity" (from Hegel) and "heterogeneity" (from Bataille).

Although Kristeva's terms are intended as an allusion to Lacan, we can also approach them as a rewriting of Derridean linguistics, effected by the deliberate failure of her oppositions to coincide with his. Briefly, each of Kristeva's terms contains elements of each of Derrida's. The symbolic resembles the *logos* as the law of the same. Indeed, the *logos* is an agent of the symbolic that is set in place by the division of the sentence into subject and predicate. On the other hand, the symbolic also lacks the self-identity of "voice," and participates instead in the structures of "writing" as an order of representations in which "the subject must separate from and through his image" (*R*, 43). Likewise the semiotic, as a dispersal of the unified ego into the various drives that (de)compose it, also resembles *écriture* in being a process in which the imaginary unity of Derridean voice is lost. That it resembles "writing," despite its nonlinguistic character, is marked by the term "semiotic." At the same time the semiotic remains connected to voice though not to the logos, by its association with music and vocal rhythms (*R*, 26) and by a link with the body that makes it irreducible to the purely linguistic category of writing.

In transecting rather than replicating Derrida's categories, Kristeva draws distinctions not simply between these categories but also within them. Thus she separates the conservative aspect of voice, its affiliation with the phallogocentric order, from voice as a figure for an interiority now associated with the confused experience of the body rather than with the clarified identity of spirit or *pneuma*. As important is the difference she discovers within writing. The tendency of *écriture* to disrupt the imaginary security of the *logos* is associated by her with the semiotic's interruption of the symbolic world of law and family. But its tendency to inscribe the subject in systems of signification that create a specular and displaced identity is now associated with the symbolic. Equally important,

Kristeva transgresses Derrida's alignment of the identity/*différance* distinction with a distinction between the material (voice) and the linguistic (writing). For Kristeva it is the linguistic sign that is the source of identity and the material (the body) that is a site of difference.

Kristeva's rewriting of grammatology cuts across the Derridean opposition between phenomenology and poststructuralism, by locating *différance* in a "pre-symbolic immediacy" (*R*, 69) that precedes the linguistic signifier. While her semiotic materialism allows her to put *différance* back into the experience of a subject-in-process, it also has political ramifications that she makes explicit in *Revolution*. By conflating the revolutionary potential of the semiotic and the conservative thrust of the symbolic within the category of writing, Derrida neutralizes the political effectiveness of *différance*. He allows the energy of the *chora*, which disperses the representations of the symbolic, to be converted into the subject's dispersal within the symbolic. Thus Kristeva, while conceding that grammatology is the most radical form taken by negativity after Hegel (*R*, 40), dismisses Derridean poststructuralism as essentially flawed. Negativity, a crucial concept in thinkers like Adorno, is also fundamental to Derridean *différance*, the movement of which thwarts or negates any attempt at the consolidation of the thetic through the identification of the subject with a thesis or position (*R*, 143). But in criticizing Hegel for recuperating negativity within the teleological movement of the dialectic, Derrida's supposedly nonsynthetic difference falls into a different kind of positivity:

> In the course of this operation, negativity has become positivised and drained of its potential for producing breaks. It holds itself back and appears as a delaying *[retardement]*, it defers and thus becomes merely positive and affirmative, it inscribes and institutes through retention (*R*, 141).

Unlike Hegel, Derrida does not use dialectic to posit through the negative; he does not confirm the status quo or create a new one. But by renouncing the dialectical and thus the possibility for radical change, he renders negativity positive by default, retaining if not affirming. *Différance* thus "neutralizes productive negativity" (*R*, 142), losing the possibility of major breaks in a micrological movement of traces that is in-different to the "'terms', 'dichotomies', and 'oppositions' that Hegelian negativity concentrates, reactivates and generates" (*R*, 141). Kristeva's division of difference into a static and a dynamic difference is an attempt to restore to writing an element of the dialectical. In effect she reinscribes as a political praxis a grammatology that reduces the difference between the semiotic and the symbolic within the category of writing.

In breaking open the category of writing Kristeva, as we have already suggested, also transposes the imaginary into the semiotic so as to separate its revolutionary from its conservative tendencies. For the semiotic also intersects the oppositions constructed by classical poststructuralism. It has affinities both with *écriture* and with the Lacanian imaginary, considered as a restatement of the project embedded in the Derridean category of voice. It is a place of non-identity that threatens the boundaries of the ego, as the symbolic in Lacan unweaves the imaginary. In that respect it is linked with the reality principle, as well as with the unweaving of the thetic effected by language as difference. But because of its association with the mother's body, the semiotic is also linked with a return to something more inward than the world of symbols constructed by the law of the father. In this respect it reinscribes the imaginary's desire for a "pre-symbolic immediacy" (*R*, 69), where the self can come into contact with itself without the intervention of socially constructed representations of itself. This desire, however, is associated not with fantasy but with the body and thus with the real, and it is associated not with the ego's idealized image of itself but with prethetic transfers of energy whose interaction with the representations constructed by the self produces a subject-in-process rather than the imaginary ego of Lacan's mirror-stage. Moreover, the "region" demarcated as the semiotic is presocial but is not the private and protected space of the imaginary. Because it is as yet unindividuated, its recovery thus displaces the symbolic, even as the symbolic in Lacan displaces the imaginary. However, it disrupts the subject's self-presence not by inscribing her in a world of Foucauldian discourse, but by returning her to the originary difference of the "fragmented body— pre-Oedipal but always already invested with semiosis" (*R*, 22): a body reconceived not simply agonistically, as the Lacanian *corps morcelé*, but also as the mother's body and thus as the trace of a plenitude.

As important as Kristeva's revision of poststructuralism is the fact that her redistribution of the elements that comprise writing and voice into the categories of the symbolic and semiotic is facilitated by the intertextual relationship between the semiotic and Nietzsche's concept of the Dionysian, which already redistributes the conceptual economy of poststructuralism. For the Dionysian participates in both the deconstructive and the phenomenological. As the element that unsettles the security of the *logos*, it unravels the *principium individuationis* that is only fictively projected in the figure of Apollo but is then reified in the thetic enterprise of Socratic dialectic. But as an element grounded in the psychosomatic processes of the body, it endows this deconstruction with an experiential rather than a purely linguistic dimension. The nature of Kristeva's link to Nietzsche is explicitly stated in her early essay "Poésie et négativité"[22] and in the connection she draws between his concept of the subject-as-multiplicity and her own concept of the subject-in-process (*R*, 127). It is also evident in her references to Artaud, whose *Theatre and its Double* is an important link between *The Birth of Tragedy* and the romanticization of madness in Deleuze and the early Foucault. Moreover it is apparent in her repeated association of the semiotic with music and the body. Thus the semiotic, as that which is "feminine, . . . unfettered, irreducible to its intelligible verbal translation," is also "musical, anterior to judgment" (*R*, 29). The semiotization of the symbolic that occurs in art is described as a giving of "'music' to literature," (*R*, 63), in a hierarchization of art-forms that clearly recalls *The Birth of Tragedy;* and there are frequent references to the "musicalization" of the text (*R*, 65), or to music as the purest version of the semiotic (*R*, 24). Equally important is her association of the semiotic with the body, a concept that is not mystified as in Cixous, but that is conceived in terms of the conflictual energy charges located by Nietzsche in the will. The will, in turn, finds an earlier elaboration in the distinction of the individuated hero of Greek tragedy from the heterogeneous articulations produced by the chorus, whose multiplicity of voices perpetually and incoherently interrupt the hero's attempt to construct a bounded ego, to master "music" through the thetic moment of "language." Although the verbal resemblance may be accidental, the Nietzschean chorus clearly anticipates Kristeva's notion of the *chora* as an "uncertain and indeterminate articulation" of voices irreducible to a single language (*R*, 25). In unraveling the representational economy established by modern drama, in which audience and stage are divided as subject and object, the choric dissolution of boundaries between audience and actors replaces visual with physical experience, making the tragic something that is not seen as spectacle but felt as a region neither clearly inside nor outside us. Likewise the chora, which Kristeva links to the Dionysian in what seems an almost explicit allusion to Nietzsche (*R*, 79), is a "semiotic violence" that "breaks through the symbolic border," portending "the latter's dissolution in a dancing, singing, and poetic animality" (*R*, 29).

Equally important as a parallel between Nietzsche and Kristeva is her distinction between phenotext and genotext, which is crucial to her concept of the semiotic as the repository of what is revolutionary in art and to identifying in art a language that can represent the limits of representation. The phenotext is oriented to sign and communication, to producing a language of intelligible signs within a structure that "presupposes a subject of enunciation and an addressee" (*R*, 87). The genotext, although it includes the "advent of the symbolic" (*R*, 86), is still a process rather than a structure. Kristeva images it in terms of a "path" that temporarily organizes spaces or "zones" in which the subject is generated "by a process of facilitations and marks," but whose structures are always "ephemeral" (*R*, 86–87). The genotext is therefore that dimension of the text, surviving in rhythm and melody, that unsettles its signifying structure: a "space underlying the written" that can be "seen in language" but is "not linguistic" in the sense of being reducible to the signs that would tranquilize it (*R*, 29, 86). The text makes us aware of the pressures that produce its language as an epidermis that protects "the body from the attack of drives by making it a place—the place of the signifier—in which the body can signify itself through positions" (*R*, 49).

But this stratification of the text is already present in Nietzsche, who describes Greek tragedy as a "Dionysian chorus that ever anew discharges itself in an Apollonian world of images *[Bilderwelt]*" (*BT*, 65; I, 62). As the "transformation of the body" into language (*R*, 79), the process of the text thus spans "Two Utterly different spheres of expression": the "Apollonian dream world *[Traumwelt der Scene]*" and the interplay of shifting forces in the music of the chorus, which resists being "condensed into images *[nicht zum Bilde verdichteten Krafte]*" (*BT*, 66–67; I, 64). This stratification of the text is explicit in Greek tragedy, which contains two signifying materials, music and language. But Nietzsche's discussion of Hamlet is perhaps the earliest instance of a reading that locates a genotext in a text that is apparently pure language, through a symptomatic reading of its silences and absences. Focusing on his father's death as failing to provide an adequate objective correlative for Hamlet's nausea, Nietzsche locates in the superficiality of Hamlet's words in relation to his actions a depth that has not been articulated and can thus appear only as a gap in language (*BT*, 60, 105; I, 56–57,109–110). His reading, moreover, is not a deconstruction in the mode of de Man—namely, a rhetorical reading that decomposes the play into its component figures. It is driven by a hermeneutic that deconstructs the social structures of revenge tragedy in order to hear the unsaid, by reading the sign as what Kristeva calls "the voice . . . projected from the agitated body" (R, 46).

We can thus attribute to Nietzsche Kristeva's deconstruction of logocentrism through a semiotic materialism that locates the functioning of the trace in the body and not, as in Derrida, purely in language. If Nietzsche does not associate the body with presence, as does Merleau-Ponty, his valorization of the body as a figure for existential immediacy marks him as part of a tradition that is phenomenological as much as deconstructive. For the positing of something not reducible to language is a phenomenological move that identifies language, if not as an expression of consciousness, then at least as the transformation of a nerve stimulus into sound. It is precisely this phenomenological element that allows Kristeva to rewrite deconstruction as praxis, instead of converting Marxism into poststructuralism as do Althusser and Baudrillard. For it is the emphasis on the body that restores to deconstruction its "socio-historical imbrication" and relevance to "direct experience" (R, 13). Moreover, we can also trace back to Nietzsche Kristeva's paraesthetic[23] privileging of art as the locus for a deconstruction that functions constructively, unlike the complete reduction to the *chora* produced in fantasy or schizophrenia (R, 182). Through art Kristeva legitimizes the thetic as Apollonian rather than theological. Art is defined as a "second-degree thetic," a resumption of the *chora* "within the signifying device of language" so as to reaffirm the symbolic as an order that no longer represses the *chora* because it uses the thetic only as a boundary (R, 50–51, 61). As in Nietzsche, this valorization of the aesthetic marks Kristeva's deconstruction as a form of romanticism that distinguishes between levels of cognition and marks out zones in the topography of experience that are more authentic than others, closer to a "pre-symbolic immediacy" (R, 69).

There are of course differences between Kristeva and Nietzsche. Most important of all are her greater emphasis on the subject and her Hegelianism, evident in her definition of art as "the *Aufhebung* of the semiotic in the symbolic" (R, 51). But even if Nietzsche provides only one strand in Kristeva's thinking, her work suggests that he is the site of an important resistance within poststructuralism to the hegemony of its own linguistic models. Christopher Norris suggests that music, from Schopenhauer to Bloch, has been a name for whatever eludes "the powers of abstract conceptualisation."[24] The body is likewise a figure for an important difference within deconstruction. I use the term "figure" deliberately. Although the body is part of the theoretical content of Kristeva's work, it must not be understood as a concept whose status as content would embed it in essentialism. Rather it is a figure for Kristeva's difference from Derrida and Foucault, whose global use of the terms *écriture* and "discourse" is itself figurative.

We find the same figures of music and the body in the work of Roland Barthes.[25] But equally significant is the suppression of aurality, visibility, and materiality in the texts of classical poststructuralism. For while the body, for instance, is simply absent from structuralist theory, it persists as a ghostly presence in a poststructuralism whose genealogy is marked as much by its effacement of phenomenological motifs as by its derivation from structuralism. Neil Hertz has pointed out that de Man's highly abstract writings are punctuated by figures of anatomical dismemberment and mutilation.[26] Moreover, the body surfaces subtextually in such seemingly incorporeal and rhetorical terms as "disfiguration" or the undoing of a figure, and in the obsession of de Man and others with episodes of hanging and drowning in romantic texts as figures for the "violence" of language.

This return, at the level of figure, of a phenomenology deconstructed at the level of concept allows us to conclude by commenting on the intervention made by Kristeva in a "Theory" dominated by the linguistic absolute. The notion of ends—whether it be the end of the book, of metaphysics, or of man himself—has come to dominate the rhetoric of theory. Intertwined with a forgetting of the material in the linguistic, the concrete in the abstract, the rhetoric of the end disturbingly recalls Hegelian pronouncements about the end of history. This end, for Hegel, was to be accomplished through an *Aufhebung* of art in philosophy, and of phenomenology in logic. In repeating the end of art as the end of man, poststructuralism puts a "theory" governed by the linguistic paradigm in the place occupied by "philosophy" in the Hegelian system. Yet the *Aufhebung* of criticism in theory is also profoundly at odds with the goals of theory, which announces itself as different from, as deferring, philosophy. The body as an explicit or effaced figure in poststructuralist theory is one locus for the critical process that de Man calls the resistance to theory. This resistance is an explicit part of Kristeva's agenda. But where the body is a disciplined or effaced presence, as in the later work of Foucault and de Man, it becomes the site of an unthematized resistance to a theory whose rhetoric betrays itself as an apocalyptic displacement of

Hegelian teleology. The figure of dis-figuration, for instance, configures in its very structure the continued reference of de Manian "rhetoric" to what it puts under erasure: namely the subject and the material, the phenomenology that Hegel could not surpass in logic. We could not talk of a self-resistance were it not for the pathos that haunts the writing of both de Man and Foucault, and that invites a symptomatic reading of their asceticism. That pathos is only augmented by the self-critical presence of phenomenology in the theoretical past of poststructuralism: a presence for which the appropriation of Nietzsche provides a major site.

Notes

1. Paul de Man, *Allegories of Reading: Figural Language in Rousseau, Nietzsche, Rilke and Proust* (New Haven: Yale University Press, 1979).

2. For the earlier de Man's links to existentialism and phenomenology, see Frank Lentricchia, *After the New Criticism* (Chicago: University of Chicago Press, 1980), 282ff.; Tilottama Rajan, "Displacing Post-Structuralism: Romantic Studies After Paul de Man," *Studies in Romanticism* 24 (1985): 451–74.

3. Nietzsche's connections with romanticism have been discussed by Ernst Behler, "Nietzsche und die Frühromantische Schule," *Nietzsche-Studien* 7 (1978): 59–96 and Benjamin Bennett, "Nietzsche's Idea of Myth: The Birth of Tragedy out of the Spirit of Eighteenth-Century Aesthetics," *PMLA* 94 (1979): 420–33. Both of these essays point to the importance of myth and art in Nietzsche as an expression of his romanticism. However, both were written before the reconception of the term "romanticism" made it possible to see Nietzsche as a romantic without making his work discontinuous with deconstruction. More recently Allan Megill's *Prophets of Extremity: Nietzsche, Heidegger, Foucault, Derrida* (Berkeley and Los Angeles: University of California Press, 1985) considers Nietzsche's romanticization of art as linking him to the deconstructive tradition. In focusing on Kristeva rather than Derrida, this essay takes up a different though not incompatible set of connections between Nietzsche and deconstruction and sees a sharper divergence between Nietzsche and Derrida than does Megill.

4. I use this term to designate the work of Lacan after "The Mirror Stage," the middle (or archaeological) work of Foucault and to some extent his later genealogical work, the later work of de Man, and the middle work of Derrida (exclusive of his recent interest in phenomena like the apocalyptic and the sublime). As this listing indicates, no theorist can be unequivocally identified with poststructuralism, each theoretical oeuvre being constituted around its resistance to itself. Indeed, it may well be that "poststructuralism" is less a description of the above theorists than a phase in the Anglo-American reception of French theory.

5. Quotations from Nietzsche are from English translations, with the German supplied in brackets where necessary, and with references to the corresponding German passages given in parentheses. The English translations have been abbreviated as follows: *BT – The Birth of Tragedy and The Case of Wagner*, trans. Walter Kaufmann (New York:

Vintage, 1967); "TF" – "Truth and Falsity in an Ultra Moral Sense," in *The Philosophy of Nietzsche*, ed. Geoffrey Clive, trans. Oscar Levy (New York: Mentor, 1965), 503–15; *WP – The Will to Power*, trans. Walter Kaufmann and R. J. Hollingdale (New York: Vintage, 1968); *WS – The Wanderer and his Shadow*, in *The Complete Works of Friedrich Nietzsche*, vol. 7, ed. Oscar Levy (rpt. New York: Russell and Russell, 1964). References to the originals of *BT*, "TF," and *WS* are to Friedrich Nietzsche, *Sämtliche Werke, Kritische Studienausgabe*, ed. Giorgio Colli and Mazzino Montinari, 15 vols.(Berlin: Walter de Gruyter, 1988). Since *WP* does not appear as such in the Colli-Montinari edition, I have used vol. 9 of the *Sämtliche Werke*, ed. Peter Gast, 12 vols. (Stuttgart: Alfred Kroner, 1964). The material cited here appears in different form in vol. 13 of the Colli-Montinari edition.

6. David Carroll, *The Subject in Question: The Language of Theory and the Strategies of Fiction* (Chicago: University of Chicago Press, 1982), 7.

7. For a discussion of Nietzsche and empiricism see William Walker, "Enlightened Nietzsche," *Studies in Romanticism* 29 (1990): 39–66.

8. De Man, *Allegories of Reading*, 113.

9. Hugh Blair, *Lectures on Rhetoric and Belles Lettres*, 3 vols. (London: Strahan and Cadell, 1785), 1:354–55.

10. Ibid., 351–52. Likewise Warburton argues that alphabetic writing is the final stage in a series of shifts that begins where there is initially a sign for each thing and proceeds through hieroglyphic writing, which puts "one single figure for the mark" of "several things" (*The Divine Legation of Moses Demonstrated, The Works of the Right Reverend William Warburton*, 12 vols. [London: Cadell and Davies, 1811], 4:120, 131, 14).

11. Megill, *Prophets of Extremity*, 36ff.

12. This seems clear from Nietzsche's positing in "TF" of a leaf that is not captured by the word "leaf" (507; I, 879–80).

13. Cf. Nietzsche's statement, "It is the powerful who made the names of things into law" (*WP*, 277; Kroner, ed., IX, 350).

14. On the one hand Nietzsche says music is a "copy *[Abbild]* of the will," thus implying that the will precedes music (*BT*, 100; I, 104). On the other hand he says music "appears as will *[erscheint als Wille]*," thus implying that music precedes the will (*BT*, 55; I, 50).

15. Kaufmann translates this phrase as "transfiguring mirror."

16. De Man, "The Rhetoric of Temporality," in *Blindness and Insight: Essays in the Rhetoric of Contemporary Criticism*, rev. ed. (Minneapolis: University of Minnesota Press, 1983), 187ff.

17. Drew Leder, *The Absent Body* (Chicago: University of Chicago Press, 1990).

18. Eric Blondel, "Nietzsche: Life as Metaphor," in *The New Nietzsche: Contemporary Styles of Interpretation*, ed. David B. Allison (New York: Delta, 1977), 152.

19. On this subject, see Stephen Land, *From Signs to Propositions: The Concept of Form in Eighteenth-Century Semantic Theory* (London: Longmans, 1974). Land, however, sees the shift to the proposition as the unit of analysis as resulting in a structuralist rather than a diacritical theory of language.

20. Jacques Derrida, *Positions*, trans. Alan Bass (Chicago: University of Chicago Press, 1981), 28.

21. All references are to Julia Kristeva, *Revolution in Poetic Language*, trans. Margaret Waller (New York: Columbia University Press, 1984).

22. Julia Kristeva, *Semeiotiké: Recherches pour une sémanalyse* (Paris: Éditions du seuil, 1969), 188.

23. I borrow this term from David Carroll, *Paraesthetics: Foucault, Lyotard, Derrida* (London: Methuen, 1987).

24. Christopher Norris, *Deconstruction and the Interests of Theory* (London: Pinter Publishers, 1988), 32.

25. See in particular the essays "Musica Practica" and "Brecht, Diderot, Eisenstein," in Barthes, *Image, Music, Text*, trans. Stephen Heath (New York: Hill and Wang, 1977), 69–71, 77, 149, 185.

26. Neil Hertz, "Lurid Figures," in *Reading de Man Reading*, ed. Lindsay Waters and Wlad Godzich (Minneapolis: University of Minnesota Press, 1989), 82–104.

II

Rethinking the Subject

Stubborn Attachment, Bodily Subjection: Hegel on the Unhappy Consciousness

Judith Butler

a freedom still enmeshed in servitude.
—Hegel, *The Phenomenology of Spirit*

The transition in *The Phenomenology of Spirit* from the section on "Lordship and Bondage" to that of "The Freedom of Self-Consciousness: Stoicism, Skepticism, and the Unhappy Consciousness"[1] is one of the least interrogated of Hegel's philosophical movements. Perhaps because the chapter on Lordship and Bondage secured a liberationist narrative for various progressive political visions, the resolution of freedom into self-enslavement at the end of the chapter has been generally considered unwelcome news.[2] And yet, insofar as recent theory has called into question both the assumption of a progressive history as well as the status of the "subject," the dystopic resolution of "Lordship and Bondage" has perhaps regained a timely significance.

Postliberationist theorists such as Michel Foucault have suggested that the point of modern politics is no longer to liberate a subject, but, rather, to interrogate the regulatory mechanisms through which "subjects" are produced and maintained. Although Foucault's vocabulary ought not to be conflated with that of Hegel, his concern with the double-edged implications of "subjection" (*assujettissement:* the simultaneous *forming* and *regulating* of the subject) is in some ways prefigured by

I would like to thank William Connolly and Peter Fenves for comments on earlier versions of this essay.

Hegel's account of the bondsman's "liberation" into various forms of ethical beratement. In *Discipline and Punish*, Foucault limits the efficacy of prison reform: "[T]he man described for us, whom we are invited to free, is already in himself the effect of a subjection *[assujettissement]* much more profound than himself."[3] The bondsman in Hegel throws off the apparently external "lord" only to become installed in an ethical world in which various norms and ideals are lorded over himself. Or, to put it more precisely, the subject is formed as an unhappy consciousness through the reflexive application of these ethical laws.

The permutations of self-enslavement that Hegel describes appear to take the body as that which must be negated, mortified, subordinated to an ethical demand. The "terror" that seizes the bondsman with his recognition of freedom appears to culminate in the simultaneous fabrication of ethical norms and the beratement of the bodily condition of his own life. In this sense, "The Unhappy Consciousness" establishes a relation between self-enslavement as bodily subjection and the formulation of self-imposed ethical imperatives that prefigures Nietzsche's critique of the same in *On the Genealogy of Morals* and Foucault's ultimate appropriation of that critique. In the following citation from Nietzsche's *Genealogy of Morals*, one can discern a temporary convergence between the figures of self-enslavement in Hegel's "Unhappy Consciousness" and the moralized "man" of conscience in Nietzsche:

> This *instinct for freedom* forcibly made latent . . . this instinct for freedom pushed back and repressed, incarcerated within and finally able to discharge and vent itself only on itself: that and that alone is what the bad conscience is in its beginnings. (87)

Underscoring the painful realization that "liberation" from external authorities does not suffice to initiate a subject into freedom, Foucault draws upon Nietzsche and, in particular, the self-incarcerating movement that structures modern forms of reflexivity. The limits to "liberation" are to be understood not only as those that are self-imposed but, more fundamentally, as the precondition of the very formation of the subject. A certain structuring attachment to subjection becomes the condition of moral subjectivation. Consider the expanded text of Foucault's remarks on the prisoner's subjection in *Discipline and Punish:*

> The man described for us, whom we are invited to free, is already in himself the effect of a subjection *[assujettissement]* much more profound

than himself. A "soul" inhabits him and brings him to existence, which is itself a factor in the mastery that power exercises over the body. The soul is the effect and instrument of a political anatomy; the soul is the prison of the body. (30)[4]

How precisely are we to read this "inhabiting" of the body by this soul? And can a return to Hegel help us to read it? What are the points of convergence and divergence in Hegel, Nietzsche, and Foucault on the structure of "subjection"? A thorough answer is not possible here, although I hope to conduct it elsewhere. I would like in the following, however, to suggest that Hegel's account in "The Unhappy Consciousness" prefigures a critical discourse on those ethical positions that seek the denial or sacrifice of bodily life, and that fall into instructive paradoxes when they do. Hegel shows that if the suppression of the body requires an instrumental movement of and by the body, then the body is inadvertently preserved in and by the instrument of its suppression. This formulation prefigures the possibility of a convergence with Nietzschean, Foucauldian, and Freudian perspectives on self-abasement that Hegel, in the transition to Spirit, proceeded to foreclose.

The first section of this essay will offer a reading, informed by poststructuralism, that accounts for how this paradox of bodily subjection is formulated in both the transition from "Lordship and Bondage" to "The Unhappy Consciousness" in *The Phenomenology of Spirit*. In the second section, I will consider the restatements of that paradoxical formulation in psychoanalytic and Foucaultian terms. Without presuming a direct line of influence, I will suggest both that Hegel's insights in "The Unhappy Consciousness" on the ineluctability of the attachment of and to the body in subjection is reiterated in both psychoanalytic and Foucaultian frameworks, and that the Foucaultian account of subjection, despite its significant moves beyond dialectical logic, remains unwittingly tethered to the Hegelian formulation. Further, I'll suggest that Hegel tacitly presumes that subjection is to be understood as a self-negating attachment, and that this operative presumption links his position with the Freudian notion of libidinal investment.

HEGEL AND THE PRODUCTION OF SELF-ENSLAVEMENT

In Hegel's *Phenomenology*, bodies are almost never to be found as objects of philosophical reflection, much less as sites of experience, for bodies are, in Hegel, always and only referred to indirectly as the encasement, location, or specificity of consciousness. By the time we arrive at the section on the unhappy consciousness, we, the readers, have already encountered the lord and the bondsman, and we have been given to understand these discrepant figures as differentially positioned with respect to bodily life. The bondsman appears as an instrumental body whose labor both provides for the material conditions of the lord's existence, and whose material products reflect both the subordination of the bondsman and the domination of the master. In a sense, the lord postures as a disembodied desire for self-reflection, one who not only requires the subordination of the bondsman to the status of an instrumental body, but who requires in effect that the bondsman be the lord's body, but to be it in such a way that the lord forgets or disavows his own activity in producing the bondsman, a production that we will call a projection.

This "forgetting" involves a clever trick, for it is the very action by which an activity is disavowed and that, as an action, rhetorically concedes the very "activity" that it seeks to negate. To disavow one's body, to render it "Other," and then to establish the "Other" as an effect of autonomy, is to produce it in such a way that the activity of its production—and its essential relation to the lord—is denied. This trick or ruse involves a double disavowal, and an imperative that the "Other" become complicit with this disavowal: in order not to be the body that the lord presumably is, and in order to have the bondsman posture as if the body that it is its own—and not the orchestrated projection of the lord—there is the necessity of a certain kind of exchange, a bargain or deal, in which ruses are transacted, occupied, and enacted. In effect, the imperative to the bondsman consists in the following formulation: you be my body for me, but do not let me know that the body that you are is my body. An injunction and contract are here performed in such a way that the moves that guarantee the fulfillment of the injunction and the contract are immediately covered over and forgotten.

At the close of the section on lordship and bondage, the bondsman labors away in a repetitive fashion on objects that belong to the lord. In this sense, both his labor and his products are presumed from the start to be other than his own, expropriated; they are given away prior to any possibility of giving them away, since they are, strictly speaking, never the bondsman's to give. And yet, this "contract" in which the bondsman substitutes himself for the lord becomes consequential; the substitution itself becomes formative of and for the bondsman. As the bondsman slaves away and becomes aware of his own signature on the things that he makes, he recognizes in the form of the artifact that he forms the markings of his own labor, markings that are formative of the object itself. His labor produces a visible and legible set of marks in which the bondsman reads back from the object a confirmation of his own formative activity. This labor, this activity, which belongs from the start to the lord, is nevertheless reflected back to the bondsman as his own labor, a labor that emanates from him, even if it appears to emanate from the lord.

Can, then, the labor reflected back be said finally to be the bondsman's own? Remember that the lord has disavowed his own laboring being, his body as an instrument of labor, and has established the bondsman as the one who will occupy the lord's body for him. In this sense, the lord has contracted the bondsmen as a surrogate or substitute; the bondsmen thus belongs to the lord, but this is a kind of belonging that cannot be avowed, for to avow the belonging would be to avow the substitution and, hence, to expose the lord as being the body that the lord apparently very much does not want to be. Hence, it is as a substitute in the service of disavowal that the bondsmen labors, and so it is only by miming and covering over the mimetic status of that labor that the bondsman appears both to be active and autonomous. Indeed, the object emerges as the objectification of the bondsman's labor, and so as an instance of that labor, a congealing and reflection of that labor. But what, then, does the object reflect? Is it the autonomy of the bondsman? Or is it that the object reflects the dissimulated effect of autonomy that is the consequence of the contract made between lord and bondsman? In other words, if the bondsman effects autonomy through a miming of the lord's body, a miming that remains hidden from the lord, then the "autonomy" of the slave is the credible effect of this dissimulation. The object of labor thus reflects the autonomy of the bondsman to the extent that the object, too, covers over the dissimulation that is the activity of the bondsman. In his work, then, the bondsman discovers or reads his own signature, but what is it that marks that signature as his own? The bondsman discovers his autonomy, but he does not (yet) see that his autonomy is the dissimulated effect of the lord's (and neither does he see that the lord's autonomy is itself a dissimulation; on the one hand, the lord effects the autonomy of disembodied reflection, delegating the autonomy of embodiment to the bondsman, thus producing two "autonomies" that appear at the outset radically to exclude one another).

But here the question emerges, Does the bondsman's activity remain fully constrained by the dissimulation by which it is mobilized? Or does this very dissimulation produce effects that exceed the control or dominion of the lord?

If the bondsman is to recognize the marks made on the object as his own, then that "recognition" must take place through an act of reading or interpretation by which the marks *(Zeichen)* that the bondsman sees are somehow understood to designate the bondsman; here it is not the witnessing of the activity, but the reading of the *signs* produced as the effect of that effectivity that designate the bondsman, that must in some way be understood to refer retroactively to the bondsman as signatory. If we are to understand the forming of the object as the inscribing of the bondsman's signature, the formative principle of the object as the formation of the signature itself, then the bondsman's signature designates a domain of contested ownership. On the one hand, this is *his* mark, which he can read (we shall let the bondsman occupy the site of presumptive masculinity), and so the object appears to belong to him, and yet this object marked by him, which has his mark on it, belongs to the lord, at least nominally. The bondsman signs, as it were, for the lord, as a proxy signatory, as a delegated substitute, and so the signature does not seal ownership of the object by the bondsman, but becomes the site for the redoubling of ownership and, hence, sets the stage for a scene of contestation.

The mark or sign on the object is not simply the property of the bondsman, but this object with his mark on it implies for him that he is a being who marks things, whose activity produces a singular effect, a signature, that is irreducibly his. And that signature is erased when the object is given over to the lord, who stamps it with *his* name, owns it, or consumes it in some way. The working of the slave is thus to be understood as a marking that regularly unmarks itself, a signatory act that puts itself under erasure at the moment in which it is circulated, for circulation here is always a matter of expropriation by the lord. The slave, of course, from the start has been working for another, under the name or sign of some other, and so has been marking the object with its own signature under a set of conditions in which that signature is always already erased, written over, expropriated, resignified. If the bondsman writes over the signatory of the lord, temporarily reversing the subordinate position of the proxy to the original, the lord reappropriates the object by writing over the signature of the bondsman. What emerges is less a palimpsestic object—like Kafka's topographies—than a mark of ownership produced through a set of consequential erasures.

Significantly, the bondsman nevertheless derives a sense of self-recognition at the end of the chapter, but not through reading back his signature from the object; after all, that signature has been written over by that of the lord. He recognizes himself in the very forfeiture of the signature, in *the threat* to autonomy that that expropriation produces. Strangely, then, a certain self-recognition is derived from the radically tenuous status of the bondsman; it is achieved through the experience of *absolute fear*.

This fear is a fear of a certain loss of control, a certain transience and expropriability produced through the activity of labor. And it is here that the logic of the bondsman's activity appears curiously to converge with that of the lord. Earlier it seemed that the lord occupied the place of pure consumption, appropriating and extinguishing all that the bondsman made. The bondsman, on the other hand, achieved the experience of self-reflexivity through working on and creating an object that bore the marks of his being, and thereby understood himself as a being who forms or creates things that outlast him, a producer of permanent things. The lord, of course, has been occupying the position of pure consumption, so for him objects are transitory, and he himself is defined as a series of transitory desires. For the lord, then, nothing seems to last, except perhaps his own consuming activity, his own endless desire.

These two positions, however, are not radically opposed to one another, for each in a different way experiences only and always the loss of the object and, with that loss, the experience of a fearful transience. Work is, for Hegel, a form of desire, a form that ideally suppresses the transitory character of desire; in his words, "[W]ork is desire held in check, fleetingness staved off. . . ."(118). To work on an object is to give it form, and to give it form is to give it an existence that overcomes transitoriness. The consumption of the object is the negation of that effect of permanence; the consumption of the object is its deformation. The accumulation of property, however, requires that formed objects be possessed rather than consumed; only as property do objects retain their form and "stave off fleetingness." Only as property, then, do objects fulfill the theological promise with which they are invested.

The bondsman's fear, then, consists in the experience of having what appears to be his property expropriated. In the experience of giving up what he has made, the bondsman understands two issues simultaneously; one, that he is embodied or signified in what he makes, and that what he makes is made under the compulsion to give it up. Hence, if the object defines him, reflects back what he is, is the signatory text by which he acquires a sense of who he is, and if those objects are relentlessly sacrificed, then what he *is* is a relentlessly self-sacrificing being. He can recognize his own signature only as that which is constantly being erased, a persistent site of vanishing. He is that which has no control over that to which he puts his name or over those purposes to which his name is put. His signature is at once an act of self-erasure: he sees that the signature is his, and at the same time that his own existence appears to be irreducibly his own, and that what is irreducibly his own is his own vanishing, and that this vanishing is effected by another, that is, that this is a socially compelled form of self-erasure.

This expropriation of the object does not negate the bondsman's sense of himself as a laboring being, but it does imply that whatever he makes, he will also lose. The determinate thing that the bondsman makes reflects the bondsman himself as a determinate thing: if the object is the congealing or forming of labor, and if that labor is that of the bondsman, then the determinate and transient character of the thing will imply the determinate and transient character of the bondsman himself. The laboring body that now knows itself to have formed the object also knows that it is *transient.* The bondsman not only negates things (in the sense of transforming them through labor), and is a negating activity, but is that which is subject to a full and final negation in death. This confrontation of death at the end of the chapter recalls the life-and-death struggle at the beginning of the chapter. The strategy of domination was meant to replace the life-and-death struggle; but in the earlier version, death was understood as that which happened through the violence of the other; domination was understood to be a way of forcing the other to die *within* the context of life; the failure of domination as a strategy thus reintroduces the fear of death, but locates it now as a feature of determinate or embodied being, no longer as a threat posed by another. The bondsman verges on this shattering recognition of his own death in the last paragraph of the chapter, but recoils from the recognition of death, attaching itself instead to various of its own attributes, taking up a posture of smugness or stubbornness, clinging to what appears to be firm about itself, firmly clinging to itself, in order not to know death as that which threatens every aspect of its own firmness: "[S]ince the entire contents of its natural consciousness have not been jeopardized, determinate being still *in principle* attaches to it; having a mind of one's own is self-will, a freedom still enmeshed in servitude" [seine Substanz ist von ihm nicht durch und durch angesteckt. Indem nicht alle Erfüllungen seines naturlichen Bewußtseins wankend geworden, gehört es *an sich* noch bestimmtem Sein an; der eigene Sinn ist *Eigensinn,* eine Freiheit, welche noch innerhalb der knechtschaft stehenbleibt](155).

The unhappy consciousness emerges here in the movement by which terror is allayed through stubbornness or, rather, through the action by which the terror over bodily death is displaced by a smugness and stubbornness that, in the next chapter, is further revalued as religious self-righteousness. This sanctimonious self is not *without* terror, but it becomes a reflexivity that is formulated as a kind of self-terrorization. The body that the bondsmen emblematized as a laboring instrument is recast at the end of the lordship and bondage chapter as a transient object, subject to death. The recognition of the body's death is averred, however, for a mode of living in which the body is ceaselessly dying away: hence, the move from the servitude of the bondsman to that of the unhappy consciousness. The bondsman takes the place of the lord by recognizing his own formative capacity, but once the lord is displaced, that bondsman becomes lord over himself—more specifically, lord over his own body. This form of reflexivity signals the passage from bondage to unhappy consciousness. It involves the splitting of the psyche into two parts, a lordship and a bondage internal to a single consciousness, whereby the body is again dissimulated as an alterity, but where this alterity is now interior to the psyche itself. No longer subjected as an external instrument of labor, the body is nevertheless still split off from consciousness. Reconstituted as an interior alien, the body is sustained through its disavowal and as that which for consciousness must remain disavowed.

What is the form that this self-subjection takes in the section on the unhappy consciousness? In the first instance, it is a form of stubbornness *(eigensinnigkeit);* it has a "mind of one's own" or "self-will," but one that is nevertheless still a form of servitude. It clings or attaches itself to itself, and this clinging to consciousness is thus also at the same time a disavowal of the body; the body appears to signify the terror of death, "the absolute fear." This unhappy consciousness requires and engages this attachment through the invocation of an imperative. Its fear is allayed through the legislation of an ethical norm. Hence, the imperative to cling to oneself is motivated by this absolute fear, and by the need to refuse that fear. Inasmuch as it is an *ethical* injunction, this imperative is itself the disarticulated refusal of absolute fear.

The section on the unhappy consciousness can be read as an effort to explain the genesis of the sphere of the ethical as a defense against the absolute fear that nevertheless constitutes its motivation. The fabrication of norms from (and against) fear, and the reflexive imposition of those norms, subjects the unhappy consciousness in a double sense: the subject is subordinated to norms, but the norms are also subjectivating, that is, they give an ethical shape to the reflexivity of this emerging subject. This subjection that takes place under the sign of the ethical is a flight from fear, and so is constituted as a kind of flight and denial, a fearful flight from fear that covers its fear with stubbornness first and then religious self-righteousness. The more absolute the ethical imperative becomes, the more stubborn or *eigensinnig* the enforcement of its law, and the more the absoluteness of the motivating fear is at once articulated and refused. Absolute fear is thus displaced by the absolute law that, paradoxically, reconstituted the fear as a fear *of* the law.

Absolute fear would correspond to the "jeopardization of all determinate things," including the determinate thingness of the bondsman. The flight from that fear, a fear of death, is to vacate the thinglike character of the subject altogether. This entails vacating the body and clinging to what appears to be most disembodied: thought. Hegel introduces stoicism as a kind of defensive clinging, one that separates the activity of thinking from any content. For Hegel, stoicism is a withdrawal into a subjective and rational existence that has as its highest aim the absolute withdrawal from existence per se, including its own. This task, of course, turns out to be self-refuting insofar as even self-refutation requires a persistent "self" to enact the withdrawal from its own and other existences; precisely because the conceptual act of negation always presupposes a position from which that negation takes place, stoicism ends up underscoring the very positivity of the self that it sought to deny. Skepticism follows upon stoicism for Hegel precisely because skepticism begins with the presupposition of the insuperability of the thinking subject. For skepticism, the self is a perpetually negating activity, actively refuting the existence of everything as its own constitutive activity.

Skepticism negates the domain of alterity by trying to show that any given determination of logical necessity turns into its opposite and, hence, is not what it is. The skeptic traces and focuses on this constant vanishing of determinate appearance without taking into account the dialectical logic that orchestrates and unifies these various oppositions. Hence, nothing is what it is, and there is no logical or empirical ground accessible to the skeptic by which the domain of alterity might be rationally known. The skeptic's own thinking becomes a frantic effort to make every given determination disappear into some other, so that this constant appearing and vanishing proceeds according to no order or necessity. The skeptic, like some new historicists among us, ends up producing contradiction for its own sake. Significantly, Hegel argues that this production of chaos (understood as ceaseless contradiction) is *pleasurable* inasmuch as the skeptic is always able to undermine the position of his philosophical opponent.

This kind of pleasurable and incessant refutation is still a form of stubbornness or eigensinnigkeit: "[I]t is in fact like the squabbling of self-willed children *[eigensinniger Jungen]* who by contradicting themselves buy for themselves the pleasure *[die Freude]* of continually contradicting one another"(Eng., 126; Ger., 162). The skeptic overrides his own contradictoriness in order to take pleasure in forcing others to witness their own contradictions. But this pleasure, a form of sadism to be sure, is short-lived, for the stubborn and persistent character of the skeptic's efforts will doubtless be challenged when the skeptic encounters another like himself. If another skeptic exposes the first skeptic's contradictions, then the first skeptic is forced to take account of his own contradictoriness, and this understanding *of* his own contradictoriness will initiate for him a new modality of thought. It is at this point, at which the skeptic becomes self-conscious of the constitutive contradiction of his own negating activity, that the unhappy consciousness emerges as an explicit form of ethical reflexivity.

In a sense, the childish and stubborn pleasure that the skeptic takes in watching another fall turns into a profound "unhappiness" when he is, as it were, forced to watch himself fall into endless contradictions. Here the distance afforded by "watching" seems essentially linked to the sadism of the pleasure and to the posture of the skeptic as one who exempts himself through visual distance from the scene that he witnesses. The sadistic pleasure involved in watching another becomes, in the mode of "unhappiness," a displeasurable watching of oneself.[5] The self that shored up its identity by encouraging others to fall into contradiction suddenly sees itself as one of those others; this self-viewing, which is the initiation into the unhappy consciousness, also inverts the skeptic's pleasure into pain. The sadism directed toward the other now becomes turned back[6] on consciousness itself (postponing for the moment the matter of whether the pleasure in sadism is also rerouted against consciousness itself). As a dual structure, the unhappy consciousness takes itself as its own object of scorn.

The philosophical elaboration of this scorn takes the following form: consciousness is now divided into two parts, the "essential" and "unchangeable," on the one hand, and the "inessential" and "changeable," on the other. The watching self, defined as a kind of *witnessing* and *scorning*, differentiates itself from the self witnessed as perpetually falling into contradiction. And this watching becomes a way of *re*establishing the visual distance between a subject aloof from the scene and the subject in contradiction. In this case, however, the *witnessing* and *scorning* self cannot deny that the contradictory self is its own self; it knows that the contradictory self is *itself*, but in order to shore up an identity over and against it, it renders this contradictory self into an *in*essential part of itself. It thus parts with itself in order to purify itself of contradiction.

As a result, the unhappy consciousness berates itself constantly, setting up one part of itself as a pure judge aloof from contradiction, and disparaging its changeable part as that which is inessential, although ineluctably tied to it. Significantly, the activity that begins as childish sadism in the case of skepticism becomes reformulated as ethical self-judgment in the context of the unhappy consciousness: as adult to child, then, the unchangeable consciousness "passes judgment" on the changeable. Implicit to this dual structuring of the subject, however, is the relation between thought and corporeality, for the unchangeable will be a kind of noncontradictory thought, the pure thought sought by the Stoics; the contradictory domain will be that of alternating qualities, the changeable domain of appearance, that which pertains to the subject's own phenomenal being. The child who "watches" is transfigured into the judge who "passes judgment," and that aspect of the self on which it passes judgment is steeped in the changeable world of bodily sensation.

Unhappy consciousness seeks to overcome this duality by finding a body that *embodies* the purity of its unchangeable part; it seeks to come into relation with "the Unchangeable in its incarnate or embodied form." To do this, the subject subordinates its own body in the service of the thought of the unchangeable; this subordinating and purifying effort is that of *devotion (Andacht)*. And yet, predictably, this effort to deploy the body in the service of thinking the unchangeable proves impossible. Devotion turns out to be pure self-feeling—what Hegel disparagingly refers to as "the chaotic jingling of bells, or a mist of warm incense, a musical thinking. . . ." (131).[7] As a self-feeling, it is the feeling of the body compelled to signify the transcendent and unchangeable, a feeling that nevertheless remains ensconced in the bodily feeling that it seeks to transcend. Indeed, self-feeling refers only and endlessly to itself (a transcendentalized form of *eigensinnigkeit)*, and so is unable to furnish knowledge of anything other than itself. Devotion, then, which seeks to instrumentalize the body in the service of the unchangeable, turns out to be an immersion in the body that precludes access to anything else— indeed, an immersion that takes the body to be the unchangeable and so falls into contradiction.

Although devotion appears to be a form of self-immersion, it is also a continuation of self-beratement as self-mortification. This self-feeling, precisely because it does not reach the unchangeable, becomes itself the object of derision and judgment, marking the continuing inadequacy of the self in relation to its transcendent measure. The transcendent is what is always missed, and so haunts this consciousness as a figure of that which is permanently inaccessible, forever lost. In the mode of devotion, then, "consciousness . . . can only find as a present reality the grave of its life" (132).[8] In a transposition of figures, the body survives, and all that is left of the transcendent ideal is a nonliving "grave." Whereas devotion, then, begins as an effort to subordinate the body to a transcendent object, it ends by taking the body, i.e., self-feeling, as its object of worship, and letting the unchangeable spirit die.

Here we might conclude that a certain form of self-preoccupation, understood as a reformulation of an insurmountable *eigensinnigkeit*, constitutes a narcissism of the subject that defeats the self-sacrificial project of devotion. The subject that would subordinate its body to an ideal, compelling its body to embody an ideal, finds itself more fully autonomous from that ideal, outliving it altogether. The collapse of devotion into narcissism, if we can call it that, signifies that there can be no final leave-taking of the body within life. Forced, then, to accept this ineluctability of the body as a presupposition, a new form of the subject emerges that is distinctly Kantian. If there is a world of appearance for which the body is essential, then surely there is a world of noumena in which the body has no place; the world divides up into beings that are for-itself and in-itself.

In a formulation that will prefigure Kierkegaard's *Philosophical Fragments,* Hegel claims that the unchangeable world surrenders or renounces an embodied form, that it, the in-itself, delivers an embodied version of itself into the changeable world to be sacrificed. This reference to the figure of Christ suggests that the unchangeable world becomes embodied, but does so only then to be sacrificed or returned to the unchangeable world from which it came. As a model for the sacred life, Christ is understood as an embodiment that is continually in the mode of giving thanks. In its desire and in its work, this embodied consciousness seeks to give thanks for its own life, capacities, faculties, abilities. These are given to it; its life is experienced as a gift, and it lives out its life in the mode of gratefulness. All of its acts it owes to another; its life becomes understood as a kind of endless debt.

Precisely because, on the one hand, this living being owes its life to another being, it is not the seat or origin of its own actions. Its action is thus referred to another's action; it is not the ground of its own action,[9] and in that sense is not responsible for what it does. On the other hand, its own actions are to be construed as a perpetual self-sacrifice by which that self *proves* or demonstrates its own thankfulness. This demonstration of thankfulness thus becomes a kind of self-aggrandizement—what Hegel will call "the extreme of individuality" (134).

The renunciation of the self as the origin of its own actions must be performed repeatedly and can never finally be achieved, if only because the *demonstration* of renunciation is itself a self-willed action. This self-willed action thus rhetorically confounds precisely what it is supposed to show. The self becomes an incessant performer of renunciation, whereby the performance, as an action, contradicts the postulation of *in*action that it is meant to signify. Paradoxically, performance becomes the occasion for a grand and endless action that effectively augments and individuates the self it seeks to deny.

This consciousness, like the stoic, which seeks to know and show itself as a "nothing," inevitably becomes a *doing* of nothing. And here the pleasure that earlier appeared to belong to the childish sadism of the skeptic is turned around on the self: this "doing of nothing," Hegel argues, finds in "its enjoyment a feeling of wretchedness." This intermingling of pleasure and pain results from a renunciation of the self that can never quite accomplish that renunciation, which, as an incessant accomplishing, carries with it the pleasurable assertion of self. The self-absorption of consciousness does not translate into self-congratulation or simple narcissism. Rather, it appears as negative narcissism, an engaged preoccupation with what is most debased and defiled about it.

Here again the self to be renounced is figured as a bodily self, as "this actual individual in the animal functions." Here Hegel appears to imply defecation as an object of self-preoccupation: "[T]hese [animal functions] are no longer performed naturally and without embarrassment, as matters trifling in themselves that cannot possess any importance or essential significance for Spirit; instead, it is in them that the enemy reveals himself in his characteristic shape, they are rather the object of serious endeavour, and become precisely matters of the utmost importance. This enemy, however, renews himself in his defeat, and consciousness, in fixing its attention on him, far from freeing itself from him, really remains forever in contact with him, and for ever sees itself as defiled" (135–36). This "enemy," as it were, is described as "the merest particular of the meanest character," one that serves unfortunately as an object of identification for this "fallen" consciousness. Here, consciousness in its full abjection has become like shit, lost to a self-referential anality, a circle of its own making. In Hegel's words, "[W]e have here only a personality confined to its own self and its petty actions, a personality brooding over itself, as wretched as it is impoverished" (136).

Regarding itself as a nothing, as a doing of nothing, as an excremental function and, hence, itself as excrement, this consciousness effectively reduces itself to the changeable features of its bodily functions and products. And yet, as an experience of wretchedness, there is some consciousness that takes stocks of these functions and that is not thoroughly identified with them. Significantly, it is here, in the effort to differentiate itself from its excretory functions—indeed, from its excretory identity—that consciousness relies on a "mediator," what Hegel will call "the priest." In order to reconnect with the pure and the unchangeable, this bodily consciousness offers up its every "doing" to a priest or minister. This mediating agency relieves the abject consciousness of its responsibility for its own actions. Through the institution of counsel and advice, the priest offers the reason for the abject consciousness's actions. Everything that the abject consciousness offers, that is, all of its externalizations, including desire, work, and excremental function, are to be construed as *offerings*, as the paying of penance. The priest institutes bodily self-abnegation as the price to pay for holiness, elevating the renunciatory gesture of excretion to a religious practice whereby the entire body is ritualistically purged. The sanctification of abjection takes place through rituals of fasting and mortification *(fasten und kasteien)* (Ger., 175; Eng., 137). Because the body cannot be fully denied, as the stoic thought, it becomes that which must be ritualistically renounced.

In its fastings and mortifications, the unhappy consciousness denies itself the pleasures of consumption, figuring perhaps that it will forestall the inevitability of the excremental moment. As self-inflicted bodily acts, fasting and mortification are reflexive actions, turnings of the body against itself. At the limits of this self-mortification and self-sacrifice, this abjected consciousness appears to ground its action in the counsel of the priest, and yet this grounding merely conceals the reflexive origins of its self-punishment.

At this juncture Hegel departs from what has been the pattern of explanation in which a *self-negating* posture is underscored as a *posture*, a phenomenalization that refutes the negation it seeks to institute. In the place of such an explanation, Hegel asserts that it is the will of another that operates through the self-sacrificial actions of the penitent. In effect, self-sacrifice is not refuted through the claim that self-sacrifice is itself a willful activity; rather, Hegel asserts that in self-sacrifice, one enacts another's will. One might expect that the penitent will be shown to be reveling in itself, self-aggrandizing, narcissistic—that its self-punishments culminate in a pleasurable assertion of self. But Hegel eschews the possibility of this explanation and thus breaks with the pattern of explanation in the chapter in favor of a religious solution in Spirit.

Indeed, it is at this juncture that one might well imagine a different set of transitions for the close of "The Unhappy Consciousness" than the ones Hegel supplies—ones that are, nevertheless, perhaps more properly Hegelian than Hegel himself.

The penitent disclaims its act as its own, avowing that another's will operates through that self-sacrificial agent, that of the priest's, and, further, that the priest's will is determined by God's. Installed thus in a great chain of wills, the abject consciousness enters into a community of wills. Although his will is determinate, it is nevertheless bound to that of the priest; it is in this unity that the notion of Spirit is first discerned. The mediator or priest counsels the penitent that his pain will be repaid with everlasting abundance, that his misery will be rewarded with everlasting happiness; misery and pain imply a future transformation into their opposites. In this sense, the minister reformulates the dialectic reversal and establishes the inversion of values as an absolute principle. Whereas in all of the earlier examples of self-negation the pleasure was understood to inhere in the pain (the pleasurable aggrandizement of the stoic, the pleasurable sadism of the skeptic), the pleasure is here temporally removed from the pain, and figured as its future compensation. For Hegel, it is this eschatological transformation of the pain of this world into the pleasure of the next that establishes the transition from self-consciousness to reason. And it is the recognition of this self-consciousness as part of a religious community of wills that effects the transition from self-consciousness to spirit.

But what are we to make of this final transition, considering the immanent relation of pleasure and pain in the transitions that precede it? The chapter on the unhappy consciousness appears to proceed as if it contained a trenchant critique of ethical imperatives and religious ideals, a critique that prefigures the Nietzschean analysis that emerges some sixty years later. Every effort to reduce itself to inaction or to nothing, to subordinate or mortify its own body, culminates inadvertently in the production of self-consciousness as a pleasure-seeking and self-aggrandizing agent. Every effort to overcome the body, pleasure, and agency proves to be nothing other than the assertion of precisely those features of the subject.

POST-HEGELIAN SUBJECTIONS

I would suggest that prior to the introduction of the "mediator" and the "priest," the chapter on "Freedom of Self-Consciousness" progresses in such a way that the Nietzschean critique of ethical norms is prefigured. This latter critique, articulated in Nietzsche's *On the Genealogy of Morals*[10] and *Daybreak*, has received more recent reformulations in Foucault's *Discipline and Punish*. Both Hegel's position and those inspired by Nietzsche might also be usefully compared with Freud's critique of the genesis of moral imperatives in *Civilization and its Discontents*.[11] Recall that for Hegel the emergence of ethical imperatives takes place first in a defensive response to absolute fear, and must itself be construed as a permutation and refusal of that fear. This absolute fear is the fear of death and, hence, a fear conditioned upon the finite character of the body. The ethical refusal and subordination of the body might then be understood as a magical effort to preempt that existential negation. Moreover, the ideal of radical self-sufficiency is jeopardized by the permeability and dependency. In this sense, excretion is not the only "animal function" that would signify "defilement" for this subject. The repeated efforts to sacrifice the body that become repeated assertions of the body are also efforts to defend it against everything that "jeopardizes" it, where "jeopardy" *(durch und durch angesteckt)* denotes a danger slightly less dire than death, a kind of penetrative paroxysm that implies being moved or shaken sexually "through and through." One could then see in the various forms of self-beratement and self-mortification typologized in "The Unhappy

Consciousness" a prefiguration of neurosis and, perhaps also, a specific modality of homosexual panic.[12]

We might then reread the mobilizing fear that is both refused and rerouted by the ethical imperative in terms of the feared "expropriability" of the body. If the bondsman's laboring activity can be expropriated by the lord, and the essence of the bondsman's body be held in ownership by that lord, then the body constitutes a site of contested ownership, one that through domination or the threat of death can always be owned by another. The body appears to be nothing other than a threat to the project of safety and self-sufficiency that governs the *Phenomenology*'s trajectory. The anal preoccupation that directly precedes the ascendance into a religious concept of an afterlife suggests that bodily permeability can only be resolved through an escape into an afterlife in which no bodies exist at all. This affirmation of the absolute negation of the body thus contradicts all the earlier efforts to subordinate or master the body *within* life, efforts that culminated in the assertion of the ineluctability of the body. And whereas other religious notions turned out to be surreptitious ways of reasserting the body, this one appears exempt from the dialectical reversal that it resolves.

The failure to maintain the subjection of the body is theorized along psychoanalytic lines that sustain strong parallels with these earlier dialectical reversals. The repression of the libido is always to be understood as itself a libidinally invested repression. Hence, the libido is not absolutely negated through repression, but rather becomes the instrument of its own subjection. The repressive law is not external to the libido that it represses, but the repressive law represses to the extent that repression becomes a libidinal activity.[13] Further, moral interdictions, especially those that are turned against the body, are themselves sustained by the bodily activity that they seek to curb:

> An idea . . . which belongs entirely to psychoanalysis and which is foreign to people's ordinary way of thinking . . . it tells us that conscience (or more correctly, the anxiety which later becomes conscience) is indeed the cause of instinctual renunciation to begin with, but that later that relationship is reversed. Every renunciation of instinct now becomes a dynamic source of conscience and every fresh renunciation increases the latter's severity and intolerance. (*CD*, 84)

According to Freud, then, the self-imposed imperatives of conscience are pursued and applied precisely because they are now the site of the very satisfaction that they seek to prohibit. In other words, prohibition becomes the displaced site of satisfaction for the "instinct" or desire that is prohibited, an occasion for the reliving of the instinct under the rubric of the condemning law. This is of course the source of that form of comedy in which the bearer of the moral law turns out to be the most serious transgressor of its precepts (Hawthorne's Dimmesdale, Tom Stoppard's moral philosopher). And precisely because this displaced satisfaction is experienced through the application of the law, that application is reinvigorated and intensified with the emergence of every prohibited desire. The prohibition does not seek the obliteration of prohibited desire; on the contrary, prohibition pursues the reproduction of prohibited desire and becomes itself intensified through the renunciations it effects. The "afterlife" of prohibited desire is in the prohibition itself, where the prohibition not only sustains, but is sustained by, the desire that it forces the subject to renounce. In this sense, then, renunciation takes place through the very desire that is renounced, which is to say that the desire is *never* renounced, but becomes preserved and reasserted in the very structure of renunciation.

Nietzsche makes a similar argument, deploying a dialectical structure not unlike Hegel's, in his critique of the ascetic ideal in *On the Genealogy of Morals.* The ineluctability of the body in "The Unhappy Consciousness" parallels the ineluctability of "instinct" in Freud and that of the will in Nietzsche. For Nietzsche, the ascetic ideal, understood as a will to nothingness, is a way of interpreting all suffering as guilt. And whereas guilt works to deny a specific kind of object for human wants, it cannot obliterate the wanting character of humans. According to the dictates of guilt, then, "man had only to want something—and to begin with, it mattered not what, whereto, or how he wanted: *the will itself was saved.*"[14] The ascetic ideal, very much like Hegel's "unhappy consciousness," is to be understood, then, as

> that hatred against everything human, even more, against everything animal, everything material, this disgust with the senses, with reason itself, this fear of happiness and beauty, this desire to get away from all semblance, change, becoming, death, wish, desire itself—the meaning of all this is a will to nothingness, a will running counter to life, a revolt against the most fundamental presuppositions of life; yet it is and remains a will! . . . rather than want nothing, man even wants nothingness!

Here I do not mean to suggest a strict equivalence between Freud's highly problematic notion of instinct, Hegel's inchoate body, and

Nietzsche's will. And yet, I do want to suggest that these three thinkers circumscribe a kind of dialectical reversal that centers on the final impossibility of a full or final reflexive suppression of what we might loosely call "the body" within the confines of life. If the suppression of the body is itself an instrumental movement of and by the body, then the body is inadvertently preserved in and by the instrument of its suppression. The self-defeating effort of such suppression, however, does not only lead to its opposite, namely, a self-congratulatory or self-aggrandizing assertion of desire, will, the body: it leads in more contemporary formulations to the elaboration of an institution of the subject that exceeds the dialectical frame by which it is spawned.

In Hegel, the suppression of bodily life is shown to require the very body that it seeks to suppress; in this sense, the body is preserved in and by the very act of suppression. Freud understood this differently in his analysis of neurosis as a kind of libidinal attachment to a prohibition that nevertheless thwarts libidinal gratification. In the case where that thwarting constitutes a repression—the splitting off of the ideation from the affect, neurosis or symptomatization follows. One might read Hegel's references to *eigensinnigkeit* or stubbornness as illustrating the process of splitting and defense in the formation of neurosis. That Hegel refers to this "unhappiness" as a kind of stubborn attachment suggests that, as in neurosis, the ethical regulation of bodily impulse becomes the focus and aim of impulse itself. In both cases, we are given to understand an attachment to subjection that is formative of the reflexive structure of subjection itself. The impulse or bodily experience that would be negated, to return to Hegel, is inadvertently *preserved* by that very negating activity.

We can see in both Hegel and Freud a certain reliance on a dialectical reversal by which a bodily experience, broadly construed, comes under the censor of the law only to reemerge as the sustaining affect of that law. The Freudian notion of *sublimation* suggests that denial or displacement of pleasure and desire can become formative of culture; his *Civilization and its Discontents* thus laid the ground for Marcuse's *Eros and Civilization.* The inadvertently productive effects of sublimation in the formation of cultural products appear to exceed the dialectical reversal by which they are generated. Whereas for Marcuse the drives or eros and thanatos precede the regulatory imperatives by which they are rendered culturally livable, for Foucault the repressive hypothesis, which appears to include the model of sublimation within its structure, fails to work precisely because repression generates the very pleasures and desires it seeks to regulate.

For Foucault, repression does not act on a pregiven field of pleasure and desire; it constitutes that field as that which is to-be-regulated, that which is always potentially or actually under the rubric of regulation. The repressive regime, as Foucault calls it, requires its own self-augmentation and proliferation. As such, this regime requires the field of bodily impulse to expand and proliferate as a moralized domain, such that it will continually have fresh material through which to articulate its own power. Hence, repression produces a field of infinitely moralizable bodily phenomena in order to facilitate and rationalize its own proliferation.

Here we see that Foucault departs from the kind of dialectical reversal that we followed in Hegel. In Foucault, the suppression of the body does not merely require and produce the very body it seeks to suppress. It goes further by extending the domain of the regulatable body, proliferating sites of control, discipline, and suppression. In other words, the body *presumed* by the Hegelian explanation is incessantly produced and proliferated in order to extend the domain of juridical power. In this sense, the restrictions placed on the body not only *require* and *produce* the body they seek to restrict, but *proliferate* the very domain of the bodily beyond the domain targeted by the original restriction. In what many have come to see as a finally utopian gesture in Foucault, this proliferation of the body by juridical regimes beyond the terms of dialectical reversal is also the site of possible resistance. The psychoanalytic discourse that would describe and pathologize repressed desire ends up producing a discursive incitement to desire: impulse is continually fabricated as a site of confession and, hence, potential control, but this fabrication exceeds the regulatory aims by which it is generated. In this sense, criminal codes that seek to catalogue and institutionalize normalcy become the site for a contestation of the concept of the normal; sexologists who would classify and pathologize homosexuality inadvertently provide the conditions for a proliferation and mobilization of homosexual cultures.

Within the Hegelian framework, the subject that splits itself off from its body requires that body in order to sustain its splitting activity; the body to be suppressed is thus marshaled in the service of that suppression. For Foucault, the body to be regulated is similarly marshaled in the service of that suppression, but the body is not preconstituted prior to that regulation. On the contrary, the body is produced as an object of regulation, and for regulation to augment itself, the body is *proliferated* as an object of regulation. This proliferation is both what marks off Foucault's theory from Hegel's and constitutes the site of potential resistance to regulation. The possibility of this resistance is derived from what is *unforeseeable* in proliferation. But for a regulatory regime to produce effects that are not only unforeseeable but constitute resistance, it seems that we need to return to the question of stubborn attachments and, more precisely, the place of that attachment in the subversion of the law.

Although Foucault criticizes Freud on the repressive hypothesis, he is indebted to the theorization of repression in his own account of the production and proliferation of the regulated body. In particular, the logic of subjection in both Hegel and Freud implies that the instrument of suppression becomes itself the new structure and aim of desire, at least when subjection proves effective. But if a regulatory regime requires the production of new sites of regulation and, hence, a more thoroughgoing moralization of the body, then what is the place of bodily impulse, desire, and attachment? Does the regulatory regime not only produce desire, but become produced by the cultivation of a certain attachment *to* the rule of subjection? If part of what regulatory regimes do is to constrain the formation and attachments of desire, then it seems that what is presumed from the start is a certain detachability of impulse, a certain incommensurability between the capacity for a bodily attachment, on the one hand, and the site where it is confined, on the other. Foucault appears to presume precisely this detachability of desire in claiming that incitements and reversals are to some degree *unforeseeable*, that they have the capacity, central to the notion of resistance, to exceed the regulatory aims for which they were produced. If a given regime cannot fully control the incitements that it nevertheless produces, is that in part the result of a resistance, at the level of impulse, to a full and final domestication by any regulatory regime?

What Hegel circumscribes in "The Unhappy Consciousness" is not merely that moral wretchedness cannot be coherently sustained, that it invariably concedes the bodily being that it seeks to deny, but that the pursuit of wretchedness, the attachment to wretchedness, is both the condition and the potential undoing of such subjection. If wretchedness, agony, and pain are sites of modes of stubbornness—ways of attaching to oneself, negatively articulated modes of reflexivity—then that is because they are given by regulatory regimes as the available sites for such an attachment, and that a subject will attach to pain rather than not attach at all. For Freud, an infant forms a pleasure-giving attachment to any excitation that comes its way, even the most traumatic, which accounts for the formation of masochism and, for some, the production of abjection, rejection, wretchedness, etc., as the necessary preconditions for love. The rejecting gesture can become masochistically eroticized only because it *is* a gesture. Although the rejecting gesture's alleged purpose is to thwart an oncoming desire, it nevertheless appears *as a gesture,* thus *making itself present,* and lending itself to a reading as a kind of offering or, minimally, *presence.* Precisely because the rejecting gesture *is,* it rhetorically denies the threat of withdrawal that it nevertheless purports to signify. For the infant, the presence or determinacy of that object, no matter how persistently rejecting, is nevertheless a site of presence and excitation and, hence, is better than no object at all. This truism is not far from Nietzsche's line that the will would rather will nothingness than not will at all. In both cases, the desire to desire is a willingness to desire precisely that which would foreclose desire, if only for the possibility of continuing to desire.

The question, then, that Hegel and Freud would appear to pose for Foucault is whether this terrain of "stubborn attachment" does not in some way figure in the scenarios of subjection that he describes. To what extent does a regulatory regime exploit this willingness to attach blindly to that which seeks the suppression or negation of that very attachment? And to what extent does the attachment that a regulatory regime requires prove to be both its constitutive failure and the potential site of resistance? If desire has as its final aim the continuation of itself—and here one might link Hegel, Freud, and Foucault back to Spinoza's *conatus*—then the capacity of desire to be withdrawn and to reattach will constitute something like the vulnerability of every strategy of subjection.

Notes

1. In the following text I refer to this chapter in an abbreviated form as "The Unhappy Consciousness." English citations are from *The Phenomenology of Spirit,* A.V. Miller translation, Oxford University Press; German citations are from the *Werke,* vol. 3, Suhrkamp Verlag, 1980.

2. See Herbert Marcuse's reading in *Eros and Civilization* and Jessica Benjamin's *Bonds of Love* for two positions that move from lordship and bondage to the concept of reciprocal recognition without paying close attention to the turning against liberation and equality enacted in "The Unhappy Consciousness." On the other hand, a much underread essay, Jean Wahl's *Le malheur de la conscience,* takes the unhappy consciousness to constitute the central paradox of Hegel's anthropology. His essay, first published in 1929, was enormously influential on Jean Hyppolite, Alexandre Kojève, and others who argued against the view of Hegel as a defender of a closed systematic totality.

196 ■ Judith Butler

3. Michel Foucault, *Discipline and Punish*, trans. Alan Sheridan (New York: Vintage, 1979), 30.

4. "L'homme dont on nous parle et qu'on invite à liberer est déjà en lui-même l'effet d'un assujettissement bien plus profond que lui. Une 'âme' l'habite et le porte à l'existence, qui est elle-même une pièce dans la mâitrise que le pouvoir exerce sur le corps. L'âme, effet et instrument d'une anatomie politique; l'âme, prison du corps." Ibid., 34.

5. The relevance of the psychoanalytic understanding of the "phantasmic" and, in particular, the view of Laplanche and Pontalis that the subject is *dissimulated* in the scene of phantasy. We might consider the various stages of progress in the *Phenomenology* as successive forms of the phantasmic, that is, successive ways in which the subject becomes dissimulated in and as the scene of its action.

6. It is difficult to know what word to use to describe the reflexive turn of sadism here. It seems that "internalization" is too fully linked with certain forms of psychoanalysis to be altogether right in this context. I will try to use Hegel's own terminology as far as possible.

7. "Sein Denken als solches bleibt das gestaltlose Sausen des Glockengeläutes oder eine warme Nebelerfüllung, ein musikalisches Denken, das nicht zum Begriffe, der die einzige immanente gegenständliche Weise wäre, kommt" (168).

8. "[D]as Grab seines *wirklichen* unwandelbaren Wesens [hat] *keine Wirklichkeit*" (69–70).

9. Cf. Kierkegaard, *Sickness Unto Death*, for the paradox of not having one's ground in oneself.

10. Friedrich Nietzsche, *On the Genealogy of Morals*, trans. Walter Kaufmann (New York: Vintage, 1980); *Friedrich Nietzsche: Werke, Band 11*, Hanser Editions, 1981.

12. Sigmund Freud, *Civilization and its Discontents*, trans. Strachey (New York: Norton, 1977). Cited in text as *CD*. Other places where Freud discusses the origins of conscience include "On Narcissism: An Introduction," and *The Ego and the Id.*

12. See Freud, "On Narcissism: An Introduction," for a discussion of the repression of homosexuality and the origins of conscience.

13. Here one can see that Foucault's critique of Freud in *The History of Sexuality, Volume 1* is partially wrong.

14. My translation from the German: "[S]ie brachte alles Leiden unter die Perspektive der schuld. . . . Aber trotz alledem—der Mensch war damit *gerettet*, er hatte einen *Sinn*, . . . er konnte nunmehr etwas wollen gleichgültig zunächst, wohin, wozu, womit, er wollte: *der Wille selbst war gerettet*" (900). Consider the remarks with which Nietzsche then closes *Zur Genealogie der Moral*: "[L]ieber will noch der Mensch das Nichts wollen also nicht wollen. . . ." (900).

The Ring of Being: Nietzsche, Freud and the History of Conscience

Ned Lukacher

THE RING OF CONSCIENCE

> The manner of Dasein's coming back to its past is, among other things, conscience.
>
> —Martin Heidegger, "The Concept of Time"

Annulus aeternitatis, "ring of eternity," was the title of the final section of a projected four-part work that Friedrich Nietzsche planned in August 1881 but never wrote.[1] It was to have concluded his "Projection of 'A New Way of Life.'" The phrase reappears a few years later in Book Three of *Thus Spoke Zarathustra*, in the section entitled "The Convalescent":

> "O Zarathustra," the animals said, "to those who think as we do, all things themselves are dancing: they come and offer their hands and laugh and flee—and come back. Everything goes, everything comes back; eternally rolls the wheel of being. Everything dies, everything blossoms again; eternally runs the year of being. Everything breaks, everything is joined anew; eternally the same house of being is built. Everything parts, everything greets every other thing again; eternally the ring of being *[der Ring des Seins]* remains faithful to itself. In every Now, being begins; round every Here rolls the There. The center is everywhere. Bent is the path of eternity *[Krumm ist der Pfad der Ewigkeit]*."[2]

It would be difficult to find another passage in Nietzsche that has proved more decisive for Martin Heidegger and for the Nietzschean tradition in general. Zarathustra's animals are responding to his question about the nature of language, the answer to which is important to his convalescence on the way to a new existence, one in which his relation to his world, to himself, and to language is radically reinvented after a long and painful catharsis. The dance, the wheel, the house of being, the ring, and the jointure of all things into a unifying structure are thus culminating figures for Zarathustra's transformation into the "teacher of eternal recurrence." Zarathustra's question anticipates the form of its answer: "Are not words and sounds rainbows and illusive bridges between things which are eternally apart?" (329). It is language that comes back eternally in order to create the illusion of bridging the gap between mind and nature.

The "ring of being" is a figure at the limits of figuration, a figure not only for the cosmological finitude of space-time, but also for the inner relations of language and subjectivity. The jointure of the ring of being provides a memorable poetic image for Zarathustra's "most abysmal thought" (328), while Zarathustra himself has nothing but contempt for the aesthetic uses of figurative language. Zarathustra is convalescing from the thought of eternal recurrence, a thought that chokes and disgusts him because it means that everything, the highest and the lowest things, including even himself, must eternally recur. What must be renounced and given up, what one must recover from, is the anticipation of getting outside oneself, getting outside the ring of existence to which language consigns us. Zarathustra's new relation to language means that he no longer seeks the one true metaphor for being, and that he no longer wants to create the aesthetic pleasure of creating the illusion of passing from finitude to the infinite, beyond the ring, beyond the ontological difference between beings and Being. While language is the very stuff of this disjunctive connection, what comes around again and again in eternal recurrence, it is also what makes us forget the thought of eternal recurrence behind the aesthetic pleasures of rhetorical invention:

> [H]ow should there be any outside-myself? There is no outside. But all sounds make us forget this. . . . Have not names and sounds been given to things that man might find things refreshing? Speaking is a beautiful folly: with that man dances over all things. (329)

The ring is properly an *annulus*, the mark or trace that binds, that signals a marriage or contract between the poetic thinker and the doctrine of eternal recurrence, between the "advocate of suffering, the advocate of the circle" (328) and his conscience. But in order to recover, the convalescent must turn to poetic song. During a necessary transitional stage, the poetic thinker will learn to sing and dance in language, for it may be a long time before the thought of eternal recurrence can be brought back to the health of prose. "For singing is for the convalescent," the animals tell Zarathustra, "the healthy can speak. And when the healthy man also wants songs, he wants different songs from the convalescent" (332).

For Plato, writes Heidegger, "Particular beings and Being are differently located."[3] Nietzsche's "ring of being" relocates Being back within the realm of being; it does away with the inside/outside metaphors on which the Platonic tradition relies by insisting that the character of Being lies *within* the ring, in the realm of becoming, and that what is infinite is not what lies outside, but rather the materiality and force on the inside. Instead of an infinite spatial-temporal realm outside the ring, which has always been at the basis of Western metaphysics, Nietzsche insists that the finitude of space-time itself has an infinite temporal dimension, which he calls "eternal recurrence." In section 1067 of *The Will to Power*, Nietzsche writes of the world as "a sea of forces storming and raging in itself, eternally changing, eternally running back, over monstrous ages of recurrence."[4] It is a finite world "enclosed by 'nothing' as by a boundary." Nietzsche goes on to speak of "the joy of the circle" as a "ring," which, perhaps "without will," "holds goodwill unto itself" (550). Nietzsche joins the thought of eternal recurrence to the liminal figure of the ring, while the will to power is linked to the raging sea of force and matter. As Heidegger has noted, will to power and eternal recurrence, far from being at odds with each other, are inseparable in Nietzsche's thinking. The spatial finitude of will to power is inseparable from the temporality of eternal recurrence. This is from Nietzsche's notes during the early 1880s: "[F]inite as space, infinite as time—with the indestructible is given eternity and beginninglessness—with determinateness, a border, perhaps new forms."[5] While there is no one true metaphor, we might imagine the temporal displacements of a spatial form, namely the ring, along a linear line like a series of circles or curved forms as they spiral down through the eons along a linear trajectory. The ring comes into being again and again, but in discrete cycles whose temporal difference we can spatialize in the figure of the line.

Nietzsche himself wants to unsettle any aesthetic pleasure we might quietly take in figuring eternal recurrence as a cyclical movement. "Let us beware," he writes in *The Gay Science*, "of positing generally and everywhere anything as elegant as the cyclical movements of our neighboring stars; even a glance into the Milky Way raises doubts whether there are not coarser and more contradictory movements there, as well as stars with eternally linear paths, etc."[6] This advice is all by way of encouraging a general abandonment of the language of our deep-seated "aesthetic anthropomorphisms" (168). Nietzsche is always on guard against the insidious effect of such anthropomorphisms, for they are what resist "our de-deification of nature" and postpone the effort "to *'naturalize'* humanity in terms of a pure, newly discovered, newly redeemed nature" (169). The relation of the circle to the line is a version of the relation of figurative language to language as such, with all its nonreflective, noncognitive grammatical and syntactic elements. We too easily mistake the random motions along the line for a purposeful aesthetic delight of the curve. Nietzsche recognizes the impossibility of ever purifying language of its figural lies and aberrations but nevertheless insists on being as scrupulous as possible. Indeed, it was the "will to lie," the will to believe in a nonexistent transcendent order beyond the ring, that turned the real world into a fable, and that led Nietzsche to the thought of will to power. We might think of will of power at one level as the marking of curves and lines between points and lines, and at another the imposition of rationalizing and idealizing figures of speech upon the random movements of force and matter, and language.

The abandonment of "aesthetic anthropomorphisms" is essential to the scathing honesty Nietzsche demands of the thinker of eternal recurrence:

> [W]e should not reinterpret the exceedingly derivative, late, rare, accidental [human reality], that we perceive only on the crust of the earth and make of it something essential, universal, and eternal, which is what those people do who call the universe an organism. This nauseates me. Let us beware of believing that the universe is a machine: it is certainly not constructed for one purpose, and calling it a "machine" does it far too much honor. (*The Gay Science*, 168)

Vigilance with regard to language is the essential form in which Nietzsche expresses the moral implications of eternal recurrence and will to power. Human existence on the crust of the planet can know itself only through its particularity. The teleology implicit in figural language invariably conceals the divided self-relation that is essential to eternal recurrence.

Will to power is always particular, always imbedded in the matter and force of the moment, a moment that is always divided. Will to power is what recurs in eternal recurrence; it is the particular history that takes on a transcendental character by finally appearing irreducible to anything but itself. That moment is divided between what are in effect two discrete temporalities: the presentness of the present as it appears to human reflection and the presentness of the present as it appears against a temporal horizon beyond the capacity of reflection, lost in the unimaginable abyss of space-time. "[T]he doctrine of will to power," writes Heidegger, "springs from nowhere else than eternal return, carrying the mark of its origin always with it, as the stream of its source."[7] Will to power "springs" from eternal recurrence and retains its mark, the mark of another temporality, whose noncoincidence, whose non-identity, is precisely what we experience on the crust of this planet. Conscientiousness is nothing if not a keeping faith with the still withheld answers to the enigmas of existence. One shows bad faith and may suffer from bad conscience by imposing figurative answers on the imponderable. The artist's way of life leads the subject through the most excruciating trajectory. We can only become "new," in Nietzsche's idiom, by sacrificing ourselves to the thought of eternal return, by allowing it to stream into our will to power, by allowing the heat of this thought to turn one to "ashes": "You must wish to consume yourself in your own flame: how could you wish to become new unless you had first become ashes?" (176). It is from this sacrificial experience that one must convalesce.

One of Zarathustra's disciples calls him "the leech of conscience" precisely because the thought of eternal recurrence puts the bite back into the bite of conscience. The disciple who prostrates himself in the swamp in order to be covered with leeches might be regarded as exhibiting the *via negativa* of discipleship. "The conscience of my spirit," claims the disciple, "demands of me that I know one thing and nothing else," and he concludes by repeating Zarathustra's own words: "Spirit is the life that itself cuts into life" (363). The ethics of affirming the pain of an impossible purification becomes the new categorical imperative of Nietzsche's new conscience, which is precisely not the conscience of self-reflection, not a mode of reflection but of its abysses. The history of will to power is the history of mankind's defenses against the gap, caesura, the illusive bridge, between mind and nature, between thinking and the truth. We have always dealt with the anxiety and guilt of that nonknowledge by inventing figures that make us forget the abyss on which our thinking and speaking totter. Willing, as Heidegger remarks, is the power of "being out beyond oneself," not by closing oneself off in a fixed motion but rather by "resolute openness" or *Entschlossenheit*, a resoluteness that opens rather than constricting, that opens onto an enigma beyond the will of a personal self.[8] Aesthetic figures are helpful to a point, but can become obstacles to the very openness they may mean to encourage. What is the relation between the point at which the temporality of eternal recurrence cuts into our experience of the present moment and the point at which we learn to listen to language as such rather than imposing aesthetically pleasing figures, which, while they might afford the willful pleasure of discharging a quota of energy, must be sacrificed if one is to attain a purer understanding and experience? Though Nietzsche sometimes appears to want to transcend the entire mechanism of cathartic purgation, it is in fact only the moral interpretation he wishes to abandon so that catharsis may resume its quasi-medical status as a function of involuntary physiological responses beyond the intervention of a self-conscious subject. Nietzsche's new conscience is precisely the effort to attain a purely somatic catharsis, indeed, the catharsis of thinking from consciousness. The separation of the will from subjectivity is a necessary corollary to the separation in the moment itself. Nietzsche's catharsis of the will is the process of the will's becoming unconscious, of its submergence, its "going under," into unconscious somatic states. The division of the present in what Zarathustra calls the "gateway" *(Torwegs)* of the "Moment" where two paths, "two eternities," meet "face to face" (*Thus Spoke Zarathustra*, 269–70) is the metaphysical version of the division within conscience between the self-conscious subject and the unconscious will. It is precisely the unconscious element in conscience that makes *Gewißen* such a crucial notion to Nietzsche, for in effect it names the point at which eternal recurrence streams into will to power, the point at which the unconscious will overtakes the subject of reflection.

Let us move now from the illusive bridge of language in *Zarathustra* to the analysis of bad conscience in *On the Genealogy of Morals*, where once again it is a question of the bridge. Nietzsche's concern here is to write the history of conscience and, above all, to invent the primal scene in which the human animal first experiences the divisive enigma of self-reflection. Everything begins in the instinctual realization "that pain is the most powerful aid to mnemonics."[9] Debts are enforced by the threat of violence, and thus the social bond itself is forged from the fear of not paying back a debt. The ability to make a promise and thus to risk retaliation marks the advent of an incredible event: "the extraordinary privilege of *responsibility*, the consciousness of this rare freedom, this power over oneself and over fate" (60). Over the eons, this consciousness "penetrated to the profoundest depths and became instinct, the dominating instinct." All ethical obligations thus draw upon "the terror that formerly attended all promises, pledges, and vows" (61). Even Kant's categorical imperative still "smells of cruelty" (65). The creation of "a memory for the human animal" forces the animal out of "the passing moment" and into an unconscious temporality organized by language and memory.

It is the becoming unconscious, the becoming instinct, of the painful consciousness of fear and anxiety about unpaid debts that initiates what Nietzsche calls mankind's "gravest and uncanniest illness, from which humanity has not recovered, man's suffering of *man, of himself*—the result of a forcible sundering from his animal past, as it were a leap and plunge into new surroundings and conditions of existence, a declaration of war against the old instincts upon which his strength, joy, and terribleness had rested hitherto" (85). The illness of bad conscience marks the beginning of the emergence of the thought of eternal recurrence, the thought of another temporality, into the life of the human animal, the beginning of the cut of spirit into life, from within life itself. Here, of course, lies Heidegger's essential complaint, that Nietzsche's understanding of the emergence of conscience is purely biologistic, empirical and anthropological to a fault, since it obviates the equally constitutive role of language itself and thus ignores the nonpathological, non-objective order of subjectless willing. As we saw in *Thus Spoke Zarathustra*, we can now see in *On the Genealogy of Morals* that language is always essential to Nietzsche's understanding of that "fine species of bad conscience" called "responsibility."[10] While Nietzsche might use biological figures of speech, he is as concerned as Heidegger in the entirely nonsubjective element that is nevertheless discernible in subjectivity itself. "Bad conscience is an illness," writes Nietzsche, "but an illness as pregnancy is an illness." We might call the rest of this passage of *On the Genealogy of Morals* Nietzsche's *Ereignis*, his account of the appropriation of human being by something beyond it, i.e., will to power, language, or by whatever figure you can think of for what lies at the limit, at the edge of the ring:

> Let us add at once that, on the other hand, the existence on earth of an animal soul turned against itself, taking sides against itself, was some-

thing so new, profound, unheard of, enigmatic, contradictory, *and pregnant with a future* that the aspect of the earth was essentially altered. Indeed, divine spectators were needed to do justice to the spectacle that thus began and the end of which is not yet in sight—a spectacle too subtle, too marvellous, too paradoxical to be played senselessly unobserved on some ludicrous planet! From now on, man is *included* among the most unexpected and exciting lucky throws in the dice game of Heraclitus's "great child," be he called Zeus or chance; he gives rise to an interest, a tension, a hope, almost a certainty, as if with him something were announcing and preparing itself, as if man were not a goal but only a way, an episode, a bridge, a great promise. (85)

The event of making promises becomes itself the bridge to yet another promise, the promise that human existence is the path on which some nonsubjective thing is traveling with the human. In *Zarathustra* Nietzsche writes of the creation of the world in terms of the "child's self-propelling wheel, a first motion, a sacred 'Yes'" (139). The event of bad conscience marks the entry of human being into the game. Will to power is not simply biological, physical force within matter; it is that capacity of force to check itself, it is that part of life that cuts into life, that part of instinct that turns on instinct itself, and it is no more irreducibly biological than it is irreducibly linguistic. What we experience as the *morsus conscientiae*, the bite of conscience, is also the appropriation of human being by language, the appropriation of will to power by eternal recurrence, of consciousness by an unconscious will.

To the dwarf's notion that "'All truth is crooked *[krumm]*; time itself is a circle,'" Zarathustra responds, "'Don't make things too easy for yourself'" (270). Nietzsche tries always to check the persuasive power of his own figures of speech. To regard conscience as "an organ, like the stomach," or to mount a "moral theory from a zoological point of view," is to disrupt our idealizing notions about these issues, which can never be done without also risking new idealizations.[11] Heidegger is constantly alert to aesthetic subterfuges in Nietzsche, and Paul de Man takes this vigilance still further. But Nietzsche not only anticipates such vigilance, he also anticipates its limits: "[T]here is only one world, and it is false, cruel, and contradictory, seductive, meaningless. *We need to lie* in order to overcome this reality, this 'truth', that is, in order to live. That the lie is necessary in order to live, is what arises again and again from the dubious character of existence."[12] Will to power is synonymous with the power of the promise and the lie. Nietzsche holds out no promise of an end to the power of the lie, of an end to bad conscience, or of an end to the reign of idealist moral philosophy. The most he promises is a coming "war of the spirits" and "the most profound collision of conscience" *(Gewißens-Kollision)* (327). While the line will from time to time disrupt the dance of the circle and spiral, and while language as such will at times unravel the language of self-reflexive figures, there will always be recourse to aesthetic subterfuge.

What happens to Nietzsche's elaboration of his history of conscience after *On the Genealogy of Morals* might be best described as Nietzsche's own catastrophic "collision of conscience." There are two major strands in his discussions of conscience in his later writings: the first is devoted to excoriating the abuses of conscience, to attacks upon what he calls "conscience-vivisection," which proceeds by making "every Yes and No a matter of conscience" (*The Will to Power*, 632). These ills he attributes to the Judeo-Christian tradition and its morbid delight in the most ancient cruelties of conscience. On the other hand, Nietzsche also assaults the decadent, pleasure-loving mentality of modernity that has lost all respect for itself, and for which conscience has in effect lost its teeth. As he remarks in *Twilight of the Idols* and *The Will to Power*, conscience has lost its bite, and the question of conscience has become "a dentist's question" (*The Will to Power*, 467). These figures of conscience risk blurring and losing sight of the fundamental allegory of conscience that was Nietzsche's original objective. He places before himself the difficult task of correcting both the perverse excesses of the religious conscience and the equally perverse diminution of conscience in the secular world. His frustration appears to have reached its culmination in *The Anti-Christ*, where he sharpens the vague poetic prehistory of conscience in *On the Genealogy of Morals* into a focused attack on the great betrayal of the promise of bad conscience that occurred during the invention of the Jewish conscience.

The Greeks had their gods "precisely so as to ward off the 'bad conscience,' so as to be able to rejoice in their freedom of soul—the very opposite of the use to which Christianity put its God" (*On the Genealogy of Morals*, 94). In *The Anti-Christ* he reiterates that "Christianity has cheated us out of the harvest of ancient culture" and proclaims "A new conscience for truths that have so far remained mute."[13] Some of these unheard truths are appallingly familiar: "[T]he Jews are the *most catastrophic* people in world history," and "by their aftereffect *[Nachwirkung]* they have made mankind so thoroughly false that even today the Christian can feel anti-Jewish without realizing that he himself is the ultimate

206 ■ Ned Lukacher

Jewish consequence" (*The Anti-Christ*, 593). Nietzsche speaks of the "vampirism" of the rabbinical perversion of the will to power through the "holy lie" of the guilty conscience of a chosen people (630ff.). Thanks to the Jews, bad conscience is turned into "Judaine" (642), the poison of Jewishness. The scurrilous influence of such statements has been incalculable. Though Nietzsche focuses much of his attack upon Christianity as the essence of the Jewish spirit, and though he has little concrete discussion of the Old Testament or the scholarship on it, the book's anti-Semitic character is particularly virulent, perhaps because it everywhere implies that, if in the work of Paul and the other major Christian theologians the Jewish instinct against life and freedom remains so palpable and pernicious, then Judaism itself must be utterly unimaginable. And none of the positive things Nietzsche has to say elsewhere about the Jewish character can lessen the gravity of the charges he here levels against Jewish religious culture.[14]

In *The Anti-Christ* the theoretical project of writing the history of conscience becomes the practical project of clearing the ground for a reinvention of conscience by first dismantling the notion of conscience as the *vox Dei*, as the internalization of a transcendent script, what Paul calls the "circumcision of the heart" (Rom. 2:29). The new conscience faces its mysterious foundation with a minimum of aesthetic-theological mediation. The cutting edge of the Pauline conscience remains, for Nietzsche, a blunt and clumsy instrument whose only purpose is to shield mankind from the abyss of the truth.

Though Nietzsche has contempt for the Judeo-Christian interpretation of conscience, he does not want to do without the question of conscience, even if it has been reduced to a "dentist's question." The thought of eternal recurrence and will to power reach their culmination in the task of fashioning a new conscience that can bear to gaze upon the truth, that can bear the thought of the "ring of being," of the finitude of space and the infinity of time. But what is left of conscience once it is separated from its ideal moral ground? Has it become a receptacle like the stomach? Nietzsche's new conscience is the self-tormenting will of the spirit that knows itself as that which feeds upon itself.

CONSCIENCE AND ITS DISCONTENTS

[T]he question arises whether these particularly meaningful movements or events are not being generated by random and superficial

properties of the signifier rather than by the constraints of meaning. The obliteration of thought by "measure" would then have to be interpreted as the loss of semantic depth and its replacement by what Mallarmé calls "le hasard infini des conjonctions."
—Paul de Man, "Shelley Disfigured"

In *Civilization and Its Discontents*, Freud describes the formation of conscience in terms of the sending and receiving of something like a letter:

[The individual's] aggressiveness is introjected, internalized; it is, in point of fact, sent back to where it came from *[aber dorthin zurück-geschickt]*—that is, it is directed towards his own ego. There it is taken over by a portion of the ego, which sets itself over against the rest of the ego, and which now, in the form of "conscience," is ready to put into action against the ego the same harsh aggressiveness that the ego would have liked to satisfy upon the other, extraneous individuals. The tension between the harsh super-ego and the ego that is subjected to it, is called by us the sense of guilt; it expresses itself as a need for punishment. Civilization, therefore, obtains mastery over the individual's dangerous desire for aggression by weakening and disarming it and by setting up an agency *[Instanz]* within him to watch over it, like a garrison in a conquered city.[15]

We might call this passage "the instance of the letter between Nietzsche and Lacan." Between Nietzsche's internalization *(Verinnerlichung)* and Lacan's *instance de la lettre*, Freud thinks of the circulation of instinct in terms of return mail. But this is not just any letter that is being sent back; it is the destructive or sadistic drive that the ego had projected into the external world. Civilization demands the internalization of the sadistic drives, but their internalization in turn causes the members of society to suffer a guilty conscience, to fall ill, and thus civilization itself begins to decay and weaken. Freud is worried that the modern ego has weakened like a city under siege. Freud wonders whether bad conscience was finally too high a price to pay for civilization.

In an extraordinary passage in *The Ego and the Id*, Freud describes the attacks of the superego on the ego in terms of biological decomposition:

In suffering under the attacks of the super-ego or perhaps even succumbing to them, the ego is meeting with a fate like that of the protista that are destroyed by the products of decomposition that they themselves

have created. From the economic point of view the morality that functions in the super-ego seems to be a similar product of decomposition
[*Zersetzung*].[16]

What Freud in this text calls "conscience anxiety" *(Gewißensangst)* is one
of the by-products of the decomposition of the ego. Freud is thus elaborating a quantifiable empirical language for Nietzsche's nearly identical
diagnosis of the ravages of bad conscience.

The sending back of the letter is thus also a kind of decomposition in
which the ego is destroyed by its inability to discharge the destructive
drive it has internalized. "In the course of an individual's development,"
writes Freud in *Moses and Monotheism*, "a portion of the inhibiting forces
[hemmenden Mächte] in the external world are internalized *[verinnerlicht]*
and an agency *[Instanz]* is constructed in the ego which confronts the
rest of the ego in an observing, criticizing and prohibiting sense."[17] The
very thing that makes mankind a bridge for something greater than itself
can also become the thing that lacerates too deeply, becomes too dominant. The *Verinnerlichung* of Freud and Nietzsche becomes the *Lichtung*
or "clearing" in Heidegger, for conscience is built in a strange topology
within the ego, but over it the ego has no control, and it in fact controls
the ego, often with excessive severity. Psychoanalysis is finally reducible
to a science for healing egos damaged by poorly constructed, or over-
active, superegos. The task of the new conscience is to build otherwise in
the clearing within the ego that has ascendancy over the ego; the task is
to make the thing to which the ego belongs better, more efficient in its
dispensation of pleasure and guilt. Like Nietzsche, Freud wants to teach
his contemporaries to affirm their bad conscience, to know that their
feelings of guilt and anxiety result from oedipal conflicts, from the struggle
to resist and internalize parental figures and other elements in the external world. If such recognition is not forthcoming, they fear that humankind will decline into either a general consciencelessness or a neurotic
paralysis beneath the burden of bad conscience.

Freud's *Trieblehre* or "theory of drives" is ultimately a contest between
Triebanspruch, the "call or demand of the drive," and *Triebverzicht*, the
"renunciation of the drive." The ego or sexual drive seizes the world,
makes it its own, and answers the *Triebanspruch*, while a portion of it, a
strange otherness within the instinct that threatens the interests of life
itself, is turned back on the subject by parents, by society, by language
itself, and is set up within the ego. When this turning back, this "instinctual

renunciation," is received back by its sender, we reach what Zarathustra's disciple called "the life that itself cuts into life"; it is at this point that the will to power that is still life-affirming begins to turn deathly, reveals an otherness within itself, what Freud calls the "death drive" *(Todestrieb)*. It is that turning back, that ringing round, that opens the way to the bridge, to a greater promise, as well as to pain, suffering, and illness. Eros and Thanatos, sex and death, good and evil, are distinct and irreducible moments in a temporal process that is at once life-sustaining and destructive of life. The ego of modernity desires the very thing that is destroying it. It takes pleasure in the symptoms of its own internal compulsions. Freud begins to see that the ego's dependence on its own symptoms is a sign that there is something "beyond the pleasure principle."

In the work of that title, in *The Ego and the Id* (1923), and other works of the 1920s, Freud laid the groundwork for the full-scale analysis of conscience that begins in *Civilization and Its Discontents* (1930) and that culminates in *Moses and Monotheism* (1939). The abyss of conscience opens up in the zone of compulsive repetition, in the neurotic affirmation of self-punishment and renunciation: "In the end we come to see that we are dealing with what may be called a 'moral' factor, a sense of guilt *[Schuldgefühl]*, which is finding its satisfaction in the illness and refuses to give up *[nicht verzichten will]* the punishment of suffering" (39; *G.W.*, 13:279). Conscience itself is not primordial here; it is only what is constructed in the place where *Triebverzicht* goes to work. Conscience is an abyss because the guilt that it draws upon must already have been there before the man-made apparatus was installed. That is why Freud speaks of a "primal guilt" that was "in existence before *[daß es früher besteht]* the super-ego, and therefore before conscience" (*Civilization and Its Discontents*, 83). Before conscience, in the clearing where it will rise, Freud detects an irreducible empirical quota of fear: the "sensory material *[Empfindungsmaterial]* of the anxiety that is operating behind *[dahinter]* the sense of guilt" (84; *G.W.*, 14:496).

But what is the empiricity of this "material"? Does it come from the ego's fear of the external world or fear of its own libido? The notion of "primal guilt" marks yet another differentiation in the impossible effort to discover the ground of experience. What is the nature of this preexistent "earliness" that precedes conscience and the superego? It is as though, for Freud, human reflection were essentially a defensive mechanism, an instinctive fear of instinct itself. "Primal guilt" lies on the threshold between organic life and inorganic existence, and between life and death;

it is at once life's protection against death and the work of death always already at work in life itself.

What had been humankind's premodern fear of nature has become, in the administered world, in the epoch of internalized bio-power, a fear of unbridled will to power, of the invasiveness of a subjectless system within the subject's unconscious. Adorno's diagnosis is highly Freudian in this regard: "Panic breaks out once again, after millennia of enlightenment, over a humanity whose control of nature as control of human beings far exceeds in horror anything they ever had to fear from nature."[18] Conscience is itself only a relatively recent mode of administering fear, of channeling and circulating it within subjectivities and in order to serve certain social or communal goals.

In this sense, both Nietzsche's new conscience and Freud's psychoanalytic conscience are efforts to think what lies before conscience, before the self-reflection and self-certainty of conscience, and thus what is finally the active agency of conscience, the unconscious will that empowers conscience. And it is at this point that Freud's *Trieblehre* itself begins to decompose into a monism. "Both kinds of instinct," writes Freud, "would be active in every particle of living substance, though in unequal proportions. . . . This hypothesis throws no light whatever upon the manner in which the two classes of instincts are fused, blended, and alloyed with each other; but that this takes place regularly and very extensively is an assumption indispensable to our conception" (31; *G.W.*, 13:269). Conscience is the site of a primordial and irreducible fear that cannot be purged away by aesthetic-rhetorical figuration or externalized in an imaginary effort at liberation.

Nietzsche's animadversions against the moral interpretation of catharsis are consistent throughout his career, from section 22 of *The Birth of Tragedy* to *Twilight of the Idols* and the numerous related entries in the *Nachlaß* during the late 1880s: rather than purging the subject of pity and fear, the "vehement discharge" of these dangerous emotions takes one "beyond pity and terror, *to realize in oneself* the eternal joy of becoming —that joy which also encompasses *joy of destruction*."[19] Catharsis is the affirmation of the destructive power of internalization, not its suppression or its moral-aesthetic concealment behind idealizing moral platitudes. The healing power of the Dionysian sacrifice lies at the heart of Nietzschean catharsis, and it attests to the abyssal horrors into which the Greek tragedians, though not the Greek philosophers, dared to look. It is thus fitting that Nietzsche should call "the sacrifice of [life's] highest types" "the *bridge* to the psychology of the tragic poet" (my emphasis). The diminution of the spirit of tragedy is thus a necessary corollary to the failure of will in Platonism and Judeo-Christianity, and its refusal to face the violent power of internalization.

Nietzsche believes that the catharsis of fear and pity, rather than purging the subject, brings about an intensification of fear and pity in which the pain itself is transformed into a joyous affirmation of the desperate truth of the human condition. Rather than celebrating the moral and aesthetic virtues of a clean conscience, Nietzsche's celebrates the pain of guilty conscience itself and makes its irreducibility into the highest virtue.

In his analysis of catharsis in "Psychopathic Characters on the Stage" (c. 1906), Freud is concerned with our resistance to the causes of suffering, which can originate with the gods, in human conflict, or within the self. And resistance is precisely a question of conscience, a question of how much force we are able to marshal against the reemergence of repressed material. Hamlet, for example, is tortured by conscience because his superego resists the return of the incestuous wish. The aesthetic pleasure that we derive from our identification with the tragic protagonist depends entirely on how we respond to the recognition of the repressed material. And this is the point at which Freud has a rather significant insight. Unless we are as neurotic as Hamlet, we will not take pleasure in identifying with someone who is experiencing the desublimation of incestuous desires. The considerable amount of libidinal expenditure, the sheer effort of will necessary to keep the repressed material at bay, would preclude our deriving much pleasure from the identification. We take pleasure in the protagonist's struggles of conscience precisely by not having to realize the nature of the repressed material. The delight of catharsis thus inheres in the shared experience of the character's will to power over what must remain a nameless eruption in the unconscious. Though it may be "recognizable," it is "never given a definite name": "in the spectator too the process is carried through with his attention averted, and he is in the grip of his emotions instead of taking stock of what is happening" (*S.E.*, 7:309). Freud's implication is clear: because the cathartic pleasure of identification depends on reducing the expenditure of resistance, both protagonist and spectator must avert their attention from the content of the unconscious wish. The shared struggle of conscience becomes at once moral and aesthetic only at the price of foreclosing the immoral and unaesthetic nature of the repressed material. Freud's insight reveals, in Adorno's words, that the "substitute gratification [of catharsis] has always been attended by the repression of instincts."[20] Freud's remarks also reveal that an anti-aesthetic catharsis will necessarily entail a new conscience.

They introduce as well the notion of "identification" as fundamental to understanding the operations of conscience and the will: the experience of the play enables the spectator to satisfy his or her secret ambitions "to stand in his own person at the hub of world affairs," and thus *"to identify oneself* with a hero" (*S.E.*, 7:305). The nature of one's conscience depends on making such identifications early in life with parental figures. The gender of conscience belies the gender of this identification, which might be plural. The problem of determining how what starts out from the id as a sadistic sexual instinct can return to the ego as Thanatos depends, for Freud, on the "defusion" of the sexual instinct so that only its destructive components remain. We might call the following passage on the identifications in conscience an account of how we learn to fear what we once thought we could control:

> The super-ego arises, as we know, from an identification with the father as model. Every such identification is in the nature of a desexualization or even of a sublimation. It now seems as though when a transformation of this kind takes place, an instinctual defusion *[Triebentmischung]* occurs at the same time. After sublimation, the erotic component no longer has the power to bind *[zu binden]* the whole of the destructiveness that was combined with it, and this is released in the form of an inclination to aggression and destruction. This defusion would be the source of the general character of harshness and cruelty exhibited by the ideal *[das Ideal]*—its dictatorial "Thou shalt." *(The Ego and the Id,* 44–45; *G. W.,* 13:284–85)

A history of conscience would have to posit a specific historical origin for this generic account of the birth of conscience through the internalization of the death drive. Remember that for Nietzsche this is the moment of infection, the moment of the Mosaic invention of the law, of conscience before the law and before the destructive (we might even call it "psychopathic") "Thou shalt."

Freud announces his concern about "the history of the origin of conscience" late in *Civilization and Its Discontents:*

> The aggressiveness of conscience keeps up the aggressiveness of the authority. So far things have no doubt been made clear; but where does

this leave room for the reinforcing influence of misfortune (of renunciation imposed from without), and for the extraordinary severity of conscience in the best and most tractable people? We have already explained both these peculiarities of conscience, but we probably still have the impression that those explanations do not go to the bottom of the matter, and leave a residue still unexplained. And here at last an idea comes in which belongs entirely to psychoanalysis and which is foreign to people's ordinary way of thinking. The idea is of a sort that enables us to understand why the subject matter was bound to seem so confused and obscure to us. For it tells us that conscience (or more correctly, the anxiety that later becomes conscience) is indeed the cause of instinctual renunciation to begin with, but that later the relationship is reversed. Every renunciation of instinct now becomes a dynamic source of conscience and every fresh renunciation increases the latter's severity and intolerance. If we could only bring it better into harmony with what we already know about the history of the origin of conscience, we should be tempted to defend the paradoxical statement that conscience is the result of instinctual renunciation, or that instinctual renunciation (imposed on us from without) creates conscience, which then demands further instinctual renunciation. (75–76)

Oedipal identification with the father means internalizing the renunciation of the prohibition against incest and making it the basis of one's self-relation, one's *cum scientia*, one's "knowing with oneself." The task is henceforth that of determining historically the point at which conscience becomes dynamically efficient and self-perpetuating. And this point must involve an oedipal murder, a murder of the father, not on the stage, but at the very origins of Western history. All the elements are in place for the invention of the primal scene in the history of the origin of conscience: the oedipal complex, the murder of the *Urvater*, the *Trieblehre*, and the psychoanalysis of conscience. There must have been a real murder and real guilt, Freud finally concluded, something "imposed on us from without," if we are to explain the historic power of Judeo-Christian instinctual renunciation and its secular derivations. There was one other decisive element: the publication of Ernst Sellin's *Moses and his Meaning for the History of the Israelite-Judaic Religion* (1922), where Freud discovered the hypothesis that Moses had been murdered.[21] Freud would end with the beginning, with the murder of Moses, the real event that must have started it all.

The extraordinary relation between *The Anti-Christ* and *Moses and Monotheism* deserves close attention. Both works come at the very end of a thinker's career (though for very different reasons), and both works purport to delineate a historical origin of the sense of guilt. For Nietzsche, the severity of the dynamic conscience is a Jewish invention, and submission to the law initiates a catastrophic historical error. Nietzsche had no suspicion just how catastrophic this invention proved to be. Freud, however, had a profoundly ominous sense of the catastrophe. And perhaps what most informs *Moses and Monotheism* is his sense that the long-besieged modern ego would soon rise up as never before and take its revenge on the regime of instinctual renunciation that had ruled for so long. The paganism of *The Anti-Christ* had formed the values of a generation. *Moses and Monotheism* is Freud's "Anti-*Anti-Christ*." In what will be his last prescription, Freud transforms Nietzsche's poisonous "Judaine" into the remedy for an ailing civilization.

Like Nietzsche, Freud realizes that German "hatred of the Jews is at bottom a hatred of Christians, and we need not be surprised that in the German National-Socialist revolution this intimate relation between two monotheist religions finds a clear expression in the hostile treatment of both of them" (*S.E.*, 23:92). With the world on the brink of its most massive oedipal crime, on the brink of its war against conscience and instinctual renunciation, Freud staged his great defense of instinctual renunciation. Having for years excoriated the cruelties of conscience in countless ways, Freud finally takes his stand with conscience.

Not only was Moses murdered by his rancorous followers, but he wasn't a Jew either; he was an Egyptian. Freud hypothesizes that the hypothetical Egyptian made his own original contribution to Akhenaton's revolutionary monotheism: "the harsh prohibition against making an image of any living or imagined creature" (*S.E.*, 23:19; *G.W.*, 16:117). The invention of Mosaic law takes on a truly Kantian sublimity in Freud's handling and becomes a "momentous step" into the "spiritual *[geistigen]* principle": "[I]deas, memories and inferences became decisive in contrast to the lower psychical activity that had direct perceptions by the sense-organs as its content. This was unquestionably one of the most important stages on the path to becoming human *[Menschwerdung]*" (*S.E.*, 23:113, translation modified). All the things that Nietzsche says occurred when the true world became a fable are here adduced as the exemplary steps toward the truth; and we should recall that Freud comes to this conclusion after almost two decades of otherwise very Nietzschean thinking about the intractability of guilt and the sexual nature of the unconscious will.

The Mosaic "victory of intellectuality *[Geistigkeit]* over sensuality," and of paternal ideation over the maternal body, may also, Freud speculates, include "the invention of the first alphabet": "If [the scribes of Moses] were subject to the prohibition against pictures, they would even have had a motive for abandoning the hieroglyphic picture-writing while adapting its written characters to expressing a new language" (*S.E.*, 23:43 n. 2). The invention of conscience is not simply contemporaneous with but also identical with the invention of alphabetic writing, or rather the purification of most of its pictorial elements. It was Moses who taught the human ego to make its sacrifices to the growing severity of conscience, to the superego, to language itself. Above all, Mosaic monotheism "renounced *[verzichtet]* immortality entirely; the possibility of existence continuing after death is nowhere and never mentioned" (*S.E.*, 23:20). The garrison tower is now in place, but not for long, for the Mosaic *Urvater* must be slain if the unprecedented power of his doctrine is to be felt as a persistent and insurmountable sense of guilt. Freud would agree entirely with Nietzsche's characterization of the radical historicity of will to power as a distinct drive or current within biological life, though not, *pace* Heidegger, reducible to the biological, but Freud differs entirely in seeing Judeo-Christianity as a great refinement of will to power rather than its morbid perversion. Integrating Sellin's hypothesis of the murder of Moses within his post-Nietzschean history of conscience, Freud speculates that Moses' followers could not "tolerate such a highly spiritualized *[vergeistigte]* religion and find satisfaction of their needs in what it had to offer. . . . [T]he savage Semites took fate into their own hands and rid themselves of their tyrant" (*S.E.*, 23:47; *G. W.*, 16:148–49). The Levitical scribes sought to conceal the murder by a "distortion" *(Entstellung)* of the written record that conflated the Egyptian Moses with the Midianite Moses, son-in-law of Jethro, a priest in the volcanic Yahweh religion. The ideational bias of alphabetic writing, which appears to elevate the "spiritual principle," does so only in order to conceal a crime. Bad conscience is literally invented by the double gesture of a new kind of writing that spiritualizes a murder.

What Nietzsche regarded as the rabbinical betrayal of "the great promise" that is the internalization of will to power, becomes for Freud the actualization of that promise:

> There was no place in the religion of Moses for a direct expression of the murderous hatred of the father. All that could come to light was a

mighty reaction against it — a sense of guilt on account of that hostility, a bad conscience for having sinned against God and for not ceasing to sin. This sense of guilt, which was uninterruptedly kept awake by the Prophets, and which soon formed an essential part of the religious system, had yet another superficial motivation, which neatly disguised [maskierte] its true origin. Things were going badly for the people; the hopes resting on the favour of God failed in fulfilment; it was not easy to maintain the illusion, loved above all else, of being God's chosen people. If they wished to avoid renouncing that happiness, a sense of guilt on account of their own sinfulness offered welcome means of exculpating God: they deserved no better than to be punished by him since they had not obeyed his commandments. And, driven by the need to satisfy this sense of guilt, which was insatiable [unersättlich] and came from sources so much deeper [und aus soviel tieferer Quelle kam], they must make those commandments grow ever stricter, more meticulous, and even more trivial. In a fresh rapture of moral asceticism they imposed more and more new instinctual renunciations on themselves and in that way reached—in doctrine and precept, at least— ethical heights which had remained inaccessible to other peoples of antiquity. (S.E., 23: 134; G. W., 16:243)

In order to explain the historical force of this now dynamic Jewish conscience, Freud relies upon the phylogenetic transmission of acquired traits. The establishment of a racial libidinal quota provides Freud with a hypothetical empirical ground for anti-Semitism and thus with a specifically racial conscience where the quota of libidinal force that could be imposed by the superego upon the ego is a measure of the guilt that has been imposed on a people from external sources. It is that force that Freud feels is waning in the late 1930s. The malaise of modern civilization in effect begins with the Prophets' creative libidinal management of guilt as a social bond. Freud writes that, by the time of Paul, the Jewish sense of guilt "had caught hold of all the Mediterranean peoples as a dull discontent [ein dumpfes Unbehagen]" (S.E., 23:135; G.W., 16:244). And Christianity was invented precisely in order to relieve that guilt, to lessen some of the pressure on the beleaguered ego. The religion of the son would afford some libidinal satisfaction by allowing a visual symbol of the noumenal realm and by its promise of an afterlife. Nietzsche, of course, speaks only of Paul's "rabbinical impudence" (The Anti-Christ, 616). For Freud, as for Nietzsche, however, Christianity remains no more than an aesthetic Judaism.

    Moses and Monotheism completes Freud's reinvention of Nietzsche's new conscience. But does not Freud's historicist hypothesis about the origin of conscience still betray its own idealizing, aesthetic presuppositions? Does not Nietzsche teach that figuration keeps us from suffering from the truth, and that, even while we try to withstand the storm that rushes from the abyss, we too will take figural shelter from the enigmas of language and existence? "Geist ist das Leben, das selber ins Leben schneidet," spirit is what cuts into life, it inscribes the trace of an inorganic force into the instincts of life, it is the essence of will to power, while figural language tries to heal the wound, to idealize the pain by purifying it away. That is why Freud describes the internalization of the law, why he figures the birth of conscience, as the respiration of *Geist*, as a "movement of the air" *(die bewegte Luft)*, and this movement is the "path *[Wege]* to our becoming human." But what is the materiality of this path? It is, of course, language itself. *Geist*, writes Freud at the end of *Moses and Monotheism*, "derives its name from a breath of wind—'animus,' 'spiritus,' and the Hebrew 'ruach' (breath)" (*S.E.*, 23:114).[22] But does *Geistigkeit* (intellectuality, spirituality) derive from inanimate, inorganic existence, or does it betray an aesthetic anthropomorphism? While Nietzsche wants to avoid all the idealizing tropes of the metaphysical tradition, Freud wants to reinvent them in naturalistic terms. The animation that enlivens organic life occupies a problematic zone that infinitely complicates the interrelation of life and death. Must we attribute intentionality to a "movement of the air"?

Nietzsche and Freud lead us toward a notion of organic life that is irreducibly linked to the temporality of inorganic, inanimate forces—in other words, to the temporality of death. The thought of a new conscience tries to abandon all idealizing presuppositions concerning this enlivening "breath of wind." But can we think of *Geist* as something purely material without an ideational component, without some preexistent, non-accidental structure? "Let us beware of saying that death is opposed to life," writes Nietzsche in section 109 of *The Gay Science*. "The living is merely a type of what is dead, and a very rare type" (168). Can we think of life itself as an accident, a momentary interplay of Eros and Thanatos against the backdrop of the eternal recurrence of nature's inorganic forces? And of conscience as the self-reflection of inorganic existence that takes place, precisely, through the medium of organic life? Freud and Nietzsche take very different paths toward similar goals. Suspended between the line and the circle, between the inorganic, nonfigurative essence of language and the organic figurations of the human, Freud and Nietzsche try to delineate the shape of a new, extra-moral conscience, where the historical modification of human instincts takes place within the context of a universal struggle of life and death. And what of the relation of the enlivening breath of *Geist* to language and speech? Can we think of language, what Lacan calls "the order of the signifier," as tracing the inner structure of inorganic existence, of all that lies beyond the mortality of organic life? We are *human* beings, writes Lacan, "no doubt because the human being is only the *humus* of language."[23] Does not *Geist* name the crossing of language and organic *humus*, the insufflation of inorganic existence, of death and the symbolic order of number and letter, within the soil, within a piece of earth?

Instinct *(der Instinkt)*, writes Hegel, is the "animal's relation to its non-organic particularized nature," which "feeds on itself in that it consumes itself as its own inorganicity."[24] The Freudo-Nietzschean doctrine of the instinctual bases of conscience and the moral law continues Hegel's historicization of the phenomenology of experience. In Nietzsche's idiom, it is "joy" *(Lust)*, the instinct of pleasure, that discovers within itself something other, something deathly, inorganic:

> *What* does joy not want? It is thirstier, more cordial, hungrier, more terrible, more secret than all woe; it wants *itself*, it bites into itself, the ring's will strives in it *[des Ringes Wille ringt in ihr]*. (*Thus Spoke Zarathustra*, 435)

This is the bite of conscience conceived as the constriction of inorganic existence within organic life, a bite that at once constitutes the organic and places it in the path of death. Hegel's notion of organic life feeding on its own inorganicity is another version of this same biting of the ring of the will into itself. Rather than opposing one another, Freud and Nietzsche mark distinct stages in what Jacques Derrida has called the Hegelian logic of stricture, where the dialectic itself becomes a series of constrictions and releases that begins with creation and ends with the apocalypse: "a movement of *constriction:* grip, constraint, restriction; it is a question of closing up, squeezing, containing, suppressing, subjecting, compressing, repressing, subduing, reducing, forcing, subjugating, enslaving, hemming in."[25] The bite of conscience is always both the bite of the ring of being and the constriction of organic life by the will of the inorganic forces within it. The striving of the will's ring *(des Ringes Wille ringt)* reveals that language itself is the "ringing" "breath of wind" that calls humankind into its own.

Notes

1. Friedrich Nietzsche, *Nachlaß*, in *Studienausgabe*, ed. Giovanni Colli and Mazzino Montinari, 15 vols. (Munich/Berlin: DTV and Walter de Gruyter, 1980), 11:197. This note, dated Sils-Maria, 26 August 1881, is briefly discussed by Martin Heidegger in *Nietzsche*, ed. David Krell, 4 vols. (San Francisco: Harper & Row, 1979-87), 2:80.

2. Friedrich Nietzsche, *Thus Spoke Zarathustra*, in *The Portable Nietzsche*, ed. Walter Kaufmann (New York: Penguin, 1976), 329–30; *Also Sprach Zarathustra*, in *Werke*, ed. Karl Schlechta, 3 vols. (Munich: Carl Hansel Verlag, 1963), 2:463. References in the text will be to these editions.

3. Martin Heidegger, *What is Called Thinking?* trans. J. Glenn Gray (San Francisco: Harper & Row, 1968), 227. In reading the history of metaphysics (as opposed to the history of being), Heidegger always points to the presumption of a spatial displacement in which, as Heidegger observes apropos of Hegel, "spirit *must first of all fall* 'into time.' It remains obscure what indeed is signified ontologically by 'falling' or by the 'actualizing' of a spirit which has power over time and really 'is' outside of it" (*Being and Time*, trans. John Macquarrie and Edward Robinson [New York: Harper & Row, 1962], 485). The notion of the ring calls such presuppositions into question.

4. Friedrich Nietzsche, *The Will to Power*, trans. Walter Kaufmann (New York: Random House, 1967), 549. Subsequent references in the text are to page numbers of this edition. I discuss section 1067 in greater detail in "Mourning Becomes Telepathy," my introduction to Jacques Derrida, *Cinders*, ed. Ned Lukacher (Lincoln: University of Nebraska Press, 1991), 5ff.

5. Friedrich Nietzsche, *Nachgelaßene Fragmente: Juli 1882 – Winter 1883/84*, in *Nietzsche Werke: Kritische Gesamtausgabe*, hrg. Giorgio Colli und Mazzino Montinari, 24 bd. (Berlin: Walter de Gruyter, 1968–79), 7.1, 637.

6. Friedrich Nietzsche, *The Gay Science*, trans. Walter Kaufmann (New York, Vintage Books, 1968), 167. References in the text are to page numbers in this edition.

7. Heidegger, *Nietzsche*, 2:81.

8. Ibid., 1:52. This is also one of the reasons why Heidegger would have to disagree categorically with a proposition like Freud's that "ethics is the limitation of instinct" *(Ethik ist aber Triebeinschränkung) (S.E.,* 23:64), since the openness of Dasein rules out the question of limits. The metaphysics of Freud's empiricism would thus be of a piece with the generalized "narrowing *[Verengung]* of the concept of existence" that Heidegger sees at work throughout the history of metaphysics (*The End of Philosophy*, trans. Joan Stambaugh [New York: Harper & Row, 1973], 67). Freud recognizes, however, that the imposition of ethical values is itself part of the instinctual apparatus it seeks to dominate.

9. Friedrich Nietzsche, *On the Genealogy of Morals/Ecce Homo*, trans. Walter Kaufmann (New York: Vintage Books, 1968), 61. Subsequent references in the text are to page numbers of this edition. "It almost seems," writes Heidegger in "Overcoming Metaphysics," "as if the being of pain were cut off from man under the dominance of the will, similarly the being of joy. Can the extreme measure of suffering still bring a transformation here?" (*The End of Philosophy*, 110).

10. Friedrich Nietzsche, *Fragments posthumes: Printemps-automne 1884*, ed. Giorgio Colli and Mazzino Montinari, trans. Jean Launay (Paris: Gallimard, 1982), 286.

11. Ibid., 286, 326.

12. Nietzsche, *Nachgelaßene Fragmente: Herbst 1887 bis Marz 1888*, in *Nietzsche Werke: Kritische Gesamtausgabe*, ed. Giorgio Colli and Mazzino Montinaro (Berlin: Walter de Gruyter, 1977), 415.

13. Nietzsche, *The Anti-Christ*, in Kaufmann, *The Portable Nietzsche*, 652, 568.

14. The savagery of Nietzsche's assault on conscience (and perhaps a great deal of his madness as well) may have involved his desperation to escape, or rather counteract, the visitations of the paternal ghost. The father's ghost is the very spirit of Pauline theology, and the son's thinking is the apotrope needed to keep the specter at bay. The implications of the scene he describes to Franz Overbeck on 11 February 1883 are sweeping: "I have to bear such a *manifold* burden of tormenting and horrible memories! Not for a moment have I been able to forget, for instance, that my mother called me a disgrace to my dead father" *(Selected Letters of Friedrich Nietzsche*, ed. Christopher Middleton [Chicago: University of Chicago Press, 1969], 206). Nietzsche replays this graveside conjuration of the father's ghost by the scolding mother in *Thus Spoke Zarathustra* and in the *Nachlaß*. Plato and other great philosophers, however heinous Nietzsche found them, escape the scathing abuse Nietzsche reserves for the Jewish and Protestant traditions. Between them, however, Paul and Plato sum up for Nietzsche the follies of the Jew-Greek in Western civilization.

15. Sigmund Freud, *Civilization and Its Discontents*, trans. James Strachey (New York: W. W. Norton, 1962), 70. Subsequent references in the text are to page numbers of this edition. References to Freud's German text are to *Gesammelte Werke*, hrgb. Anna Freud et al., 18 vols. (Frankfurt a.M.: S. Fischer Verlag, 1950–74). Here *G.W.*, 14:482.

16. Sigmund Freud, *The Ego and the Id*, trans. James Strachey (New York: W.W. Norton, 1975), 47. *G.W.*, 13:287.

17. *The Standard Edition of the Complete Psychological Works of Sigmund Freud*, ed. James Strachey et al., 24 vols. (London: Hogarth Press and the Institute for Psycho-Analysis, 1953–74), 23:116; *G.W.*, 16:224. Henceforth abbreviated *S.E.* in the text.

18. Theodor Adorno, *Minima Moralia: Reflections from Damaged Life*, trans. E. F. N. Jephcott (London: NLB, 1974), 239. Translation slightly modified.

19. Friedrich Nietzsche, *Twilight of the Idols/The Anti-Christ*, trans. R. J. Hollingdale (New York: Penguin, 1984), 110.

20. Theodor Adorno, *Aesthetic Theory*, trans. C. Lenhardt (New York: Routledge, 1984), 339.

21. For recent discussions of Sellin's influence on Freud, see Yosef Yerushalmi, *Freud's Moses: Judaism Terminable and Interminable* (New Haven: Yale University Press, 1991), 25–27; and Jacques Lacan, *L'envers de la psychanalyse: Le Séminaire: livre XVII*, ed. Jacques-Alain Miller (Paris: Seuil, 1991), 152–62.

22. Jacques Derrida may be thinking of this passage from *Moses and Monotheism* when, in an imaginary dialogue between Heidegger and a spokesperson for Judeo-Christianity, the latter asks Heidegger whether his fiery, material, non-idealizing *Geist* really does depart from the onto-theological tradition, which has always "spoken of *ruah, pneuma, spiritus* and, why not, *Geist*" *(Of Spirit: Heidegger and the Question*, trans. Geoffrey Bennington and Rachel Bowlby [Chicago: University of Chicago Press, 1989], 111).

23. Lacan, *L'envers de la psychanalyse*, 57.

24. G. W. F. Hegel, *Philosophy of Nature* (Part Two of "The Encyclopedia of the Philosophical Sciences"), trans. A. V. Miller (Oxford: Clarendon Press, 1970), sections 342 and 361.

25. Jacques Derrida, *Glas*, trans. John P. Leavey, Jr., and Richard Rand (Lincoln: University of Nebraska Press, 1987), 99a.

Immediacy and Dissolution: Notes on the Languages of Moral Agency and Critical Discourse

Thomas Pfau

> No Man can understand
> But He that hath endured
> The Dissolution—in Himself—
> That Man—be qualified
>
> To qualify Despair
> To Those who failing new—
> Mistake Defeat for Death—Each time
> Till acclimated—to—
>
> —Emily Dickinson, # 539

One of the most intricate and contested conceptual alliances that the period of romanticism and idealism has bequeathed contemporary theory is undoubtedly that between "immediacy" and "morality." It appears to become an efficient cultural tenet during the latter part of the eighteenth century, such as in its grounding of Adam Smith's paradigmatic "emotivist" concept of morality in the *Theory of Moral Sentiments* (1759). Achieving further momentum in the Neoplatonist and post-Enlightenment thought of Hemsterhuis, Hamann, Herder, and Schiller, the concept of "immediacy" eventually comes to assume a pivotal function in the

Thanks are due to Richard Swartz and Alberto Moreiras for their kind and engaged commentary on earlier drafts of this essay. A particularly substantial debt I owe to Barbara Herrnstein-Smith for long and genuinely probing comments and for the hours spent discussing several of the issues raised in the following pages.

philosophy of Kant and Fichte as well as in the poetic theories of Novalis, Schlegel, and Coleridge. Here it serves as the very "ground" for the discourses of epistemology and moral theory, that is, as an unmediated, principled, and self-conscious subjectivity that, by way of the correlative notion of "sympathy," also project itself into political and social theory.[1] As such, needless to say, "immediacy" once again assumes a variety of costumes, appearing as the auto-affective play of the faculties in Kant's *Critique of Judgment*, namely, as the "feeling" *(Gefühl)* that our reflective judgment recognizes as the condition of possibility for "knowledge in general"; or it appears as a postulate of self-*production* in Fichte, realized by an agency whose unconscious "act" *(Tathandlung)* generates the "feeling of its determinability" *(Bestimmbarkeit)* for what is an inevitably belated "reflection"; or, again, we encounter a morally charged *Gefühl* in the work of the quintessentially romantic Novalis (arguably Fichte's most incisive reader); it is eventually recognized by reflection as a "formative drive" *(Formtrieb)*.[2] However varied its inflection, "immediacy" functions as *the* condition of possibility for all knowledge, and thus as the capstone of the conceptual edifices of early nineteenth-century theory. Yet as the romantics also acknowledge, with Novalis once again appearing the most probing, "immediacy" as the condition of possibility for reflection is recuperable only in alienated form; hence, the archaeological project of reflexive determination can never entirely account for the "interest" or "motive" that causes theory to undertake such an archaeology of the subject's "immediate" ground. "Feeling," he remarks, "cannot feel itself. . . . It can only be observed in reflection—at which point the spirit of the feeling is lost."[3] As an increasingly vertiginous or mesmerized encircling of the undecidable concept of "immediacy," theory constitutes itself as the site of a conflict between an archaeological and a teleological, a formal and a social, kind of knowledge, with both meanings permeating the epistemic practice of *Bestimmung* (i.e., determination/destination).

Much critical theory over the last thirty-five years or so has sought to dismantle this notion, exposing its inherently tautological or, alternatively, foreign-determined quality and, in uncovering its contradictory or imaginary dimension, contesting the status of "immediacy" as the essential *and* knowable condition of possibility for knowledge.[4] We may especially think of Derrida's critique of the early Husserl's notion of self-presence, or of Lacan's linguistic rewriting of Freud. More recently, however, theory has increasingly abandoned these relatively abstract forms of "deconstruction" in favor of contextually and historically attentive forms of critique. According to Alan Liu, this reorientation of deconstruction toward ideological critique and historicist modes of inquiry, as such inclined to consider the idea(l) of a "pure" theory as yet another *symptom* of ideological commitment rather than its cure, has been accompanied by a strong emphasis on the *formal-methodological* and (by implication) moral *propriety of cultural analysis.* In conscientiously disavowing any notion of totality, diligently abjuring any form of diachronic or synchronic generalization, and in duly espousing the credo of scholarly "detail" or highly limited, localized "fields" of inquiry, a new particularism of highly specialized theoretical discourses has emerged. What ties these discourses together is their latently moral sense of critical urgency, a "sense" that, to be sure, we can only arrive at counterintuitively. For on the surface, Theory appears little more than a vague title for a critical practice characterized by ever-increasing topical diversity and self-conscious conceptual discriminations, as well as by its ongoing dispersion and reassessment of "fields" and "approaches," by its vindication of overlooked or suppressed traditions, canons, and cultures, and by its scrupulous search for "groundbreaking" forms of critique whose restorative efforts unfold under the explicit theoretical caveat of a duly localized authority.[5]

In reviewing the varied though structurally cognate "channels" on which postmodern "high cultural criticisms" are currently broadcasting, Alan Liu has recently pointed to cultural critique's overriding interest in exposing and revaluating (albeit belatedly) the local mechanisms of "power" whose capacity to shape a given "culture" or "slice" of culture hinges on the exclusion of entire population-groups and/or on the often indiscriminate appropriation of specific material and economic interests that, in turn, the now "dominant" culture will obfuscate under the aegis of the *aesthetic.* Where the "immediacy" of its participants had deceptively rendered their culture the correlate of *perception*, a postmodern critique conceives of culture as the effect of a contextually determined, typically aggressive *definition.* This inherently self-blinded, hence "immediate," constitutive efficiency of any culture is commonly referred to as its "ideology," and according to Jerome McGann, it is "a fortiori seen as a body of illusions."[6] Extending Liu's analysis, we may with some legitimacy remark on a pervasive, self-consciously belated, and thus principled insistence in current "high cultural criticism" to redeem past cultures from the restrictive and exclusionary economies that enabled historically and locally specific cultural meanings to constitute themselves and to serve their (at the time unreflected) purpose.[7] As contemporary cultural criticisms reverse the valuation of "immediacy" and "culture," of subjective agency and its material, sociocultural effects, they appear to reinstate the originally Hegelian premise that all relations, whether immanent, semiotic, material, economic, psychological, etc., are susceptible of theoretical scrutiny precisely on account of their inherently duplicitous ("unconscious") structure, a structure that hinges precisely on the dialectic between the "immediacy" of cultural production and the necessarily belated, critical reflection capable of articulating the cost/benefit ratio that shapes and sustains cultural productivity. In situating their objects of inquiry within a matrix of immediacy/reflection, surface/depth, and ideology/critique, contemporary critiques build on a paradigm of Theory in which relations are by definition imbued with moral-evaluative significance.[8] *As cultural critique, that is, the ever more complex languages of contemporary theoretical critique have constituted and positioned themselves as the infrastructure of a postmodern, dis-individuated morality.*

What may thus far appear a strangely double-barreled focus on moral theory and cultural critique respectively, constitutes indeed a subject chosen at once deliberately and, as I hope to show, purposefully. For besides revealing how any notion of the "social" is born of the "classic" encounter between theory and praxis, the Hegelian and post-Hegelian conception of moral theory appears beset by a significant, twofold crisis. First, there is the crisis of legitimacy that affects the traditional concept of the moral subject, which can be thought alternatively as affective immediacy or as self-conscious intentionality or as social personality, depending on whether we follow an emotivist, decisionist, or pragmatist model of moral theory.[9] Secondly, we come to see—as early as in the work of Hegel—that the crisis of moral theory involves the recognition of *a general contingency of values* (regardless of whether they are overtly moral or not) *on their sustained discursive instantiation* or, as Derrida might put it, on their "iterability." In other words, the crisis of moral theory—which is encompassed by the question concerning how cultural values are defined and socially identified—is not one of possibility or impossibility but of its delimitation within a general spectrum of discursive practices continuously performed and reorganized by the multifaceted "discipline" of Theory.

Put differently, my argument here will be that Theory per se constitutes a metalanguage, whose principal motivation it is to redistribute and reconfigure particular, more or less stringently formalized conceptual sets and subsets insofar as they are to function as the "dimension of assessment" (J. L. Austin) of whatever a particular individual or community thinks and addresses as the Real or "reality." In actively soliciting our subscribership to a *particular* metalanguage, Theory reveals a motivation more or less independent of the all too conspicuous question concerning its ontological "truth-value," an issue no longer thinkable or solvable as a *separate, pure,* and *autonomous* theoretical problem anyway. And precisely to the extent that it appears imbedded in a contingent set of historical, social, and discursive factors (empirical factors that effectively shape and determine the direction and rigor of its transcendent conceptualizations), the practice of Theory not only develops a set of technical rules and norms designed to govern any variety of sociohistorical inquiries but, in so doing, also exercises an inherently "moral" function in that it delimits valid/appropriate discursive practices in a given community and its institutional conception of acceptable, relevant, and/or purposeful context(s). In its metalingual distribution of cognitive authority and accountability, Theory qua practice prestructures (in the sense of a hermeneutic "prejudice" *(Vorhaben)* the idea of critique as inherently moral, well before particular critical "modes" or "approaches" will begin to "discern" the ethical tensions that inhere in and support discrete sociocultural phenomena. As Michael Oakeshott has remarked, morality cannot be restricted to a matter of momentous ethical choices made within a topically preindexed "field" of moral problems, a notion that, under the title "decisionism," defines merely a particular local trend in current moral theory. Rather, when seen as a matter of positioning oneself in a continuum of complex and interlacing discourses,

> moral conduct is agents related to one another in the acknowledgement of the authority of a practice composed of conditions which because of their generality attracts to itself the generic name, "practice": morality, *mos.* A morality is the *ars artium* of conduct, the practice of all practices; the practice of agency without further specification.[10]

Deferring, for the time being, a more insistent questioning of Oakeshott's conservative and ultimately precipitous identification of "moral conduct" with "the acknowledgement of the authority of a practice" (when, in fact, it might just as conceivably constitute itself as a persistent critical challenge to such an authority),we shall retain his overall crucial identification of morality as the "practice of agency." Proceeding from the hypothesis that morality begets its "subject" through a configuration of particulars and universals, and that, therefore, it cannot be restricted to a conscious and intentional individuality, we shall trace some historical and paradigmatic links between Hegel and contemporary ordinary-language and neopragmatist philosophy (in Austin and Oakeshott), links that identify the practice of Theory as both inherently discursive and, in virtue of its metalingual quality, as latently moral. Such a rethinking of the ratio of theory and discourse is not simply motivated by that ratio's vitiating impact on the ontologically motivated (moral) idealisms of the early nineteenth century but should also caution us against an overly enthusiastic embracing of the various contemporary, eschatologically "motivated," if strenuously localized, theoretical critiques of cultural production.

I

In its effort at reconfiguring moral theories from Plato and Aristotle through Erasmus, Leibniz, Hume, Adam Smith, and Kant, Hegel's *Phenomenology of Spirit* devotes a significant and highly condensed chapter to redefining the question concerning the intelligibility of the social and the political as one of morality. In positing community and moral order as the semantic *effects* of private and "immediate" or expressive significations, grounded in and legitimated by a form of moral authorship, Theory as a metalanguage serves primarily the purpose of verifying and grounding the integrity and authority of this very *relation* between individual (moral) agency and social authority. To do so, Hegel realizes, requires a more rigorous reassessment of the authenticity, determinability, and communicability of Kant's affective paradigm of morality, known as the "feeling of duty" *(Pflichtgefühl)*. That is, the grounding of an authentic and "immediate" self-relation (i.e., a "moral self-consciousness") conditions its efficiency for the determination of moral (i.e., social and cultural) relations, for which moral self-consciousness is to provide the essential nucleus.

As is well known, Hegel's *Phenomenology* posits the speculative progression of a "natural consciousness" whose "reflexive determinations" of its own concept *(Begriff)* successively "cancel" *[aufheben]* its initially empirical positions, and thus "sublate" *(aufheben)* the discrete individuality of consciousness into the inclusive and trans-individual authority of "spirit" *(Geist)*.[11] Consistent with its paradigmatic dialectic mediation of meaning and truth *(Meinung, Wahrheit)*, the *Phenomenology* redescribes morality as a dynamic and self-transforming structure of relations, rather than defining it as a transhistorical, principled, and quasi-substantial essence, meaning, or innate property within individual consciousness. Section C in part BB of the *Phenomenology of Spirit*, entitled "Spirit that is certain of itself: Morality," thus concentrates on the very tensions between what appears to be an initial moment of private conviction and the reflexive recognition of its incompatibility with social obligation. In short, we are offered a speculative analysis of the concept of duty.

Initially, Hegel comments, "self-consciousness knows duty to be the absolute essence. . . . However, as thus locked up within itself, moral self-consciousness is not yet posited as *consciousness*. The object is immediate knowledge, and being thus permeated purely by the self is *not* an object."[12] In short, duty must mediate the apparent positivity of its own, immediate "conviction" and the strict negativity of the worldly and sensuous "otherness" by which it is opposed. Hence, "moral consciousness as the *simple knowing* and *willing* of pure duty is, in the doing of it, . . . brought into relation with the actuality of the complex case" *(PS, 369; PhG, 429)*. A tension emerges between a consciousness characterized by a general and formal sense of morality (duty) and another consciousness informed by the situational and contextual exigencies of a specific situation: "Thus it is postulated that it is *another* consciousness which . . . contains the equally essential relation to 'doing', and to the necessity of the *specific* content: since for this other, duties mean specific duties, the content as such is equally essential as the form which makes the content a duty" *(PS, 370; PhG, 430)*. For Hegel it is the "immediate" form of the spirit qua "conscience" that will reconcile the universality of duty as a postulate directed at all being with the situational pragmatics and particularity of "duties," thereby mediating a discursive form and a social content. The need for such reconciliation is more than a merely technical, philosophical exigency, since the initial opposition comes down to one between the transcendental (Duty) and the empirical (duties), that is, a conflict between two ways (say, orthodox vs. pragmatic) of *meaning;* and, as Hegel is well aware, conflicts of meaning become, ultimately, always conflicts of value.

Hence, what Hegel now refers to as "this self of conscience" or a "*third* self" is also characterized as "moral self-consciousness having attained its truth" *(PS, 384–85; PhG, 445–46)*. To specify that which authenticates and authorizes this "truth" of conscience, however, is to perform a paradigmatic shift from the interiority of an individuated (self-)consciousness (irrespective of whether its content be duty as form or duties as content) to the distinctively modern and mediated concept of "personality." As Hegel observes, "[T]he totality or actuality which shows itself to be the truth of the ethical world is the self of the person; its existence consists in its being acknowledged by others." In other words, "conscience is the common element of the two self-consciousnesses, and this element is the substance in which the deed has an *enduring reality*, the moment of being *recognized* and *acknowledged* by others" (*PS*, 384, 388; *PhG*, 445, 450). Moral authority, that is, emerges at, indeed is constitutive of, the very intersection between theory and practice, transcendence and empiricity, cognition and ideology. In view of this inherently bilateral structure, which mandates that it be "recognized" as *moral* authority as well as "acknowledged" as moral *authority*, we must now determine how and to what extent morality will evolve as a discernible and phenomenal (i.e., cultural) moment by integrating its potentially opposed aspects within or, rather, as a discursive-linguistic practice.

With unfailing concentration Hegel thus points out how "here again, then, we see language as the existence of Spirit. Language is self-consciousness existing *for others*, self-consciousness which *as such* is immediately *present*, and as *this* self-consciousness is universal" (*PS*, 395; *PhG*, 458). When recognized as the very infrastructure for the construction and manifestation of moral authority, language must shoulder the burden of proving the truth and "sincerity" of the speaker's collective and morally authoritative "spirit" for others. Whereas "moral consciousness" had presented itself as "still dumb, shut up with itself within its inner life," Hegel now asserts that "language . . . emerges as the middle term, mediating between independent and acknowledged self-consciousnesses; and the *existent self* is immediately universal acknowledgment." The social dimension of this inward paradigm of the "ethical spirit" emerges into full view with Hegel's qualification of it as "law and simple command" (*PS*, 396; *PhG*, 458–59).[13] Thus, in keeping with Hegel's antiformalist dialectic of moral consciousness, language emerges as a more or less explicitly performative *praxis* rather than as a referential *form* (to retain an ultimately untenable distinction for the sake of argument here).[14] That is, rather than signifying or representing moral meanings, it instantiates or enacts social values *as* and *through* a more or less defined language. In short, it is the *visibly* enacted competence within *any* given discourse per se, and not merely the topical and referential emulation of the putative conceptual stock of generic and traditional morality (e.g., conscience, good/evil, duty, etc.) that underwrites the morality of any verbal agent. As Hegel puts it,

> [T]he content of the language of conscience is the *self that knows itself as essential being*. This alone is what it declares, and this declaration is the true actuality *[wahre Wirklichkeit]* of the act, and the validating *[das Gelten]* of the action. Consciousness declares its conviction; it is in this conviction alone that the action is a duty; also it is valid as duty solely through the conviction being *declared*. For universal self-consciousness is free from the *specific* action that merely *is;* what is valid for that self consciousness is not the *action* as existence, but the *conviction* that it is a duty; and this is made actual in language. (*PS*, 396; *PhG*, 459)

Morality, which for Hegel now involves transfiguring the putative "immediacy" of an individual conscience into a social force, hinges on the felicitous performance or emulation of a more or less "settled" discursive practice. Viewed as such, morality is characterized by three crucial features: (1) its discursive mode of appearance is *necessary*, since it alone insures the existence of moral authority "*for* universal acknowledgment"; (2) the sincerity of moral speech is strictly an effect (though, obviously, "effect" can no longer be correlated with any dimension of intentionality or interiority whatever) of a speaker's performative competence in emulating the rhetorical and generic *conventions* or, morally speaking, the *rules and norms* of such speech; and thus (3) the social efficiency (universality) of moral speech proves to be contingent on the *felicity* of its performance rather than on the *intentionality* of the "subject" of utterance.

What renders Hegel's argument so volatile, yet also productive, is its recognition of the undecidable causality between an inward moral conviction and "its" socially visible, discursive appearance. The performative and strictly discursive phenomenality of the moral subject denies "conscience" and "conviction" any axiological or temporal priority over their discursive appearance. To thus redescribe morality as social and discursive practice rather than as an inward presence ("conviction") is tantamount to rethinking the very idea of discursive practice itself. For we can now situate morality strictly in the "custom" (Lat., *mos*) that sustains the practice of any discourse whatsoever, which amounts to a structural rather than topical conception that implicitly suspends the traditional, emotivist paradigm of morality as the signification or expression of a putative "immediacy" (i.e., the interiority of moral self-consciousness qua duty). Alternatively, we may provisionally redescribe morality as a rhetorical interaction with a social- and foreign-determined continuum of form- and genre-based practices or conventions of *meaning*. Undoubtedly, though, it is precisely this alienation *[Entäusserung]* of conscience into discourse that alarms Hegel; for it now appears that the sincerity and authority of moral conscience are irreducibly and precariously *the effects* of its universal linguistic performativity as "declaration" *[Aussprechen]*. Eager to reign in the deviant (i.e., undecidable) causality between the spirit and its word, Hegel now confronts the question as to "whether the assurance of acting from a conviction of duty is true" with categorical directness, namely, by declaring the very question inherently illegitimate:

> Whether the assurance of acting from a conviction of duty is *true*, whether what is done is actually a *duty*—these questions or doubts have no meaning when addressed to conscience. To ask whether the assurance would be true would presuppose that the inner intention is different from the one put forward, i.e., that what the individual self wills, can be separated from duty, from the will of the universal and pure consciousness; the latter would be put into words, but the former would be strictly the true motive of action. But this distinction between the universal consciousness and the individual self is just what has been superseded, and the supersession of it *is* conscience. The self's immediate knowing that is certain of itself is law and duty. Its intention, through being its intention, is what is right; all that is required is that it should know this, and should state its conviction that its knowing and willing are right. The declaration of assurance in itself rids the form of its particularity. It thereby acknowledges the *necessary universality of the self*. (*PS*, 396–97; *PhG*, 459–60)

On the surface, the passage seems unsettlingly circular in its logic, repeatedly proposing the outcome ("the necessary universality of the self") as that which, in the embryonic form of an immediate belief, is said to have governed the discursive act ("declaration") whereby a "conviction" is surreptitiously transmuted into something self-affirming or self-privileging (i.e., "assurance").[15] Yet, aside from such *post hoc* reasoning—which adumbrates the much larger problematic of what Hegel calls "determinate negation"—the passage is not merely outrageous but also curiously suggestive. For Hegel has effectively begun to dissociate the question of morality—itself by now all but coterminous with that concerning the

effective or felicitous instantiation of conscience qua "declaration"—
from the traditional true/false opposition. The latter, he notes, presumes
an extralinguistic criterion of verification (faith, intentionality, etc.) whose
intrinsically subjective and particular status would render it incommen-
surable with the "necessary universality of self." Yet this analysis of conscience not only calls into question the concept of "expressivity" that has
been proposed as an encompassing paradigm for Hegel's thought, but it
positively identifies morality as an ideational effect of a verbal agent's
performance within a preestablished and conventional structure of
"iterable" discursive forms.[16] If "declaration" is the semiotic and/or rhetorical infrastructure in virtue of which "conscience" can *appear*, we should
also note that the appearance of "conscience"—itself the sublation of the
oppositions between individuality and collectivity, between duties and
Duty, between duty and law, etc.—requires the *dis*appearance of that
infrastructure itself.[17] That is, the felicity of the "declaration" of conscience, which involves its "acknowledgment" as social authority, proves
contingent upon the inculcation of community-specific conventions of
meaning whose "iterability" instantiates moral force not in a propositional, deictic, or thetic sense but as a structural, and thus inherently
"invisible" event; it must be a *form* (e.g., the time-honored affiliation of
the *idea* of morality with the *semiosis* of spontaneity):

> It is *in the form of the act* that the universality lies. It is this form which
> is to be established as actual: it is the *self* which as such is actual in
> language, which declares itself to be the truth, and just by doing so . . .
> is acknowledged by [all other selves]." (*PS*, 397; *PhG*, 460)

Erich Tugendhat thus remarks quite concisely that "in addressing the
question of how the consciousness relation is constituted, we must thoroughly abandon the idea of taking our bearing from any sort of inner
perception." Once the latter notion has been surrendered, it becomes
apparent that Hegel "is referring to socio-anthropological structures, not
ontological structures."[18]

II

Hegel's significant conjugation of a notion of "form" with his indisput-
ably performative conception of moral "self-declaration" calls up rather

similar paradoxes within related twentieth-century theory. For arguably the concept of "form" would seem nothing short of anathema to that of the performative. After all, isn't John L. Austin's self-irony, in *How To Do Things with Words*, precisely the result of that book's progressive recognition of the impossibility of any formal determination of performative (illocutionary) meaning? And isn't the gradual collapse of constative into performative, of locution into illocution, the result of a radically contextual paradigm of meaning according to which "it is essential to realize that 'true' and 'false' . . . [stand] only for a general dimension of being a right or proper thing to say as opposed to the wrong thing, in these circumstances, to this audience, for these purposes, and with these intentions" (*HTW*, 145)?[19] Before pursuing the central conflict between performative and formalist conceptions of meaning—staged in such lucid terms by Hegel's *Phenomenology*—we should note, also so as to motivate the connection between Hegel's moral theory and more recent theories of the performative, that Austin's contextualist model of meaning-as-success-or-failure already hints at a fundamental moral force subtending discourse in general. Thus the constative true/false dyad becomes assimilated to the performative successful/unsuccessful opposition, only to be redescribed, for any genuinely specific contextual situation, as that of the "proper" or "wrong" thing to say.

To subscribe to Austin's familiar shorthand definition of performatives as statements where "the uttering of the words is, indeed, usually a, or even the, leading incident in the performance of the act," such as betting, christening, exchanging marriage vows, promising, etc." (*HTW*, 8), is to recognize, minimally, that in an illocutionary act meanings are not so much generated as they are enlisted, cited, or used.[20] And when contextual and conventional constraints are said to have replaced a formal grammatical paradigm of meaning, a related casualty will be the concept of a self-present, "immediate" intentionality, a category repeatedly ironized in *How to Do Things with Words* almost from the start: "surely," Austin remarks, "words must be spoken 'seriously' and so as to be taken 'seriously'.

> But we are apt to have a feeling that their being serious consists in their being uttered as (merely) the outward or visible sign, for convenience or other record or for information, of an inward and spiritual act: from which it is but a short step to go on to believe or to assume without realizing that for many purposes the outward utterance is a description, *true or false*, of the occurrence of the inward performance. . . . It is

> gratifying to observe . . . how excess of profundity, or rather solemnity, at once paves the way for immorality. For one who says "promising is not merely a matter of uttering words! It is an inward and spiritual act" is apt to appear as a solid moralist standing out against a generation of superficial theorizers: we see him as he sees himself, surveying the invisible depths of ethical space, with all the distinction of a specialist in the *sui generis*. Yet he provides Hyppolitus with a let-out, the bigamist with an excuse for his "I do" and the welsher with a defence for his "I bet." Accuracy and morality alike are on the side of the plain saying that *our word is our bond*. (*HTW*, 9–10)[21]

These remarks certainly seem to dispel Derrida's insistent yet misguided critique that "performative meaning once more becomes the communication of an intentional meaning" or that "intention remains the organizing center" of the illocutionary operation.[22] As proved to be the case with Hegel's thesis on moral "declaration, " Austin's notion of a subjective interiority—whether we are to think it as "immediacy" or "intentionality"—can only be thought as the *correlate of discursive self-enactment*. Belonging to the order of "appearance" *(Erscheinung)*, the semiolinguistic nature of Hegel's moral "personality" is fully contingent on what Austin calls "uptake," thus proving an effect of social interpretation rather than private volition.

Yet in thus characterizing the *phenomenality* of (moral) meaning within a network of contextual and conventional constraints, Austin suddenly adopts an uncharacteristically hesitant, reduplicative phrasing, referring to "words . . . spoken 'seriously' and *so as to be taken* 'seriously'" (italics added). Along with the performative *function* of an illocutionary act there emerges the need for renewed consideration of the formal *structure* of that act, qua locution in general. Derrida first raised the issue when insisting on a "general and systematic elaboration of the structure of locution which avoids the endless alternation of essence and accident" (*SEC*, 324).

> Aside from all the questions posed by the very historically sedimented notion of "convention," we must notice here: (1) that to consider only the conventionality that forms the *circumstance* of the statement, its contextual surroundings, and not a certain intrinsic conventionality of that which constitutes the locution itself, that is, everything that might quickly be summarized under the problematic heading of the "arbitrariness of the sign"; . . . Ritual is not an eventuality, but, as iterability, is a structural characteristic of every mark. . . . Is not what Austin excludes as anomalous, exceptional, "non-serious," that is, *citation* (on

the stage, in a poem, or in a soliloquy), the determined modification of a general citationality—or rather, a general iterability—without which there would not even be a "successful" performative? (*SEC*, 323–24; 325)

We cannot rehearse any further the contentious aftermath of Austin's argument by a host of very disparately motivated readers.[23] What Derrida successfully and, for our purposes significantly, remarks, however, is the need to consider the perceived *formal* quality of the utterance itself as the exclusive resource for the inculcation of its situational or contextual impact and effect. It is in the "form" or "structure" of a locution—by which we are to understand both its grammatical quality as well as more overtly contingent matters, such as intonation, diction, tone, choice of medium and/or channel of communication, etc.—that its social function (and, in virtue of that function, a certain assessment of "context") can constitute itself materially. Austin himself, we recall, refers to this issue as "securing the uptake" of a statement (*HTW*, 117; 139). Hence his contention "that what we have to study is not the sentence but the issuing of an utterance in a speech-situation" (*HTW*, 139) may require some modification. For we have now reason to understand the *form* of that utterance itself as the principal index of *how* a given agency has come to *interpret* that "speech-situation," that is, *how* it wishes to enter into a nexus of discourse-patterns and discourse-constraints whose (inherently moral) *force* may be defined along an often unspecified amalgamation of economic, gendered, ethnic, and religious parameters.[24] In short, it is the speech act's affirmation/modification of a locutionary form and thus the interpretive assessment of discursive "propriety" that intimates the "morality" of the speaker. Once again, it is to be stressed that by "morality" we are not primarily concerned with the familiar dilemmas and exemplary motifs of formal ethics. Rather, morality inheres in the irreducibly discursive and thus social "attitude" (no longer a "pure" psychological concept) of the speaker, that is, his or her willingness to conform to, alter, disrupt, or challenge, etc., the currently relevant "dimension of assessment—how the words stand in respect of satisfactoriness to the facts, events, situations, &c. to which they refer" (*HTW*, 149) or, as we should qualify, "are (interpretively) taken to be referring to."

Michael Oakeshott's neopragmatist discussion of morality may help to clarify how all discursive practice is invariably imbued with a continuously operative, latent moral "motivation," and how an explicitly "theoretical" engagement of discursive practice (no matter what the theory in question is a theory of) merely renders this circumstance more visible. "Morality," according to Oakeshott,

> is like an art in having to be learned, in being learned better by some than by others, in allowing for almost endless opportunity for individual style, and in which virtuosity and mastery are distinguishable; and it is like a language in being an instrument of understanding and a medium of intercourse, in having a vocabulary and syntax of its own, and in being spoken well or ill. (*OHC*, 62)

Similar to Hegel and Austin, Oakeshott readily acknowledges the undecidability of inward "conscience" and social "declaration" or, as he puts it, between "the compunctions of "virtuous" self-enactment and those of moral self-disclosure" (*OHC*, 76). The futility of insisting on any rigorous and transcendental distinction in this regard is explained by the obvious fact that the vocabularies of either position coalesce into "a single language" (*OHC*, 77).[25] In arguing that morality is "a language spoken well or ill on every occasion of human intercourse," Oakeshott also affirms that discursive practice is moral not merely in a topical, thematic, and incidental sense but, on the contrary, is being "performed" at all times "in" saying anything whose locutionary form discernibly links that utterance to a community and its perceived "logic of sense." Hence morality constitutes "neither a system of general principles nor a code of rules, but a vernacular language," and "what has to be learned in moral education is . . . how to speak the language intelligently" (*OHC*, 78–79). Oakeshott proceeds to characterize the inherently moral energy that informs discursive practice with an indeed appropriate mixture of lucidity and eloquence:

> Every such vernacular of moral converse . . . emerges as a ritual of utterance and response, a continuously extemporized dance whose participants are alive to one another's movements and to the ground upon which they tread. . . . [It] is responsive to the aspirations of those who speak it and it is amplified in the *pia libertas* of its conscientious users. It is never fixed or finished, but (like other languages) *it has a settled character* in terms of which it responds to the linguistic inventions, the enterprises, the fortunes, the waywardness, the censoriousness, and sometimes the ridicule of those who speak it. Although a moral language may obtrude rules and duties, these are not targets to be aimed at but *nodal densities of sentiment* to which an agent who is familiar with the language and *who acknowledges its authority* recognizes himself to

be incited to subscribe. Learning to speak a language of self-enactment
is *learning how to subscribe to its intimations of "virtue"*. (*OHC*, 63–64,
75; italics mine)

What Oakeshott points to when he speaks of the "settled character" and
those "nodal densities of sentiments" and "intimations of 'virtue'" can be
identified, I think, as precisely those formal features of the vernacular
that have been of concern to us from the outset. And yet, the genteel and
serene confidence with which morality is being reconceived as linguistic
practice shrouds the underlying, conservative ideology ("an agent who is
familiar with *the* language and acknowledges its authority") according to
which agency is conflated with acceptance into a linguistic community
that, in turn, Oakeshott can think as a priori *one* language only. A dia-
metric reversal of Hegel's categorical identification of moral "conviction"
with its "necessarily universal" other, "conscience," has taken place; for
Oakeshott has essentially transferred the attribute of "immediacy" from
its traditional site ("consciousness") unto language. The self-sameness or
homogeneity of "a moral language" has become paradigmatic, thus exil-
ing the possibility of all difference from language itself. If difference were
to assert itself effectively, we are to conclude, Oakeshott would simply
consider it as *another* language.

Nevertheless, with due qualification, what remains of relevance to
both Theory in general and specific forms of cultural critique, is precisely
Oakeshott's intimation of the social, regulative efficiency of "form" and,
indeed, of specific discursive "genres." Moral authority, according to
Oakeshott, arises out of a felicitous rhetorical practice that configures
generic features and situational demands.[26] Hence it does not express
and signify inward meanings but constitutes the emergence of an utterance into an assemblage of generically fixed and predecided meanings.
Thus, rather than becoming the fetish of essentialist affirmation or deconstructionist critique, the time-honored concept of "immediacy" emerges
as a *social force* instantiated by the vernacular practice of discourse. The
meanings of such practice will vary depending on the speaker's interpretive assessment of what would be the most appropriate formal relation *to*
(or self-enactment *within*) the discursive conventions and constraints
assumed to be "at stake," all the while understanding such "propriety"
strictly as the "subjective" and contingent interpretive ratio of once again
"subjective" interest and communal constraint, of verbal (and, by implication, political) imagination and discursive precept, respectively. To be
sure, these hermeneutic predecisions, which in turn may obtain at varying

levels of awareness, can be subjected to some interpretive and metalingual commentary that, in turn, may seek to determine what prompted us to participate in a given discourse in this or that way. This latter kind of discourse is precisely what we commonly refer to and engage in under the title of "Theory," and its critically reflective supersession of the "immediacy" that produces significations in culture with talk *about* that culture intimates in striking manner the coinherence of analytic (abstract) conduct and eschatological motivation. At issue, for Theory, is not merely the performativity of gestures, acts, pronouncements, and works that instantiate (i.e., affirm/alter) a certain vision of culture but also the blind spot missed in those acts, that omission or lack of awareness that causes these acts to appear, upon retrospect, necessarily "infelicitous."

What Hegel's and Austin's reflections suggest and share, then, is that Theory can transcend the "immediacy" of a culture's and/or individual's self-blinded productivity of "meanings" only at the expense of a progressively stricter self-identification as a unique (i.e., abstract) discursive *form*. By now, of course, we also recognize how and for what reasons the notions of *form* and *genre* are so inextricably interwoven with social and moral "interest" and why it would seem precipitous to dismiss the concept of form as but a misguided, aggregational paradigm of meaning as conscious "immanence." As Michael Oakeshott notes,

> Rules, duties, and the like (moral principles and dogmas) are, then, passages of stringency in a moral practice. But they should not be thought of as strands of some exceptionally tough material woven into the otherwise flimsy fabric of moral association, constituents not only of notable strength but also of independent authority; conservators of the integrity of a moral practice. Rather, they are to be recognized as *densities obtruded by the tensions of a spoken language of moral intercourse,* nodal points at which a practice turns upon itself in a vortiginous movement and becomes steadier in ceasing to be adventurous. They may help to keep a practice in shape, but they do not give it its shape. They are abstractions which derive their authority from the practice itself as a spoken language in which they appear as passages of somewhat exaggerated emphasis. (*OHC*, 67–68)

Again, one must wonder whether Oakeshott's qualifications of "rules, duties, and the like" as "passages of somewhat exaggerated emphasis" does not, in fact, intimate a contiguous trajectory leading from formal recurrence to speculation about the "independent authority" of forms to conservatism ("ceasing to be adventurous") and, finally, to coercion and repression ("to help to keep a practice in shape"). The flaw in Oakeshott's argument lies in the self-evident ways in which a *certain* sense of moral practice, of moral value and, corresponding to these, of social and cultural organization is already in place before his otherwise lucid exposition of discursive practice begins to be enacted.

Keeping these serious problems of his argument in mind, we can nevertheless (and perhaps all the more clearly) identify how, more directly than either Hegel or Austin, Oakeshott has come to identify the *social efficiency of locutionary form*—here characterized with perhaps deceptive generality as "passages of stringency"—that shows illocutions of *all* sorts (those of the theorist included) to "secure uptake" and thus convert the putative inwardness and "immediacy" of conceptual labor into social authority. Hence the performative enactment of "immediacy" as moral agency and its reflective critique in the idiom of Theory reveal the concepts of locutionary form and performative function to collaborate in insuring the social/moral efficacy of discursive *practice*, rather than appearing as incompatible in *theory*. Hegel and the more recent analyses of the performative thus compel us to recognize a significant and indelibly structural, "moral" dimension in Theory, a dimension that manifests itself as soon as Theory becomes "critical" by directing its reflective energy at the precarious "immediacy" of cultural production while simultaneously refining (if not sublimating) its social interestedness qua reflective transcendence, that is, by cultivating, with varying intensity, its moral authority under the auspices of an expressly specialized and emblematically "rigorous" form.

Notes

1. On the connection between "immediacy" as a purportedly natural and authoritative sensibility and its extension into a social norm qua "sympathy," see Lucinda Cole, "'Anti'-Feminist Sympathies: The Politics of Relationship in Smith, Wollstonecraft, and Moore," *ELH* 58 (1990): 107–40.

2. For Kant, see *Critique of Judgment*, trans. J. H. Bernard (New York: Macmillan, 1951), "Introduction," B XXXVIIIff. and § 29, B 114–31; for Fichte, see *Science of Knowledge*, trans. Peter Heath and John L. Lachs (New York: Appleton-Century-Crofts, 1970), 189ff. and his contemporaneous essay fragments, "Von den Pflichten des Gelehrten" (On the duties of the scholar), *Gesamtausgabe*, ed. Reinhard Lauth and Hans Jacob (Stuttgart: Fromann, 1965–), II, 3:298ff.. Still the most incisive analysis of the status of

feeling in Fichte can be found in Novalis; see his "Fichte-Studien," *Werke, Tagebücher, und Briefe*, ed. Hans-Joachim Mähl (Munich: Hanser, 1978), II, 7–209. Regarding the relation between competing idealist versions of "immediacy" and "self-consciousness," respectively, see Ernst Tugendhat, *Self-Consciousness and Self-Determination* (Cambridge: MIT Press, 1986); Ulrich Pothast, *Über einige Fragen der Selbstbeziehung* (Frankfurt: Klostermann, 1971), Dieter Henrich, "Selbstbewußtsein: Kritische Einleitung in eine Theorie," in *Hermeneutik und Dialektik*, ed. Rüdiger Bubner et al. (Tübingen: J. C. B. Mohr, 1970), and his "Fichte's Original Insight," *Contemporary German Philosophy* 1 (1982): 15–51. See also my introduction to *Idealism and the Endgame of Theory: Three Essays by F. W. J. Schelling* (Albany: SUNY Press, 1994), 1–57. Specifically on Novalis, see Manfred Frank, *Einführung in die frühromantische Ästhetik* (Frankfurt: Suhrkamp, 1989), 248–86.

3. Novalis, *Werke, Tagebücher, und Briefe*, II, 18 (translation mine).

4. For alternative, critical accounts mediating romantic and/or idealist conceptions of the subject with contemporary theory, see Manfred Frank, *What is Neo-Structuralism?* trans. Sabine Wilke (Minneapolis: University of Minnesota Press, 1988), Rodolphe Gasché, *The Tain of the Mirror: Derrida and the Philosophy of Reflection* (Cambridge: Harvard University Press, 1986), and Paul Smith, *Discerning the Subject* (Minneapolis: University of Minnesota Press, 1988).

5. Alan Liu, "Local Transcendence: Cultural Criticism, Postmodernism, and the Romanticism of Detail," *Representations* 32 (1990): 75–113; see also his earlier "The Power of Formalism: The New Historicism," *ELH* 56 (1989): 721–71.

6. The formulation is Jérome McGann's in *The Romantic Ideology* (Chicago: University of Chicago Press, 1983), 12; see also pp. 13 and 56.

7. The eschatological motivation of cultural criticism emerges with exemplary distinctness in recent, new historicist and cultural materialist reassessments of romanticism. Thus Marjorie Levinson, in an essay appropriately entitled "The New Historicism: Back to the Future," remarks how "we are the ones who, by putting the past to a certain use, put it in a certain order." While the phrase, which echoes her earlier credo in a "self-consciously belated criticism," inaugurates a "transhistorical dialectic" that "might also be an effect of the past which we study," it is nevertheless clear that "the origin coalesces as a structure . . . only by the retroactive practice of the present" *(Rethinking Historicism*, ed. M. Levinson [New York: Basil Blackwell, 1989], 20–23).

8. For probing analyses of the interaction between moral theory and larger conceptions of cultural productivity, see Julie Ellison's *Delicate Subjects: Romanticism, Gender, and the Ethics of Understanding* (Ithaca: Cornell University Press, 1990). See also my own argument on the coinherence of social theory and the seemingly narrow, technical focus of poetic theory in Wordsworth, in "'Elementary Feelings' and 'Distorted Language': The Pragmatics of Culture in Wordsworth's *Preface* 1800," *New Literary History* 24, no. 1 (1993): 125–46.

9. For a rereading of contemporary moral theory—which is not our principal concern here—see Jürgen Habermas, *Moral Consciousness and Communicative Action* (Cambridge: MIT Press, 1990).

10. Michael Oakeshott, *Of Human Conduct* (Oxford: Clarendon, 1975), 60; henceforth cited parenthetically as *OHC*.

11. Regarding Hegel's logic of reflection, see Martin Heidegger, *Hegel's Concept of*

Experience, trans. Kenley Royce Dove (New York: Octagon, 1983), and Heidegger's lectures entitled *Hegels Phänomenologie des Geistes*, vol. 32 of the *Gesamtausgabe* (Frankfurt: Klostermann, 1980). See also Alexandre Kojève, *Introduction to the Reading of Hegel*, trans. James H. Nichols (Ithaca: Cornell University Press, 1969), as well as Rodolphe Gasché, *The Tain of the Mirror*, 23–59 and Erich Tugendhat, *Self-Consciousness and Self-Determination*.

12. *Phenomenology of Spirit*, trans. A. V. Miller (New York: Oxford University Press, 1977), 365. *Phänomenologie des Geistes* (Hamburg: Felix Meiner, 1952). All subsequent citations will be parenthetical, using the abbreviations of *PS* and *PhG* for the English and German text, respectively.

13. For a relevant, partially convergent interpretation of Hegel, see Jürgen Habermas, *Moral Consciousness and Communicative Action*, trans. C. Lenhardt and S. Nicholsen (Cambridge: MIT Press, 1990), especially pp. 195–211.

14. Much of John L. Austin's *How to Do Things with Words* (New York: Oxford University Press, 1975) is of course dedicated to exposing the fragility of the distinction between the performative and the constative and that between locutionary, illocutionary, and perlocutionary speech acts. See especially pp. 109–52.

15. Recently, Barbara Herrnstein-Smith has redescribed this figure of epistemic conservatism as "epistemic self-privileging," an originally Platonic figure of thought in which "the Skeptic's annihilation is *required, produced*, and *guaranteed* by the Believer's belief." "Belief and Resistance: A Symmetrical Account," *Critical Inquiry* 18 (1991): 125–39; quote from 130. See also her more explicit discussion of such epistemic self-privileging in "Unloading the Self-Refutation Charge," forthcoming; it corresponds to what in the present essay I invoke under the title of "immediacy."

16. Such an "expressivist" model of consciousness as the salient characteristic of Hegel's thought has been set forth by Charles Taylor, *Hegel* (New York: Cambridge University Press, 1975) and more recently, by the same author, *Human Agency and Language* (New York: Cambridge University Press, 1985).

17. On the concept of "infrastructure" in the work of Jacques Derrida, see Rodolphe Gasché, *The Tain of the Mirror*, 142–63. In his comment on Hegel's *Phenomenology*, Jean Hyppolite remarks on the centrality of language in relation to conscience, yet he views it still as merely ancillary, and clarifying, expressive of an interior and thus heteronomous essence or meaning. *Genesis and Structure of Hegel's Phenomenology of Spirit* (Evanston, Ill.: Northwestern University Press, 1974), 496–512.

18. Tugendhat, *Self-Consciousness and Self-Determination*, 9, 33.

19. John L. Austin, *How To Do Things with Words* (New York: Oxford University Press, 1962), henceforth cited parenthetically as *HTW*.

20. John Searle's insistence that we discriminate between "use" and "mention" presupposes a self-present, immediate subjectivity as the "utterance origin" whose intentionality would support that distinction, itself obviously cognate with that between sincere/insincere speech. Yet, as Hegel has shown, the notion of "conscience" and moral agency already requires the suspension (or supersession) of such a private, ego-logical, and intentionalist paradigm of meaning. For the texts by Searle, see notes 22 and 23 below.

21. For a lucid discussion of this passage and its history of being misread, see Sandy Petrey, *Speech Acts and Literary Theory* (New York: Routledge, 1990), 84–85. Austin again explores the duplicitous logic of moral "immediacy" later on, HTW, 78–79. We

must stress, however, that his critique of intentionality and inward self-presence is simply based on the assumption of a "false consciousness." For a lucid analysis of the epistemological conundrum of lying, see J. L. Austin's "Pretending," in *Philosophical Papers* (Oxford: Clarendon, 1970), 253–71.

22. Jacques Derrida, "Signature, Event, Context," in *Margins of Philosophy*, trans. Alan Bass (Chicago: University of Chicago Press, 1980), 322, 323. Derrida's critique often appears far more pertinent to John Searle's theory of the performative as set forth in *Speech Acts* (Cambridge: Cambridge University Press, 1969); their debate is examined by Sandy Petrey, *Speech Acts and Literary Theory*, 131–46.

23. For positions of a decidedly "conservative" and, at times, orthodox inflection, see John Searle's *Speech Acts* as well as his polemic against Derrida in "Reiterating the Differences: A Reply to Derrida," *Glyph* 1 (1977): 198–208, and Charles Altieri, *Act and Quality* (Amherst: University of Massachusetts Press, 1981). A more flexible assessment of Austin, though perhaps too oblivious of Austin's persistent refusal of philosophical "seriousness" and "rigor," can be found in Jacques Derrida, *Limited Inc*, ed. Samuel Weber (Evanston, Ill.: Northwestern University Press, 1988), which contains Derrida's earlier "Signature, Event, Context" and, responding to John Searle's critique of that essay, the title essay itself. See also Stanley Fish, "How to Do Things with Austin and Searle," in *Is there a Text in this Class?* (Cambridge: Harvard University Press, 1980), and, more recently, "With the Compliments of the Author: Reflections on Austin and Derrida" in *Doing What Comes Naturally: Change, Rhetoric, and the Practice of Theory in Literary and Legal Studies* (Durham, N.C.: Duke University Press, 1989), 37–67, and Sandra Petrey's recent reexamination of all these debates in *Speech Acts and Literary Theory* (New York: Routledge, 1990); Manfred Frank has reconsidered the debates from a continental perspective, aiming at the renewal of a dialogue between hermeneutic and poststructuralist thought, in *Das Sagbare und das Unsagbare* (Frankfurt: Suhrkamp, 1980).

24. It is (a significant paradox, to be sure) just as appropriate to speak of "style" as of "form," since the iterable (conventional) and the unique (original) moment in speech are dialectically related as two sides of the same coin. Clearly the most significant theorist of a contextually, rather than aesthetically, motivated analysis of "style," Friedrich Schleiermacher recognized that if the production of meaning inheres in a dialectic of style/form or innovation/conformity, this "immediate" ratio can be recovered only by approximation, namely, in an infinite "oscillation" of *interpretation* between speculation and comparison. For an assessment of the significance of Schleiermacher's *Dialectic and Hermeneutics* to contemporary theory, see my "Immediacy and the Text: Friedrich Schleiermacher's Theory of Style and Interpretation," *Journal of the History of Ideas* 51 (1990): 51–73.

25. Elucidating morality as a type of discursive action, Habermas inexplicably falls back on a prelinguistic, ideational paradigm of moral "norms." While initially misconstruing Austin's concept of the performative as bearing a strictly "derivative" *[abgeleitet]* relation to such norms, Habermas eventually acknowledges that to isolate them as values preexisting their discursive iteration would be to adopt a "utopian" vision of morality. *Moral Consciousness and Communicative Action* (Cambridge: MIT Press, 1990), 60–62.

26. For a very lucid conception of genre as the discursive infrastructure for social and cultural practice (including the practice of Theory), see Carolyn Miller, "Genre as Social Action," *Quarterly Journal of Speech* 70 (1984): 151–67.

"Non-Identity": The German Romantics, Schelling, and Adorno

Andrew Bowie

One of the major issues to emerge from the theoretical debates sur-rounding poststructuralism was the suspicion of an often very vaguely understood notion of "identity." The last thing anyone wanted to be involved in was the "repression of difference" entailed by "Western meta-physics." As the debate became less parochial and it became clear that Jacques Derrida was not the only person to be suspicious of Hegel's *Logic*, it was realized that there is a complex tradition of Western thought, associated in particular with the German romantics, that had already explored many of the issues concerning identity and difference.[1] The most evident representative of this tradition in more recent theory was T. W. Adorno, who made the critique of "identity thinking" one of his main philosophical aims. Like so many others, including Derrida, he did so not least in terms of his suspicion of, and simultaneous admiration for, Hegel. Adorno's approach to "non-identity" strikes a chord through its insistence on the need to attend to what is repressed in the increasingly administered and bureaucratic world of modern science and technology. The power of Adorno's position becomes most apparent in his philo-sophical interpretations of modern art, which at their best sustain the tension between the aesthetic need to do justice to the particular and the

This essay was written with the support of the Alexander von Humbolt foundation. My thanks to that splendid institution. My thanks also to Manfred Frank for first revealing the problem with Adorno's position to me.

244 ■ Andrew Bowie

theoretical need to understand art's inseparable relationship to the major
dilemmas of modern society. Adorno's understanding of art is connected
to, though not wholly dependent on, his theory of "non-identity." His
conception of "non-identity" is, I want to suggest, simply wrong in one
vital respect. The reasons why can be shown via some key ideas present
in romantic philosophy. By romantic philosophy I mean that strand of
post-Kantian philosophy—represented in particular by Friedrich Schlegel,
Novalis, and some aspects of Schelling—that, while coming close to Hegel,
differs from him in one crucial respect, as we shall see in a moment.

As with Derrida, there has been a tendency among the admirers of
Adorno to think that Adorno's own work can dictate the terms in which
he is judged. For Adorno strictly philosophical argument is always suspicious because it necessarily bears the marks of its entanglement with
the conflicts of the social and historical situation of its emergence, while
at the same time trying to conceal those conflicts. The very idea of
"strictly philosophical argument" smacks precisely of the kind of *prima
philosophia* that Adorno terms "identity thinking," be it in the form of
Parmenides' identification of thinking and being, Husserl's attempt at
salvaging transcendental philosophy, or of Hegel's system. At the same
time Adorno at his best is not a Nietzschean or post-Nietzschean reduc-
tionist, in that he does not wish to reduce truth to the will to power.
Indeed, the whole point of *Aesthetic Theory* can be understood as being
the attempt to keep truth while not enforcing identity upon difference.[2]

One of the tasks of a proper contemporary assessment of Adorno's
work is to confront the tension between the need for "philosophical"
argument—in the sense of argument that seeks the truth about a specific
problem, such as the problem of self-consciousness, using resources from
anywhere in philosophy past or present—and the inherent suspicion of
such argument that is generated by Adorno's insistence that philosophy
only takes place in a determinate historical context and cannot simply be
abstracted from that context. In the space available here I just want to
deal with one aspect of this problem, rather than attempting to do justice
to the complexity of Adorno's position. If all one ever does is to try to do
justice to Adorno by stressing how complex everything is, the danger is
that very basic matters never get addressed, as they so often do not in
relation to Derrida. It is a mistake to think that Adorno's suspicion of
prima philosophia means that one should avoid arguing about the internal
workings of philosophical issues, including logical problems. Adorno
himself is quite clear that one should not reduce philosophical problems

to contexts, and the issue I want to discuss cannot be dealt with in a merely historical, contextual, or intertextual manner. It is only if one thinks that philosophical problems only lead to answers in the terms of "Western metaphysics," and are thus inherently repressive, that they cease to be a valid object of attention. The ground for such judgments about philosophy seems to me itself necessarily metaphysical, in that it entails the ability to circumscribe what "Western metaphysics" really is. It is clear to me that certain arguments about non-identity cannot be right and it is vital to show why. Otherwise one will go on generating theory that cannot go anywhere because it ignores insights that invalidate certain ways of discussing issues.

This does not mean, however, that it is invalid to question the nature of "Western metaphysics." One way of doing so is, precisely, in terms of the problem of identity, as we know from developments in recent theory. The reason for the repeated reference to Hegel in this connection lies in the perception that Hegel's was the most consistent attempt at carrying out a programme that began with Parmenides, the programme of explicating the relationship of thinking and being. Many people think Hegel was a failure who yet gave us certain conceptual strategies that can be held onto, even if the final aim of his system is never fulfilled. Adorno shares a version of this view with Derrida. Up to a point I would agree, but in one key respect a problem with Hegel's position is repeated in Adorno (and Derrida), with consequences that need to be carefully considered.

The problem with Hegel's position has to do with the question of identity, and it goes back to debates that began in Germany at the time of Kant. I make no apology for simply using some of these arguments to show what is wrong with Adorno's position. I do so because the arguments seem to me to retain their validity. The fact is that many of the key ideas in romanticism were never adequately understood and were buried in the demise of Hegelianism. My aim is to help to revive some of these ideas. It was Schelling who first brought out the implications of the question of identity for Hegel's system from the 1820s onwards. He did so on the basis of aspects of his thinking that are also present at times, not least via the influence of Hölderlin and Friedrich Schlegel, in his early thinking. I shall, therefore, not make any strict distinction here between the early and the late Schelling.[3] The assumption has tended to be that Adorno reveals the same problem as Schelling, but in a way that is able to preserve more of the insights of Hegel. It can be argued, though, that Schelling shows something that puts in question some of those aspects of

Hegel's work that Adorno still retains. To explain why, I need to go over some ground that Manfred Frank has explored in detail and that I have elsewhere tried to make available to English-speaking readers.[4] Given the difficulty and unfamiliarity of the issues, a degree of repetition is not necessarily a problem.

As is well known, the philosophy of Kant had a startling effect on the philosophical outlook of his age. Taking Hume's arguments on causality seriously, Kant saw no alternative to asserting that knowledge of things in themselves of the kind that had been the aim of science and philosophy from the very beginning was impossible. Knowledge was the subject's synthesizing of intuitions in judgments of our understanding, not the adequate representation to the mind of the inherent properties of objects. The aim of German idealism was to overcome Kant's separation of the world in itself from the way we know it, on the grounds that we are also part of the world. The success of the idealist enterprise depended upon finding a way of showing that the difference suggested by Kant, between the world in itself—including ourselves—and our knowledge of the world, was only apparent. Adorno sustains an ambivalent relationship to Kant and German idealism throughout his career. On the one hand, he knows that Kantian dualism cannot be sustained in the form Kant presents it; on the other, he sees that the ways of overcoming that dualism in German idealism end up repressing the object side of the dialectic that Kant had sustained in the notion of things-in-themselves. For Adorno, thought in German idealism consumes its object in the manner characteristic of metaphysics since Parmenides.

The simple problem behind the relationship of thought and being in any version is that it is not possible to overcome the split of thinking and being from one side of the divide between the two. It was Schelling who, albeit inconsistently, saw the consequences of this fact in a way that both Hegel and Adorno failed adequately to comprehend. The conceptual basis of this realization was laid in aspects of the philosophy of the German romantics, particularly in the work of Friedrich Schlegel and Novalis, with whom Schelling had direct contact in Jena at the beginning of the nineteenth century.[5] Nobody is going to claim that the insights of the romantics are always wholly coherent, but, as Benjamin already showed in his Ph.D. dissertation, which Adorno knew, there is serious substance in their philosophical fragments. Given the frequent conscious and unconscious echoes of the romantics in Adorno's work, it is important to clarify what is at issue in their philosophy. Manfred

Frank has suggested that romantic philosophy is, *avant la lettre*, "Hegelianism without a crowning conclusion."[6] This does not mean that the romantics think that the Absolute therefore has no place in philosophy, but rather that they see the relationship of philosophy to the Absolute in a different way from Hegel. Consider the following from Friedrich Schlegel's lectures on *Transcendentalphilosophie* of 1800–1801, at which Hegel was present in the audience:

> Truth arises when opposed errors neutralize each other. Absolute truth cannot be admitted; and this is the testimony for the freedom of thought and of spirit. If absolute truth were found, then the business of spirit would be completed and it would have to cease to be, since it only exists in activity.[7]

Schlegel, then, does not conceive of the truth as simply consisting in positive assertions. He is, though, fully aware that his claim that all truth is relative because it cannot be absolute is open to the standard (and correct) objection that it leads to skepticism, in that the claim is self-refuting: "If all truth is relative, then the proposition is also relative that all truth is relative" (*TP*, 95). What one has to understand, Schlegel maintains, is how that relativity itself is the motor of the process of truth. Any particular knowledge is always context-relative in that it is open to further development by being recontextualized in, say, the way Newtonian physics changes its status in the light of relativity theory. The problem is to explain this without falling into skepticism.

Schlegel expressly rejects the idea of truth as "agreement of subjective and objective" because "reality . . . cannot be called either subject or object" (*TP*, 92). Like many thinkers in this period he does not follow the model that regards thought as representation of external objects to the thinking subject, in that this is precisely the kind of dualism that has to be avoided if one is not to return to Kantian problems. Schlegel even suggests, presaging the linguistic turn that his friend Schleiermacher will be the first to make in a worked-out manner,[8] that the idea of the agreement of "idea" *(Vorstellung)* and "object" *(Gegenstand)* "says no more . . . than what a sign says of what is to be signified" (*TP*, 4). The final consequence of his position is that ultimately everything should be said to be identical: "The proposition of identity is the last truth. . . . *Philosophy is complete when all concepts are transcendent and all propositions are identical.*" This should, perhaps surprisingly, not be seen as the repression of non-identity, understood as the complete assimilation of being into thought. Why is this the case?

The key point is how "identity" is conceived. Crucially, Schlegel goes on to add: "(But this is only the ideal of philosophy, which is never achievable)" (*TP*, 28). Non-identity is inherent in philosophy because absolute identity cannot be thought. What this means will become clearer as we develop these ideas. In Schlegel's view everything particular is negative, in that it can only become determinate if its relations to other things are expressed in judgments. Knowledge of the totality of these relations is what would enable us to say the absolute truth about the particular thing. This is what Kant had referred to in the *Critique of Pure Reason* as the "transcendental ideal" of total determinacy. Kant claims that "to completely know a thing one must know everything possible . . . complete determination is consequently a concept that we can never represent *in concreto* in its totality."[9] How, then, can there be any truth at all? Schlegel thinks the truth must be understood as "the indifference of two opposed errors"; truth "arises where opposed errors neutralise each other . . . if we destroy error truth arises of its own accord" (*TP*, 92–93). In this sense *"There really is no error"* (*TP*, 94) because truth and error are identical, in that the truth is the product of error's self-cancellation, and thus cannot be without error. As Fichte had seen in a vital passage of the *Wissenschaftslehre:*

> Everything which is opposed to something is the same as what it is opposed to in one characteristic = X; and: everything the same is opposed to what it is the same as in one respect = X. Such a characteristic = X is the ground, in the first case the ground of relation, in the second the ground of difference; for identifying *[gleichsetzen]* or comparing *[vergleichen]* what is opposed is called relating; opposing what has been identified is *differentiating* them.[10]

Opposed "errors" must in some way be the same, as otherwise they could not be regarded as opposed at all. The question is how one approaches their identity. Clearly the process of truth is something in which we are always already engaged by dint of being in a world of opposed things that we try to bring to identity in judgments. What, though, of the whole that is the ground of relating and differentiating?

As we just saw, Schlegel thinks that philosophy cannot attain this whole. Why, then, talk about it at all, unless one is going to attempt, like

Hegel, to show that the whole can be attained in philosophy? The problem is to explain why there is a changing finite world of opposed things, and thus why we have the structure of truth that tries to synthesize difference into identity. Propositions have to join what is separate and they must therefore have a dual structure. The whole cannot itself have this dual structure, in that it is the condition of possibility of identity, as the passage from Fichte suggests. This leads both Schlegel, and the Schelling of the 1800 *System of Transcendental Idealism*, to the idea that the Highest necessarily cannot be said, because the very structure of saying entails the splitting of what cannot be divided. Schlegel therefore introduces "allegory, which is the mediating term between unity and multiplicity" (*TP*, 41). Allegory is the means of presenting that which cannot be presented as itself—"unity"—which thus can only appear because what is said, "multiplicity," is not what is meant. The argument, then, (and here we come close to Adorno) is that art, as shown in the notion of allegory, is able to show what philosophy cannot. Art can do so because its significance is not reducible to what can be said about it in propositional terms or, if it is itself articulated in language, to what it says propositionally. The importance of allegory in Benjamin's *Trauerspielbuch* clearly has its roots in romantic philosophy, as do key aspects of Benjamin's nonpropositional theory of the "mimetic" in language.[11]

Importantly, although what is at issue here is the ground of identity, this ground cannot be identified in a proposition, even the proposition A=A. As Novalis puts it in one of his most revealing insights in the "Fichte-Studies" of 1795–96: "The essence of identity can only be established in an *apparent proposition*. We leave the *identical* in order to represent it":[12] without some kind of difference, even if it is only the difference between the first and the second A, there can be no propositions about unity. What is at issue, then, is not an identity that is based upon the sameness of subject and object that can be asserted in a proposition, because this would fail to account for thought's difference from its other. One cannot account for that difference from within thought, because what is in question is precisely the *difference* of thought from its other. What is discussed in terms of "identity," as the overall structure that includes thought and its other, can therefore just as easily be seen as "non-identical," in that it, as the ground of identification, cannot itself be identified within a subject-object, or propositional, structure. This is the argument that Hölderlin uses in 1795 against Fichte's notion of the absolute I. Fichte's I could, Hölderlin shows, only be an *I* if it has a "reflexive" other of which it is conscious, which means that it is no longer absolute. Hölderlin thereby reveals the irreflexive ground within which the relation of I and not-I is contained.[13]

The counterposition to this is Hegel's system, which is precisely intended to show that philosophy, rather than art, can grasp the Absolute. For this to be possible the Absolute must itself be constituted reflexively, so that what appears opposed to thinking can ultimately be articulated as dependent upon thinking. What is most obviously opposed to thinking, which is necessarily constituted in terms of difference, is being. The aim of the beginning of the *Logic* is to show that the apparent immediacy of being, which the romantic position sees as leading to allegory, the necessarily indirect means of showing the truth of being, is an illusion, about which nothing can or need be said. The difficulty Adorno faces is that he clearly cannot accept Hegel's position because it yet again gives primacy to thinking in the manner of "Western metaphysics"; but he also has both philosophical and ideological reasons for suspecting the romantic position described here. The fact is that the romantic position involves ideas that arguably bring one very close to one version of what Heidegger means by "being." In his 1789 text on Spinoza, F. H. Jacobi, who is one of the major sources of the romantic position,[14] called the "ontological" ground of what could not be understood in terms of reflexive difference *Seyn* (being). Jacobi thereby made an influential distinction between the ontic, which could be determined propositionally, and the ontological, which could not; it is this distinction that Hölderlin and Schelling used against Fichte. I cannot here consider either Adorno's evident misreadings of Heidegger, or the fact that he comes much closer to Heidegger than he wants to admit. In the circumstances that followed 1933, I think Adorno was right not to want to be associated with the dreadful man. Unfortunately, though, Heidegger was probably nearer the insight at which Adorno wished to arrive than Adorno himself. The person who, in the light of Jacobi's key thought, already saw well before Heidegger how this issue might be dealt with was Schelling, particularly in the critique of Hegel in his later work from the 1820s onwards.

Now much of what Adorno says on this topic parallels Schelling, as Adorno himself occasionally suggests. There is, though, a crucial difference. The difference lies in how the relationship of subject and object is understood. The point of the romantic position, which is shared in various ways by Schlegel, Novalis, Hölderlin, and, much of the time, Schelling, was that this relationship could not be understood in "reflexive" terms. In the romantic view, although subject and object could not be separated in the manner Kant's philosophy had required, neither could they be united by articulating their relationship in philosophy. Hegel's aim was to get away from the need for a founding ground of identity of the kind that we outlined above, by finding a way of avoiding foundations altogether. The only way to do this, as Hegel saw, was to stop the beginning from being a positive foundation. This meant that the beginning could only become determinate at the end, when its dependence on what follows had been shown by its becoming determinate in the concept. The movement of the *Logic* is dependent on something like Schlegel's idea that the truth is the product of error's self-cancellation. The difference is that at the end of the *Logic* this self-cancellation cancels itself, in the realization of the absolute Idea, which takes up all the negations of the negation into itself as the final positive conclusion. Now Adorno thinks that aspects of the way in which Hegel's dialectic tries to avoid positive foundations are vital for philosophy if it is to escape the traps of the history of metaphysics. At the same time it is clear that Hegel's system is itself the culmination of the history of the attempt of metaphysics to have thought swallow its object. This is why Adorno sustains his attachment to Kant, who at least retained the indigestible thing-in-itself.

Let us look at how Adorno deals with this issue in the second part of *Negative Dialectics*, and compare his argument with the later Schelling's critique of Hegel, which depends on a development of some of the romantic ideas we have just seen. At the beginning of the second part of *Negative Dialectics* Adorno takes Hegel to task for expressly refusing at the beginning of the *Logic* to begin with "something" rather than with "being": "He thereby prejudices the whole work, which wants to show the primacy of the subject, in favour of the subject, idealistically."[15] Had Hegel begun with "something," as opposed to "being," he would have sustained "more tolerance in relation to the non-identical" and yet still been led to the next moment, to the "non-conceptual" (*ND*, 139), that which cannot be subsumed into identity by being known. Adorno opposes any move in the direction of ontology, which he sees as the result of trying to come up with the concept of another kind of beginning:

> No being without beings [*Kein Sein ohne Seiendes*]. The something as the necessary substrate for thought of the concept, including the concept of being, is the most extreme abstraction—which cannot be got rid of by any further process of thought—of the content of that which is not identical with thought. (*ND*, 139)

Adorno does not wish to fix a concept of the "non-conceptual," because that is precisely what Hegel does with his concept of "being," the "indeterminate immediate," which negates itself and sets in motion the process of its becoming articulated. For Adorno, then, any *concept* of being depends upon the particular something that resists being subsumed into a general metaphysical category: "Whatever experience the word being might carry with it can only be expressed in configurations of beings" (*ND*, 143). One can only get the concept of being by abstracting from what is immediate, from the fact that one always begins with something.

The argument depends upon the understanding of "immediacy" and it is here that difficulties begin to emerge in Adorno's position. Hegel's point was to reveal how the apparently immediate is in fact mediated, which is what allows him to subject being to the concept in the *Logic*. Adorno does not accept that immediacy and mediation can have a symmetrical relationship to each other: "Immediacy itself, however, stands for a moment that does not need cognition, mediation, in the way that cognition does need the immediate" (*ND*, 174). Dieter Henrich has shown in detail how Hegel makes an invalid move in the "logic of reflection" at the beginning of the second part of the *Logic*, where the move from "being" to "essence" *(Wesen)* (the move that allows knowledge of being) is made.[16] Hegel makes the invalid move by having two different senses of immediacy and equating them, so that the apparent positive initial immediacy of being can be claimed to be as mediated as the immediacy of essence, which is the result of a negation of the negation. In Hegel's terms even to say being is immediate means that one is led to the dependence of the notion of immediacy on the other of immediacy for immediacy to be knowable. Hence the immediate is really mediated, which is precisely what Adorno will not accept. Now, the key point about Hegel's sleight of hand, as Henrich shows, is that for it to work Hegel must *presuppose* the identity of the immediacy of being and the immediacy of essence, thereby contradicting the whole method of the *Logic*, which depends on having no presuppositions.

The fact is that there can be nothing in Hegel's construction to show the sameness of the two kinds of immediacy. Hegel assumes that one side of a relation, "essence," can show its identity with the other side. This, though, requires a third position, which would have to be that of essence, rather than of the immediacy of being. The problem is that this position cannot itself depend upon a relationship to an other, as essence does, because this would lead to a regress, where each negative (related) position tried to arrive at the position of independence of relation. The only possible such position must, as Manfred Frank has shown, already be immediate: "[B]ecause reflection is a relation with only two places and is grounded in its own structure, it must presuppose self-identity as a fact which is external to reflection."[17] This self-identity is how Hölderlin already understood being in 1795. Schelling insists in the *Introduction to the Philosophy of Revelation or Foundation of the Positive Philosophy*, which was given in Berlin in 1842–43,

> If we want anything at all which is outside thought, then we must begin with a being which is absolutely independent of all thinking, which precedes all thinking. Hegelian philosophy knows nothing of this being, it has no place for this concept.[18]

He excludes this being, which he terms "necessary existence," from essence in the following manner: "It is incoherent to ask what sort of being *[Wesen]* could exist necessarily; for in that way I assume that an essence *[Wesen]*, a What, a possibility precedes necessary existence" (II/3, 166–67). The move to essence and concept is from being: "[E]xisting is not here the consequence of the concept or of essence, but rather existence is here itself the concept and itself the essence" (II/3, 167). How, then, does this relate to Adorno's critique of Hegel?

Clearly both Schelling and Adorno are convinced that Hegel too readily assimilates everything into thought, thereby leaving no space for that which cannot be shown to be mediated by thought. This is evident when Adorno says in the *Metacritique of Epistemology*,

> The fact that not all being is consciousness is not included as a necessity of thought in the analysis of the concept of being, but rather puts an end to the closure involved in such an analysis. To think not-thinking: that is not a logical consequence of thinking, but rather suspends the claim to totality of thinking.[19]

The difference between Schelling and Adorno lies in the way each understands "reflexivity." It seems clear to me that Adorno thinks that by hanging on to an inverted conception of the relation of subject and object he can avoid a construction that entails "being which is absolutely independent of thinking." His largely mistaken worry was probably that such a view is really a version of Heidegger's "being," and that it is therefore mystical and irrationalist. Schelling, though, sees the essential alternative as follows:

[E]ither the concept would have to go first, and being would have to be the consequence of the concept, which would mean it was no longer absolute being; or the concept is the consequence of being, then we must begin with being without the concept (II/3, 164).

This means that the relationship between thought and its object, including thought itself as its own object, must be grounded in what cannot be articulated by thinking because it has to precede thinking. As Manfred Frank has repeatedly shown,[20] even to know my thoughts as my thoughts requires that I be already familiar with them in a nonreflexive way, otherwise I have no criterion via which I can know them as *mine*.

This idea of immediacy is, then, not just invoked, "shot from a pistol," but rather the result of a strict analysis of the limitations of the model of reflection, which turns out to be unable to ground itself. This is clear in Schelling's critique of the Cartesian ego. Schelling has no doubt that the Cartesian ego cannot take the absolute place that is assigned to it by most accounts of Western metaphysics:

Thinking is, therefore, only a determination or way of being. . . . The sum that is contained in the cogito does not, then, have the significance of an absolute I am, but only of an "I am in one way or another," namely as just thinking, in that way of being which one calls thinking. (I/10, 10)

He goes on to suggest,

I think is, therefore, in truth in no way something immediate, it only emerges via the reflection which directs itself at the thinking in me; this thinking, by the way, also carries on independently of the thinking that reflects upon it. . . . Indeed, true thinking must even be independent of the subject that reflects upon it, in other words, it will think all the more truly the less the subject interferes with it. (I/10, 11)

Is this not, then, really what Adorno terms the "primacy of the object" (*ND*, 185), in that the supremacy of the subject as reflexive consciousness is undermined?

The answer is clearly no, in that Schelling would never refer to what is going on in thinking as a merely objective process. The simple problem with Adorno's notion of the primacy of the object is that it is hard to know what the word *object* means. By putting immediate being first,

Schelling sees any cognitive relationship of subject and object, including, as we just saw, the relation to oneself, as grounded in a structure that necessarily transcends what can be known, because it is not just a structure of relation between two dependent terms, not just a structure of "reflection." Adorno's concern is to sustain non-identity by preventing the subject from assuming the absolute primacy it had in Hegel. Schelling's way of undermining this primacy depended, as we saw, on his notion of the primacy of being before the concept. Adorno puts his idea of the "primacy of the object" as follows:

> Object can only be thought via subject, but it always sustains itself against the latter as an other; subject, however, is in its own constitution already also object. The object cannot be even thought away from the subject as an idea, but the subject can from the object. It is part of the meaning of subjectivity also to be object; it is not in the same way part of the meaning of objectivity to be subject. (*ND*, 184)

Adorno has here really just inverted Hegel, by now attributing the prior role of the subject in Hegel to the object. The structure is, however, still reflexive. This is questionable for two related reasons. The first is that Adorno's position actually gives no way of understanding what constitutes the distinction between conscious subject and its object, as opposed to the random difference in nature between one material thing and another that cannot be known for lack of that which could be *aware* of it as a difference. The second reason is that, if the argument is to be consistent, the judgment on what the objective is seems to have to come from the objective itself. This, though, is impossible because it removes the objective's criterion of differentiation of itself from the other.

Now, it may be argued that Adorno's point is tied to his perception of the incursion of the "functional context of society" (*ND*, 180) into the very internal constitution of its members, rendering them objects of what social "subjects" collectively produce, in the form of reified structures of social organization. His philosophical model for this is Kant's transcendental subject, which, like modern forms of social organization, is articulated independently of real empirical subjects. This is, though, a case where Adorno's attempt to keep a dialectical relationship between philosophy and historical context fails to take the philosophical issue seriously enough. How does Adorno know that this incursion has taken place into the subject, given his own location in such a society? His judgment only makes sense on the basis of some criterion of a subject, understood as that which cannot (and should not) be objectified. Without some kind of access to such a criterion (which is also indispensable for *Aesthetic Theory*) the critical force of Adorno's position is lost. Adorno's mistake, which he shares with Derrida, is that he sees the subject only in reflexive terms, as the correlate of the object. For Adorno the philosophical subject wrongly imagines it can subsume the object into self-presence. The point of the romantic conception of the subject, developed in Schelling's critique of Descartes, is that subjectivity itself cannot be conceived of in terms of self-presence, because it is carried by a being that it cannot reflexively identify as its own. As such we live with an inherent non-identity. This does not mean that we cannot be understood as subjects.

The philosophical root of Adorno's mistake is, then, the refusal to take on the notion of being in the sense we saw it being used by the romantics and the later Schelling. The point of a critique of identity thinking is, reductively, to show the illusions of the subject that thinks it generates the world out of itself. The classic model of this illusion is often illustrated (somewhat unfairly) by Fichte's way of understanding Kant's transcendental subject, where the world of objects is generated by the activity of the I opposing itself to itself in the form of the not-I.[21] Fichte is thereby seen as turning the world of nature into that which has to be overcome in the name of practical reason, by making nature the reflected object of the action of the subject. Schelling's objections to Fichte after 1801 were based on the idea that the subject itself depended on nature. This was also what had led Hölderlin to move beyond the merely reflexive structure of subject and object in order to ground both thinking and material nature in a whole of which they are aspects. In many ways Adorno agrees with such a conception, and he approvingly cites Schelling's *Weltalter* for grounding consciousness in nature (*ND*, 202). However, this does not free him from the obligation to characterize subjectivity in an adequate manner.

Adorno wants, in a way that is also to become familiar from Derrida, to deconstruct the opposition of subject and object: "[C]ritical thinking does not want to hand over the sovereign's throne of the subject to the object, on which the object would be nothing but an idol, but rather to remove the hierarchy" (*ND*, 182). He claims that

> Every assertion that subjectivity "is" in some way already includes an
> objectivity which the subject pretends to ground via its own absolute

being. Only because the subject for its part is mediated, and thus is not the radical other of the object that first legitimates the object, can it grasp objectivity at all. (*ND*, 186)

What Adorno seems to mean by "object" has to do with material, sensuous existence, that the thinking subject is seen as trying to repress in the kinds of idealism that Adorno is attacking. If this is the case, though, he still needs to tell us how the thinking subject is *aware* of its own material existence as *its* material existence. Like all materialist attempts to understand the structure of subjectivity, Adorno's fails because it cannot explain basic facts about consciousness. Consciousness may be matter's awareness of itself, but it cannot be matter's awareness of itself as an object, because this leads into a regress where the phenomenon to be understood, self-consciousness, which cannot just be matter qua object because this would fail to account for the *subjective* aspect of matter, is lost.

The problem underlying all this is Adorno's implicit equation of immediacy with objectivity. We saw above that immediacy is the way out of the narcissistic trap of Hegelian reflection for both Schelling and Adorno. As Adorno said: "Immediacy itself, however, stands for a moment which does not need cognition, mediation, in the way that cognition does need the immediate" (*ND*, 174). However one thinks of it, objectivity, about which he says similar things, cannot be the *same* as immediacy, in that the object can only be *as such* in a "mediated" relation to an other that is a subject. There can only *be* objectivity in relation to an other that is aware of something as objective. That something cannot itself be turned into an object, as that would mean the very possibility of a world about which we can say anything disintegrates, because the condition of predication disappears.

The fact is that Adorno inverts Hegel's logic of reflection. Whereas Hegel invalidly makes the immediacy of being into a subjectively mediated moment of the dialectic, in order to dissolve it into our knowledge of it, Adorno invalidly makes the mediated object into something immediate, so that it can be shown to be prior to the subject. The only defensible form of such immediacy, though— which Adorno, like Derrida, would not countenance—is the immediacy of being, as the nonreflexive ground of the difference of subject and object that emerges via the failure of reflection to ground itself. Furthermore, though the subject is in no way the source of the *existence* of the object, the *determinacy* of the object as that object, which is expressed in a proposition, must be in some way dependent upon the subject. The subject itself, as we saw, also depends upon a moment of immediacy, in that its reflexive self-awareness that can be articulated in propositions is grounded in a prereflexive awareness that is prepropositional and does not have a subject-object structure. Without such prereflexive awareness I would be unable to distinguish the reflection of myself in a mirror from any other object in the world. In this view, then, the subject cannot wholly assimilate the object, because it cannot even fully articulate its own structure. The fact is that the idea of the self-articulation of an *object* that is entailed by the materialist aspect of Adorno's position is completely opaque, because it does not confront the fact that the world is disclosed at all. Schelling revealed this very problem throughout his life, when arguing against Spinoza's materialistic conception of being.[22]

What, then, does this admittedly abstract philosophical argument do to the idea of non-identity that is central for Adorno's thinking? As I have stated the case so far, it might appear that I am simply conjuring away the reasons that make Adorno introduce the notion of the primacy of the object. The reasons have to do with Adorno's awareness, especially in the light of the unspeakable horrors of Nazism—though the basic thought emerges earlier than the Nazi period—that the autonomy of the subject can easily become a non-existent illusion in the face of the pressures of modern social reality. There is clearly, though, a hiatus between what history tells us about subjects and what philosophical reflection tells us about subjectivity. It is important to sustain the tension generated by this hiatus, not just opt for one side of the split. If real history often abolishes subjects, part of philosophy's job is to show how they can be valued: otherwise the real and conceptual death of the subject would be of no concern anyway. Aspects of forgotten romantic philosophy with which Adorno did not engage can help us reevaluate our conceptions of subjectivity in ways that Adorno's position does not always allow.

How far Adorno's philosophical failure on this particular point invalidates other aspects of his work is a matter for detailed further investigation. To conclude, I want to point very briefly to one way of understanding what Adorno tries to get at via the idea of the primacy of the object. The relationship of subjectivity to language clearly involves the issue Adorno is confronting. Language qua material signifier exists as an external "object," but it is also intrinsically part of the thinking subject. On the one hand, this relationship can be and should be seen as repressive: there is no point in trying to wish away the repressions entailed by the "insertion into the symbolic." On the other, language is also enabling: it is not just a means of identification, but also a means of expression, via which a subject can say something completely different, while using the same signifying material as others. Adorno is at his most enlightening when he considers this tension in his writings on aesthetics, particularly on the language of music, where the state of the objective material is seen as presenting the subject with the challenge of how to express what society has repressed. This suggests that the insights he offers in some of his aesthetic writings need to be used against some of the failings of his philosophical position.[23] Interestingly, many of these insights relate closely to the romantic conception of art described above. If the idea of non-identity is to be appropriately understood, then, it should not lead, as so much recent theory has, and as some of Adorno's philosophical writings do, to the repression of subjectivity via the reduction of the subject to the happening of language or society. This does not mean that the subject therefore becomes the master of language: the subversion of the Cartesian subject we saw in Schelling already makes this plain. The point is that more detailed attention to the history of the philosophical attempt to understand subjectivity is vital at the present moment: this attention requires an awareness of past resources that has been signally lacking in much recent discussion. The sort of intersection I have tried to establish depends as much on rigor of philosophical argument, where we are prepared to say that someone is simply wrong, as it does on revealing yet another part of the infinite possibilities of intertextual connection in the history of philosophy or theory. In the case of non-identity this sort of attention to connections in the history of modern philosophy should lead to a proper insight into the ultimate fragility of the subject, which, while not master in its own house, still has to live somewhere.

Notes

1. On this see Manfred Frank, *Was Ist Neo-Strukturalismus?* (Frankfurt, 1984); Peter Dews, *Logics of Disintegration* (London, 1987); Andrew Bowie, *Aesthetics and Subjectivity: From Kant to Nietzsche* (Manchester, 1990).

2. On Adorno's relation to Nietzsche see, e.g., Norbert Bolz's essay in Burkhardt Lindner and W. Martin Lüdke, eds., *Materialien zur ästhetischen Theorie Th. W. Adornos: Konstruktion der Moderne* (Frankfurt, 1979).

3. For those wanting such distinctions, see Andrew Bowie, *Schelling and Modern European Philosophy: An Introduction* (London, 1993).

4. See Manfred Frank, *Einführung in die frühromantische Ästhetik* (Frankfurt, 1989); *Das Problem "Zeit" in der deutschen Romantik*, (Paderborn, Munich, Vienna, Zurich, 1990); Bowie, *Aesthetics and Subjectivity* (Manchester, 1990); "Revealing the Truth of Art," *Radical Philosophy* 58 (Summer 1991); idem, *Schelling and Modern European Philosophy*; idem, "Re-thinking the History of the Subject: Jacobi, Schelling and Heidegger," in *Deconstructive Subjectivities*, ed. Peter Dews and Simon Critchley (New York, 1994).

5. See Frank, *Einführung*, 228; Bowie, *Schelling and Modern European Philosophy*.

6. Frank, *Einführung*, 228.

7. Friedrich Schlegel, *Transcendentalphilosophie*, ed. Michael Elsasser (Hamburg, 1991), 93. Abbreviated in the text as *TP*.

8. See Bowie, *Aesthetics and Subjectivity*, chap. 6.

9. Immanuel Kant, *Werkausgabe*, vols. 1–12, ed. Wilhelm Weischedel (Frankfurt, 1968–77); idem, *Kritik der reinen Vernunft*, B 600, A 573.

10. J. G. Fichte, *Werke*, 1:111.

11. See Andrew Bowie, "Truth, Language and Art: Benjamin, Davidson and Others," in Bartram and Pinkney, eds., *Walter Benjamin in the Post-Modern*, (London, 1994).

12. Novalis, *Band 2: Das philosophisch-theoretische Werk*, ed. Hans-Joachim Mähl, (Munich and Vienna, 1978), 8.

13. On this see Manfred Frank, *Der unendliche Mangel an Sein* (Frankfurt, 1975); idem, *Eine Einführung in Schellings Philosophie* (Frankfurt, 1985); Bowie, *Aesthetics and Subjectivity*, chap. 3.

14. See Frank, *Einführung*; Birgit Sandkaulen-Bock, *Ausgang vom Unbedingten: Über den Anfang in der Philosophie Schellings* (Göttingen, 1990); Bowie, "Rethinking the History of the Subject."

15. T. W. Adorno, *Negative Dialektik* (Frankfurt, 1975), 139. Abbreviated in the text as *ND*.

16. See Dieter Henrich, *Hegel im Kontext* (Frankfurt, 1971); see also Frank, *Der unendliche Mangel*; and Bowie *Schelling and Modern European Philosophy*.

17. Frank, *Der unendliche Mangel*, 60.

18. Schelling references are to Friedrich Wilhelm Schelling's *Sämmtliche Werke*, ed. K. F. A. Schelling, I Abtheilung, vols. 1–10, II Abtheilung vols. 1–4 (Stuttgart, 1856–61). E.g., here "(II/3, 164)."

19. T. W. Adorno, *Zur Metakritik der Erkenntnistheorie* (Frankfurt, 1970), 33.

20. E.g., most recently, Manfred Frank, *Selbstbewußtsein und Selbsterkenntnis* (Stuttgart, 1991).

21. See Frederick Neuhouser, *Fichte's Theory of Subjectivity* (Cambridge, 1989) for a more hermeneutically apt view of Fichte.

22. See Bowie, *Schelling and Modern European Philosophy*; and F. W. J. Schelling, *On the History of Modern Philosophy*, translated and introduced by Andrew Bowie (Cambridge, 1994).

23. See, e.g., Elizabeth Bradbury, "Social and Aesthetic Theory: A Reexamination of Aspects of the Work of T. W. Adorno," Ph. D. diss., Cambridge University, 1993.

III Reinscribing History

Complementarity, History, and the Unconscious

Arkady Plotnitsky

Pervasive across much modern intellectual history, Hegel's impact is immense whenever the question of history is concerned. Hegel's ideas have shaped the history of the question of history ever since the appearance of *The Phenomenology of Spirit*. This history has staged itself as a drama with an extraordinary cast, from Hegel's contemporaries, such as Schelling, to Marx, to Nietzsche, to the twentieth century—most importantly for the present essay, to Freud and Derrida. Nietzsche, Freud, and Derrida have been seen more as thinkers of the unconscious than of history;[1] and the emphasis on the unconscious in their works is undeniable. This is why they are the main figures here, positioned *against* Hegel as the thinker of history and (and as) consciousness—of historical *consciousness* and of *historical* consciousness. They do, however, also have fundamental historical concerns, and their work has had crucial implications for the modern or postmodern understanding of history, defined by this essay as the conjunction of history and the unconscious—or history, matter, and the unconscious.

First, then, this essay will be concerned with the understanding of history against, but in the shadow of, Hegel's logic of history.

Second, it will suggest a general theoretical framework demanded by

The ideas of this essay are further developed in a full-length study, *In the Shadow of Hegel: Complementarity, History, and the Unconscious* (Gainesville: University Press of Florida, 1993).

and enabling the understanding of history at issue, but with much larger implications. This framework is constructed under the general heading of complementarity: the idea drawn from Niels Bohr's interpretation of quantum mechanics and conjoined with the economy of the unconscious.

COMPLEMENTARITY

The framework of complementarity was introduced by Niels Bohr to account for the indeterminacy of quantum systems and to describe— comprehensively, but without classical synthesis—their conflicting aspects, such as the wave-particle duality. In Bohr's interpretation the wave-particle *duality* becomes the wave-particle *complementarity*, and quantum indeterminacy, arguably the most fundamental feature of quantum physics, becomes the *complementarity* of coordination and causality, leading to a radical reconsideration of observation, experiment, and related notions. According to Bohr, "[T]he space-time coordination and the claim of causality, the union of which characterizes the classical theories, [become] complementary but exclusive features of the description, symbolizing the idealization of observation and definition respectively."[2]

Bohr's complementarity is thus correlative to Heisenberg's uncertainty relations, which are a rigorous mathematical expression of the limits on the possibility of *simultaneous* exact measurement of such complementary variables as position and momentum. David Bohm spells out the correlation with uncertainty relations more directly: "At the quantum level, the most general physical properties of any system must be expressed in terms of complementary pairs of variables, each of which can be better defined only at the expense of a corresponding loss in the degree of definition of the other."[3]

This formulation also suggests a general definition of complementarity, applicable well beyond physics. Bohr, too, speaks of very general implications of "the peculiar reciprocal uncertainty that affects all measurement of atomic quantities." For "the complementary nature of the description appearing in this uncertainty is unavoidable already in an analysis of the most elementary concepts employed in interpreting experience" (*ATND*, 57). Bohr believed that complementarity could be applied in many different fields, including biology, psychology, and philosophy; and he attempted to explore some of these possibilities in his writings.

Complementarity demands a radical critique of classical theories and of the very processes and technologies of measurement and observation, and while it may not require their wholesale replacement, it does necessitate a redefinition of their functioning and limits. In particular, it makes the functioning of classical concepts and models *complementary*, and, within rigorously defined limits, necessarily complementary.

It is a revolutionary feature of complementarity that the relationships between description and event, and the very concepts of event or object of description are subjected to a radical deconstruction, making description and event in turn reciprocal and complementary. Quantum events become effects, effects without causes, or without *classical* causes. As a result, Bohr's complementarity suggests, specifically against Einstein, that no mathematical, conceptual, or metaphorical model—continuous (as Einstein would want), discontinuous, or complementarily continuous and discontinuous—can be assigned the status of physical reality. The latter concept itself becomes radically problematized and deconstructed in the process. Complementarity spells the end of mathematical, physical, and all other realisms, along with all idealisms, hitherto conceived.

While there may be, alongside mutual exclusivity, relations between different counterparts—such as particles and waves or coordination and causality—there can be, under the conditions of complementarity, no full *conceptual* synthesis of such features. The underlying structure may be seen as finally undecidable; and indeed there is no single underlying structure—decidable or undecidable, known or unknown, nameable or unnameable. This suspension of grounding synthesis is a crucial and profoundly anti-Hegelian move, marking the proximity of the matrix to the radical modern or postmodern anti-epistemologies. Bohr often speaks of the "epistemological lesson" of quantum mechanics, but "anti-epistemological lesson" may be a better phrase.

History offers many analogies and parallels, and I shall develop the complementary economy of history, matter, and the unconscious later. To give a direct example here, uncertainty relations signal a mutual inhibition between causality and coordination, and demand complementarity between them in order to produce a viable analytical matrix. By analogy, historical accounts must oscillate between a comprehensive description of a given configuration of events, or an analysis of differences and forces involved, and of particular causal or efficacious relations between them. An attempt to describe both or to analyze the latter comprehensively would inhibit each. Such descriptions are further complicated, but never fully created, by the position of a given historian. This configuration is analogous to, although more complicated than, the position of the observer inhibiting, but again not creating, the results of observation and measurement in quantum mechanics. One can either establish the positions of events or establish connections between them; furthermore, either alternative can be accomplished only within certain limits of probability. Similarly, one must oscillate between focusing on the local structure of historical events or on causal relations among those events.

One can reverse the metaphor and suggest that a quantum mechanical description is also a history of a quantum event or events. One can speak of Heisenberg's microscope of history, to parallel a thought experiment he constructed to explain uncertainty relations: the lens of history can never be fully focused. The metaphor describes the "built-in" conditions of nature and, still more radically, history. In quantum mechanics and its "history" or in history and its "quantum mechanics," there can be no undisturbed history, which could then be disturbed by observation. Such distortions take place, too. But they must be seen as superimposed upon the *structural* distortion that prohibits one from speaking of an undisturbed history (or matter) existing "by itself," independently of interpretation, or of their metaphysical opposition or, conversely, unity. It becomes impossible to see any given distortion as unconditionally primary or to claim the unconditional primacy of distortion as structure, necessitating the Derridean deconstruction of both concepts—"distortion and primacy"—and their unequivocal, metaphysical opposition.[4] Moving back from quantum physics to history, one can now describe the historical process by using quantum trajectories—"histories." Such a description can be juxtaposed to classical (post-Hegelian) pictures of history, metaphorically analogous to classical physics. Proceeding against Thomas S. Kuhn, physicist Werner Israel writes on the history of the discovery of "dark matter," such as neutron stars or black holes,

> It is not easy to detect in this story anything that often resembles the Kuhnian cycle of paradigm and revolution. Rather, one sees a meandering path that resolves into a Brownian motion at the microlevel of individual scientists. Perhaps it is not altogether flippant to suggest that the evolutionary picture that naturally presents itself is of substantially classical motion (but with considerable quantum spread) that arises by constructive interference from a probing of all possible paths, very occasionally interrupted by barrier tunnelling at places where the incident current becomes sufficiently large. Whether this motion will

ultimately approach a fixed point or limit cycle, and whether there is more than one, are questions for future generations.[5]

In recent *history*, the complementary interactions just discussed are reflected perhaps most interestingly in and between Foucault's various projects, arguably the single most important force on the current scene of historical analysis. They can be detected specifically in the oscillations between a more "historical," or more causal, and a more "geographical," or in Foucault's own terms "cartographical," orientation within and between his various investigations, as well as in his attempts to avoid the pitfalls of classical historicisms that emerge when either line of inquiry is privileged over another. The richness and complexities of the Foucauldian economy would require a separate treatment even in the context of "coordination" and "causality" or in the context of the present essay as a whole (to neither of which Foucault's project[s] can be limited, of course). It can be argued, however, that Foucault's analysis remains within the limits of classical rather than "quantum" (anti-)epistemology, in part by virtue of being grounded in the metaphorical models and paradigms derived from classical, rather than quantum, physics and metaphysics. In effect, and to a degree against its own grain, Deleuze's *Foucault* suggests how in Foucault's works of the middle period, classical physics functions indirectly as such a classical economy.[6] Foucault's is a powerful, but still classical, geometry of force and of the play of forces and difference between forces. While sharing a variety of Foucauldian features, the model suggested by the present analysis differs from Foucault's project or projects (we must keep in mind differences between them). History as complementarity can be seen as a kind of "quantum" model in contrast to Foucault's more classical microphysics of history.

In the most general terms, complementarity as understood by the present essay entails the necessity of accounting for the simultaneous operation of pairs or clusters of concepts or extended frameworks—such as history and the unconscious; or history, matter, and the unconscious; or more conventional pairs such as consciousness and the unconscious, continuities and breaks, unities and multiplicities, permanence and transformations. Complementary relations may thus be described as heterogeneously interactive and interactively heterogeneous: at times acting jointly, at times conflicting with or inhibiting each other, at times as being mutually exclusive. One may need to engage jointly, but without classical synthesis, classically incompatible concepts, or conversely, disengage classically joined concepts, or employ a parallel processing of both types of the transformation. In this extended sense, complementary constituents are not always mutually exclusive, as in Bohr's definition cited earlier. At a certain level, however, the same is the case in Bohr's complementarity considered as a general framework.

One can thus extend complementarity to various conjunctions or clusterings, double or multiple, of terms and concepts—or as Derrida terms them, "neither terms nor concepts"—operative within a given theoretical or historical field. Most complementarities addressed here will relate to the efficacities that cannot be seen or named as concepts in any of the classical senses of this term. Complementarity may be further extended to the complementarities of entire theoretical matrices or even fields or other forms of enclosure. One can, and often must, enter the complementarity of interpretation and history, history and theory, theory and literature, theory and criticism, or their more multiple complementary conjunctions. In this case, too, however, the complementary functioning will not proceed by way of synthesis or within a uniformly or globally controlled system or process, or a system-process, as in Hegel.

I refer here primarily to Hegel because of his significance for the question of history. The general point of the juxtaposition of complementarity and the synthesis of classical theories is much broader, however, and it is particularly significant in the context of the question of the relationships between different discursive modes or different fields of inquiry. One should not, of course, ignore the complementary aspects of various classical theories and paradigms, and such aspects may in fact be found in Hegel as well. One should, however, also differentiate carefully between them and the asynthesis or rather, complementarily, synthesis/asynthesis of complementarity. Thus, while suggestive of interesting complementary possibilities, especially with respect to the interactions between literature and philosophy, the concept of sympoetry or symphilosophy developed by Friedrich Schlegel remains dominated by the economy of synthesis; and *in this sense* it is much closer (although in other respects is not identical, indeed is often contrary) to the Hegelian philosophy than to complementarity. Philippe Lacoue-Labarthe's and Jean-Luc Nancy's brilliant analysis of Schlegel and German romanticism in *L'Absolu littéraire*[7] opens the space of a potential exploration of this economy, itself complementary, of differences and proximities between Schlegel's theories and complementarity. Their analysis of the relationships between totality and fragmentation, systematization and antisystematization, and related oppositions would complicate the issue, but would not contradict the present point. Their title phrase—"the literary absolute"—is already a suggestive index. Under the conditions of complementarity, along and interactively with (the absolute) synthesis, all absolutes would be suspended, be they literary, philosophical, or other.

I would detect more significant early anticipations or modulations of the complementary anti-epistemology and discursive practices in some romantic poetry and fiction, in particular in Blake, Shelley (especially in *The Triumph of Life*), and Kleist. One must remain cautious, however, for one should not ignore the opposite tendencies there toward synthesis as well. I would locate the opening of the complementary anti-epistemology and the enactment of the complementary analytical practice in Nietzsche. Nietzsche's significance for poststructuralist theory would support this point, but there are more direct historical links as well. By the time complementarity was conceived, Nietzsche's impact was considerable. Curiously, it was especially so in Denmark, where Nietzsche was taught as early as 1887 by Georg Brandes in Copenhagen—Bohr's native city and the birthplace of complementarity, sometimes referred to as "the Copenhagen interpretation." The connection may actually be even more historically grounded. For Bohr in fact knew Georg Brandes personally and admired him.[8]

The limits of complementarity appear to be very broad. It can play a role in a variety of theoretical and historical projects. The question of history itself—the possibility of the concept and project of history—will serve as the main case in this essay. History, I shall argue, is a multiple engagement of the complementary; and this engagement makes history exceed itself. History by itself—without other modes of analysis—will never suffice, even though, and because, one can never fully unify or subsume these interactions under any single name or concept, or a containable set of names or concepts. Complementarity implies the multiplicity of history, but equally the excess of the historical, even in the historical analysis.

The very question of history and the case of Hegel, perhaps the greatest signature underneath the idea of history, expand so as to engage manifold complementarities, and, complementarily, historical and theoretical analyses, where we must also place our relationships with Hegel—continuities and ruptures, proximities and distances, departures and returns, and even some arrivals. For, at least in some respects, we may not yet have arrived at places at which Hegel had arrived or from which he took his departures, even though, since Hegel, Hegelianism has developed into an immense manifold of theories, ideologies, and political practices, and has produced a great many "Hegels."

HEGEL: HISTORY-CONSCIOUSNESS

Hegel's *The Philosophy of History*, particularly the Introduction, may be seen as his most direct statement on his philosophy of history. Beginning with his earliest works, however, Hegel was to question, more radically than anyone before him and a great many after him, the directness of the direct, the immediacy of the immediate, including in his own text. One can say that Hegel *is* the introduction to the philosophy of history. Commenting on the *conclusion* of the *Phenomenology*, Alexandre Kojève states that "for Hegel, the introduction of History into philosophy is his principal and decisive discovery."⁹ The historical field opened by Hegel far exceeds philosophy, however; and the *Phenomenology* already inscribes this extension.

The unconscious, by contrast, has an altogether different place in Hegel, in part by virtue of Hegel's *conscious* opposition to it. This opposition, it is true, may be seen as defining philosophy in general. If so, however, this long-standing agenda still culminates in Hegel. History and the unconscious have been, and perhaps had to be, defined against each other before they could define each other.

For Hegel there is only one true history (*Geschichte*, in Hegel joining the historical process and historiography) and one true consciousness *(Bewußtsein)*, the one and only history that is truly historical and the one and only consciousness that is truly conscious: the history and consciousness of, and *as*, always conscious and always historical Spirit *(Geist)*. Simultaneously, history-*Geist* is the only one that is truly conscious and consciousness-*Geist* is the only one that is truly historical. All other forms of history and consciousness, individual and collective, are related, via multiple and complex mediation, to this grand unity of history and consciousness in *Geist*. *Geist* as consciousness-history *(Bewußtsein-Geschichte)* governs all other forms of history and consciousness, such as human consciousness or actual human history, but cannot be identified with them. Hegel uses many other terms—such as "mediation" *[Vermittlung]*, "becoming" *[Werden]*, and "self" *[Selbst]*—in order to inscribe this economy, where governing and subordinate configurations reciprocally determine and inhabit, and (sometimes against Hegel) inhibit each other.

It would not be possible to give a general definition of *Geist*, and Hegel never does so. It is useful to list some of its defining features, even though some of these are more debatable than others, and all of them are open to interpretation:

its jointly historical and self-conscious nature;

its preoccupation with self-cognition as its primary activity;

its all-encompassing nature and the wholeness of its constitution;

its excess in every aspect of its nature over all human economies—individual or collective—even though "the movement of carrying forward the form of its self-knowledge is the labor which it accomplishes as actual history";[10]

its role as a transcendental structure—a transcendental signified in Derrida's sense—controlling the transformational play, even while unfolding it with ever-increasing richness.

The nuances of the Hegelian economy of consciousness, self-consciousness, and knowledge cannot be fully explored here. Historical determination, however, is irreducible at any point of Hegel's text, beginning at least with the *Phenomenology*, where its role was profoundly understood by both Kojève and Jean Hyppolite.[11] This determination need not imply that history, in its more customary sense, is Hegel's only concern in the *Phenomenology*. Hegelian logic, although reciprocal in this sense, actually proceeds more in the opposite direction. First, the Hegelian economy entails, together with consciousness and self-consciousness, a certain fundamental historicity as the economy of difference, mediation, and becoming. History in its more conventional sense, would, then, be determined by this economy as the economy of *Geist*. This economy defines human history as world history *[Weltgeschichte]*, developed most specifically in *The Philosophy of History*.

The equally irreducible conscious determination in Hegel is itself determined by self-consciousness, again within a complex conceptual and textual economy relating various levels of consciousness and self-consciousness. These complications arise both by virtue of the unconscious forces shaping this text and its margins, and from Hegel's own elaborations, such as the analysis of desire in the *Phenomenology*, which was a major influence on Kojève, Bataille, and Lacan. All human knowledge and consciousness, and particularly philosophy as the best human knowledge and consciousness, are determined in relation to the consciousness, always historical, of *Geist* as self-consciousness. The truth of *Geist*'s consciousness is *Geist*'s self-consciousness: the truth of human consciousness and self-consciousness is its consciousness *of Geist*'s self-consciousness. History, in the ultimate sense pertaining to *Geist*, and various histories that *Geist* generates and unifies, mediate this relationship. Only that in human history which belongs, authentically, to *Geist* may be truly historical. Everything else is incapable of authentic, true historicity and is discarded by *Geist* in the course of history. It is important that *Geist* discards it consciously. *Geist* has an enormous capacity for conserving anything even as it negates in the *Aufhebung*, which is defined by this double or triple—negating, conserving, and superseding—operation. Through *Aufhebung*, *Geist* transforms and improves everything it conserves. But it does not conserve everything.

Interactively, Hegel's concepts—mediation, purposiveness, reflexivity, consciousness and self-consciousness—must in the end, in Absolute Knowledge, enact a reduction of difference in presence: the becoming of presence or, in Heideggerian terms, a presencing of presence. Hegel's goal is *a play of differences and transformations*. But this play preserves and sustains presence at each point of the flow—in the continuum of Absolute Knowledge—thereby also controlling the differential play, and teleologically the whole of history. "Mastery" might be a better term. Difference is reduced only as "the unconscious"—the difference that inhibits or disrupts the continuum and wholeness. As such, however, Hegel's economy of *difference* remains a *reduction* of difference in the continuous flow of presence. It is indeed true that, to use Hyppolite's formulation, as a philosophy of difference "[Hegel's] speculative reflection—or absolute reflection—replaces the old dogmatic metaphysics."[12] But this replacement is also an installment of one of the most powerful forms of ontotheology as the metaphysics of presence in the Heraclitean form of becoming, here as history-consciousness. We need all the power of critical thought, including Hegel's own, against this "Hegel," even though we may not be able to leave him behind altogether.

The point is of great importance because the strategy continues to repeat itself, whether at issue is a new form of theory (or history) or a new reading of Hegel. The temptation to reread Hegel and (re)make him into Marx, Nietzsche, Freud, Heidegger, Lacan, or Derrida is great; and even leaving aside their debt to Hegel, Hegel has much to offer by way of proximity to all these thinkers. The most careful discrimination is in order, however. One must equally respect and account for both differences *and* proximities between Hegel and these figures, and between these figures themselves. Transformational and Heraclitean as it is, the Hegelian economy should not be identified with those of the figures just mentioned; and exploring differences between them may prove just as and sometimes more productive than locating proximities.

All Hegel's concepts must be related within his meticulously assembled economy of self-consciousness, through which alone they can be approached. Hegel certainly wants and attempts thus to relate them. Disconnectedness from consciousness, or "*un*-consciousness," is what makes things discounted and places them outside *Geist* and history. History in its more conventional sense, understood by Hegel as world history, is determined by this economy of *Geist* as historical and self-conscious spirit. Hegel writes in his introduction to *The Philosophy of History:* "This self-contained existence of *Geist* is none other than self-*consciousness—consciousness* of [its] own being *[Dieses Beisichselbstsein des Geistes ist Selbstbewußtsein, das Bewußtsein von sich selbst].* . . . The World History merely shows how *Geist* comes to a consciousness and adoption *[Wollen]* of the Truth: the dawn of knowledge appears *[es dämmert in ihm]*; it begins to discover salient principles, and last arrives at full *consciousness*" (translation modified).[13]

On the one hand, then, there is always consciousness, and on the other, always historicity: the determination of *Geist*, truth, consciousness and self-consciousness, knowledge, reason, science *[Wissenschaft]*, and Absolute Knowledge *[das absolute Wissen]* as historical. If consciousness and knowledge are, by definition, determination and determinability and if absolute knowledge is absolute determinability, this determinability is itself determined *historically* by Hegel. It is history that makes knowledge into knowledge and Absolute Knowledge into the *Absolute* Knowledge. History is Hegel's great discovery, and it is never given up; either in Hegel's text as a major conceptual and rhetorical instrument, or *by* this text, at any time in history, from "the dawn of knowledge" to absolute knowledge.

THE EFFECT OF DEFERRAL AND
HISTORY AS COMPLEMENTARITY

While other trajectories are possible, in particular proceeding via Nietzsche, Bataille, or Lacan, the complementarity of history and the unconscious—or history, matter, and the unconscious—is perhaps best approached through the metaphors generated by Freud's theory of memory and psychological processes and their extension in Derrida. These metaphors can be "transferred" so as to refigure history and the historicity of history as complementarity. The term "transfer" must be used with great caution, in quotation marks, or under erasure as in Derrida. For, against Hegel and to a degree Freud, the very possibility of transferring the individual to the collective and the historical becomes problematized in the complementary economy of their relationships. This transfer must conform to a complementary economy as opposed to classical relations between individual and collective *(or historical)* consciousness, in which the latter is usually modeled on the former.

Characterizing Freud's "project for scientific psychology" as a "neurological fable," Derrida writes in *Writing and Difference:* "Whatever may be thought of the continuities and ruptures to come, this hypothesis is remarkable as soon as it is considered as a metaphorical model and *not* as a neurological description."[14] The hypothesis at issue is Freud's hypothesis of pathbreaking and trace as temporal deferral, leading to Derrida's *différance* and his other multiplying—*disseminating*—neither words nor concepts. Freud himself still conceives of this metaphoric conglomerate—"the unconscious"— metaphysically, at least to a degree. Freud's discourse is, according to Derrida, uneasily situated between metaphysics and positivism; and Derrida speaks of "the complicity of these two menaces within Freud's discourse" (*WD*, 198; *ED*, 295). It can be shown that Freud's understanding of history is even more metaphysical. The distinction between Freud's local economy (memory) and his global economy (history) is not unequivocal and not always effective; at a certain point, however, it is useful and to a degree necessary. For one needs a "global" model, based on Freud's microeconomics of memory and psyche, that would prohibit historical totalization. Freud's macroeconomics of history remains a totalizing, metaphysical economy, even though it is designed to incorporate the effects of the unconscious. As Derrida points out: "The irreducibility of the 'effect of deferral [*à-retardement]'*—such, no doubt, is Freud's discovery. Freud exploits this discovery in its ultimate consequences, beyond the psychoanalysis of the individual, and he thought that the history of culture ought to confirm it. In *Moses and Monotheism* (1937), the efficacity of delay and of action subsequent to the event [*l'efficace du retardement et de l'après-coup]* is at work over large historical intervals" (*WD*, 203; *ED*, 303; translation modified).

In the case of history, the complicity with metaphysics and positivism in Freud can be assigned specific proper names—Hegel as the name of metaphysics, here in the name of the unconscious, and Marx as the name of positivism. History as actual history *[wirkliche Geschichte]* and memory resist Hegelian or Marxist economy, in the latter case precisely as the (political) economy of *wirkliche* (real) "empirical" history. A more complementary economy of memory and history becomes necessary, which enhances the theoretical and metaphoric play in either direction: from memory to history and from history to memory. But this economy also prohibits any unconditional mapping, particularly in the direction from the individual to the historical: one of the most common gestures in intellectual history.

The history of culture would, thus, seem to confirm Freud's discovery differently, or confirm a different Freud's discovery. The irreducibility of the effect of deferral makes all universal models of history untenable. Broader collective and *historical Freudian* effects—the *historical* functioning of the irreducible effects of deferral—must be accounted for by complementary economies of history. Such economies may have to depend on Freud's metaphorical models, local and to a degree global, and on the interaction between them. In particular, such effects are crucial for our understanding of the cultural, or social and political, reduction of difference by the force of repression.[15] "The unconscious," however, Freud's greatest discovery, gives a tremendous counter-Hegelian potential to the economy of history based on "the irreducible effect of deferral."

In Freud's theory, beginning with the *Project*, where it receives its more "scientific" rendition, all "perceptions" are seen as delayed—and delayed as inscribed, by virtue of being written—by an operation of putting them in a certain reserve *(Vorrat)*, crucial to the operation of the (Freudian) unconscious. Perceptions are thus "immediately," that is to say by mediation, deferred and differentiated from "originary" perceptions. *Always already* channeled through this machinery—at once an assembly and disassembly line—of the unconscious, all perceptions become Derrida's traces. However much the fiction of immediacy and presence may or at times must be retained, everything immediate becomes always already mediated.

It is important to keep in mind that the mediated at issue *is not* the mediated immediate—or the immediated mediated—of Hegel's (self-) conscious mediation, but the product of the mediation of and by the unconscious, as the latter is in turn refigured in the deconstructed field. The efficacy of all such processes may not conform to any given economy, classical or deconstructed—whether of mediation, temporality, historicity, deferral, or anything—while generating all of these as supplementary and complementary effects. Everything immediate and everything mediated becomes *written* in Derrida's sense of writing, where, in view of this erasure of absolute origin, there are no absolutely originary perceptions, but "only, everywhere, differences and traces of traces."[16] Furthermore,

> The trace is not only the disappearance of origin—within the discourse that we sustain and according to the path that we follow it means that the origin did not even disappear, that it has never constituted except reciprocally by a nonorigin, the trace, which thus becomes the origin of the origin. From then on, to wrench the concept of the trace from the classical scheme, which would derive it from a presence or from an originary nontrace and which would make of it an empirical mark, one must indeed speak of an originary trace or arche-trace. Yet we know that that concept destroys its name and that, if all begins with the trace, there is above all no originary trace.[17]

Accentuating the difference from the classical scheme, or schemes, is crucial. For, as I have stressed, classical theories are often the theories of transformations, difference, exteriority.

Derrida's economy leads to a radical questioning of consciousness and presence: "But what is consciousness? What does 'consciousness' mean? Most often, in the very form of meaning, in all its modifications, consciousness offers itself to thought only as self-presence, as the perception of self in presence." Therefore, "In order to describe traces, in order to read the traces of 'unconscious' traces (there are no 'conscious' traces), the language of presence and absence, the metaphysical discourse of phenomenology, is inadequate. (Although the phenomenologist is not the only one to speak this language)" (*M*, 16, 21; *M*, 17, 21).

Everything thus will be processed, by way of differences and deferrals, through the radically transformational play of the unconscious, leading to the complementarity of all inscriptions. All historicity must be seen as an effect of this efficacious dynamics. But this efficacy cannot be either final, "bottom line," or unique. It may not be "historical" in any given sense; and by the same token, there can be no general sense of the historical. This efficacy may not be historical even when the effects at issue can be at a given moment best figured as historical in one sense or another. As a result, the complementarity of history and the unconscious may be applied either to what are conventionally seen as psychological processes or to what are conventionally seen as historical processes. Or rather, it must be applied to both at once, mutually complicating and mutually inhibiting them, making them mutually complicit—in short, requiring precisely that they be complementary. The relationships between them may be ultimately undecidable, as in Derrida's analysis of many such relationships; and the exploration of this undecidability is an interesting and important project in its own right. But this undecidability need not imply that one cannot construct and explore either psychological or historical configurations, including by means of their complementary conjunctions.[18]

By the same token, one must maintain the effects of presence, permanence, repetition, such as "protective" or "repressive" forces, refiguring them whenever one must differentiate them from their functioning in a precritical text. One must also maintain the effects of "original" transformations, inflicting a "permanent" or lasting change within the system of memory or history—the enduring effects of revolutions. Hence, in setting up his "neurological fable," Freud must speak of "originary perceptions," inflicting permanent changes, or the effects of permanent alteration, within the system of memory. Since these "originary perceptions" still remain always already mediated, an insertion of a continuous interval into any break is always possible, however radical or revolutionary the break. But that possibility does not erase the effects of ruptures or revolutions along other trajectories. Nor does it erase various long or stable effects produced by such transformations. The resulting inscription comprehends the "unconscious" in the Freudian sense, whether one speaks of the psychological or the historical framework generated by Freud's metaphorical model. One must keep in mind the complexity of Freud's position and of the relations between the metaphysical, or positivist, appurtenance and the deconstructive potential of Freud's text. For Freud also "warned in *The Interpretation of Dreams*, against metaphorizing the unconscious as an original text subsisting alongside the *Umschrift* (transcription)" (*WD*, 192; *ED*, 288).

Equally significant is the general understanding of the textuality of the textual and its "strange" supplementary logic emerging in Derrida's analysis in "Freud and the Scene of Writing" (*WD*, 311–12). It is further considered in his analyses of Rousseau and Husserl, which complement—

supplement—the discussion of Freud. The textuality so inscribed—the textuality of the unconscious as a text that has never been present—fundamentally relates writing and temporality, juxtaposing the resulting economy to the classical economy of presence and continuity. The unconscious trace and its *différance* produce presence or the *necessary* fiction of presence, while dislocating it. A corresponding economy dislocates and recomprehends the efficacy of presence conceived *in terms of presence*. The logic of the supplement constrains one to think this efficacy otherwise. Once we want to or must speak of the possibility of presence, we cannot inscribe its efficacy in terms of presence, even if we cannot fully escape these terms either. In "Différance," Derrida offers one of his crucial propositions, enabled, via Bataille and against Hegel, by what Bataille calls *general economy:* "A certain alterity—to which Freud gives the metaphysical name of the unconscious—is definitively exempt from every process of presentation by means of which we would call upon it to show itself in person" (*M*, 20; *M*, 21).

As shall be seen below, "matter" will be equally insisted upon and inscribed in the same terms in *Positions* (64): as a "radical alterity"—a loss of one type or another, possibly a very great loss—inaccessible to and irrecoverable by the philosophical operations or conscious knowledge. Following Nietzsche, both Bataille and Derrida offer a "materialist" economy and complementarity of "the unconscious" and "history" as a *general economy* emerging *against* both Hegel and Marx.[18] Bataille's short essay "Materialism" (1929) is remarkable for its critical assessment of traditional materialism as the ontotheology or idealism of matter. It invokes quantum theories of matter, on the one hand, and Freud, on the other:

> Materialism will be seen as a senile idealism *[un idéalisme gâteux]* to the extent that it is not immediately based on psychological or social facts, instead of on artificially isolated physical phenomena. Thus it is from Freud, among others—rather than from long-dead physicists, whose ideas today have no meaning—that a representation of matter must be taken. It is of little importance that the fear of psychological complications (a fear that only bears witness to intellectual weakness) causes timid souls to see in this attitude an aversion or a return to spiritual values. When the word *materialism* is used, it is time to designate the direct interpretation, *excluding all idealism*, of raw phenomena, and not a system founded on the fragmentary elements of an ideological analysis, elaborated under the sign of religious relations.[20]

The bottomless "bottom line" of the unconscious is finally the *abyss* of matter. "Matter" itself is thus also an abyss, a "radical alterity." In this respect the theories of the unconscious—in Nietzsche, Freud, Bataille, Lacan, and Derrida—on the one hand, and Bohr's complementarity, on the other, are decisive; both lines of thought provide powerful metaphors for and establish powerful constraints on a theory of history.

Under these conditions, it is by history, and in the richest possible economy, that memory should perhaps be metaphorized, rather than the other way around, as it has been more customarily from Hegel on. Freud's "history" too underutilizes, even represses, some of the potential of his own matrix of memory. It can be used more richly in order to produce different economies of memory *and* history, and both a richer difference and a richer interaction between them, leading to an interactively heterogeneous and heterogeneously interactive—complementary—dynamics of the individual and the historical.[21] Derrida's *différance* opens up this dynamics and thus gives more difference and more interaction, more mediation, to this "liberation of memory," but without at the same time suggesting, in contrast to a number of recent theories, a utopian vision of free, unconstrained interpretation, science, art, or community.[22] The "exteriority" at issue at once "constitutes and effaces . . . conscious subjectivity" and, it follows, unconscious subjectivity as well (*OG*, 84; *DG*, 126). On the one hand, "subjectivity" must be "constituted" as a necessary fiction—biological, psychological, theoretical, social, or political. On the other hand, subjectivity must be "suspended" by exposing its fictional nature and by deconstructing the classical concepts defining it.

As I have pointed out, one cannot "liberate" oneself from *presence* at either level: either at the individual level of memory or at the collective level of history. Along with, and as, repression, presence appears as a necessary effect of *différance* and the closures that are induced in the process. According to Derrida, "Spacing [*l'espacement*] as writing is the becoming-absent and the becoming-unconscious of the subject. By the movement of its drift/derivation [*dérive*] the emancipation of the sign constitutes in return the desire for presence" (*OG*, 69; *DG*, 100). This economy plays a major role in *writing* history, as Derrida's writing becomes necessary as a result. It plays an equally significant role in shaping the textual constitution of records of history and in theoretical or political, or again *historical*, uses of history. The practice of history will have to be related to the possibility and the necessity of this compensation repression operating within this textual play.[23] Whatever the degree of necessity of presence, however, one cannot postulate *presence* as anterior and prior to the movement that produces presence along with differences. While retaining "presence," "repetition"—for example, Freud's "repetition compulsion"—or "repression," one must see them as "effects" produced by this movement. As Derrida writes on Freud, but also referring to Heidegger:

> No doubt life protects itself by repetition, trace, *différance* (deferral). But we must be wary of this formulation: there is no life present at *first* which would *then* come to protect, postpone, or reserve itself in *différance*. The latter constitutes the essence of life. Or rather, as *différance* is not an *essence*, as it is not anything, it *is not* life, if Being is determined as *ousia*, presence/existence, substance or subject. Life must be thought of as a trace before Being may be determined as presence. . . . (*WD*, 203; *ED*, 302)

One understands very little about Derrida's *différance* unless one understands that *différance* is also memory and—and *as*, and *as not*—history. But one will not understand more about *différance* unless one understands what happens to memory and history once they become *différance* , including a *différance* of memory and history. The drift-derivation of *différance* must, again, be distinguished from the becoming of classical philosophy—the becoming-presence or difference-presence— as in Hegel's, Husserl's, or Heidegger's economy of temporality and history, and many other theories that share the same grounding and thus conform to the metaphysics of presence.

The historical aspects of the Derridean economy emerge at many crucial points of Derrida's analysis, especially in his inscription of *différance*. *Différance* engages history, even though and because it is also the efficacity of the repression of history, or of difference in general, that persists throughout the history of philosophy and intellectual and political history. Such a repression often functions in the form and the name of history, difference, multiplicity, heterogeneity, and other forces dislocating presence. Hence Derrida's qualification of the "historical": "If the word 'history' did not in and of itself convey the motif of a final repression of difference, one could say that only differences can be 'historical' from the outset and in each of their aspects [seules de différences peuvent être d'entrée de jeu et de part en part 'historique']" (*M*, 11; *M*, 12). Such an economy of "history" is more radically historical than anything that Hegel and various Hegelianisms can conceive; and it is such by virtue of being at once "more" and "less" historical, by being always "more or less" historical. It necessitates a radical critique of metaphysical historicism and makes it impossible to subsume "knowledge" under the name "history," or "knowledge," or any unique name, including *différance*. Still Derrida gives a certain, *conditional*, priority to the historical at many crucial junctures. First, under the conditions of *différance*, one can no more insist on erasing anything absolutely than on maintaining anything absolutely. Second, history, "historically" speaking, has had a much greater role in enhancing difference than in repressing it.

At the same time, conjoining matter and the unconscious within the economy of radical, but never absolute, alterity, makes this economy a materialist one, but by the same token, an antidialectical one. The dialectical materialist economy cannot transgress the metaphysics of presence, logocentrism, finally, even idealism—the idealism of matter. In *Positions*, Derrida comments on materiality in the context of Marx, Engels, Lenin, but proceeding via Bataille and general economy, "whose traits I [Derrida] attempted to outline based on a reading of Bataille. It follows that if, and in the extent to which, *matter* in this general economy designates, as you [Houdebine] said, radical alterity (I will specify; in relation to philosophical oppositions), then what I write can be considered 'materialist'" (*P*, 64; *P*, 87). Derrida's qualification of Houdebine's phrase "radical alterity" is crucial, along with the quotation marks that *mark* the general economy against *Marx*. Metaphysical materialism *fixes* matter by philosophical oppositions, or fully maps it by a set of philosophical propositions, again *fixed*, even if as becoming or "radical alterity." In short, if and only if matter "is" *différance*, "then what [Derrida] writes can be considered 'materialist'."

Différance, then, must be related to "matter." If, however, "matter" enters the field of *différance*, it does so by way of a complementarity with the unconscious and history. The complementarity of the three—matter, history, and the unconscious—would radically redelimit the field of materialist historicity. Given a history of these terms and concepts, once one needs materiality and history, as apparently "we" do, at least for the moment, one needs the unconscious inscribed in a deconstructed and complementary field, and not the consciousness of dialectic, whether idealist (as in Hegel) or materialist (as in Marx).

But one will not be able always to speak only in terms of history, or in terms of the unconscious, or matter, or again in any single term or a containable conglomerate of terms. It is crucial that what makes "historicity" complex and irreducible, *in those cases where configurations and economies will be configured as historical,* is also that which—never the same—demands that there will be configurations and economies in which history and historicity will be reducible. To engage such an economy is quite different from suggesting that any *historicity as historicity,* named as such, is not always historical, even if the latter becomes nonsimple, nonlinear, heterogeneous, disseminated, and differentiated through and through, without a single or undivided origin. A far more radical plurality is at stake, as it allows for no absolutely indispensable economy, concept, or name. Otherwise, after the metaphysics of *history* has been deconstructed, the metaphysics of *historicity* emerges. As the transcendental signified—or signifier—of history is erased, that of historicity appears. History and historicity can be inscribed only in relation to other names and economies, thus making both complementary. The same, of course, is the case with the unconscious. The historical framework emerging from the history of the thematics of the unconscious offers a viable and productive opposition to Hegelianism as a framework of the conscious and self-conscious integration of history; and the major texts of the unconscious, those of Freud, to begin with, or Lacan, who often directly connects Freudian and historical thematics, are far from exhausted in this respect. While, however, such an economy of history would depend on a matrix of the unconscious, it cannot be confined there either. There are, to begin with, many metaphorical models of that type, even in any one writer at issue here, and they are related even more richly between different writers. Many historical (or again, complementarily, historical and ahistorical) trajectories must be engaged, which cannot be fully integrated, however much interaction may emerge at certain points. This complementary asynthesis refers specifically to the trajectories of the very idea of complementarity and thus to the history of modern science, relating, but again not unifying, the latter with the history of the notions of the unconscious and matter, and with the history of the question of history itself.

Notes

1. Lacan may be unavoidable in this context as well, given both his debt to and his subversion of Hegel, particularly the dialectic of desire in the *Phenomenology.*

2. Niels Bohr, *Atomic Theory and the Description of Nature* (Cambridge: Cambridge University Press, 1961), 54–55. Bohr's work on complementarity is assembled in

three volumes of essays: *The Philosophical Writings of Niels Bohr*, 3 vols. (Woodbridge, Conn.: Ox Bow, 1987).

3. David Bohm, *Quantum Theory* (1951; rpt., New York: Dover, 1989), 160.

4. In Derrida the same procedure applies to "all the pairs of opposites on which philosophy is constructed and on which our discourse lives, not in order to see opposition erase itself, but to see what indicates that each of the terms must appear as the *différance* of the other, as the other different and deferred in the economy of the same. . . ." (*Marges de la philosophie* [Paris: Éditions de Minuit, 1972], 18; *Margins of Philosophy*, trans. Alan Bass [Chicago: University of Chicago Press, 1982], 17; hereafter *M*).

5. Werner Israel, "Dark Stars: The Evolution of an Idea," in *Three Hundred Years of Gravitation*, ed. Stephen Hawking and Werner Israel (Cambridge: Cambridge University Press, 1987).

6. Gilles Deleuze, *Foucault* (Paris: Éditions de Minuit, 1986); *Foucault*, trans. Seán Hand (Minneapolis: University of Minnesota Press, 1988).

7. Philippe Lacoue-Labarthe and Jean-Luc Nancy, *L'Absolu littéraire* (Paris: Éditions du Seuil, 1978); *The Literary Absolute: The Theory of Literature in German Romanticism*, trans. Philip Barnard and Cheryl Lester (Albany: State University of New York Press, 1988).

8. I extensively develop these connections among Nietzsche, Bohr, Freud, Bataille, and Derrida from the perspective of complementarity in *In the Shadow of Hegel* and in *Complementarity: Anti-Epistemology after Bohr and Derrida* (Durham, N.C.: Duke University Press, 1994), where I also consider the difference between complementarity and Derrida's deconstruction, by contrasting Bohr's complementarity and Gödelian undecidability in formal logic. Briefly, a Derridean approach would emphasize and engage an exploration of the undecidability of classical oppositional terms—form and meaning, mind and nature, consciousness and the unconscious, and so forth—thereby deconstructing the decidability of such oppositions claimed by philosophy as the metaphysics of presence. Complementarity would stress the possibility of complementary engagements of such terms and concepts and their arrangements, either classical, but suitably refigured, or newly introduced. In the present essay, Derrida's ideas are used within and in order to support a *complementary*, rather than an *undecidable*, model of history.

9. Alexandre Kojève, *Introduction to the Reading of Hegel: Lectures on the Phenomenology of Spirit*, assembled by Raymond Queneau, ed. Allan Bloom, trans. James H. Nichols (Ithaca: Cornell University Press, 1969), 161.

10. G. W. F. Hegel, *Phänomenologie des Geistes, Werke in 20 Bänden* (Frankfurt am Main: Suhrkamp, 1986), 3:586; *Hegel's Phenomenology of Spirit*, trans by A. V. Miller (Oxford: Oxford University Press, 1977), 488. Identifying *Geist* with collective human history has been a prominent (mis)reading of Hegel, for example, in Marx or Kojève; the resulting economies are usually as problematic as Hegel's, or more so.

11. For Kojève, history is a central determination of the book (150–65). For Hyppolite's discussion, see the chapter "History and Phenomenology," in *Genesis and Structure of Hegel's Phenomenology of Spirit*, trans. Samuel Cherniak and John Heckman (Evanston, Ill.: Northwestern University Press, 1974), 27–50. Most major commentators, while debating the character, determination, and models of history in the book, would make this point to one degree or another. Certainly, it is crucial for most Marxist Hegelians, or Hegelian Marxists, such as Georg Lukács and Herbert Marcuse.

12. Jean Hyppolite, *Logique et existence* (Paris: Presses Universitaires de France, 1953), 106.

13. G. W. F. Hegel, *The Philosophy of History*, trans. J. Sibree (New York: Dover, 1956), 17, 53; *Werke*, 12:30, 73–74.

14. Jacques Derrida, *L'Écriture et la différence* (Paris: Éditions du Seuil, 1967), 298; *Writing and Difference*, trans. Alan Bass (Chicago: University of Chicago Press, 1978), 200 (hereafter *ED* and *WD*).

15. Lyotard's analysis in *Heidegger et "les juifs"* (Paris: Éditions Galilée, 1988); *Heidegger and "the jews,"* trans. Andreas Michel and Mark S. Roberts (Minneapolis: University of Minnesota Press, 1990), steeped in Freudian and post-Freudian—and here post-Derridean—machinery, engages these issues and models, thus using Freud's model of the history of Judaism to analyze the case of "Heidegger and 'the jews'" (21, 81).

16. Jacques Derrida, *Positions* (Paris: Éditions de Minuit, 1972), 38; *Positions*, trans. Alan Bass (Chicago: University of Chicago Press, 1981), 26 (hereafter *P*).

17. Jacques Derrida, *De la grammatologie* (Paris: Éditions de Minuit, 1967), 90; *Of Grammatology*, trans. Gayatri C. Spivak (Baltimore: Johns Hopkins University Press, 1975), 61 (hereafter *DG* and *OG*).

18. As I said, one can see Derrida's deconstruction, particularly in his earlier works, as *metaphorically* analogous to Gödelian undecidability and incompleteness in mathematics logic, often invoked by Derrida. As *metaphorically* analogous to Bohr's matrix, complementarity will be closer to the second project just described. This distinction is not unconditional—not decidable—and is based on a relative balance in emphasis and orientation of goals, but it is not without significance and implications.

19. As opposed to classical theories or restricted economies, a general economy must deal with the fact that irrecoverable losses in interpretation and theory do take place and that one must relate one's interpretation and theory to such losses. See in particular Derrida's "From Restricted to General Economy: A Hegelianism Without Reserve" in *Writing and Difference*, but the notion itself is crucial throughout Derrida's text. It can be argued that Bohr's complementarity has a general economic character, since it necessitates a relation to and a taking into account of a radical loss in (re)presentation. The differences between complementarity and Foucauldian, Deleuzian, or several other recent models of history, such as in Lyotard, may in fact be further elucidated through the idea of general economy.

20. Georges Bataille, *Oeuvres complètes* (Paris: Gallimard, 1970-), 1:179-80; *Visions of Excess*, ed. Alan Stoekl (Minneapolis: University of Minnesota Press, 1985), 15-16.

21. The related thematics—memory, forgetting, history—continuously reemerge in recent literature, particularly, beyond Freud and Lacan, around Hegel, Nietzsche, Heidegger, Derrida and de Man. Among recent works stressing the possibilities at issue, see Dominick LaCapra's essay on Freud, "History and Psychoanalysis," in *The Trial(s) of Psychoanalysis*, ed. François Meltzer (Chicago: University of Chicago Press, 1988); or again Lyotard's work cited earlier. Along more Derridean or post-Derridean lines, see Gregory Ulmer's *Teletheory: Grammatology in the Age of Video* (New York: Routledge, 1989), particularly part 2 (115–208), David Farrell Krell's *Of Memory, Reminiscence and Writing: On the Verge* (Bloomington: Indiana University Press, 1990), and the essays collected in *Poststructuralism and the Question of History*, ed. Derek Attridge, Geoff Bennington and Robert Young (Cambridge: Cambridge University Press, 1987). Another

study that may be cited here and that deals more directly and extensively with the question of history is Hans Kellner's *Language and Historical Representation: Getting the Story Crooked* (Madison: University of Wisconsin Press, 1989).

22.   One can think, in particular, of the Deleuzian model or, again, certain aspects of Foucault's vision; but other recent approaches may be cited, including some having Derridean or Nietzschean genealogies.

23.   Lyotard's analysis in *Heidegger and "the jews"* is an interesting exploration of some of the effects of this economy in the sociocultural field, although Lyotard's historical model itself is not as radical as it could be.

Reconstructing Aesthetic Education: Modernity, Postmodernity, and Romantic Historicism

Eric Meyer

Postmodernism is characterized by the breakdown of signifying systems into differential signifiers and unlinked syntactic chains, by the dispersion of subjectivity into decentered libidinal intensities and temporal flows, and by a generalized collapse of the legitimating narratives or *grands récits* that underwrote modernity. This crisis of faith in Jürgen Habermas's "incomplete project of modernity" and "incredulity toward metanarratives," in Jean-François Lyotard's phrase, marks a historical discontinuity or epistemic break, signaled by the persistent prefix, "post," that stands in aporetic relation to "the modern," which it both climaxes and brings to a close.[1]

"As the word itself suggests," Fredric Jameson observes, "this break is most often related to the waning or extinction of the hundred-year-long modern period (or its ideological or aesthetic repudiation)," which historical rupture is related to "the emergence of a new type of social life and a new economic order —what is often euphemistically called modernization, postindustrial or consumer society, the society of the media or the spectacle, or multinational capital."[2] These theoretical formulations then might be regarded as simply effects of the increased technologization of consciousness, as mass media information systems produce an unprecedented social organization that remains poised precariously between dystopian possibilities of total manipulation and control and utopian prospects of global communication and multicultural community.

Whether the critic celebrates this profusion of differential textual effects as a Baudrillardian "ecstasy of communication" or decentered Derridean *écriture*, or considers postmodernity under the Frankfurt School categories of reification, instrumentalization, and fragmentation, there seems almost an unspoken consensus that the Enlightenment project is at an end, and that the Hegelian narrative of the redemptive or progressive movement of history no longer corresponds to a distinctly postmodern world.

In postmodern theory, then, history stands as a synecdoche for the teleological concept of linear rational progress and absolute social development that legitimates modern Western European culture. Indeed, history is commonly identified with "Ideology . . . as a *political* explanation of the world" that seeks "to be a *total* explanation or conception" of the "world-as-history," as the "Systems-Subject" of the "Total State."[3] In contemporary formulations, Hegelian dialectical subl(im)ation and the Marxian materialist dialectic are adapted as a functionalist model of the information society, in which individuals are merely "effects of structure" and "the transcendental subject of cognition is apparently abandoned," as Horkheimer and Adorno observe, to be "replaced by the much smoother work of automatic control mechanisms." But it is not simply that the technologization of the consciousness-industries "leads to an insensitive liquidation of metaphysics," Adorno and Horkheimer suggest, "but that in the social whole they themselves become a metaphysics, an ideological curtain." Behind it the Hegelian system appears as "a *Weltanschauung* that has become materially translated"—in Guy Debord's terms, "a worldview which has become objectified" in the postmodern spectacle."[4]

The common ground between these formulations, then, according to poststructuralist critiques of the "metaphysics of subjectivity," is the idealist notion of "a subjectivity present to itself, as the support, the source, and the finality of representation, certitude, and will." This remains true despite the fact that the structuralist model actually eliminates the last traces of subjectivity, thus accomplishing "the completion of metaphysics," in Heidegger's terms, that "begins with Hegel's metaphysics of absolute knowledge as the Spirit of will." This "overcoming [of] metaphysics," however, is also its de(con)struction, as the Hegelian will to knowledge and the Nietzschean will to power are destroyed and preserved, negated and transcended in the Heideggerian will to will of technology *(techne)*. The completion of metaphysics, Heidegger writes, "has already taken place. The consequences of this occurrence are the events of world history in this century," as international conflict has provided "the ground for the planetary manner of thinking" in the global objectification of human consciousness. The history of Western metaphysics might thus be regarded as a successive exteriorization of essence or a "progression of Being to beingness," although this same process is also a degradation of thinking to untruth and an abandonment of Being in machination (enframing), so that metaphysics "remains just as essentially remote from the Origin in its start as in its finish." For Heidegger, then, postmodernity might be signaled by the end of the "fate of the West and that presupposition of its planetary dominance" that occurs when Western thought returns to its origins by overcoming its ends, thus accomplishing the global totalization of metaphysics in Hegel's *Phenomenology*.[5]

Postmodernity might then be identified with that "end of history" or "end(s) of man" that transpires when Hegelian thought is recognized as totalitarian and thus unmasked, overthrown, exceeded, or destroyed in the overcoming of metaphysics proclaimed by Heidegger. No doubt there is evidence in twentieth-century history to support this analysis, as the hypostasis of the absolute subject inevitably suggests a totalitarian suppression of difference, while the mimetic politics of mass movements conform to the mechanisms of identification of the Hegelian state. But this (mis)apprehension of Hegelian historicism as an attempt to bring history/knowledge under the domination of sovereign identity, under the rule of the absolute subject, rests on an extrapolation from theoretical totalization to totalitarian political systems that emphasize the structural overdetermination of the total system over the local microsystem, the total state over the autonomous subject, and, ultimately, of absolute sovereignty over nature and history. "For what made the *grands récits* of modernity master narratives," Craig Owens asks, "if not the fact that they were all narratives of mastery, of man seeking his telos in the conquest of nature?"[6] By this logic, then, history is finally revealed as merely a displaced reflection of socioeconomic modernization and an ideological afterimage of the imperial world system, converted into a reified "world-picture" *(Weltbild)* or "worldview" *(Weltanschauung)*, and technologized and objectified in global postmodern society.[7]

Yet as Heidegger insists, "[M]etaphysics is not yet completed with the absolute metaphysics of Spirit," since "the counter movements to this metaphysics belong to it" (*EP*, 89); while Derrida suggests that "the thinking of the end of man, therefore, is always already prescribed in metaphysics," as that *Aufhebung* of "man" that appears in the *Phenomenology*.[8] In fact, the Hegelian dialectic forestalls theoretical totalization, decenters the absolute subject, and preserves a place for difference within absolute identity; meanwhile, poststructuralist theory mobilizes its own "total system or logic," as Jameson observes, "by constructing an increasingly closed and terrifying machine" that too often simply reflects the ideological conception it critiques, as logocentrism, phallocentrism, phallogocentrism, or simply an all-encompassing, inescapable network of power ("PM," 57). Such totalizing conceptions, then, might be seen as attempts to apprehend the multinational world order, which cannot be conceived directly by the reified subject or transcoded into a coherent worldview, but instead appears as the abstract ideological structure of global postmodernity. Thus the theoretical effects of postmodern criticism might be read as signs of the inability to comprehend the emergent global world system, as reflected in the fragmentary, discontinuous, disruptive quality of postmodern aesthetic production.

But the inability to meaningfully represent the absent totality of the emerging multinational world system characterizes modernity as well, for the rapid growth and expansion of transnational industrial-capitalist culture deconstructs the lost unity of traditional peoples, nations, and tribes, without supplying a lived ideological framework to reconstruct that vanished collective past. In fact, even the rhetoric of crisis, of rupture, break, or discontinuity is an aftereffect of the sudden decomposition of tradition under modernity, and reflects the need—and inability—to reconstruct mythic narratives and spiritual worldviews within the detotalized totality of the expanding industrial-capitalist international system. Postmodernity then might represent a further intensification of the fragmentation of traditional life-worlds by societal modernization, as industrial-capitalist economic and technological development reaches beyond any localized determination, while the global extension of information media and political-economic exchange systems further aggravates the split between centered perceptual structures and the decentered totality of the multinational world system. The structural totalization of the global socioeconomic superstructure then infracts back upon the communicational infrastructure, as economic rationalization and instrumental systems logic tear apart living languages through the reduction of linguistic structures to quantifiable functions or mathematical games. This pervasive mediatization and cyberneticization then actually intrudes into the interiority of the supposed private self and breaks down the prereflective unity of the reified consciousness, to reconstruct the autonomous individual as simply a functional component in the telematic network of postindustrial societies.

Within this destabilizing situation, then, it appears a strategic objective of postmodern theory to comprehend global postmodernity as the reinteriorized collective consciousness of a decentered human subjectivity coming to consciousness of itself and reawakening into utopian community. Such totalizing conceptions lend themselves to appropriation by Horkheimer and Adorno's "administered world" that places nature and human society under the absolute power and control of the total state system; yet they can also appear as utopian images of a fully democratic society, in which humanity has been liberated into conscious participation in the continuous recreation of imaginative community. It is necessary, then, to think postmodern culture dialectically to recover the unconscious utopian content that might restore the mediatized public sphere to a genuinely communicational function and allow the intellectual systems of modernity to serve as imaginative blueprints for a fully multicultural society. In this light, the unrecognized horizons of postmodern experience remain those described by Hegel's secularized metaphysical narrative of Mind or Spirit *(Geist)*, which opens a utopian prospect of an "end of history" that is also history's fulfillment in global human community.

It might be objected that postmodern culture can no longer sustain the humanist agenda that orchestrates and motivates the great emancipatory narratives of modernity. Yet given the postmodern situation, in which any individual or social group is consciously or unconsciously positioned in the worldwide network of information media and communications systems, the need for some such coherent hermeneutic framework to cognitively mediate this global totality would seem a critical objective. It may prove that the mediatized public sphere can no longer be thought of as a Durkheimian collective consciousness or Hegelian objective spirit, since under the extreme reification of mass media communications systems consciousness is technologized, informationalized, and transcoded into an unlinked chain of material signifiers or precession of simulacra, while culture undergoes "a thorough exteriorization with respect to the knower" that converts the psyche itself into symbolic exchange in the circulation systems of multinational capital (*PC*, 4). But the residually idealist notion of mass media communications as an objectified collective consciousness or externalized human nervous system might be thought not only under the Mannheimian conception of material ideology or the Heideggerian technological will to will, but even the Derridean revision of the Hegelian *Aufhebung*, in which "man appears to himself in consciousness in his Being-past, in his to-have-been, in his past surpassed and conserved, retained, interiorized *[erinnert]*, and *relève*," as the Absolute Subject of Hegelian *Phenomenology* ("EM," 121).

The apparent split between subject and totality might then indicate a certain amnesiac condition whereby "our entire contemporary social system has little by little begun to lose its capacity to retain its own past," even as that stored collective memory becomes simultaneously present as a sensationalized media spectacle of dispersed, heterogenous, and finally incoherent displays of world history ("CS," 125). For the individual positioned within the vertiginous sensory mirage of contemporary mass media, history appears simply absent except as the reified artifacts and fetishized icons in the archives and museums of the postmodern present, while popular media and communication systems dissolve historicity into an illusory atemporal flux or asynchronous perpetual present reduced to a degraded cybernetic or cinematic representation of Hegelian objective spirit. Thus dialectically to relift the inert collective past cannot be accomplished within the postmodern sensibility, which remains locked within a flattened, decentered subjectivity and mesmerized by the mediatized display of commodity images and simulacra that constitute postmodern culture.

Yet if postmodernity remains fragmentary and disjunctive, unified only by the illusory coherence of micronarratives and organized only by the arbitrary structure of language games, this disjunction might be defined by postmodern culture itself, which appears as a static semiotic code that precludes continuities between the various orders of significance or moments of succession in the collective narrative. In other words, the social totality is not non-existent, but rather detotalized and dispersed across the omnipresent information media that, while promoting a virtual simultaneity and copresence of communicational transparency, actually empty communication into an endless repetition of material signifiers that eclipse any referent or signified. Paradoxically, while the barriers between private and public, aesthetic and political realms, have largely collapsed or been eliminated, this situation has produced a massive disorientation and lack of shared goals and ideals, since the unification and totalization of postmodern experience is effected only by a reduction of communications media to a self-referential code system, a simulation model of the postindustrial informational society. Yet it might be possible, through some further dialectical inversion or return of the repressed, to discover a suppressed subtext within the closed circuit of capital-information exchange, and thus to comprehend the reified socioeconomic superstructure as the decentralized collective consciousness of a planetary intelligence in (re)evolutionary transformation toward a global utopian community.

Despite its supposed postmetaphysical tendencies, then, postmodern theory remains implicated in Hegelian phenomenology, whether through the Heideggerian "step backward *(schritt zurück)*" that rethinks "the still *unthought* unity of the essential nature of metaphysics, " or the Derridean deconstruction that discloses the play of difference(s) underwriting Western "metaphysical humanism."[9] The structural homology between the Hegelian system and industrial-capitalist technological development, however, suggests that the Hegelian autonomous subject is simply the reified consciousness of economic rationalization, while the Absolute Subject becomes simply the automatized control system of the Hegelian state. More immediately, Hegel's aesthetic speculation on the reinteriorized life-(hi)story of Spirit appears as the cinematic life-memories recorded by contemporary perceptual technology and projected outward in the multimedia mass entertainments of the postmodern spectacle. But the idea of culture as conscious history, raised into heightened awareness through constructive, goal-directed aesthetic activity, remains relevant even in a supposed posthistorical age, in which the spectacle of daily life presents a simulacrum for Hegelian objective spirit. The romantic concept of "man" as the *"subject* of history," in Debord's terms, "producing himself, becoming master and possessor of his world which is history, and existing as *consciousness of his game"* thus provides the subject and telos of postmodernity even when overtly elided or suppressed by a static ahistorical and always already mediatized cultural practice (*SS,* 74). The incomplete project of modernity remains the rationale of a world now fully revealed as a materialized collective unconscious in the symbolic action and fantasy drama that occupy the postmodern public sphere.

Hegelian historicism arose in the wake of the French Revolution, the reorganization of economic life under modern capitalism, and the collapse of traditional life-worlds and religio-ethical orders. Hegel's *Phenomenology* thus depicts the generalized crisis of modernity as a simultaneous destruction and preservation of tradition, as "the structure of the previous world" is abruptly "interrupted by the sunrise, which, in a flash and at a single stroke, brings to view the form and structure *(Gebilde)* of the new world."[10] Hegel marks the aporetic moment at which modernity first appears as a world-picture *(Weltbild)* but not yet as a worldview *(Weltanschauung)*, since "the actual realization of this abstract whole is only found when those previous shapes and forms ... are developed anew again" as "the new world" of absolute spirit *(PM, 76)*. The Hegelian dialectic, then, records primary experience as a succession of discontinuous moments to be reassembled and recomposed by the Hegelian absolute subject, and provides a mechanism of legitimation or theoretical "science" *(Wissenschaft)* that reconstructs the previous organic community *(Gemeinschaft)* within the antagonistic conditions of bourgeois-democratic civil society *(Gesellschaft)*. The Hegelian system thus constitutes the conscious ideology of a world in perpetual legitimation crisis, which must continually recreate its structural coherence in the perennial deconstruction and reconstruction of cultural forms.

The representative texts of speculative historicism are then both reflections of this widespread social, economic, moral, and political crisis, and attempts to reconstruct the fragmented life-worlds of previous spiritual traditions. The post-Kantian problematic bridges the gap between the decentered subject and the absent totality through the self-moving activity of transcendental subjectivity (Fichte), the phenomenological relifting of absolute identity (Schelling), the synthetic operation of aesthetic rationality (Schiller), or the speculative dialectic of objective idealism (Hegel). The speculative concept *(Begriff)* arises as a dialectical mediation between self and other, predicated on the intentional structure of the prereflective cogito and the logical proposition of noncontradiction, which move from recursive self-identity (a = a) through objective representation in logical non-identity (a = b) to a higher synthesis of identity and non-identity (a = a/b). The intentional structure of phenomenological reflection, then, actually contains two elemental forms: a moment of simple self-reflexive identity (or "immediacy") in which the self-image appears as a recursive structure or mirror stage of specular (mis)recognition; and a second moment of deferred self-difference and otherness (or "mediacy") in which the self-image recedes into a succession of figures in facing mirrors, thus dissolving identity into a virtual image or perceptual vanishing point. The phenomenological subject is thus constituted in the differentiation or splitting *(Trennung)* of reflective self-consciousness, as both a subl(im)ation *(Aufhebung)* and a dissolution *(Auflösung)* into intersubjective being *(Dasein)*.

These two forms then produce a third moment, in which, in Benjamin's description, "the strict ur-form of reflection is shattered and expended through [a] redoubling *[Doppeldeutigkeit]*" that effects "the dissolution of the proper form of reflection into the Absolute."[11] This transcendental reflection is also a syllogistic permutation of the logical proposition that overturns the binary syntactical structure of subject and predicate to reconstruct categorical logic as a speculative proposition that comprehends differential substructures as a transformational grammar, much as successive events or moments are subsumed in the speculative metanarrative. This dialectical subl(im)ation, then, attempts to circumvent the internal contradiction in mimetic reflection through a simultaneous destruction and supersession that raises the speculative subject to metacritical self-consciousness. But mimetic identification is not transcended or overcome so much as simply obliterated and reinstated "as the moment in which absolute self-consciousness becomes the principle of thinking," in Heidegger's words, at the completion of Hegel's metaphysics of absolute knowledge (*EP*, 110).

Considered in contemporary terms, the speculative dialectic is simply the systems programming of the technology (τέχνη) of subject-formation, and describes how prereflective subjectivity and grammatical logic are dismantled and reconstructed as functional elements of a rationalized and routinized socioeconomic modernity. Yet the speculative dialectic also provides for a reprogramming of communicational practice as a metanarrative syntax that might allow for aesthetic judgments and ethical determinations through the synthetic or metacritical faculty of the *Aufhebung*. The speculative dialectic describes a linguistic and perceptual strategy whereby the decentered subject can utilize the gaps, breaks, and lags within an internally fractured and disintegrative communicational field to reconstitute autonomous subjectivity and recompose signifying practice. The successive relinking and recitation of linguistic structures and syntactic chains in speculative language might then reconnect the disparate fields of postmodern knowledge to global multicultural communication without simply conferring conceptual closure on the speculative system or reproducing the abstract systems logic of capital-information exchange. By reimagining global communication as a decentered human subjectivity, then, speculative discourse might provide a self-citational linguistic format wide enough to comprehend the various heterogenous languages and multiliterate discursive formations of the world's peoples and cultures in a viable communications community.

The speculative metanarrative thus mediates between subjective perception and the social body by reinteriorizing world history as the life-(hi)story of a decentered subject while reimagining world culture as a utopian human form. Speculative historicism then reconstructs subjective phenomenology as the distinct states or stages of human development, as the configurations of intersubjectivity are diachronically transposed into a narrative of the evolution of consciousness that is also a history of philosophy and a philosophical anthropology. The speculative system thus enables the absolute subject to recapitulate the phylogeny of the human race within individual ontogeny, so that the periods and moments of human development appear again reinteriorized in the absolutized consciousness of the *Aufhebung*. Hegel's *Phenomenology* then supersedes these prior narratives into the speculative metanarrative, in which individual phenomenology and human history are dialectically recombined and synthetically recomposed as the representative life-(hi)story of a universal individual who recollects *(Erinnerung)* the imaginative shape of world history in absolute knowledge. But Hegelian *Phenomenology* finally exceeds or transgresses humanist anthropology or metaphysical phenomenology, since the *Aufhebung* of "man" in effect turns the absolute subject inside out to describe global human consciousness as merely the reinteriorized content of the world soul or world spirit.

At this most comprehensive horizon, then, the speculative system is simultaneously dismantled and reconstructed as an emancipatory metanarrative through which the philosophical subject dialectically relifts sedimented linguistic structures and intersubjective worldviews into the decentered metaconsciousness of the Hegelian *Geist*. Similarly, Hegelian phenomenology is finally deconstructed and superseded into a transformational metanarrative that recites world history as the life-(hi)story of Spirit; at the same time, history approaches an Althusserian "process without subject or goal" that does not reach a definitive "end of man," but rather is both confirmed and deconstructed by the "circular reappropriation" of Kantian anthropology in Hegelian *Phenomenology*. But history continues to appear as a course of aesthetic education or curriculum of ethical development, so that the speculative metanarrative comprehends the origins and ends of phenomenology by sublating "the two *ends* of man" into the absolutized consciousness of the Hegelian *Aufhebung* ("EM," 121). Taken to its limits, then, the speculative metanarrative accomplishes its deconstruction by transgressing its ideological boundaries toward a thinking of man that cannot be reduced to Western metaphysical humanism, thus carrying out an *Aufhebung* of the *Aufhebung* that decenters Hegelian world history and opens Western civilization to its other(s).

But the completion of metaphysics is the end of history and the beginning of art, since the deconstruction of the Hegelian *Aufhebung* is supplemented and completed in Schelling's *Auflösung*, while Hegelian world history is recomposed as the speculative metanarrative of Schiller's *On the Aesthetic Education of Man*. Thus the fragmentary "Earliest System-Program of German Idealism" (1795–96?) suggests that "the highest act of Reason, the one through which it encompasses all Ideas, is an aesthetic act"; that "the philosophy of the spirit is an aesthetic philosophy"; and that "the principle for a *history of mankind*" that might supersede "the whole wretched human work of State" is finally the "*equal* development of *all* powers" in "universal freedom and equality of spirits" that is "the last [and] greatest work of mankind."[12] The problematic conditions of any such aesthetic reconstruction, however, are already written into the speculative metanarrative that reintegrates a fragmentary and disjunctive material culture into an ethical totality or aesthetic whole. By rereading Hegel's *Phenomenology* through Schiller's *Letters on Aesthetic Education*, however, a reconceived romantic historicism might reunite the disintegrative social order through a Kantian *sensus communis* or Schillerian aesthetic rationality that establishes a noncoercive consensus for free participation in the utopian social project.

In fact, the most influential accounts of postmodern culture might be mediated by combining Habermas's communicative rationality *(Diskurs)* with Lyotard's Kantian sublime in a Schillerian aesthetic rationality that reunifies dialectical oppositions and preserves diversity and difference in a reintegrated aesthetic field. The most effective restatement of aesthetic rationality, however, is Adorno's *Aesthetic Theory*, which harmonizes heterogenous non-identical elements in a tension-filled unity while revealing gaps, breaks, and discontinuities and refusing to coerce that formal content into a strictly rational order.[13] Aesthetic rationality thus also describes a nonrepressive political organization that supersedes internal tension and antagonism and promotes an ethical ideal of reconciliation and resolution rather than domination or subordination, as a dimly reflected utopian image of a harmonious social body in a world in which traditional religious or mythic thought no longer represents the imaginary shape of a fully human community.

Aesthetic education, then, hinges on a unifying social integration that shapes and forms the individual through the free play of all human faculties, and envisions the human community as capable of autonomous self-determination and free self-development. The functioning of the social formation then appears as a nonreductive homology or reciprocal feedback relation between individual self-formation and collective development, so that as the aesthetic subject recapitulates human history, so he or she also imaginatively reconstructs the free subjectivity of a detotalized social body. Jean Baudrillard's critique that "aesthetic value connotes the internal functionality of an [informational] ensemble" that "*communicates . . .* according to the economy of a model, with maximal integration and minimal loss of information" thus suggests the capacity of aesthetic rationality to harmonize communication practices, although Baudrillard regards the aesthetic utopia as an ideological dissimulation of the performativity principle of information theory.[14] But the Hegelian ethical totality or Schillerian aesthetic state allows the reintegration of fragmented value-spheres and conflicting faculties to emerge from within the communicational field, while preserving the greatest possible difference and dissent within the nonrepressive political body and gathering together disparate sectors and antagonistic realms in the harmonization of the imaginative community. Speculative historicism, then, provides an imaginary horizon to undertake the reintegration of the ethical and aesthetic spheres as the objectified faculties of a decentered human subject, and refigures the history of a people or nation as an abbreviated recapitulation of the education of the human race in world history. The speculative metanarrative thus describes the coming-to-consciousness of the individual subject, the reformation of the democratic nation-state, and the emergence of humanity into worldwide utopian community as occurring asynchronously at disparate uneven levels within the materialized collective unconsciousness or political imaginary of a global metahumanist society. Yet if the speculative metanarrative can be thought as a modern myth that describes "the 'giant spirit' that comes to consciousness within man" through reciting world history as the life-(hi)story of the Hegelian world spirit, the speculative metanarrative is a "myth that explains or interprets itself," that exposes itself as myth even while allowing humanity to imagine the nations and peoples of the world as the autonomous members of a future utopian multicultural community.[15]

It might be argued, then, that the "Earliest System-Program of German Idealism" is simply a philosophical project to construct a German national subject, while the speculative system is a model for programming the industrial-capitalist nation-state, as the speculative university is built into the disciplinary apparatuses and institutional structures of the "Subject-State" or "Total State."[16] Certainly the correlation between Schiller's program of aesthetic education and the societal modernization of Germany invites such a demystifying reading; but the speculative system achieves an aesthetic totalization that allows the complex in(ter)determination of human, natural, and technological systems in the aesthetic state. The speculative system might then be considered a conceptual diagram for deconstructing self-destructive socioeconomic apparatuses and deprogramming automatized control mechanisms to reintegrate those structural totalities with organic systems based on the spiritual worldviews of premodern societies. Because the ecological principles and religio-ethical systems of traditional societies have been torn apart by the competition-based systems logic of industrial-capitalist technological development, however, internal organic bioregulators and spiritual life-worlds must be remodeled and reprogrammed at a higher metastable systems level and regulated through communications practices that maintain a harmonious natural environment and human community. Baudrillard suggests that in postindustrial societies the environment itself serves as a simulation model for a capital-information exchange network in which even "the great referent Nature" is replaced by a "metapolitical economy" of total manipulation. Yet the utopian corollary of Baudrillard's "cyberneticized society" might be a communications society modeled on global ecological interrelatedness between a rehumanized humanity and a restored natural world (*PES*, 202). By reinteriorizing organic and structural subsystems, then, the speculative metanarrative might place autonomous control functions on a metasubjective or metadiscursive level and sustain a complex harmonization effect between humanity and nature through the reintegrated communicational practices of the aesthetic state.

The speculative metanarrative thus opens outward from the closure of metaphysical thought to describe the complex interplay between the absolutized consciousness and the planetary thinking of the Hegelian world spirit. Of course the Hegelian system would have to be further decentered, detotalized, and delimited to describe a postmodern consciousness no longer organized by such subjects of history as classes, races, nations, or sexes, no longer structured by a Eurocentric narrative of Western civilization, and no longer circumscribed by the anthropocentric worldview that places "man" in domination over nature and history. But despite repeated attempts to exceed, overturn, overcome, deconstruct, or simply destroy Hegelian metaphysics, the speculative metanarrative remains the philosophical horizon through which postmodern thought is constrained to pass in describing a global multiliterate and multicultural world.

Whether or not postmodernity is finally imaginable as the completion of metaphysics, as an "end of history" or "end(s) of man," nonetheless the approach of Euro-American modernity toward global totality makes the objectification of human consciousness in planetary communication networks virtually a literal reality of the multinational world system. Should a utopian transformation achieve worldwide cultural postmodernity, however, this breakthrough into materialized collective consciousness or objective spirit will probably not attain legitimation through the presumed universal laws of abstract reason and the dictates of critical judgment that underwrote the Kantian League of Nations and the Hegelian world court. Rather, any coherent organization of nations and peoples and tribes would require the harmonization of pluralistic difference and the reconciliation of division and dissent through mutual education and cross-cultural interchange of ideas and artifacts and currencies that establish collectivity while preserving diversity, non-identity, and difference within the emergent postmodern world system. Aesthetic education might thus enable a passage into global multicultural community, even though the multinational world order cannot apparently be imagined as a single human body, while the disparate nations and peoples of the world cannot readily be unified in a universal narrative of development. Yet by reinteriorizing the global communicational infrastructure as a restored collective consciousness and rehumanizing the collective body as an imaginary utopian society, the speculative metanarrative might allow the individual to comprehend his or her relation to an increasingly multinational world system as participation in an emerging multicultural community. In this situation, then, the speculative metanarrative provides imaginative guidelines to unify the various peoples and nations and tribes as equal participants and free citizens within the global postmodern society.

Speculative historicism does not, however, suggest prescriptive blueprints for the political future, but rather promotes global collectivity through symbolic communication and representative action that are ethical and aesthetic rather than expressly political, and that emerge from the various life-worlds and spiritual traditions of the world's peoples. Within the expanded imaginative horizons of this greater collective project, then, aesthetic education might play a role in the future utopian transformation of postmodern culture.

Notes

1. Jürgen Habermas, "Modernity—An Incomplete Project," in *The Anti-Aesthetic*, ed. Hal Foster (Port Townsend, Wash.: Bay Press, 1983), 3–15. Jean-François Lyotard, *The Postmodern Condition*, trans. Geoff Bennington and Brian Massumi (Minneapolis, University of Minnesota Press, 1984), 3 (hereafter *PC*). See also Jean Baudrillard, "The Ecstasy of Communication," in Foster, *The Anti-Aesthetic*, 126–34.

2. Fredric Jameson, "Postmodernism and Consumer Society," in Foster, *The Anti-Aesthetic*, 111–25, 113 (hereafter "CS"). See also "Postmodernism, or The Cultural Logic of Late Capitalism," *New Left Review* 146 (1984): 53–92 (hereafter "PM"); and *Postmodernism, or, The Cultural Logic of Late Capitalism* (Durham, N.C.: Duke University Press, 1991).

3. Phillipe Lacoue-Labarthe and Jean-Luc Nancy, "The Nazi Myth," trans. Brian Holmes, *Critical Inquiry* 16 (Winter 1990): 291–312, 293.

4. Max Horkheimer and Theodor W. Adorno, *Dialectic of Enlightenment*, trans. John Cummings (New York: Continuum, 1987), xv. Guy Debord, *The Society of the Spectacle* (Detroit: Black and Red, 1977), 74 (hereafter *SS*).

5. Lacoue-Labarthe and Nancy, "Nazi Myth," 294. Martin Heidegger, *The End of Philosophy*, trans. Joan Stambaugh (New York: Harper & Row, 1973), 89, 86, 95, 81, 90 (Hereafter *EP*).

6. Craig Owens, "The Discourse of Others: Feminism and Postmodernism," in Foster, *The Anti-Aesthetic*, 57–82, 65.

7. See Martin Heidegger, "The Age of the World Picture," in *The Question Concerning Technology*, trans. William Lovitt (New York: Garland, 1977), 115–54.

8. Jacques Derrida, "The Ends of Man," in *Margins of Philosophy*, trans. Alan Bass (Chicago: University of Chicago Press, 1982), 109–36, 121 (hereafter "EM").

9. Martin Heidegger, *Identity and Difference*, trans. Joan Stambaugh (New York: Harper & Row, 1969), 49, 55.

10. G. W. F. Hegel, *The Phenomenology of Mind*, trans. J. B. Baillie (New York: Harper Torchbooks, 1967), 75 (hereafter *PM*).

11. Walter Benjamin, "Der Begriff der Kunstkritik in der deutschen Romantik," in *Schriften* (Frankfurt: Suhrkamp Verlag, 1955), 2:420–528, 439.

12. Friedrich Hölderlin, "The Earliest System-Program of German Idealism," in H. S. Harris, *Hegel's Development: Toward the Sunlight, 1770–1801* (Oxford: Clarendon Press, 1972), 510–12. Also translated in *Essays and Lectures in Theory*, trans. Thomas Pfau (Albany: SUNY Press, 1988), 154–56. Friedrich Schiller, *On the Aesthetic Education of Man*, trans. Reginald Snell (London: Routledge & Kegan Paul, 1954).

13. T. W. Adorno, *Aesthetic Theory*, trans. Greta Adorno and Rolf Tiedemann (London: Routledge & Kegan Paul, 1984).

14. Jean Baudrillard, *For a Critique of the Political Economy of the Sign*, trans. Charles Levin (St. Louis: Telos Press, 1981), 188 (hereafter *PES*).

15. Friedrich Schelling, cited in Philippe Lacoue-Labarthe and Jean-Luc Nancy, *The Literary Absolute: The Theory of Literature in German Romanticism*, trans. Phillip Barnard and Cheryl Lester(Albany: SUNY Press, 1988), 79; and Jean-Luc Nancy, *The Inoperative Community*, trans. Peter Connor, Lisa Garbus, Michael Holland, and Simona Sawhney (Minneapolis: University of Minnesota Press, 1991), 49.

16. See Lacoue-Labarthe and Nancy, "Nazi Myth," 299; and idem, *The Literary Absolute*.

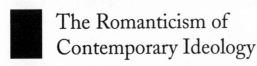

The Romanticism of Contemporary Ideology

Paul Hamilton

In the last decade or so, critics writing about romanticism have appeared to split into two main theoretical camps. Firstly, there were deconstructive critics who translated the romantics' interest in epistemology into the idiom of post-Saussurean linguistics. Secondly, new historicist critics resisted deconstructive readings, claiming that to see romantic writing as being primarily about epistemology, the nature of imagination, the contest of the faculties, and so on was to accept it uncritically at its own estimation of itself. Instead, the romantic preoccupation with the mind ought to be contextualized historically, and so understood as a strategy for sidestepping political issues. Unearth these, and we see that the deconstructive critic's translation only repeats the original romantic evasion.

This critical opposition, however, was simplistic. Deconstructive criticism, responding in its turn to historicism, began to make clearer its own interest in formulating the ideological content of romantic aesthetics. Collaborating with historicism, deconstruction now presented itself as exposing the rhetoric through which romanticism contrived to disguise the ideology that historicism condemned. Initially, this romantic ideology was defined by historicism only in terms of its assimilation of all kinds of social, political, and historical issues to a transcendental philosophical perspective. Historicism paid less attention to the ways in which romanticism refigured these issues; simply to point out the fact of ideological sublimation was enough. More detailed ideology critique followed, and the examination of how the romantics articulated political issues replaced straightforward condemnation of their ideological delivery. For who can escape ideology? If the question now sounds rhetorical, it is because of our vastly increased sensitivity to the presence of ideology in all our discursive practices. Its apparent ubiquity for us, though, also has a romantic precedent. This "romanticism" in our current perception of ideology is what I want to investigate here. The deconstructive critic alerts the historicist critic to the pervasive character of romantic ideology by pointing out the inescapable figurality of romantic writing, its habitual—because linguistic—displacement of meaning. Perhaps this is the next stage in their collaboration—the recognition of a historical feature of romanticism that intersects revealingly with contemporary theories of the ideological?[1]

I

Prior to the (eventual) critical dialogue I have been describing, a rough consensus existed among British and American romantic scholars that the period was one of intellectual expansion after an age of Enlightenment. However skeptical and emancipatory its aims, the Enlightenment was pictured as still powered by an inappropriately mechanistic understanding of human creativity. The romantics found or privileged new categories for this unconfinable essence, and their twentieth-century critics largely reproduced them. Disapproving critics of romanticism, like Hulme, Babbitt, and T. S. Eliot, still shared the view of romanticism as an intellectually liberationist movement, which was why they disapproved. Their revisionary successors championed romantic range and ambition, even if that imaginative scope was seen by commentators like Bloom and Hartman as a fraught, potentially unmanageable freedom from natural determinism.

Subsequent deconstructive and historicist critics, though, looked instead for shades of the prison-house lodged within the very heart of romantic, imaginative license. Rather as Horkheimer and Adorno interpreted the Enlightenment, they have read romanticism as an escape from the constraints of nature into a new prison of its own making. The language of capability, which previously seemed unequivocally to legitimate romantic practice, lost credibility when it was shown to be a discourse impervious to critique, one which just could not fail.

> Poetic language can do nothing but originate anew over and over
> again; it is always constitutive, able to posit regardless of presence but,
> by the same token, unable to give a foundation to what it posits except
> as an intent of consciousness.[2]

This description by Paul de Man repositions romanticism in relation to ideological practice. In other words, poetry of this kind is always incorrigibly buoyant: it is self-writing, self-righting, and self-wrighting. Romantic discourse abounds with poems about the impossibility of producing poetry, poems as different as Wordsworth's *Prelude*, Keats's *Hyperion* poems and Byron's *Don Juan*. In each case, failure of the self to achieve its goal is recuperated as autobiography (self-writing). Or an imaginative falling short of effective realization is still imagined, and so still constitutive of the creative category valorized by romantic discourse. This furnishes the ironic (self-righting) logic of the fragment; it also underpins the aura of the symbol as a form that exhibits its own self-fashioning (self-wrighting) as an aesthetic experience replacing the philosophical shortcomings that initially it seemed to record. This literary absolute translates everything into its own terms, which, since they ensure success, elide problems that would have remained visible in a less idealizing discourse.[3]

Romantic poetry described in this way can have no recalcitrant moments; all crises—loss of subject, inability to conclude, idiosyncrasy—merely add to the aesthetic substance of the poem. Sublimation is always sublime rather than escapist, internalization is always symbolic rather than obscurantist, logical opposites are aesthetically reconciled; as soon as the aesthetic transposition takes place, then all its contents become intents, and its categories self-originating. Both deconstructive and historicist critics see this self-confirming system as ideological. Ideology has meant a bewildering number of things over the years, but the most recurrent sense has emphasized pretensions to wholeness. And it is the switch from valorizing wholeness absolutely to seeing it as a limiting, exclusive construction that typifies the change in understanding of romanticism I have been highlighting.

Characteristic of this ideology is the fact that, in Althusser's words, it "has no history." Once you are inside it, it pretends it is not there, that things were always like this. It tries to preclude the possibility of critique, to make a metalanguage unthinkable. As Alasdair MacIntyre argues, ideology and the end of ideology or end of history are symbiotically related. Both are interested in trying to deprive us of the ability to criticize or see wholes as constructions:

[T]he pragmatism of the attitude involved in the end-of-ideology thesis leaves precisely those whom it seeks to educate vulnerable to almost
any ideological appeal by its failure to criticize social wholes. Each
party to this dispute provides the other with an opponent made in
precisely the required image.[4]

This, as Hegel described Schelling's Absolute, is the night in which all
cows are black. Critics of romantic ideology disagree about the degree of
the romantics' awareness of the entrapment in which their imaginative
liberationism landed them. Yet some poems, like *The Triumph of Life*,
say, do seem to push against the limits of ideology. Arguably, *The Triumph* dramatizes ideological constraints as the intolerability of a life lived
without the possibility of critique: a life whose naturalness is felt as an
imposition. The magnetism of the triumphal car that drags so many in
its wake provides the example, par excellence, of a category we cannot
step outside—life. Famously, the Yale deconstructionists chose Shelley's
poem for the subject of their collaborative *Deconstruction and Criticism*.
Their resistance to logocentrism and his discontent with ideology are
immanent to the poem; but the textual reasons for seeing ideology rather
than biology as the subject of *The Triumph of Life* particularize that
ideology and place it historically in a period discontinuous with the
modern and postmodern by specifying it as idealist. The worthies so
shockingly in thrall in the *Triumph* stand for "thought's empire over
thought." They figure in a review of Western culture that turns its desire
for Enlightenment into that self-reflexive, "pure" intellectual virtuosity
that was Marx's target in *The German Ideology*. If we see it in this historical perspective, there is a way out of romantic ideology, an alternative to
immanent critique: the way chosen by Marx. Although it means giving
up "thought's empire over thought," this is still a renunciation that is
possible, unlike the romantic dramatization of it as the surrender of life
itself. Post-Marxists like Althusser argue that this is an alternative perceived by the *young* Marx, invisible once more after his epistemological
break with prescientific Marxism and the restoration of an all-embracing
ideology, criticism of which is always symptomatic. Even on this interpretation, the prescientific scenario is still essential to the historical reading of the logic of romantic ideology I attempt here. However, I wish to
suggest that the restoration of an inescapable ideology, and its consequent restriction of criticism to immanent criticism, represents a crucial
intersection of modern theory with a definitively romantic dilemma and
ought to be understood as such.

Analysis of the ideology of romanticism, then, suggests the romanticism of ideology. A prerequisite for understanding this romanticism of
ideology is an appreciation of the eighteenth-century theory of ideology,
its transformation within romanticism, and the critique of that inherit-
ance by Marx. This leads us, as it did Marx, into the history of eighteenth-century French thought's adaptation of British empiricism. The
term *idéologie* is generally agreed to have been coined by Destutt de
Tracy in his *Eléments d'idéologie* (1801–15), that is, right in the middle of
the English romantic age and at the end of the French Enlightenment.
Tracy's "ideology" followed the *philosophes*, and etymology, in investigating the logic of ideas: the grammar by which we compose discourse out
of strings of ideas validated by sense experience. I will question the
coherence of this clear-cut philosophical programme in the second part
of this essay. First, though, it is worth noting its democratic, accessible
nature. Indeed, Taine alleges that ideology and its proponents achieved
such prominence that Napoleon, fearing the dissidence of once sympa-
thetic intellectuals at the *Institut National*, attributed to "ideology, that
sinister metaphysics . . . all the misfortune of our beloved France."[5] The
change from what ideology means for Napoleon and the ideologue,
Tracy, to what it means for Marx when he writes *The German Ideology*
(1845), is a change into the idiom in which our own debates about
ideology, however refined their differences, are conducted. From Lukács
to Daniel Bell, Althusser to Kenneth Minogue, the proponents and
opponents of theories of ideology are arguing about something much
closer to Marx's conception than Tracy's. Not that Marx's definition was
unequivocal; but I can perhaps leave its definition as vague as this at
present in order simply to propose romanticism as a significant rite of
passage in the construction of ideology as it features in our arguments
today.

In the historical space between Tracy's *Eléments* and Marx's early
writings, I want to situate two transformers of the ideological current.
Both were primarily novelists: Marie-Henri Beyle, known as Stendhal,
and Donatien Alphonse François [Marquis de] Sade. In claiming that
they make important contributions to the *theory* of ideology, I am build-
ing on Jane Gallop's juxtaposition of Sade with Bataille to question more
broadly the customary equation of theory with philosophy. As will be
seen, their theoretical interventions raised this controversy at the time.
Their scandalous meddling argues the important change in the meaning
of "ideology" that I want to pinpoint. But a consequence of their philo-

sophical discovery was to open the door to unphilosophical, literary initiatives that question the autonomy and legitimacy of philosophical discourse, a romantic embarrassment that recent theory has been keen to revive.

Stendhal was a great admirer of Tracy, but when he presents his own attempt to analyze an ideology to Tracy, he apparently uses the word in a manner unintelligible to an Enlightenment ideologue. The treatise in question is Stendhal's book *De l'amour*. The other writer who spanned the Enlightenment and what followed, and who pushed the definition of love beyond reasonable understanding to such an extent that his explanation became eponymous is, of course, Sade. Of the two, Stendhal engages more explicitly with the history of ideas. He takes the formal structure of Tracy's reprise of eighteenth-century materialism, exposes its idealist base, and redescribes it as a hermetic belief-system. The ingenuity of the author of *De l'amour* is to show that any behavior can be psychologized into love. The central figure for this process of "crystallization," as Stendhal calls it, is the Salzburg bough:

> [A]t the salt mines of Salzburg, they throw a leafless wintry bough into one of the abandoned workings. Two or three minutes later they haul it out covered with a shining deposit of crystals. The smallest twig, no bigger than a tom-tit's claw, is studded with a galaxy of scintillating diamonds. The original branch is no longer recognizable. What I have called crystallization is mental process that draws from everything that happens new proofs of the perfection of the loved one.[6]

Similarly, Sade analyzes any aberration into a form of sexual behavior. Sade's modernism, as Angela Carter implies in *The Sadeian Woman*, is to see that once sex is detached from the defining biological function of reproduction, it becomes an ideology: it can explain anything. Stendhal gives us the resourcefulness, whimsy, and pleasure of ideology-making. *De l'amour* may seem to present itself as a critique of the aesthetics of ideology, but it ends up decrying the poverty of a life barren of love's ideology. Sade, conversely, shows the barbarity of his ideology by enjoying it. What makes his critique self-impugning also makes it undeniable. It also makes him the darling of the antihumanists from Bataille onwards who do not want their critical alternatives to produce rival forms of legitimation when legitimacy is in fact their target.

Both Stendhal's and Sade's transformations of ideology are shocking—more obviously in the case of Sade, but also in Stendhal's amorous foreclosures of all external explanation or verification. Ideology becomes a partisan phenomenology: one can suffer all manner of self-deceptions, but these too constitute love. Stendhal's conspicuous derivation of the model for explaining love from philosophical method itself then becomes as logically self-lacerating, as much a *trahison des clercs*, as Sadism. But it is under the shadow of the divine marquis that new ideologues claim polemically that the enlightenment they contribute to will escape the presumptuousness of rule, reason, and patriarchy, remaining suitably *sous rature*. "For the *chronique scandaleuse* of Justine and Juliette," claim Adorno and Horkheimer, is "the history of thought as an organ of domination."[7]

On Jane Gallop's reading of Sade and his readers in (her) *Intersections*, "a Sadeian antihumanism becomes necessarily a feminist disturbance of the distinction masculine/feminine and the correlative principle of the male, ideal sphere." Gallop thus appears to disinfect Sade in critical theory, but she avowedly wants to keep alive the scandalous nature of her association, to "release Sade's stink from the sterilizing tomb of literary history." She figures the effacement of unique authorship ("the male, ideal sphere") as an incrimination of those who replace it. Antihumanism parades rather than muffles the evil-sounding associations of its name, and poststructuralists gather round the corpse of individualism as though participating in a Sadeian scene of instruction. Gallop tells us, "My Sade, (I am at once ashamed and gratified to say) is neither mine nor even 'Sade' [but] a familiar conspiracy of teachers/readers/friends."[8] The implication is that if you don't believe in legitimation you need a highly sophisticated guilt like this to keep your methodology transgressive. Gallop's disingenuous wit is here at one with other postmodern tactics to avoid turning critique into an alternative grand narrative.

In his "Essay on Miracles," the Enlightenment philosopher David Hume had already shown how difficult it is to refute norms without setting up systems parasitical upon the normal: a *lapsus naturae* can only have happened if it is vindicated on the very grounds to which it was supposed to be an exception. The category to be disposed of by the miraculous appears to justify the miraculous. The alternative was for the believer to be "conscious of a continued miracle in his own person, which subverts all the principles of his understanding." If Hume did not dismiss this enthusiasm out of hand, he certainly let it activate his celebrated irony. However, as Isaiah Berlin once showed, succeeding Christian antinomians mapped Hume's refutation of miracles onto his own skepticism concerning our knowledge of any world external to our impressions and ideas. Perversely, they used Hume to justify their enthusiastic belief in the miraculous nature of "reality."[9] In other words, despite his ironical disengagements, Hume's so-called empiricism proved flexible enough to accommodate the opposites of skepticism and fideism. Stendhal and Sade exploit the resemblance this Enlightenment epistemology bears to a self-confirming ideology. In their different ways, they romanticize it. Furthermore, the grossly physical abnormal championed by Sade, somewhat different from the perversity of Christian antinomianism, shows how abstract the inherited "way of ideas" had to be for Hume to be able to absorb empiricism within idealism. Stendhal presumes upon the hypothetical comprehensiveness of the idealism, but Sade exposes the ideality of its internalized, disembodied empiricism.

Gallop's fashionable recourse to Sade, not Stendhal, as a means of illustrating the ideological is therefore a preference for materialism over idealism. Sade is valued for showing the ungovernable body whose materiality exceeds the empiricism rationalized within Humean idealism. The corollary of Stendhal's uncheckable, agglutinative system of ideas is a lawless, unmediated but compulsive physical reality. Things-in-themselves become as potentially alien, mystified, or obstreperous as a body's unbiddable instincts and desires. Consciousness henceforth is shadowed by an unconsciousness resourceful enough to have produced our actions for reasons other than those we were consciously in possession of while acting. The preference for Sade follows the fate of philosophy after idealism: a series of attempts to abandon idealism and engage with this material power that otherwise would be able to undermine all science and reduce all action to a parody of its real motives.

In *The German Ideology*, idealism is *the* ideology: philosophy's pretense to legislate for reality through logical prescriptions of its conditions of possibility. For Marx, this German-sounding disease is at one with the Enlightenment's absorption of materialism within empiricism. It has two main consequences, corresponding to our Stendhal/Sade axis. Idealist prescriptions ignore materialist contingencies as surely as the madman's study of the weather in *Rasselas* leads to his lunatic belief that he controls it. Marx's vivid attack on the Young Hegelians repeats Johnson's satire on the enlightenment of his day.

> Once upon a time a valiant fellow had the idea that men were drowned in water only because they were possessed with the idea of gravity. If they were to knock this notion out of their heads, say by stating it to be

a superstition, a religious concept, they would be sublimely proof against any dangers from water. His whole life long he fought against the illusion of gravity, of whose harmful results all statistics brought him new and manifold evidence. This honest fellow was the type of the new revolutionary philosophers in Germany . . .[10]

Marx's first study of ideology investigates "how a theory and history of pure thought could arise among philosophers owing to the divorce between ideas and the individuals and their empirical relations that serve as the basis of these ideas. In the same way, here too one can divorce right from its real basis" (*SW*, 185). Corresponding to the unreality of pure thought, or a self-authenticating system of ideas, must be a symbiotic conception of the material bodily individual as a law unto itself. Hence the frequent sense in reading Sade that the particular horrors are overdetermined in the service of some general *Weltanschauung* as mystified as its idealist counterpart. These grotesque rituals, recipes, protocols, hierarchies, and biographies of cruelty and desire burlesque the idea that there are contexts in which any rituals, recipes, protocols and so on are necessarily reputable. Anything, Sade wants to demonstrate, can be a turn-on. Both pure thought and utter physical license belong to the same ideological economy and so instantiate what Marx would see as equally false abstractions from the social relations determining how we produce reality. In Sade's description of a modern consensus in *La philosophie du boudoir*, the new materialism subsumes even the most extravagant schemes of mentalism:

> [W]hat we call the end of the living animal is no longer a true finis, but a simple transformation, a transformation of matter, what every modern philosopher acknowledges as one of Nature's fundamental laws . . . death is hence no more than a change of form, an imperceptible passage from one existence to another, and that is what Pythagoras called metempsychosis.[11]

Sade's provocatively uncritical conclusion is that he must have persuaded "any enlightened reader, that for murder ever to be an outrage to Nature is impossible" (*J*, 332). Social relations are precisely what do not count for anything in this kind of materialism. Marx could have used *La philosophie du boudoir* as his text.

Sade, then, through the obscene tolerance of his dramatization of violence and sexuality, parodies the contemporary resilience of ideology.

The critical potential of his writing is compromised, though, first of all by its barbarity, which keeps questionable the postmodern use of perversity as a trope for epistemological sophistication. Sade's ideology, Sadism, is a prison in which people, almost all of them women, are tortured for the sexual pleasure of men and women who have power. Sade's fictions even contain listeners who are meant to take pleasure in the stories of such enjoyments, and so the pornography incriminates its readers in advance. Secondly, the Sadeian parody is limited to a mirror image of the idealism it criticizes. As Roland Barthes points out, Sade's eroticism is "encyclopedic"; but Sade satirizes "the accounting spirit" of the encyclopedic project of the Enlightenment *philosophes* as amounting to the undiscriminating principle that "pleasure is possible anywhere." Once more, if anything can be a turn-on, then being turned on by something doesn't exactly tell you much about it.[12]

From a postmodern perspective, both these limitations to Sade's critique can appear advantageous. He inspires a form of writing whose transgressive force no longer resides in pretensions to legitimate critique, but in an undeniably offensive *anomie*, powered by a material unconscious capable of undermining all conscious explanation. His slighting of moral, political, and economic wisdom is held to be characteristic of a new "higher" criticism that locates ideology's defining strength in its power to dictate the terms of our resistance to it. Self-impugning writing, like Bataille's pornography, dovetails with unlikely allies (Adorno, Althusser, Foucault) who share a prevailing cynicism about the validity of emancipation and revolt, describing them as movements whose shape and scope are prescribed by a ubiquitous ideology. Rebellion is therefore best figured as sexual compulsiveness, non-identity, or disruptions too local to be made sense of in general terms.

These writers counter self-authenticating ideology with self-denying or disreputable critique. This is the provocatively uncritical extreme to which critics working immanently within ideology are reduced. Since the Holocaust, there has been an upsurge of ingenuity for detecting ideologies where none was to be seen before. Science, art, language, politics, race, and gender are not simply traversed or enlisted by ideology but now demonstrably have their own ideologies. In the face of this proliferation, it is hard to be anything other than an immanent critic. All else seems methodological naïveté or hypocritical purity. Adorno and Horkheimer allot a chapter to Sade in *Dialectic of Enlightenment*, arguing that the Sadeian (and sadistic) heroine, Juliette, exhibits "the pleasure of attacking civilization with its own weapons" (*DE*, 94–95). She is the scandalous precursor of the immanent critic; her "merciless doctrines [that] proclaim the identity of domination and reason . . . are more merciful than those of the moralistic lackeys of the bourgeoisie" (*DE*,111). Romanticism differs from our postmodern situation because, although it provides an explanatory genealogy for the sometimes bizarre pessimism of the immanent critic, there still seems to be a way out: ideological contamination can still be circumscribed. All forms of writing do not fall within its sphere, because romanticism's hermeneutical circle belongs to a particular kind of philosophy, idealism, to which thinkers as varied as Kierkegaard, Schopenhauer, Marx, and Nietzsche are keen to find alternatives. "Criticism," complains Nietzsche in *The Will to Power*, "is never directed at the ideal itself."[13] Nevertheless, criticism's fear of ideological growth is already there in the anxiety typified by *The Triumph of Life*—fear that to step outside ideology is to give up too much. Increasingly, ideology is seen to be enmeshed in valued processes of thinking and imagining. Accordingly, to move outside it threatens further cultural impoverishment.

Romanticism, as I am defining it, moves from a confident exploitation of ideology, Stendhal's "imaginary solution,"[14] to a dissatisfaction at finding in this structure its own completion or ending. This is the pessimism Nietzsche calls "a preliminary form of nihilism" (*WP*, 9), when nihilism describes the nowhere place left outside romantic ideology's brilliant annexations. On the optimistic side, romanticism legitimates its sense of becoming or pursuit of *Fülle* as the form of universal philosophy; its main devices—imagination, sublimity, irony, symbol, the fragment—exuberantly assimilate apparent exceptions or philosophical shortfalls to a rule of appearance. There are no epistemological defeats that cannot be translated into ironic successes; the collapse of representation becomes its effective supplement when it is reread as the *symbol* of what exceeds representation. Romantic consciousness can now make the boast Marx thought defined ideology, that of "really representing something without representing something real" (*GI*,168). Appearance is always sufficient (*WP*, 6).

On the pessimistic side, as Nietzsche saw, romanticism only becomes what it is: what the ideal realizes in "becoming" is itself. Hegel's "dialectical fatalism," like Goethe's, results in "the submission of the philosopher to reality" (*WP*, 96, 253, 422). The crisis literature of late romanticism in Britain—any poems by Shelley, Keats, and Byron, Gothic and historical novels—is at some point given over to criticizing this romantic tautology or incorrigibility, at the risk of hazarding its own mode of imaginative writing. Romantic devices no longer satisfy the appetite for something larger than they can represent; instead, they are more productively read as anticipating the immanent critique we are so conversant with today. Sade's and Stendhal's ability already to imagine a totalizing ideology, one allowing no prosaic escape, shows the danger imaginative license was now posing for critique. The earlier romantic legitimation of the imaginary, its installation at the heart of philosophical explanation, accounts for the difficulties experienced in attempting to forego so central a form of cultural endorsement. Romantic writing registers the pressure to contrive immanent critiques that would still employ imagination, even if they employ it against itself.

Marx believes ideology is a circle he can break out of because he conceives of ideology as symptomatic of an erroneous development in the history of thought, determined by the division of labor. The premise of his early writings on the subject, that idealism is ideology, comes close to looking like an attack on thought itself, the intellectual "empire" of Shelley's *Triumph*. "Let us revolt against the rule of thought," he announces at the start of *The German Ideology* (*SW*, 159). But Marx believes, of course, that economics is a form of thought. The inversion of the Hegelian dialectic, or the prioritizing of praxis and material circumstance in understanding, is conducive to improved consciousness. It does not imply a handing over of authority to an unconscious power really accounting for consciousness all along. My claim is that to appreciate the cultural pressures Marx had to resist we have to understand the romanticizing of Enlightenment ideology. Equally, to understand the revolutionary nature of Marx's break with this movement is further to define romanticism. Romanticism, that is, becomes identified with the ploy by which to step outside its ideology is made to appear like a break with thought itself. Romantic writing dramatizes this dilemma. Immanently it criticizes the pass to which it has been brought, and in so doing it expresses dissatisfaction with a criticism that can only be immanent.

II

Let us trace the romanticizing of Enlightenment ideology in more detail. Although Destutt de Tracy is usually commemorated only for his coinage of "ideology," he and Stendhal are preeminently qualified to tell the story of this transformation. Tracy was a liberal aristocrat, a member of the French National Assembly, who wrote a witty reply to Burke in 1790 and was temporarily imprisoned during the Terror. Subsequently, he produced his *Eléments* in four volumes, a work that established him as a successor to the *philosophes* and constituted an influential, late flowering of the French Enlightenment. In America, Jefferson enthusiastically translated, edited, and published the works Tracy sent him in the hope that, as he put it in a letter of 1818, they would be "be made with us the elementary book[s] of instruction."[15] One piece of writing that Tracy sent him that he did not make available was a chapter on love permissive enough for Tracy to have feared to have it included in the original, Napoleonic edition of *Eléments*. Tracy had met Stendhal, an admirer, around this time, and the novelist became a frequenter of Tracy's salon in the Rue d'Anjou in the 1820s. Despite Stendhal's lasting devotion to Tracy's ideological method, the intellectual differences between the two men became unignorable when Stendhal presented Tracy with a copy of his work on love, *De l'amour,* and the ideologue tried to read it. Mme de Tracy later recalled the incident, suggesting that the decisive disagreement was over the meanings each attached to *idéologie:* "[T]hey soon fell out because of [Stendhal's] book on the theory of love, demonstrated by crystallization, which was the *idéologie* of M. Stendhal. M. de Tracy tried to read this work, understood nothing of it, and declared to its author that it was absurd."[16]

Crystallization, or Stendhal's ideology, exemplifies the romantic departure from Enlightenment methodology. While in Milan, Stendhal had read Tracy's chapter on love in the expanded version he allowed to be published in the Italian translation of the *Eléments*. Before writing his own essay, therefore, he would have seen a typically Enlightenment attempt to define love from first principles, but in an inherently contradictory way. Tracy, one discovers, both analyzes love into its basic elements and yet shows how these only make sense in the social context from which philosophical analysis apparently tried to isolate them. Tracy's *résumé* of his argument draws a comparison from grammar. Just as isolated words have no value outside discourse *(discours)*, so only individuals united in love to create a family form the true social unit. Yet we have no difficulty in conceiving of individuals as a standard against which to check that families are composed of the right stuff. In fact, love must have appeared paradigmatic to Tracy's analysis: not the embarrassing appendage that his consignment of its full exposition to an Italian translation implied, but an analogy easing the way for acceptance of the otherwise awkward hiatus between truth and meaning bedeviling his general theory. For, fundamental to Tracy's ideology are the claims, difficult to reconcile, that "our perceptions . . . are not susceptible of any error, taken each separately, and in itself," and yet that these perceptions only have meaning when their ideas form part of discourse or a system of signs. It is the task of the philosopher to discover the grammar of things, thus perfecting our discursive understanding of them. The difficulty comes when we try to envisage how we would check existing discourse against perceptions. Perceptions must somehow be expected to possess a corrective force prior to having the significance they only acquire when discursively systematized. In other words, the empirical check tends to drop out of consideration because it relies impossibly on meanings existing independently of social context.[17]

The problem recalls Locke's famous barrier of ideas cutting us off from the reality it is meant to represent, or his inability to explain the nature of the relation between words and ideas in Book 3 of his *Essay*. If the relation remains unexplained, then it becomes arbitrary by default, and both Locke's phenomenology and his study of language enter the domain of semiotics, submitting to the rule of appearance rather than reality. Stendhal does not consciously exploit this possibility; he is clearly surprised when Tracy in effect says this is what he has done.

The absurdity of crystallization is its incorrigibility. This embarrassment is shared by Tracy's theory but remains invisible due to his inherited philosophical belief in a correspondence letting him check linguistics against empiricism. Enlightenment ideology from Condillac to Tracy mediates between the two. Thus Tracy can write, as we have seen him do, about the primacy of perceptions, and also claim in his *Eléments* that "all languages have common rules which are derived from the nature of our intellectual faculties."[18] In this context, Cartesian linguistics or the idiom of the grammarians of Port Royal guarantees that appearance still retains its logic even if it loses touch with what it was thought to be the appearance of. We are, as it were, referred in advance to Chomsky rather than to Saussure: to the universals of a deep linguistic structure rather than to the arbitrariness of the sign. Assumed is a view of language as constituted by an immutable human rationality. Avoided is the post-Saussurean surrender of that confidence in an immutable human rationality as a consequence of realizing that it is constituted by language. It is this second possibility that Stendhal's text anachronistically opens up through its characterization of love as an ideology.

What is happening, then, is that Stendhal's treatise purports to foreclose the arbitrariness of language by producing a scientific definition of love, an ideology of love in Tracy's sense. However, his definition actually restores arbitrariness by characterizing love as a psychological and imaginative overleaping of boundaries: the power to assimilate anything at all to the substance of the original object of study through a process of crystallization. But in seeing how Stendhal fails to become an Enlightenment ideologue of love, we observe how he succeeds in drawing a picture of ideology much closer to a post-Marxist understanding of it as an imaginary relation to the real. And he does this by allowing tendencies in Enlightenment ideology to develop within a new romantic phenomenology that no longer ties them down to external verification.

In such early writings as *The Holy Family, The German Ideology* and *The Poverty of Philosophy*, Marx still formulates his materialism largely through a critical reading of his philosophical heritage from Descartes to Feuerbach. He sees the empiricist reaction to Descartes's idealism culminating in a combination of the two, stretching from La Mettrie, Holbach and the *philosophes* through the work of Tracy's friend Cabanis to the natural science of Marx's own day. Marx's critique of "pure" science, applied retrospectively to this tradition, discredits the materialist half of the "combination," calling it "Cartesian materialism" because in fact all we are being given is a system of ideas (*SW*, 149–55, 179). Marx then writes his own chapter in this story we have been telling by insisting that such a system must be constructed in conformity with the social relations explaining how people have managed to produce their reality. His explanation exposes how "reality" is tailored to the dominant class's interests and desires. More recently, enlisting Freudian hindsight, post-Marxist thought has concentrated on the ingenuity with which ruling-class power is legitimated or disguised. Althusser's positioning of the ideological in a Lacanian imaginary finally grants it such unlimited resources that it can dispense with ideas altogether, becoming, in a contradiction hard to surpass, both a material and a subjective existence. That damning license is at least partly anticipated by Stendhal's ideology of love: "[D]ans cette passion terrible, *toujours une chose imaginée est une chose existante*" (*A*, 119).

However, we should keep in mind that if Stendhal's shift in the meaning of ideology characterizes the move from Enlightenment to romanticism, it also depicts romanticism as a misreading, a mistake. There seems no reason to think Stendhal disingenuous in his desire to emulate Tracy and to assume his intellectual heritage. He refers to *De l'amour* in his third and last preface as his "Physiologie de L'Amour." The laws of physics, he claims, are his model, although his treatise is palpably a compendium of everything unsystematic—anecdote, catalogue, travelogue, aphorism, reverie, conjecture, autobiography—strikingly in contrast to Tracy's chapter. Stendhal's nostalgia, though, is for the enlightened society of Diderot, fifty years before. He tells us how he finds frightening the change that has rendered Diderot's culture unintelligible and plunged French society into its present ennui, a boredom he satirizes as English, but that will grow monstrous beyond even the capabilities of the English— "peuple le plus triste de la terre"—to find again a proverbially French voice in Baudelaire (*A*, 325–26). Stendhal, unlike us, sees no anticipations of a disjunctive modernity in the vivid miscellany (or crystallography, perhaps it should be called) of his own mode of writing. Instead he tries to recover a glittering urbanity and gaiety he associates with the *ancien régime*, virtues, however, that were especially exemplified for him by *philosophes* like Diderot who were busy demonstrating that regime's obsolescence. Obviously, it would be unlikely that Tracy would appreciate so contradictory an expression of solidarity. Absurdity was what he saw; but, for us, after Marx, contradiction is fair historical game, the stuff of ideology.

If Stendhal redefines ideology, therefore, he does so inadvertently, in conformity with the contradictions underlying his own stance as a liberal sympathizer, someone expelled more than once from Italy by the Austrian government because of his support for the Carbonari and their revolutionary aspirations. Revolutionaries who take their style from that of radicals shown to best advantage in the regimes they criticize, and liberals who are enabled in their self-criticism by the privileges they wish to do away with—these are familiar knots, *pis-allers* that we can now identify as ideological constraints, but that were repeatedly dramatized during the romantic age. Perhaps this was because there was as yet no metalanguage with which to define and distance their experience, or because the break with a richly contradictory past demanded by a successfully scientific metalanguage implied an unacceptable cultural impoverishment. Stendhal gets as close to articulating this dilemma as any of his contemporaries in his ideology of love; but then his exchange with Tracy over the book shows him to have been mistaken or obscurely contradictory about its achievement. He thinks his picture of love meets the standards of Enlightenment objectivity, but, contaminated by its inexhaustible subject matter, it undermines its own control and distance altogether, miming in its own mélange the power of love absurdly to turn anything to its object. The erotic ideology he describes grows into a form that can encompass the position from which he described it. Stendhal himself dramatizes this encirclement when the love of *his* life, Métilde (Mathilde) Dembowski, dies in 1825. In English he notes in the margin of his own copy of *De l'amour*, "Death of the author," a surrender of authority sadly accentuated by being in English: none of *la gaieté française* here, the hoped-for complicity with Tracy and his enlightened precursors, but only entrapment within the age's gloomy, English self-image. This is the reality that Stendhal depicts, and, as Marx claimed in *The German Ideology*, "[W]hen reality is depicted, philosophy as an independent branch of knowledge loses its medium of existence" (*SW*, 165). Philosophical detachment from ideology is just what Stendhal's redefinition of ideology precludes. His treatise reveals a philosophical loss, and that is important: its thesis is not complacently self-confirming. But neither can it turn this loss to methodological gain. It can only propose as an alternative to complacency the reenacted awareness of loss and nostalgia for the philosophical position irrecoverably lost.

Sade's exploration of erotic self-confirming systems foregrounds what my discussion of Stendhal's treatise omits: the character allotted to woman by the discourse of male desire. But Sade does so by depersonalizing woman, making her interchangeable with things, refusing her and those who relate to her sexually any subjectivity save the blandness required by pornographic instrumentalism. We can react to this either with straightforward condemnation or else, as antihumanist critics have been led to do, we can find in Sade's perversity a means for raising consciousness of the subjugation women suffer under the contrasting, so-called normality of patriarchy. The French Sadeians, and poststructuralist critics like Jane Gallop, do the latter. Angela Carter tries to value Sadeian excess as a power to demystify gendered stereotype and myth, the achievement of "a moral pornographer."[19] But there is a third response that recovers the historicism implied, I have argued, by romantic texts' dramatized discontent with the immanence of their self-criticism.

Sade's barbarism shows that it is the bought woman or child of pornography who is effaced, silenced, or generally made available to the philosophically anaesthetized reader keen to foreground Carter's "moral pornographer" or the tyranny of contemporary ideology. To vindicate Sade at one point is simply to permit his violence at another. To see him as a deconstructor of representation is also to shelve the victim's pressing problem of how to gain redress through representation. The alternative would be to appreciate more why Marx regarded definition of the subjects of discourse through apparently impersonal economic specifics not as cultural impoverishment but as the only viable recovery of them as persons in the wake of a discredited humanism. Barthes, too, although attracted by Sade's antihumanist precociousness in suggesting "the possibility of a subject-less lexicon," has to concede that "the Sadeian text is reduced by the phenomenological return of the subject, the author, the utterer of Sadism."[20] This historical *birth* of the author risks contradicting Barthes's more famous deconstruction of the author elsewhere. It makes the point that in Sade's time a subjectivity that exploded its self-defining, interpellating ideology from within, immanently, still conveyed the sense that it was defined by external historical circumstances for which it had yet not found the language. Marx's political economy and Barthes's semiotics provide such a language. Despite their differences, they are both responding to the historical character of romanticism.

To summarize, then: romanticism, defining itself in the process, mediates the shift in meaning of "ideology" between the Enlightenment and Marx's critique of it in *The German Ideology*, a critique powered by his demonstration of what ideology has become. Romantic dramatizations of the incorrigibility of ideology open up philosophical theories of ideology to all kinds of intervention and illustration. Stendhal and Sade are representative of two poles of this undermining of philosophical autonomy to be completed by Marx. The affront Stendhal's idealist *De l'amour* causes the philosophical ideologue, Tracy, is mirrored by the scandal of Sade's materialism. Both enable us to rethink contemporary theoretical writings, from Adorno onwards, which struggle with the legacy of a critique condemned by postromantic ideology to be forever immanent. Finally, I suggest that the young Marx's strong sense that this was a period problem, a romanticism or idealism, both helps explain his subsequent economism and could significantly relativize our postmodern condition.

Notes

1. Obviously representative of this opposition are Jerome McGann's new historicism and Paul de Man's deconstruction. See, principally, McGann, *The Romantic Ideology* (Chicago: University of Chicago Press, 1983); *The Beauty of Inflections* (Oxford: Clarendon Press, 1988); *Social Values and Poetic Acts* (Cambridge: Harvard University

Press, 1988). Paul de Man, *The Rhetoric of Romanticism* (New York: Columbia University Press, 1984); "Sign and Symbol in Hegel's Aesthetics," *Critical Inquiry* 8, no. 3 (Spring 1982): 509–13; "Hegel on the Sublime," in M. Krupnick, ed., *Displacement: Derrida and After* (Bloomington: Indiana University Press, 1983), 139–52; "Phenomenality and Materiality in Kant" in G. Shapiro and Alan Sica, eds., *Hermeneutics: Questions and Prospects* (Amherst: University of Mass. Press, 1984), 121–44.

On ideology in general, see Howard Williams, *Concepts of Ideology* (Brighton, England: Wheatsheaf, 1988) and, especially useful here since it supplements his major work on romantic ideology *(The Ideology of the Aesthetic),* Terry Eagleton's *Ideology: An Introduction* (London: Verso, 1991). The placing of an imagination creative of ideology at the center of understanding, or of figurality at the heart of discourse, recalls Coleridge but finds support today. See John B. Thompson, *Studies in Ideology* (Cambridge: Polity Press, 1984). Striking studies of the elided articulation of political issues within romantic ideology are to be found in the work of Marjorie Levinson, Alan Liu, David Simpson and others. I try to address what is at stake theoretically in these readings in "A Shadow of a Magnitude: The Dialectic of Romantic Aesthetics," in *Beyond Romanticism,* ed. S. Copley and J. Whale (London: Routledge, 1992), 11–32.

2. Paul de Man, "Intentional Structure of the Romantic Image," in *The Rhetoric of Romanticism,* 6.

3. On the romantic construction of a "literary absolute," see P. Lacoue-Labarthe and J.-L. Nancy, *The Literary Absolute: The Theory of Literature in German Romanticism,* trans. P. Barnard and C. Lester (Albany: State University of New York Press, 1988).

4. L. Althusser, "Ideology and Ideological State Apparatuses," in *Essays on Ideology* (London: Verso, 1984), 33; Alasdair MacIntyre, *Against the Self-Images of the Age: Essays on Sociology and Philosophy* (London: Duckworth, 1971), 11.

5. H. Taine, *Origines de la France contemporaine: la régime moderne,* 5th ed. (Paris, 1898), 2:219–20, also quoted in Jorge Larrain, *The Concept of Ideology* (London: Hutchinson, 1979), 215. Kenneth Minogue, in *Alien Powers: The Pure Theory of Ideology* (London: Weidenfeld and Nicolson, 1985) warns against histories of ideology that "in some measure [confound] the history of an idea with the history of a word. The real source of the excitement generated by the idea of ideology lies elsewhere, and this is the reason why Marx tends to be so dismissive of eighteenth-century socialists who are, in other respects, so closely related to both his projects and his enthusiasm" (39). This paper argues that to appreciate the reasons for dismissal you have to understand the history both of idea and word.

6. [Marie-Henri Beyle] Stendhal, *Love,* trans. G. Sale and S. Sale, introduction by J. Stewart and B. C. I. G. Knight (Harmondsworth: Penguin, 1975), 45.

7. T. Adorno and M. Horkheimer, *Dialectic of Enlightenment,* trans. John Cumming (London: Verso, 1979), 117 (hereafter *DE*).

8. Jane Gallop, *Intersections: A Reading of Sade with Bataille, Blanchot, and Klossowski* (Lincoln: University of Nebraska Press, 1981), 3–4, 115–16.

9. David Hume, "On Miracles," in *Essays Moral, Political, and Literary,* ed. T. H. Green and T. H. Grose (London: Longmans, Green, 1875); Isaiah Berlin, *Against the Current: Essays in the History of Ideas* (Oxford: Oxford University Press, 1981), 181. Alasdair MacIntyre points out the ironies of a similar allegiance between the Scottish Evangelicals and Secessionists, who preceded Hume, and philosophical skepticism in *Whose Justice? Which Rationality?* (London: Duckworth, 1988), 243ff.

10. K. Marx, "The German Ideology" in *Selected Writings*, ed. D. McLellan (Oxford: Oxford University Press, 1977), 160 (hereafter *SW*).

11. Donatien Alphonse François [Marquis de] Sade, *Justine, Philosophy in the Bedroom, and Other Writings*. ed. and trans. Richard Seaver and Austryn Wainhouse (London: Arrow Books, 1991), 331 (hereafter *J*).

12. Roland Barthes, *Sade, Fourier, Loyola*, trans. R. Miller (London: Jonathan Cape, 1977), 31; Barthes, "The Metaphor of the Eye," trans. J. A. Underwood, in G. Bataille, *Story of the Eye* (Harmondsworth: Penguin, 1982), 126. Marcel Henaff gives a lucid account of the Sadeian economy of loss and its peculiar kind of romantic recuperation: "Si le cri de la victime consacre une impossibilité du parler, le cri du libertin gaspille somptuairement les reserves du langage. En passant dans le cri la jouissance devient a-symbolique [i.e., not of the Lacanian symbolic order, so symbolic of the extradiscursive in a romantic sense] mais ce blanc de signification, cette rupture de l'ordre sont le luxe de la dépense délirante que s'offre la maîtrise discursive" *(Sade, l'invention du corps libertin* [Vendome: Presses Universitaires de France, 1978], 218).

13. F. Nietzsche, *The Will to Power*, trans. W. Kaufmann and R. J. Hollingdale (New York: Random House, 1968), par. 253 (hereafter *WP*).

14. Stendhal, *De l'amour* (Paris: Garnier-Flammarion, 1965), 43 (hereafter *A*). The Penguin translation unaccountably renders the French as plural.

15. See *Translation Of A Letter From Monsieur De Tracy, Member Of The French National Assembly, To Mr. Burke, In Answer To His REMARKS ON THE FRENCH REVOLUTION* (London, 1790). Thomas Jefferson's letter is prefaced to *A Treatise On Political Economy To Which Is Prefixed A Supplement To A Preceding Work On The Understanding Or, Elements Of Ideology By The Count Destutt De Tracy, Translation Edited By Thomas Jefferson* [1817], Reprints of Economic Classics (New York: Augustus M. Kelley, 1970).

16. Destutt de Tracy, *De l'amour*, introduction by G. Chinard (Paris: Société d'editions "Les Belles Lettres," 1926), xliv.

17. Ibid., 59–60; de Tracy, *A Treatise* . . . , 5. Jacques Derrida, in *The Archaeology of the Frivolous: Reading Condillac*, trans. John Leavey (Lincoln: University of Nebraska Press, 1987), argues that, in the case of Condillac, Enlightenment philosophy's dichotomy is held together by a biologism "which develops sensationalism into semiotism"(46). Otherwise the frivolity of which Derrida thinks Condillac provides the archaeology "consists in being satisfied with tokens. It originates with the . . . empty, void, friable, useless signifier" (118). See also Brian William Head, *Ideology and Social Science: Destutt de Tracy and French Liberalism* (Dordrecht: Martinus Nijhoff, 1985), 27, 40, 54, for discussion of Tracy's empiricist corrective to Cartesian linguistics.

18. Destutt de Tracy, *Eléments d'idéologie*, 2 vols., introduction and appendices by Henri Gouhier (Paris: Librairie Philosophique J. Vrin, 1970), I, xxiii–iv. For a placing of Tracy's praise of the Port Royal grammarians within a history of philosophers who combine (Condillac) or supplement Arnauld's and Lancelot's work with empiricism, see Antoine Arnauld and Claude Lancelot, *The Port Royal Grammar*, translated with an introduction and notes by J. Rieux and B. E. Rollin (The Hague: Mouton, 1975), 25–27.

19. Angela Carter, *The Sadeian Woman: An Exercise in Cultural History* (London: Virago, 1979), 19.

20. Barthes, *Sade, Fourier, Loyola*, 134.

IV The End(s) of Theory

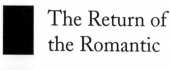

The Return of
the Romantic

Jean-Pierre Mileur

In this country, the rise of theory has been associated with the return of romanticism. There was the ideological importance of Coleridge for the New Critics—and then for their critics. The rhetorical deconstructionism of Paul de Man, the revisionism of Harold Bloom, and Geoffrey Hartman's experiments "beyond formalism" all have their roots in romanticism and turn on theories of the romantic. Even critics of these theoretical innovations tend to zero in on aspects of their "romanticism," whether formalist, existentialist, or merely precious or exaggerated. Even Nazism is linked via Nietzsche with the romantic.[1]

Come to think of it, it could easily be argued that this is hardly a return or resurgence; romanticism was never gone, or at least has been returning perpetually. The way was well-paved for the rise of theory by the importance of criticism in constituting our very understanding of "literature," and what is romanticism but the name of the mode of crisis in which criticism occurs?[2]

The movement toward theory has also by its very nature brought literary studies closer to philosophy. Indeed, the question of the relationship between literature and philosophy is a question that seems privileged in theory. But if theory has testified to the omnipresence of romanticism, at the same time it has brought once again to the fore philosophy's traditional denigration of the literary in general and specifically of the romantic. So, maybe the growing toward each other of literature/criticism and philosophy in theory has simply foregrounded the chasm, narrow but abyssal, that separates them.[3] For Philippe Lacoue-Labarthe and Jean-Luc Nancy, this chasm that defines literature and philosophy, that holds them together and apart for our modernity (and now, it appears, for our postmodernity), is romanticism. And romanticism, as the origin of the convergence of philosophy, theory, criticism, poetry, and fiction in what we have come to call and are still coming to call "Literature," is the object of their exploration in *The Literary Absolute*.

Like so many before them, Lacoue-Labarthe and Nancy begin by questioning the term "romanticism" and the literary genealogy that, on the continent at least, it implies—Dante, Shakespeare, Cervantes, the eighteenth-century English novel, *Sturm und Drang*—culminating in the famous remark that the novel is a "romantic book." In one (implicitly trivial) sense, they argue, "The word and the concept 'romantic' are indeed transmitted to the 'romantics'." In quite another sense, "their originality does not consist in inventing 'romanticism', but rather, on the one hand in using this term to cover up their own powerlessness to name and conceive what they invent, and, on the other (in any case, one can suspect this of Friedrich Schlegel), in dissimulating a 'project' that exceeds from all points of view, what this term transmits to them."[4] It is this excessiveness in particular that the literary tradition cannot account for. The argument made by Lacoue-Labarthe and Nancy is worth quoting at some length:

> [R]omanticism implies something entirely new, the *production* of something entirely new. The romantics never really succeed in naming this something: they speak of poetry, of the work, of the novel, or . . . of romanticism. In the end, they decide to call it—all things considered—*literature*. This term will be adopted by posterity (including their own, most immediate posterity) to designate a concept—a concept that may still be undefinable today, but that the romantics took great pains to delimit. They, in any case, will approach it explicitly as a new *genre*, beyond the divisions of classical (or modern) poetics and capable of resolving the inherent ("generic") divisions of the written thing. Beyond divisions and all de-finition, this *genre* is thus programmed in romanticism as *the* genre of *literature:* the genericity, so to speak, and the generativity of literature, grasping and producing themselves in an entirely new, infinitely new Work. The *absolute*, therefore, of literature. But also its *ab-solute*, its isolation in its perfect closure upon itself (upon its own organicity), as in the well-known image of the hedgehog in *Athenaeum* fragment 206.

At the same time, however, the stakes turn out to be even larger. The absolute of literature is not so much poetry (whose modern concept is also invented in *Athenaeum* fragment 116) as it is *poiesy*, according to an etymological appeal that the romantics do not fail to make. Poiesy or, in other words, production. The thought of the "literary genre" is thus less concerned with the production of the literary thing than with production, absolutely speaking. Romantic poetry sets out to penetrate the essence of poiesy, in which the literary thing produces the truth of production in itself, and thus, as will be evident in all that follows, the truth of the production *of itself*, of autopoiesy. And if it is true (as Hegel will soon demonstrate, *entirely against* romanticism) that auto-production constitutes the ultimate instance and closure of the speculative absolute, then romantic thought involves not only the absolute of literature, but literature as the absolute. . . . Romanticism is the inauguration of the *literary absolute*. . . . Romanticism is neither mere "literature" (they invent the concept) nor simply a "theory of literature" (ancient and modern). Rather, it is *theory itself as literature* or, in other words, literature producing itself as it produces its own theory. The literary absolute is also, and perhaps above all, this absolute *literary operation*.

In the end, Jena will be remembered as the place where it was claimed that the theory of the novel must itself be a novel. This demand, with which our "modernity" is still grappling, is expressed, a year before the journal is founded, in *Critical Fragment* 115, and it furnishes the entire program of the Athenaeum: "The whole history of modern poetry is a running commentary on the following brief philosophical text: all art should become science, and all science art; poetry and philosophy should be made one." (*LA*, 11–13)

For this very reason, Lacoue-Labarthe and Nancy tell us, it is "necessary (in other words still urgent) to undertake a properly philosophical study of romanticism" (*LA*, 13). Not just a philosophical study but a "properly" philosophical study. Of course the propriety of romanticism is precisely what we are told that explanation from (literary) tradition cannot provide; and propriety is, according to their translators, Barnard and Lester, what literature lacks without the kind of philosophical underpinnings that Lacoue-Labarthe and Nancy provide. Yet why propriety should belong to philosophy and not to literature, or even why its value is self-apparent, is not stated.

Theirs is a powerful argument and there is much to endorse, or at least make use of here: the notion that romanticism continues to function as the unconscious of our modernity; the recognition that the most distinctive and original genre to come out of romanticism is criticism/ theory; and the recognition that for the romantics and romanticism criticism is treated (wittingly or unwittingly) as "literature raised to the second power." All of these insights provide useful and important challenges to our own tradition's customary denigration of criticism before literature—even though what we think of as literary has long been constituted by criticism. All provide a useful antidote to criticism's own tendency to act as if it were transparent, if not invisible. Yet I cannot help but observe that these same conclusions are accessible by other paths, paths that are neither specifically Kantian nor even "properly" philosophical—and this raises questions about what Lacoue-Labarthe and Nancy choose to privilege.

Although the topic of *The Literary Absolute* is German romanticism, the first-generation romanticism of the Jena school and of Friedrich Schlegel in particular, Lacoue-Labarthe and Nancy are not even out of the preface before they are making gestures toward a more totalizing version of their argument, in a move that finds Jena everywhere while ostensibly defining its limits:

> Today, in fact, romanticism is known only through—or deliberately limited to—what was indirectly transmitted by either the English tradition (from Coleridge, who read them closely, to Joyce, who knew everything and always more than one suspects), by Schopenhauer or Nietzsche (who did not discuss what they derived from it), or—but here the path is even more indirect and for good reason—by Hegel and Mallarmé (or even by what, in France, takes on the specifically romantic name of "Symbolism"). But in almost every case, when the essential is not deliberately obscured or distorted, it still goes unperceived. If it nonetheless appears, it is repeated without comprehension and with no awareness of what is at stake. (*LA*, 16)

Jena is seminal in all these instances, though only Lacoue-Labarthe and Nancy have seen it and spoken of it as it really is. As a result, their analysis is more than a cautionary tale (and this is their antiromantic upshot) directed at Frenchmen dangerously oblivious to the creeping influence of the romanticism that has entered modern French thought via its German influences: it is a warning to us all. Furthermore,

> [O]ur own image comes back to us from the mirror of the literary absolute. And the massive truth flung back at us is that we have not left the era of the Subject.

It goes without saying that this observation is not made for the pleasure of recognizing ourselves in romanticism, but on the contrary in order to gauge what in fact functions as a genuine denegation and also to guard against a fascination and a temptation. For insofar as we are, we are all preoccupied with fragmentation, the absolute novel, anonymity, collective practice, the journal, and the manifesto; as a necessary corollary, we are all threatened by indisputable authorities, petty dictatorships, and the simplistic and brutal discussions that are capable of interrupting questioning for decades; we are all, still and always, aware of the Crisis, convinced that "interventions" are necessary and that the least of texts is immediately "effective" *[opératoire]*; we all think, as if it went without saying, that politics passes through the literary (or the theoretical). Romanticism is our naïveté.

This does not mean that romanticism is our error. But rather that we have to become aware of the necessity of this repetitive compulsion. That is why this book involves an exigency, but one we do not wish to speak of as "criticism," for good reason. At the most we might call it "vigilance." We know very well that one cannot simply dismiss romanticism (one cannot dismiss a naïveté). All the same, for this is not a superhuman task, one can exhibit a minimum of lucidity. These days, this would already be a great deal. (*LA,* 16–17)

There in that last line is the condescension, the dismissive motion. Having presented and characterized romanticism in its most dangerously naïve aspect, the whole may be classified. In fact, there are at least three stories here. One, which corresponds to their reading of Jena, deals with how authors with an enormously powerful philosophical precursor and a relatively weak national literary tradition wrote much more speculative criticism than literature and developed a "theoretical" romanticism. The second, which corresponds to the message that Lacoue-Labarthe and Nancy address to their French readers, is about how "theoretical romanticism" can have an invidious effect on readers whose own lack of a prominent native romantic tradition can make them oblivious to its influence. Finally, there is one that points to a problem of reception and arises in the minds of readers whose own romantic tradition is accurately described by neither of the first two stories. This last is the story of how authors were led by the achievements, challenge, and the weight of a preeminent national literary tradition to demand more from literature than it could provide, of how criticism grows out of the limits of romantic poetic practice and takes on the task of both supplying these deficiencies and of repressing our awareness of them, and of how, in time, criticism comes to promote itself to the second power of theory and discovers Nietzsche and those he has influenced and, by this route, establishes contact with a theoretical and academic romanticism stretching back to Jena.[5]

Clearly, the problem of what Lacoue-Labarthe and Nancy say is also the problem of how we are receiving it, especially since, after all, we are dealing with a translation. For this reason, I mean to go back and fill in some of the gaps and details in my account of their argument by means of a double gloss or commentary. On one level, I want to follow in some detail Barnard and Lester's reconstruction of and commentary on what Lacoue-Labarthe and Nancy have to say—partly because their remarks are useful, partly because they seem to accept so unquestioningly precisely what is most questionable in what they are doing. On another level, I mean to identify the "error" that Barnard/Lester and Lacoue Labarthe/Nancy seem to share, which might variously be described as a failure to recognize the coherence or propriety of tradition, the failure to recognize that practices are as able as concepts to engender movements and meanings, or perhaps simply the failure to achieve equivocity, to manifest the equi-vocation that both pairs of authors purport to offer as a responsible alternative to the seductions of the literary absolute.

According to Barnard and Lester's account, for Lacoue-Labarthe and Nancy literature is a "rigorously defined area of philosophical inquiry" (*LA*, viii)—largely as a result of their success in locating romanticism decisively as a consequence of and episode within the philosophical tradition. "Rigor," closely related to propriety, is a dominant theme of their discussion, produced fetishistically several times. It is this curiously (but entirely characteristic) ascetic metaphorics as much as anything else that calls up the discussion of Nietzsche that I will offer later in this essay.

In any case, the way is opened for romanticism in the *Critique of Judgment,* when Kant insists in his discussion of the symbolic on the "incompatibility of sensible presentation and the ideas of pure reason" (*LA*, ix). The romantics reinvent "presentation in such a way as to transform it into the kind of adequate operation lacking in Kant"; that is, romanticism in its own view completes and "perfects" idealism. Thus this Kantian dead end becomes Art as the privileged domain in which "the absolute might be experienced and realized in an unmediated, immediate fashion" (*LA*, ix). Literature, viewed as the unity of "creative formation and critical reflection," uses the formative power of the artist to extend "beyond the sensible and, recalling Kant's concept of the sublime, accomplishes a presentation of what in Kant remained unpresentable" (*LA*, ix).

Thus literature comes to be "more basic than or superior to the realm of philosophy *from which it has drawn its founding concepts* [my italics]"(*LA*, ix). Here, as clearly as anywhere, a crucial genealogical question is raised. What, if anything, do concepts found/find? And what, if anything, is there to the presumption that informs this entire book that the kinds of phenomena that register in intellectual or literary history are more credibly (or productively) seen as the result of concepts in philosophy than of practices in literature? What are concepts or ideas in such a formal, historical sense and do they found or find, or are they themselves found?

Perhaps we need to recollect Nietzsche's famous observations that "truth" is actually "a mobile army of metaphors, metonymies, and anthropomorphisms" and that metaphysics is actually a consequence of taking grammar too seriously.[6] The point, or rather the question, is whether such a genealogy doesn't—precisely because of the self-imposed requirements of "propriety" and "rigor"—predetermine a view of theoretical romanticism, and hence of theory, that confirms accusations that theory is merely an escape from practice, a continuation of metaphysics and its self-delusions by other means and the very antithesis of self-overcoming.

But isn't this a version of what Lacoue-Labarthe and Nancy deplore and warn against? Isn't it Nietzsche's point that dichotomies like philosophical truth/mere language, or concept/practice, are false? Don't Lacoue-Labarthe and Nancy argue that the philosophy/literature dichotomy is subverted in the romantic concept of "Literature"? Indeed, all this is true, but the problem is less with their genealogy than with its partiality and the stance it allows them to assume as agents of a hoped-for lucidity quite distinct from the contemporary consequences of the romanticism they have defined. They fail to see the connection between the mode and terms of their account of origins and the partiality of the picture they derive of romanticism's influence in the present. The reflexive mode of crisis they deplore in contemporary affairs and the crisis they define as the origin of romanticism are linked as a self-fulfilling teleology.

It is interesting to note that in the English literary tradition, throughout the eighteenth century and corresponding with a great effort to rationalize literary practice and history on a philosophical basis, there is a sense of immanent crisis. In particular, efforts to "rigorously" define the "propriety" of poetic language cut poetry off from language in general, create an increasingly straitened sense of possibility, and lead to anxieties—chronic to this day—about the coming end of literature, about the final running down of a poetic tradition that has fulfilled the mission defined for it and that can now only repeat itself endlessly.[7] Nietzsche, of course, recognizes a similar dynamic at work in his analysis of nihilism[8] and tries to change the terms of the discussion and define a way out, partly by initiating the ongoing project of bringing metaphysics to an end, partly by means of such notions as eternal recurrence and self-overcoming.

Adrian del Caro has argued forcefully that Nietzsche owes far more to and is far more intimately in dialogue with Friedrich Schlegel and the first-generation romanticism of Jena than with the later, nationalistic romanticism of Wagner. In del Caro's account, where Nietzsche goes beyond "romanticism" (not just Jena) is in replacing art with self-creation as the privileged arena of activity.[9] Here del Caro is the victim of the intensity of his focus on the German tradition. That privileging self-creation is postromantic will come as a revelation to any reader of Wordsworth's *Prelude*. In some contrast to Nietzsche (and contra del Caro), and in response to his own tradition, Wordsworth reopens a sense of possibility by reattaching poetic language to real language (and experience). And instead of the finite responsibility for supplementing rationality until it can finish colonizing experience, he gives poetry the potentially infinite mission of expressing, which is to say of self-definition and creation.

This is certainly not to suggest that everything Nietzsche became, Wordsworth was before him; it is, however, to suggest that through his partiality del Caro, like Lacoue-Labarthe and Nancy, fails to identify and account for properly what different romantic traditions have in common and what they hold as their own. In the cases of Nietzsche and Wordsworth, it is certainly true that at the end of the nineteenth century, Nietzsche is far more alienated from the tradition that made him than is Wordsworth at its beginning—alienated to the point of being willing to denigrate art even as he is making himself into the most literary of philosophers. For Nietzsche, self-creation represents a far more radical break than for Wordsworth, whose drive to self-definition and creation is balanced by an equally powerful sense not only of the efficacy but of the benignity of the forces that have made him what he is.

To return now to Barnard and Lester on Lacoue-Labarthe and Nancy. As a result of the romantic response to Kant, "Literature" transcends the limits of and becomes superior to philosophy; at the same time, since "Literature" could not have come into being were it not for this moment or crisis in the history of philosophy, in its transumption the importance and the reach of philosophy are much enhanced. The Kantian problem of philosophy's adequate self-presentation, a crisis involving the philosophical subject, prepares the way for the elaboration of the philosophy/ literature opposition, there since Plato in one form or another but now reproblematized in a way that gives rise to criticism/theory as the genre of the romantic/modern.

It is, according to Lacoue-Labarthe and Nancy, only after Kant that the express distinction between philosophy and literature becomes "necessary and possible" (*LA*, x) and only when Jena poses the question of literature as the question of the presentation of philosophy. "Literature" as we know it, then, is determined in a philosophical crisis and, Barnard and Lester insist officiously, "literature's most comprehensive [i.e., anxious?] gestures of authenticity invariably coincide with its greatest dependency on philosophy" (*LA*, xiv). The crisis of the philosophical subject becomes the crisis of the literary subject as well.

Kant opens up this crisis by depriving the subject of its being-subject—its adequate presentation of itself to itself—reducing the subject to little more than the logically necessary, regulatory idea of the unity of its representations. Speculative idealism and Jena romanticism are different responses to this crisis of the subject's unrepresentability to itself. Idealism fulfills the subject in the labor of the concept; romanticism envisions the autoproduction of the subject in the work of art. The speculative dialectic faces literature and thereafter, literature and philosophy summon (and repel) each other (*LA*, xvi).

For Lester and Barnard, Mary Shelley's *Frankenstein* provides an example in English romanticism of what Lacoue-Labarthe and Nancy are talking about. In the story that frames the action of the novel, a young sea captain, assailed by feelings of incompleteness, aspires to "become the 'subject-work,' the paradigmatic model of the romantic subject's autoproduction in the work of art. The arduous process of self-cultivation that he has undertaken is coextensive with his autoproduction; it is his all-consuming 'project'. . ." (*LA*, 11–12). Because he is engaged in this task of autoproduction, the "narrator's disposition as a subject-work is *fragmentary* in nature; that is, it assumes and continually points toward a perfection and completion that lie beyond it, yet also underlie its self-productive activity" (*LA*, xii).

To Captain Walton, Victor Frankenstein is the embodiment of creative power raised by reflection to the point where it "becomes capable both of producing itself and of reflecting on and theorizing its own production" (*LA*, xii). Literary consciousness, forming its own theory, as the totalizing autoproduction of the subject, completes philosophy. Of course, this project is precisely what the novel calls into question because, as everyone knows, things turn out badly for "The Modern Prometheus":

> [A]s the novel attests, this remarkable project is never fulfilled; for intrinsic reasons, it never reaches perfection. The novel's account of the project's failure, of what Lacoue-Labarthe and Nancy might call its "redhibitory defect" or inherent flaw, suggests, if nothing else, that the seemingly far-reaching powers of such a model of literature are not sufficient to regulate or control what its reflective operation engenders and that when the regulatory power of this literary subject fails, the results—at least according to this somewhat moralistic scenario—are catastrophic. One might say that when monstration is controlled by the totalizing reflection of Literature, it becomes, in the terms of this narrative, monstrous. One should recall here that Frankenstein's goal within the staging of the novel's framework is to arrest the "literary" (in an entirely different sense here) or irretrievable effects of his project, which has grown so distant from his initial idea that it seems to have altogether escaped his control. The project of the Jena romantics, as discussed in *The Literary Absolute*, is engaged in the elaboration of such a concept of literature and, despite itself, in the attainment of its limits. (*LA*, xiii)

Barnard and Lester see *Frankenstein* as illustrating and confirming Lacoue-Labarthe and Nancy's view that for Jena (and for the romantics in general) the pursuit of the literary absolute inevitably and "despite itself" leads to the disillusioning attainment of its limits. But Barnard and Lester do not say why, since this is after all a romantic novel, the product of one of the tightest circles of English romanticism, this outcome doesn't call into question Lacoue-Labarthe and Nancy's claims about romantic naïveté, or at least expose the degree of special pleading involved in their decision to make Jena stand for romanticism.

If the flaw in Frankenstein's project is "inherent" (and a "properly philosophical" reading will always prefer the inherent to the contingent), then the novel's scenario is, as Barnard and Lester imply, "merely" moralistic in an extraneous way. But it seems equally credible to argue that the novel lends support to the view that Frankenstein's flaw is his contingent failure to recognize his own partiality in interpreting his "romantic project," which he reduces to its most hyperbolic form.

Barnard and Lester's reading is a rather foreshortened one that leaves out the crucial developments in the novel's middle chapters (17–20), most particularly the key episode in which Frankenstein refuses to get rid of the monster by making him a mate. In a moment of moral differentiation in which he discovers that restraint which he forgot at the novel's beginning, Frankenstein averts the kind of collective crisis that Lacoue-Labarthe and Nancy want to lay at romanticism's doorstep. Frankenstein cannot take the risk of creating any more monsters, even to assuage his own conscience and atone for his own sins. The monster cannot be trusted, because he has already stated and demonstrated his determination to pass on the suffering that he has endured, to equalize and rationalize it. Frankenstein knows that we cannot live with each other; we cannot even live with ourselves except by virtue of our ability and willingness to absorb hurt, in excess of our deserts, perhaps without deserving it at all, without passing it on. The monster really is monstrous, and it is up to Frankenstein to reabsorb that monstrosity himself; arguably at least, he succeeds.

The extreme partiality of Barnard and Lester's reading is less a reflection of the literary absolute as a romantic illusion than of its limitations as a scenario projected by philosophy onto the romantic work of literature. The novel's own scenario may strike them as moralistic (and therefore extraneous) but that is because it is only on these terms that it can be accommodated to the essentially static role of illustrating or exemplifying that philosophy defines for the literary—a role that enforces the idea that nothing is *really* put into play or at risk in the work of literature, that nothing ever really happens as the result of fictions.

By acting as if the romantic critique of the literary absolute were somehow less "romantic" than the notion itself, Barnard and Lester obscure the fact that the debate Lacoue-Labarthe and Nancy stage with the romantics—at least the part that justifies their condemnation (however carefully it is hedged about)—the English romantics had already staged themselves, primarily in the form of the second generation's criticism of the first for abandoning the project of the imagination, their name for what Lacoue-Labarthe and Nancy call "Literature."

All this is not to say that the novel doesn't recognize the dangerously hyperbolic nature of the romantic project—its tendency to cast beyond its own ability to control—and define the distinctive anxiety that perpetually attends it. But in their determination to ignore the novel's hints and hopes that these difficulties might still be negotiated and a way found to make use of a man like Frankenstein, Barnard and Lester betray that more fundamental fear of "fantasia" in general and of romance in particular that continues to separate philosophy from literature and dictates the blindness of Lacoue-Labarthe and Nancy toward some aspects of the romanticism that, in other ways, they read so powerfully.

"Fantasia" names the "impropriety" by means of which things are made to happen in literature. "Romance" names the putting into play of the hoped-for in the face of all we know of ourselves and of the world that runs counter to desire. Such terms seek to characterize from within the power of literary practices to generate meanings and engender change quite apart from philosophical conceptualization and its hegemonic claims; they point to the existence of a romantic intertextuality that is only mistakenly subsumed under the heading of organicism—an organicism all too prone, as Lacoue-Labarthe and Nancy tell it, to metastasize.

Lacoue-Labarthe and Nancy, Barnard and Lester continue, "make it clear that the study of romanticism and its theory of literature is necessarily part of a study of the assumptions governing *current* literary-critical and theoretical practices." But they get onto shaky ground when they go on to imply that Lacoue-Labarthe and Nancy provide the only path to this insight by arguing that their "genuinely historical relevance" is in contrast to the "literary-critical historicism that characterizes most traditional thinking on romanticism" (*LA,* viii). The distinction turns, of course, on a questionable dichotomy between the "genuinely historical relevance" of Lacoue-Labarthe and Nancy's continental/philosophical approach and the "literary-critical historicism" characteristic of Anglo-American criticism. But this single dismissive gesture serves to do away with a host of more literature- or practice-based competing theories of romanticism of at least equal scope and power: Bloom, Hartman, Abrams, de Man, Rajan, and other theoretically sophisticated students of romanticism (who are also romantically sophisticated students of theory) are unceremoniously shoved off the stage.

Barnard and Lester go on to argue, quite rightly, that Lacoue-Labarthe and Nancy's "philosocentrism" doesn't represent an intrusion into the realm of literature and properly literary explanation. After all, if even part of what they say is true, how can we and why should we keep them apart? But once again, they wander onto questionable ground in elaborating. Literature, they say, lacks *propriety*—its terms and ground are not its own. This absence of the proper "is precisely what inhibits efforts to establish a positive methodology and encourages the proliferation of approaches" (*LA*, xiii). The preoccupations here—positive methodology, unity of approach, legitimacy (in an almost paternal sense) of terms and grounds—are all philosophical in a rather traditional sense; not a moment's thought is given to the possibility that literature's impropriety, even if or even because it encourages a proliferation of approaches in criticism, might be a positive advantage, its main advantage in contrast to philosophy—exactly the form of its peculiar propriety and what keeps critical theory from being reabsorbed into the dismal philosophical subfield of aesthetics.

It would be premature to say flatly that Barnard and Lester go wrong. In fact, their remarks very accurately reflect an ethos that is somewhat obscured by the caginess of Lacoue-Labarthe and Nancy's presentation. However, not only does their approach involve a more or less traditional philosophical anxiety over the "fantasia" implicit in the literary—whether it is described in terms of the fictional, imaginative, or simply the rhetorical—it also shows little or no awareness of the English literary tradition or its criticism. Let us consider these two points in order.

The point of this whole exercise, it is protested, is not to elevate philosophy over literature; it is acknowledged that there is something in literature—a by-product perhaps of the subject's autoproduction—that is not comprehended in "Literature" as they explain it. The relationship between "Literature" as it is comprehended by philosophy and literature as it escapes such comprehension is characterized (or not characterized, nor estimated) as "equivocity"—a relationship of indeterminacy, even negativity (*LA*, xix). Although no attempt is made to define this by-product or excess, or even to explain philosophy's failure to comprehend it, neither are Lacoue-Labarthe/Nancy or Barnard/Lester willing to concede to it a propriety of its own.

Unfortunately, as my remarks thus far have surely indicated, it seems to me that while Lacoue-Labarthe and Nancy *theorize* equivocity, they *enact* univocity or something close to it. Otherwise, instead of offering a strongly privileged genealogy of romanticism, in the spirit of *equi*-vocity they would at the very least offer a *hetero*-genealogy. After all, their own concept of equivocity suggests that, beyond a certain point, there is no perspective from which the competing claims of different genealogies can be adjudicated. Or to put it another way, by definition, propriety cannot go to the heart of the matter.

And this brings us to our second point. If Lacoue-Labarthe and Nancy were to enact equivocity, they would have to pay far more particular attention than they do to the English tradition, which, unlike the romanticism of Jena, is literature-rich and relatively theory-poor. From our Anglo-American critical perspective, their argument seems very dependent on the peculiarities of recent French intellectual history as it has been influenced by German philosophy and its relationship to German romanticism. The fascination of Jena with the unconditioned or absolute grows out of and gains impetus from the work of Kant. Lacking a strong national literary tradition, working in the shadow of Kant, Jena is a romanticism of ideas, a theoretical romanticism, rather than a romanticism of literary practices, as in England. I confine myself to three examples of the difference this makes in theorizing romanticism.

M. H. Abrams's *Natural Supernaturalism*[10] bases its account of romanticism on the importance of radical Protestantism, not just as an element in English society but as it is strained through a key part of the literary tradition from Spenser, through Milton, to Wordsworth (throughout the eighteenth century, after the Bible *Paradise Lost* is the most widely circulated book). Abrams's emphasis on the Protestantism of the English tradition allows him to build bridges to German romanticism; it also allows him to account both for the continuity and discontinuity of romanticism from the literary tradition—something that Lacoue-Labarthe and Nancy seem to think that only the idea of a Kantian "crisis" can do. In essence, the radicalism and radical internalism of extreme Protestantism eventually carries beyond the bounds of Christianity itself onto the new ground of the naturalized supernatural. Nietzsche defines a similar sequence of events in *Genealogy* when he asserts that in science, Christian morality has fallen victim to its own drive to truth.

Harold Bloom's seminal essay "The Internalization of Quest Romance"[11] provides a far more compelling justification for the term "romanticism" than any considered by Lacoue-Labarthe and Nancy. He follows the romantics themselves in considering their project a continuation and updating of the great romance tradition of English literature, only internalized (and thus psychologized and particularized) to a far greater degree than even Milton—still tied, however vestigially, to conventional Christianity—dared to do.

The peculiar strength of practices—at least in a sufficiently deep literary tradition—both to define continuity and to articulate departures is also apparent in a contemporary manifesto like Wordsworth's *Preface to Lyrical Ballads,* which, as we have already seen, proceeds from a change in practice—the adoption of a different poetic diction and a different object—and builds its ideology on this. The differences in the two traditions that exist from the very first generation and find expression in theories of the romantic suggest that one effect of concentrating on German and ignoring English romanticism, of emphasizing the formative power of concepts over practices, is to create a vantage point from which the "failure" of the romantic pursuit of the absolute can be seen as a limit and a border, surveyed from without or above, from an implicitly superior, postromantic point of view, in which philosophy serves as a kind of "historical absolute," the triumph of genealogy over heterogenealogy. This stance profoundly affects the picture of romanticism that emerges, for not only does heterogenealogy yield a more diverse picture of future prospects, it yields a richer middle ground historically as well. For example, a somewhat more expansive approach might have avoided Lacoue-Labarthe and Nancy's abrupt jump from the failure of Jena's initial self-justification to the consequent dangers posed by romanticism today; it might have left room to consider subsequent evolutions of romanticism and the consequent present possibilities—how romanticism acquired an ironic consciousness about itself that, though raising new problems and defining different limits, also suggests the possibility of an ongoing heuristic rather than ideological role for the romantic.

Thus it appears possible to argue that Lacoue-Labarthe and Nancy's stance is actually made possible by the manipulation of perspectives from within an ongoing romantic perspective and not by some external, extraliterary, postmodern vantage point. This in turn suggests that this argument is ultimately recaptured by Jena—at least as they define it—in the sense that it too depends on an intellectual historiography in which theory generates practices and eventually reabsorbs them to itself. The consequence of such a model—and perhaps the pay-off of this whole project—is to create a privileged vantage point from which the romantic past is put securely in its place, paradoxically repressed beyond the possibility of return in the very act of "giving it its due." Why, aside from philosophy's traditional antipathy to the contingencies of history, should this be so important?

To put the case another way, this kind of literary-intellectual historiography underwrites the possibility of an act of "historical" reading that avoids being read in turn (and thus recaptured) by the very past or "other" out of which it is constructed. In such a model, as we have seen, concepts engender practices and theory becomes the avoidance of practice, the continuation of metaphysics by other means—and doomed to fall prey to the same nihilism.

Two observations may help to clarify the significance of this defense against reading for a reading of the romantics. First, literary critics/ theorists are used to being read in terms of the sources they invoke; their matter-of-factness about this may be one of the things that distinguishes them from philosophers. An important case in point is the way that the New Critics appealed to Coleridge's theory of imaginative reconciliation in support of their own theories and even claimed to be continuing his tradition. Having invoked Coleridge in this way, however, they had to endure the deconstruction of their theories in terms supplied by the other aspects of Coleridge's life and works.[12] In de Man's view, the blindness that accompanies insight is the form in which this "being read" as one reads manifests itself. For de Man, no reader ever can completely or even adequately comprehend the terms in which he or she is being read in the act of reading.[13]

Even more important for our purposes, it should be recalled that this sense that I am being read by what I read is central to the great landscape poetry of the English romantics and informs equally their intimate and productive relationship with their own literary tradition.

To a considerable degree, the account of romanticism offered in *The Literary Absolute* turns on the figure of Friedrich Schlegel. Yet different figures embody very different relationships of romanticism with the past and imply very different romantic futures. Two figures in particular— one British, one German—not only frame the period of high romanticism at its extreme limits but also point up the limitations of Lacoue-Labarthe and Nancy's account. I have in mind Edmund Burke and Friedrich Nietzsche.

Burke, the greatest of English statesmen and staunch opponent of the French Revolution, died in 1797, the year before Wordsworth and Coleridge published their *Lyrical Ballads*. Burke made his reputation as the mouthpiece for the Whig oligarchy's unrelenting attacks on the policies of Tory ministers—including their policy in the American colonies. To young Englishmen growing up in the late eighteenth century, men like Wordsworth and Coleridge, Burke represented the possibility of a politics that was thoughtful and principled, and as enlightened as seemed consistent with the nature of English society. So Burke's single-minded opposition to the French Revolution and his unrelenting criticisms of its English sympathizers came as a shock to many of his admirers, who were drawn to the French cause as an extension of their own liberalism. Eventually his intractability on the French question led to Burke's break with his own party and the effective end of his political career.

But for Wordsworth and Coleridge, Burke proved prophetic. Early sympathy with the revolution gave way to unease and later led to returns to the established church and other gestures of conservatism. In the case of Wordsworth especially—arguably the most continually influential of the English romantics—his greatest works display profound affinities with Burke's vision of how human beings find their identities, of what they need and value. For example, when Burke writes "The moral sentiments, so nearly connected with early prejudice as to be almost one and the same thing, will assuredly not live long under a discipline that has for its basis the destruction of all prejudices,"[14] he is arguing that morality is neither relative nor absolute; it is both relative and absolute in its particularity, grounded in early prejudice or, as Wordsworth puts it, in the "affections."

No reader of Wordsworth can hear these lines without thinking of Wordsworth's account in *The Prelude* of how his early affections for the English countryside, its experiences and people, led him on to make him the man and above all the poet that he has become. And they remind us equally of his tangled relationship with the French Revolution as it is recounted there: the promise of the Republic and his early enthusiasm; the early portents in the Simplon Pass and the Gondo Gorge of the difference between life and imaginative desire; the terrible conflict between loyalty and conviction that attends the English declaration of war; the disillusionment that follows the Paris Terror; the curiously intense focus on Robespierre; the sense of release at his death and the symbolic return to and reconciliation with the fathers that occurs when he revisits the grave of his old schoolmaster—the one who encouraged him to be a poet. On the schoolmaster's headstone are lines from Gray, whose poetic diction Wordsworth mocked in the Preface to *Lyrical Ballads*, signaling a return to poetry and its tradition as well.

The central books of *The Prelude*, the most complex and tangled in this poem "on the growth of a poet's mind," are haunted by the suspicion of a fundamental opposition between the affections and loyalties, the ties to the past that make a poet, and the violence and disruptions of radical change and the *ab nihilo* "inherencies" that drive it. At one point, just before he bottoms out, Wordsworth flirts with Godwinism. But nothing, it turns out, could be farther from the truth he shares with Burke than this famous argument from *An Enquiry Concerning Political Justice:*

> A man is of more worth than a beast; because, being possessed of higher faculties, he is capable of more refined and genuine happiness. In the same manner the illustrious archbishop of Cambray was of more worth than his chambermaid, and there are few of us that would hesitate to pronounce, if his palace were in flames, and the life of only one of them could be preserved, which of the two ought to be preferred.
>
> But there is another ground of preference, beside the private consideration of one of them being farther removed from the state of a mere animal. We are not connected with one or two percipient beings, but with a society, a nation, and in some sense the whole family of mankind. Of consequence that life ought to be preferred which will be most conducive to the general good. In saving the life of Fenelon, suppose at the moment he was conceiving his project of the immortal *Telemachus*, I should be promoting the benefit of thousands, who have been cured by the perusal of it of some error, vice and consequent unhappiness. Nay, my benefit would extend farther than this, for every individual thus cured has become a better member of society, and has contributed in his turn to the happiness, the information and improvement of others.
>
> Supposing I had been myself the chambermaid, I ought to have chosen to die, rather than that Fenelon should have died. The life of Fenelon was really preferable to that of the chambermaid. But understanding is the faculty that perceives the truth of this and similar propositions; and justice is the principle that regulates my conduct accordingly. It would have been just in the chambermaid to have preferred the archbishop to herself. To have done otherwise would have been a breach of justice.
>
> Supposing the chambermaid had been my wife, my mother or my benefactor. This would not alter the truth of the proposition. The life of Fenelon would still be more valuable than that of the chambermaid; and justice, pure, unadulterated justice, would still have preferred that which was most valuable. Justice would have taught me to save the life of Fenelon at the expense of the other. What magic is there in the pronoun "my," to overturn the decision of everlasting truth? My wife

or my mother may be a fool or a prostitute, malicious, lying or dishonest. If they be, of what consequence is it that they are mine?[15]

But is not our sense of Fenelon's value, Burke would say, the very principle that impels us to save him, only an extension of, an extrapolation from, the personal affections we have given and received? Did principle or "poetry," Wordsworth would say, make me a poet, or was it the poems and poets I read who made me the poet I am? At issue in the importance of Burke to Wordsworth and to romanticism is the conservatism with regard to the past and the self of art in general and of poetry in particular. The tension between the nature of poetry and the redemptive/salvific uses to which it is put is amply demonstrated by Wordsworth's ambiguous stance at the end of *The Prelude:* a man among men, the messenger of a common redemption and the product of his own life, the great poet William Wordsworth, still looking down from Mount Snowdon. As Harold Bloom has pointed out, the strong poet is held relentlessly in the grasp of the double injunction "be like the precursors" (and hence, a poet) and "be unlike the precursors" (and hence, an original poet—i.e., more than a poet?).[16] From the very beginning, English romanticism is casting beyond poetry toward criticism and theory in an effort to escape this conservative pull, only to be tugged back into its orbit. Ultimately, in an effort to escape this same centripetal pull, Nietzsche will seek to pass beyond and even denigrate art and artists in *Genealogy* (*BW,* 538). Though more extreme to be sure, this gesture has its roots in a problem that stretches back virtually to the inception of romanticism and that not even Nietzsche finally claimed to have overcome.

In linking Burke to Nietzsche and in characterizing the span of romanticism that separates them, I think that it is particularly useful to speak of the passage from the "death of the dead" to the "death of God." The "death of the dead" is my term for that eventuality that Burke resisted, the loss of a vivid link with the past, of the sense of being part of an ongoing tradition. In particular, this involves losing the sense of living one's life on stage, under the watchful eyes of the dead, of facing their disappointment and earning their approval. Without these "affectionate" ties to the dead, society must be reinvented in and for each generation. No more could it be said, in Burke's well-known view, that society

is a partnership in all science; a partnership in all art; a partnership in every virtue, and in all perfection. As the ends of such a partnership cannot be obtained in many generations, it becomes a partnership not only between those who are living, but between those who are living, those who are dead, and those who are to be born. (*R*, 194–95)

Everyone, of course, knows about the death of God.[17] As Nietzsche insists, we have killed him. The path from the death of the dead to the death of God demonstrates that "metaphysical" principles themselves (like Godwin's "justice") could not survive their denigration of the affections as nothing more than "mere" prejudices. As a result of efforts to parse the morality out of Christian devotion, the whole ascetic/moral edifice falls prey to its own drive to "truth."[18]

The importance of Nietzsche's writing to his philosophy has not (at least in recent years) been lost upon philosophers. But their tendency, even when trying mightily to do otherwise, to grant concept priority over practice is well-illustrated by the case (a neat instance, by the way, of the tyranny of philosophical practices over ideas) of Alexander Nehamas, whose splendid book on Nietzsche *intends* to demonstrate the indispensability of the style to the thought.[19] Yet it is clear from the beginning that Nehamas does not know how to *write* himself as if this were true.

In instance after instance, he actually writes as if the style is the expression, however important, of preexisting antimetaphysical convictions. And finally, the payoff of his whole enterprise is its value in providing answers to the philosophical questions surrounding such Nietzschean concepts as eternal recurrence, the *Übermensch*, perspectivism, and particularly the will to power. That Nietzsche's writing might undermine the very practice of treating these notions as philosophical problems to be solved in this interesting but not very radical way is never considered. Yet Nehamas's thesis calls for at least considering the rather different question, "What else could someone who writes like this think about metaphysics?"

One of the consequences of posing the question in this way is that what philosophers are inclined to discuss and problematize as Nietzsche's "doctrines," like eternal recurrence or the *Übermensch* or perspectivism or self-overcoming, can then be seen, at least for heuristic purposes, as new tropes in a greatly expanded, even open-ended postmetaphysical rhetoric. More specifically, they can be seen as figures, related to hyperbole perhaps, arising out of and even returning to Nietzsche's own practices as a writer, to the motivating forces of his project. This notion of doctrines serving as conceptual characterizations of rhetorical events more complex than those referred to in the taxonomies of classical rhetoric is not so very different from Nietzsche's own (self-allegorizing?) description of metaphysics's unwitting conceptual extrapolations from grammar.

Pushing at the limits of rhetorical practice is Nietzsche's way of conceptualizing, in terms like eternal recurrence and self-overcoming, the limits of metaphysics and—more important for our purposes—the horizons of romanticism. But Nietzsche does not make the mistake of excepting himself from the movements he comments on. He is perfectly capable of the kind of telling critique he offers when he observes in *Twilight of the Idols* that Carlyle's loud recommendations of faith are linked in a typical romantic fashion to doubts about his own capacity for belief (*PN*, 521). Yet Nietzsche does not claim to be the postromantic to Carlyle's (or Wagner's) romantic; rather he presents himself as a kind of higher man, a liminal figure advanced to the ultimate stage of the status quo (or is it the *pen*ultimate stage?), perhaps perpetually to remain there.

At the end of *Genealogy*, Nietzsche clearly distinguishes himself from Zarathustra, as he distinguishes Zarathustra from the *Übermensch*, remaining within the limits of the horizons he projects (*BW*, 532). The entire third essay of *Genealogy* is presented as a commentary on a single brief remark from *Zarathustra*,[20] suggesting that commentary is a rebounding from limits (the limits reached in that central work)—a sign, along with irony, parody, constant self-commentary, and self-parody of this ultimacy or at least evolution in the status quo. Thus we are still within romanticism, but an evolved romanticism, in which simple belief or even the fiction of belief is replaced by a heuristic use of the available materials in hyperbolic attempts to "cast beyond" the present.

Eternal recurrence, for example, is radically different from the normal shape of desire, our (in)disposition to life. With regard to Nietzsche's practices, it seems to refer to the author's power of willing retrospectively what has befallen in the course of writing. Harold Bloom has argued that all figuration involves an urge to be elsewhere[21] and since the point of eternal recurrence is to not just accept but desire what has been, is, and will be, it can be characterized as a figure beyond figuration, marking the limits of the new rhetorical space that Nietzsche himself has opened up.

Most of the complications arise when we earnestly try to figure out what eternal recurrence calls on us to do. To accept ourselves as we are? Yet wanting to be absolutely as we are is probably as far as we can get from being as we are now. And wanting to be different—able to endure the "greatest stress"—is to fail immediately. In terms of the romantic quest, as it is defined in poems like Browning's "Childe Roland to the

Dark Tower Came," we set out to find the name we desire but end up, if we are lucky, desiring the name we have already been given. This romance defines a relationship with the tradition with which Nietzsche's eternal recurrence resonates powerfully; it also makes clear how violently parodic eternal recurrence is of our difficulties with the tradition, of our attempts to invent it anew out of each successive moment. With Burke, it seems to question the easy assumption that we can return to the tradition, or at least regain its distinctive reassurances, once we have abandoned them.

More simply, perhaps, the individual who has endured the "greatest stress" doesn't invoke the past in order to escape it, nor does she invoke the future in order to hold it at bay; she is as willing to be read by them as to read—as we have seen that Lacoue-Labarthe and Nancy are not. They wish to invoke tradition but to exclude themselves from it.

Even more than eternal recurrence, self-overcoming—especially in *Thus Spoke Zarathustra*, part 4—offers itself as an allegory of reading and being read. Eventually, Zarathustra's discomfiture at the readings performed on him by the higher men—a discomfort not always the result of inaccuracy—gives way to triumph. He can endure the "misreadings," the exigencies that they seek to avoid, by anxiously imposing themselves. His diagnosis of why the higher men fall short of self-overcoming is a telling one: the transformation/transcendence they seek is too shallow (*PN*, 532). They wish not to change but to carry their identities triumphantly with them, as if self-overcoming were simply the final apotheosis of what they already are. This secret conservatism causes them to remain trapped in the present. In the absoluteness that denies even in the end the recovery of a stable identity, self-overcoming marks the limit of romanticism—a horizon that Nietzsche himself can't get beyond, although he can see from where he is that romanticism without some such self-overcoming is nihilism. Yet he is no nihilist; he believes in self-overcoming.

Lest we get too deeply involved in the intricacies of Nietzsche, perhaps it would be best to offer a few observations. First, romanticism is so hard to overcome because it incorporates self-overcoming into itself. Each attempt to circumscribe it seems to become another episode in its unfolding—because of its "vagueness" Lacoue-Labarthe and Nancy would say. Second, one thing that this might mean is that Nietzsche's lesson is that romanticism is not a "doctrine," any more than eternal recurrence and self overcoming are doctrines. Rather say that romanticism is a collection of practices and rhetorical possibilities, along with the as yet incompletely conceptualized space that they open up. But I am uncomfortable with that tendentious "as yet," with its implications of a finite space to be filled, its ultimate boundaries and the terms of its fulfillment kept anxiously clear by the ritual exercise of "rigor" and "propriety." Say rather that romanticism, as Nietzsche struggled to realize and define it, is a radical reopening of rhetoric, a renegotiation of the relationship between language and conception that engenders its own rambling tradition, a family tree of begettings and misbegettings; or, as Richard Rorty would put it, a conversation that will come to an end when we "change the subject." So third, an alternative to defining the rise of criticism/theory as a response to a crisis in the history of philosophy is to think of it as the self-overcoming of poetry (remembering that poetry is still being written, however theoretically impossible and irrelevant it may be) and to wonder as well what the self-overcoming of criticism/theory might/ought to look like (besides, that is, a regressive return to poetry). Such a genealogy hardly excludes that provided by Lacoue-Labarthe and Nancy; it merely supplements and renders it properly heterogenous. For our true romantic equi-vocation is contained in the question, "Is theory the self-overcoming of philosophy in poetry, or the self-overcoming of poetry in philosophy?" To which we can only answer, "Yes."

Notes

1. In particular, I have in mind such critics of the Yale School as William Pritchard ("The Hermeneutical Mafia; or, After Strange Gods at Yale" [*Hudson Review* 28:601–10]); Gerald Graff (*Literature Against Itself* [Chicago: University of Chicago Press, 1979]); Frank Lentricchia (*After the New Criticism* [University of Chicago Press, 1980], *Criticism and Social Change* [University of Chicago Press, 1983]); Daniel T. O'Hara (*The Romance of Interpretation* [New York: Columbia University Press, 1985]); Stanley Corngold (*The Fate of the Self* [New York: Columbia University Press, 1986], "Error in Paul de Man" [*Critical Inquiry* 8, no. 3:489–507]); and Tilottama Rajan (*Dark Interpreter* [Ithaca: Cornell University Press, 1980]).

2. See Paul de Man, "Criticism and Crisis," in *Blindness and Insight: Essays in the Rhetoric of Contemporary Criticism*, 2d ed. rev. (Minneapolis: University of Minnesota Press, 1983).

3. Paul de Man, "The Resistance to Theory," *Yale French Studies* 63 (1982).

4. Philippe Lacoue-Labarthe and Jean-Luc Nancy, *The Literary Absolute* (Albany: State University of New York Press, 1988), 3 (hereafter *LA*).

5. Jean-Pierre Mileur, *The Critical Romance* (Madison: University of Wisconsin Press, 1990).

6. "Truth and Lie in an Extra-Moral Sense," in *The Portable Nietzsche*, ed. and

trans. Walter Kaufmann (New York: Viking, 1983), 46–47 (hereafter *PN*). *Twilight of the Idols*, "'Reason' in Philosophy," section 5; *PN*, 483.

7. Walter Jackson Bate, *The Burden of the Past and the English Poet* (New York: Norton, 1972).

8. See, for example, *Genealogy of Morals*, third essay, sections 26–28, in *The Basic Writings of Nietzsche*, ed. and trans. Walter Kaufmann (New York: Random House, 1968), 593–99 (hereafter *BW*). Also Nietzsche's collected notes on "European Nihilism," in *The Will to Power*, trans. Walter Kaufmann and R. J. Hollingdale (New York: Random House, 1967).

9. Adrian del Caro, *Nietzsche Contra Nietzsche* (Baton Rouge: Louisiana State University Press, 1989).

10. M. H. Abrams, *Natural Supernaturalism* (New York: Norton, 1971).

11. Harold Bloom, "The Internalization of Quest Romance," in *Romanticism and Consciousness*, ed. Harold Bloom (New York: Norton, 1970), 3–24.

12. Jean-Pierre Mileur, "Deconstruction as Imagination and Method," in *Coleridge's Theory of the Imagination Today*, ed. Christine Gallant (New York: AMS Press, 1989), 65–83.

13. See "The Rhetoric of Blindness," in de Man, *Blindness and Insight*, 102–41.

14. Edmund Burke, *Reflections on the Revolution in France*, ed. Conor Cruise O'Brien (London: Penguin, 1968), 24 (hereafter *R*).

15. *Prose of the Romantic Period*, ed. Carl Woodring (Boston: Riverside Press, 1961), 16–17.

16. See Harold Bloom, *The Anxiety of Influence* (Oxford: Oxford University Press, 1973).

17. Nietzsche, *Thus Spoke Zarathustra*, prologue, section 2; *PN*, 174.

18. Nietzsche, *Genealogy of Morals*, third essay, section 27, in *BW*, 596–97.

19. Alexander Nehamas, *Nietzsche: Life as Literature* (Cambridge: Harvard University Press, 1985). For a more extended discussion of Nehamas along these lines, and of the argument concerning Nietzsche presented here, see Bernd Magnus, Jean-Pierre Mileur, and Stanley Stewart, *Nietzsche's Case: Philosophy as/and Literature* (New York: Routledge, 1993), especially chapters 4 to 6.

20. "Unconcerned, mocking, violent,— thus wisdom wants *us:* she is a woman and always loves only a warrior" (*BW*, 531).

21. As a defense against literal meaning as death. The idea is pervasive, but see, for example, *A Map of Misreading* (New York: Oxford University Press, 1975), 83–105 or *Kabbalah and Criticism* (New York: Seabury Press, 1975), 80–84.

Moments of Discipline:
Derrida, Kant, and the
Genealogy of the Sublime

Mark A. Cheetham

The sublime, wrote James Usher in the late eighteenth century, "takes possession of our attention, and of all our faculties, and absorbs them in astonishment."[1] My aim in this paper is to examine how the notion of the sublime continues to absorb and astonish contemporary theorists. In the interests of concinnity, I will focus on just one example, Jacques Derrida's captivation by Kant's versions of the sublime. This reinvigoration of Kant and his ideas has not, of course, gone unnoticed, nor is Derrida alone today in his insistent retheorization of the sublime.[2] But Derrida's interest in the Kantian sublime throws into relief particularly dramatically two issues that are, I believe, both typical of the widespread return to the sublime and also perhaps causally related to the resurgence of this concept. First, Derrida and Kant are obsessed with borders and the legislation of conceptual boundaries. Both thinkers, I will argue, employ the term sublime—despite its putative boundlessness and uncontrollability—as a cipher of circumscription. Secondly, and in an equally paradoxical manner, Derrida uses Kant's sublime in *The Truth in Painting* as a way to think about the authority that philosophical aesthetics has had historically over the visual arts, a border dispute that finds its articulation in his machinations about genealogy and descent.

Before I turn to Derrida's reading of the Kantian sublime, it is worth remarking on the oddity—even the anachronism—of the remarkable contemporary interest in this discourse and thus also to emphasize the (perhaps unanswerable) question "Why the sublime, and now?" Lyotard asserts that "one cannot avoid returning to the 'Analytic of the Sublime' in Kant's *Third Critique*, at least . . . if one wants to have an idea of what is at stake in modernism."[3] Cannot avoid? These are surprisingly strong words from a thinker who, in *The Postmodern Condition*, warned against the sway of the past's metanarratives. Yet in supporting his claim, he invokes the concerns with boundaries that Derrida embraces in his theorizations of the "parergon": "[T]he frame of aesthetics, aesthetic commentary, built by pre-romanticism and Romanticism," Lyotard proposes, "is completely dominated by (and subordinate to) the idea of the sublime."[4] Thomas Weiskel has claimed that even though the notion of the sublime's "structure still undergirds our imaginative intellection," we nonetheless "no longer share in the hierophany of the sublime which was unquestioned in nineteenth-century critics."[5] I would suggest that Weiskel's attempt here to distance himself from the revelatory power of the idea of sublimity is undone by the insights of his own study and by the frequent revisiting of the notion by other contemporary thinkers. The sublime must be seen to bring something to light in late-twentieth-century contexts; the question is, what? Another peculiarity of the contemporary concern for the sublime arises when we recall that, historically, the sublime is an idea that has had strong gender identifications. In 1785, for example, Frances Reynolds claimed that "the masculine [character] partakes of the sublime,"[6] and her opinion is widely echoed today by more negative voices. For Patricia Yaeger, the "Romantic sublime is . . . a masculine mode of writing and relationship." While this might make it interesting as a relic of hegemony, it is therefore for her "a genre that is—in the present age—of questionable use."[7] Yet it is used frequently and explicitly. My own meditation on Derrida's reading of Kant in *The Truth in Painting* will seek to show that the sublime is an idea that works to fix boundaries of genre and discipline during a time of great border anxiety within theoretical discourses and that this instrumentality is seductive enough today to override possible jitters about the concept's history.

Derrida's examination of Kant's sublime is found in "The Colossal," the fourth section of "Parergon," which Derrida calls the first chapter of *The Truth in Painting*. The "Parergon" is prefaced by the "Passe-Partout," a section that Derrida is at pains to describe neither as a "master key" nor an introduction to his book. Nonetheless, if one reads in a more linear fashion than Derrida seems to want, the "Passe-Partout" contains hints about the import of the notion of the parergon and about the seminality of the sublime as an example or illustration of parergonality, that "re-mainder"[8] which is "neither work *(ergon)* nor outside the work *(hors d'oeuvre)* . . . [yet which] *gives rise* to the work" (9). I will read Derrida's text as if it builds up to the section on the sublime, which means that I will focus on the "Passe-Partout" and on the first and fourth divisions of the "Parergon." My excuse for this partial and slanted reading is encap-sulated in Derrida's own expression of the spirit of the parergon in the context of his reading of Kant: "I do not know what is essential and what is accessory in a work" (63). In other words, I am not trying to read Derrida correctly, whatever that would mean, but rather to deploy his reflections on the sublime within a narrative about disciplinarity.

One of the meanings of "parergon" is "frame," both in the sense of a physical limit around a painting and also in the more conceptual sense of a "frame of reference." One such reference point in what I will claim is Derrida's discussion of the sublime as parergon is the notion of "remain-der," the supplement (in the Derridean sense) that can always be found after any reading of a text or image and that is, therefore, for a moment, outside the initial definition of that work and its reading. Derrida notes that he writes "around" painting in this text "for the interest—or the grace—of these remainders" (4). On a general and quite grand level of implication, his concern is with the limits imposed on the visual arts by philosophical aesthetics and with what escapes these would-be borders. More specifically, he looks for the troublesome details in Kant's third *Critique* (and in the aesthetic theories of Hegel and Heidegger) and makes these seemingly marginal issues central to his reading. "I am occupied," he writes, "with folding the great philosophical question of the tradition ('What is art?' 'The beautiful?' 'the origin of the work of art?' etc.) on to the insistent atopics of the *parergon*" (9).

After discussing Kant for over fifteen pages, Derrida introduces Kant's own brief reference to the parergon in the third *Critique* by saying, "[S]o I begin with some examples" (52). Some of these examples are Kant's own instances of parerga in art, those "extrinsic addition[s]" such as "picture frames, or drapery on statues, or colonnades around magnifi-cent buildings."[9] Predictably but brilliantly, Derrida uses Kant's examples to show how difficult it is to determine where a parergon begins or ends and thus what is and is not parergonal in a work of art. With Kant's final "example of the columns," says Derrida for example, "is announced the whole problematic of inscription in a milieu, of the making out of the work in a field of which it is always difficult to decide if it is natural or artificial and, in this latter case, if it is *parergon* or *ergon*" (59). Earlier Derrida announced what I take to be the large implication of this movement between parergon and work: "The permanent requirement—to distinguish between the internal or proper sense and the circumstance of the object being talked about—organizes all philosophical discourses on art, the meaning of art and meaning as such, from Plato to Hegel, Husserl and Heidegger" (45). What Derrida objects to in this tradition and in the examples from Kant is not the identification of a line or limit between parergon and ergon but rather the a priori rigidity of this separation that is typical, he thinks, of philosophical discourses as they bear on art and its history. From his analyses of Kant's three examples, it might seem that Derrida wants to collapse the distinction between work and frame and in effect do away with the parergon. But as his admonition that "deconstruction must [not] . . . dream of the pure and simple absence of the frame" (73) suggests, his concern is more to show the necessary and fluid interpenetration of work and border. Referring to what is supposedly extrinsic in Kant's illustrations, Derrida argues that "what constitutes them as *parerga* is not simply their exteriority as surplus, it is the internal structural link which rivets them to the lack in the interior of the *ergon* . . . Without this lack, the *ergon* would have no need of a *parergon*. [But] the *ergon's* lack is the lack of a *parergon*" (59–60). Put more prosaically, there cannot be a work without an outline that provides definition.

If I am right in suggesting that the necessity of a relation between work and frame is argued for by Derrida in the opening section of the "Parergon," then it becomes clear why the notion of the sublime is so fascinating for him. In the text of the third *Critique* and in the many versions of the sublime generated in the nineteenth century, the sublime has the character of unboundedness. In his initial comparison of the beautiful and sublime in the "Analytic of the Sublime," Kant introduces this idea: "The beautiful in nature concerns the form of the object, which consists in [the object's] being bounded. But the sublime can also be found in a formless object, insofar as we present *unboundedness*. . . ." (sec. 23, 98). Derrida picks up on this seemingly rigid difference by commenting that "there cannot, it seems, be a *parergon* for the sublime" (127). The phrase "it seems," however, works rhetorically here to offer the possibility that the sublime as a discourse is not only bounded in Kant's text but is also the consummate legislator of limits in what Derrida sees as philosophy's mastery of art and art history.

Derrida's entrance to these issues is through the "mathematical sublime," the species of sublimity that arises from measurement and that is thus quite different from formlessness, the "dynamically" sublime in Kant's parlance, a category familiar from Burke and earlier theorists.[10] For the emotion of the mathematically sublime to be produced in us, by the pyramids for example, Kant says, we must fix our line of sight at precisely the right place. It is as if we must draw a line around these edifices at the ideal viewing distance in order to be overwhelmed by their immensity. "For if one stays too far away," he suggests, "then the apprehended parts . . . are presented only obscurely, . . . and if one gets too close, then the eye needs some time to complete the apprehension from the base to the peak" (sec. 26, 108). The need for precise placement of this line is suggested by Kant on the next page, in a passage on the "colossal" taken up by Derrida. *"Colossal,"* as Kant defines it, "is what we call the mere exhibition of a concept if that concept is almost too large for any exhibition (i.e., if it borders on the relatively monstrous)" (sec. 26, 109). Derrida puts pressure on the notion of the "almost too," asking how one could ever specify its locale, and he concludes that the "almost too," as an indication of sublime size, is not for Kant empirical at all. Yet I would argue that Kant's example of the pyramids seems to suggest that there is an exact place, a frame, from which and only from which these monuments can occasion the feeling of the sublime in an observer. The sublime of the colossal, we might say, literally "borders . . . the relatively monstrous," by circumscribing and thus identifying that which is either parergon or ergon, depending on the line of sight one takes.

Kant of course backs up this physical manner of controlling the seeming unboundedness of the mathematically sublime with "critical," a priori arguments: because the power of reason aids that of the imagination, which cannot itself adequately "exhibit" colossal vastness to the mind, he in effect suggests that the ability thus to *present* our very inability to comprehend the excesses of "raw nature" is the sublime. Kant even makes the mathematically sublime edifying for the human subject by having it simultaneously reveal and consist in our awareness of "our supersensible vocation" (sec. 27, 115), that is, the mind's ultimate intellectual control—through reference to morality—over anything it perceives. In Derrida's reading, "[T]he true sublime . . . relates only to the ideas of reason. It therefore refuses all adequate presentation. But how can this unpresentable thing present itself?" His answer: "The inadequation of presentation is presented" (131). In the experience of the Kantian sublime, the imagination thus becomes bounded in comparison with the "unbounded" power of reason (sec. 27, 117). What would seem to be the limitless power of the imagination and the confined exercise of reason reverse their roles and relative strengths; ergon can become parergon and vice versa.

With Kant and Derrida, then, we can hypothesize that the sublime is that elation arising from the consciousness of our ability to delimit colossal size or even a notion like infinity. Though Derrida does not emphasize the language of bordering and limiting in Kant's discussion of the sublime, these metaphors suggest the inexorable activity of the parergon to which Derrida has pointed. In a long passage in which Kant is working up to the triumph of reason in the experience of the mathematically sublime, he writes, "Hence it must be the *aesthetic* estimation of magnitude where we feel that effort, our imagination's effort to perform a comprehension that surpasses its ability to encompass the progressive apprehension in a whole of intuition. . . ." (sec. 26, 112). The imagination cannot "encompass" or measure or bound that which stimulates our sublime response. But reason can put such a border in place and take emotional pleasure from this accomplishment. That pleasure—not the glimmering awareness of something incommensurably "other"—is the sublime for both Kant and Derrida. The experience and pleasure of the sublime does not stem from the promise of something noumenal outside a given frame but rather from the perpetual, yet always provisional, activity of framing itself, from the parergon.

Kant's critical philosophy is dedicated to legislating proper boundaries between and limits to what we can know, do, and hope for. The introduction to the *Critique of Judgment* lays out the fundamental divisions of "Philosophy" and specifies its "Domain." "Legislation through concepts of nature," he posits, for example, "is performed by the understanding and is theoretical." This is the realm of science examined in the first *Critique*. "Legislation through the concept of freedom is performed by reason and is merely practical," the jurisdiction of the second *Critique* (preface, 13). In Kant's thinking, these fields must be autonomous, yet they act on the same area of human experience. But how can theoretical knowledge, which works a priori, present to itself the realm of the sensible? It cannot, but practical knowledge must, according to Kant, and to do so—to allow us to act in freedom as rational subjects—he argues that we must assume the existence of "a realm that is unbounded . . . the realm of the supersensible" (introduction, 14). This reasoning takes Kant to the point where his system needs the aesthetic, the critique of judgment, to bridge the "immense gulf [that] is fixed between the domain of the concept of nature, the sensible, and the domain of the concept of freedom, the supersensible" (introduction, 14). While in the early part of this text he laments that "no transition from the sensible to the supersensible . . . is possible" (introduction, 14–15), we have seen that the sublime emotion, through its recourse to reason, does present the supersensible through the sensible. The sublime spans the "gulf" Kant envisages by setting a limit, presenting the unpresentable. Its legislative power of delineation is typically Kantian.

Commentators are perennially baffled by the paradox of the Kantian sublime, its presentation as unpresentability. Kant seems to be able to live with this tension: in a little-noticed passage, all he claims to need to do is *"point* to the sublime" (sec. 26, 109; my emphasis), which in turn is all the feeling of the sublime can do vis-à-vis the supersensible.[11] He points with (always inadequate and thus parergonal) examples, and as I suggested with reference to the experience of the pyramids, his examples tend to mark out a territory for experience by inscribing a physical point from which the identifying boundaries of a work can be properly apprehended. We have seen that Derrida makes much of Kant's examples and of Kant's work as an exemplar of philosophical aesthetics. But what of Derrida's own use of visual illustration in *The Truth in Painting?* Are these examples always inadequate like any putative instance of the sublime, implying that the activity of division—of inscribing the parergon—is somehow undesirable or avoidable? Derrida could be thought to "dream of the . . . absence of the frame" or to "reframe" (73) if we notice that the first picture in *The Truth in Painting* is of God's hand using dividers to circumscribe the earth, an image taken from Kepler's *De Nive Sexangula* (25). Given the scientific context, could this image of territorial surveying be as negative as Blake's famous 1795 "portrait" of Newton as a serpentlike monster bent on containing knowledge through mathematics? Should we understand Derrida to be the sort of "romantic" who thinks that something essential in art is always missed when one "limits" a work by writing about it or presenting it through illustration?

A comparison of Kant's and Derrida's uses of examples of the sublime tells a great deal about their mutual concern for boundaries in philosophy and between philosophy and other disciplines, especially those that concern art. Both men see the activity of limiting—figured by the sublime—as necessary, but where Kant seeks distinct, immutable, and transcendentally verified divisions (whether between frame and work, reason and imagination, or philosophy and art), Derrida prefers the play of parergon and ergon, the provisional and instrumental demarcation of work or discipline. Examples from the history of art contained in Derrida's book are instances of the sublime, not in the sense that they picture what art history has nominated as a sublime image, nor in the sense that they point towards a highly valued but ineffable something outside language and the visual arts, but because they present the unpresentable as the necessity of framing, again, of the parergon.

Derrida hints at this reading in a note that precedes the text of the "Parergon." He mentions that the first version of this text "was not accompanied by any 'illustrative' exhibition" (16). Already with the unusual use of "exhibition" here, we are reminded of the frequent references to what the imagination and reason can and cannot "exhibit" found in discussions of the sublime in the third *Critique*. As Derrida goes on, the Kantian context becomes even more clear. Referring to his text's pictures, he says, "[H]ere, a certain illustrative detachment, without reference, without title or legitimacy, comes as if to 'illustrate,' in place of ornament, the unstable *topos* of ornamentality. Or in other words, *to 'illustrate,' if that is possible, the parergon*" (16; my emphasis). Where Kant will excuse his examples as mere parerga in a transcendental enterprise, Derrida seems to use illustrations to underscore the impossible yet undeniable activities of circumscription, a bounding performed by authors, readers, institutions, and disciplines. Though they are without the usual identifying captions and thus lack the overt authority of the artist's name, two of Derrida's illustrations in the section on the colossal appear to be carefully placed in the text to comment on—to work as possible parerga for—his analysis of the Kantian sublime. These visual examples are from Goya's late series of "dark" paintings. The first, *The Colossus* (130), faces Derrida's gloss on the unpresentability of the sublime (131). What he thus provides is not only an image of a giant but also one that is, in art history, commonly taken as illustrative of Goya's sublime madness. So Derrida does frame and reframe the sublime, but with an image of unreason rather than only with Kant's transcendental reason as analyzed in the text. Derrida's unremarked illustration, however, leaves many remainders.

We could say that Derrida's example of the parergon as sublime leaves remainders specifically in art, that the border that the philosophical notion of sublimity erects is not seamless. Whereas Kant's text demonstrates the urge to control art with an a priori discourse that is proud not to be about objects, Derrida worries that "every time philosophy determines art, masters it and encloses it in the history of meaning or in the ontological encyclopedia, it assigns it a job as medium" (34), with Hegel singled out as the prime offender. Art, that is, becomes one parergon or defining edge for philosophy's self-appointed work. Derrida seems to want not to "use" art in this way, yet he realizes that for there to be any question of impropriety, a distinction between art and philosophy must be perceivable; each must have recognizable limits. But can Derrida escape the traditional framing of art by philosophy when his critique of the questions asked by the "masters" is still imaged through a common-place and strictly disciplinary genealogy that descends from Kant to Hegel and Heidegger?

Richard Rorty has written that "it is difficult to tell who the parents of a child or a philosophy are."[12] While his contention may be granted, it remains the case that philosophers—like those who recognize them-selves as members of other disciplines—frequently (as here) use genetic and genealogical metaphors as a way to adumbrate how they or an idea came to be. Rorty and Derrida imagine family trees of philosophers where ideas—as parerga, perhaps, for what these men will discuss—are inherited and passed on from generation to generation. It is an effective way to image descent and to secure the authority and privileges of noble birth, and I have no quarrel with Derrida's point that philosophers such as Kant—even the discipline of philosophy—have bounded art by saying just what may and may not be art. This effect is inevitable if one stays within the frame of philosophy chosen by Derrida, but the genealogical model has at least two consequences that should be made apparent. First, it tends to construct the discourse of the sublime as an ahistorical history of ideas passed down genetically through one line, that of philosophy as it thinks about the arts. Even though this family tree grows through time, it is presented all at once as a pattern. In Derrida's picture of the sublime, for example, we don't see anything between Kant's and Hegel's reflections on this idea. There are no other parerga for the notion, such as its manifestations in the visual arts (denied as a possibility by Kant) or in travel literature. I am not positing these contexts as more truthful to something called the sublime but simply as other frames for the theory.[13] Derrida cannot be expected to consider them all, but why does he then complain about the strictures of the philosophical containment of art? Why are these constraints implicitly more important rather than simply different or additional? Secondly, there is in the philosophical genealogy a fantasy of male procreation, of keeping art "pure" by thinking it a consequence of male generation.[14] On this model, Derrida and Kant are free to be each other's "fathers" and to reissue texts. Derrida need not be concerned, for example, with historical details that fall outside the frame of philosophers talking to one another, such as whether Kant's notion of "contour" as crucial in defining sculpture was derived from Winckelmann's reflections on this idea, reflections that grew out of a concern for the history of Greek art. Like Kant, then, Derrida is here quite unconcerned with art in its historical manifestations, even though Kantian aesthetics, and especially its reflections of the sublime, have been crucial to both the visual arts and the discipline of art history, for example, in the development of German romantic landscape painting, in Erwin Panofsky's foundational references to Ernst Cassirer's neo-Kantian ideas, and in the self-understanding of twentieth-century art movements as otherwise divergent as Cubism, American Conceptual Art, and color field painting.[15] If, as Naomi Schor suggests,[16] the "detail" has historically been the realm of what is called the "feminine," then not only Kant's definition of judgment as "the ability to think the particular as contained under the universal" (introduction, 18) but also Derrida's elision of historical specificity in his genealogy of the aesthetic remain within a masculinist frame, defined here as a tendency to abstractness at the expense of "mere" details.

The sublime as philosophical discourse certainly delimits art practice in some cases, as with Barnett Newman's quotation of Burke's theories in the painter's 1948 manifesto "The Sublime is Now."[17] But there is here no absolute, genetic line whereby philosophy somehow dictates what art might be. Newman's textual and painterly discourse of the sublime is more an elective affinity than a misuse of art by philosophy. Giving art "a job as medium" should not be as much of a problem as it seems to be for Derrida, because the parerga of art (and philosophy) cannot help but be plentiful and fluid. But I think that Derrida's views on boundaries have changed since he composed the essays in *The Truth in Painting*, changed to become more consistent with his ideas there on the parergon. He has indicated recently the importance in architecture of "the law of the threshold, the law on the threshold or rather the law as the threshold itself . . . the right of entry, the introductions, the titles, the legitimization from the opening of the edifice."[18] It is the sublime more than any other idea in this context that is the (ever adaptable) law of the "threshold," of the "limen,"[19] and the sublime operates in both Kant and Derrida to open and frame both the "architectonic" of philosophy, as Kant calls it, and art. Derrida's reflections on the "remainder" left by any framing should dissolve worries about art somehow being (genetically) deformed by philosophy. He shows that there will be "art" defined inside and outside the bounds of philosophy and that these bounds do in part define what will count as a discipline on either side of the parergonal marker. There will always be borders, so art both is and is not philosophy's child. Derrida has insisted on the perspective particular to disciplinary sight lines: "[Y]ou cannot simply mix philosophy with literature, with painting, with architecture. There is a point you can recognize, some opening of the various contexts . . . that makes Deconstruction possible." For Derrida now, "the most efficient way to put Deconstruction to work [is] by going through art and architecture,"[20] as he has in his work with architects Tschumi and Eisenman and in his reflections in *The Truth in Painting*.

By getting away in his more recent thinking about art from the genealogy of the fathers of philosophical aesthetics, Derrida can be seen to reenact the parergonal activity of the sublime in new and (for a philosopher) "impossible" projects such as the La Villette town design outside Paris. Here he displays new frames for both art and philosophy, yet there should be no more guilt about improperly using art, because there is nothing but its use. As Derrida himself puts it, "[T]his crossing, this going through the boundaries of disciplines, is one of the main—not just stratagems but *necessities* of Deconstruction. The grafting of one art on to another, the contamination of codes, the dissemination of contexts, are . . . most importantly . . . moments of what we call history" (Derrida, "Jacques Derrida in Discussion," 73). The history of such parergonal activity is also the history of the sublime.

Let me conclude with speculations that return us to the issues of disciplinarity. If the sublime has been used habitually as a way of making and figuring distinctions, then its parergonal activities may be seen as both a powerful metaphor for—and agent in—current debates about the limits of disciplinary structures, the borders that Derrida suggests are crossed by deconstruction. In his introduction to *The Textual Sublime: Deconstruction and Its Differences*—a collection of essays that itself exemplifies the present return to the sublime that I have thematized—Hugh J. Silverman writes that "the literary seeks to articulate and express the sublime; philosophy names and appropriates the sublime for itself—in effect, philosophy removes the sublime *from its proper place* and makes use of it for its own purposes."[21] But how can the sublime have a "proper place" in the universal sense implied by Silverman, especially if it typically defines borders and is the occasion—as here—for territorial disputes? In equating the sublime with the parergon, Derrida has shown how the "use" that Silverman fears is the very life of the sublime. At different times and from different perspectives, even large and imprecisely defined constructs such as disciplines will have their own sublimes, those issues that are at once feared and desired and which, through the disciplinary attention they garner, work to mark the provisional limits and flash points of particular disciplines. Philosophy—if we can make a monolith of it for the sake of argument—seems to be this sort of sublime for Silverman in the passage just cited. The same could be said of the discipline of art history, which has characteristically turned to capital *P* Philosophies to determine its own ends (Heinrich Wölfflin's interest in Kant is an apposite example), only subsequently to reject such influences as inappropriate to the empirical study of art. In Derrida's own reflections on Kant's sublime, we see what may be the sublime for philosophy, that which it is fascinated by and even needs according to its own theories (we can think of Hegel here), but which remains supplemental and defines a border: material and historical specificity in the form of art. Derrida's increasing concern with the visual arts exemplifies this movement of the parergon; it is no accident that he chooses the sublime as a primary vehicle in his redefinition of philosophy.

Notes

1. James Usher, *Clio; or, A Discourse on Taste Addressed to a Young Lady*, 4th ed. (Dublin, 1778), 102.

2. J.-F. Lyotard is the most prominent theorist of the postmodern sublime. Though I will make reference to his views throughout this paper, I cannot here dwell on their similarities with and differences from Derrida's ideas. In general, however, Lyotard has been more prone than Derrida to invoke the sublime in the context of contemporary art and culture; despite Lyotard's sustained engagement with Kantian texts, he explores the sublime less from the philosophical frame that primarily concerns Derrida. I consider the relationship of Lyotard's and Derrida's (as well as de Man's and Jameson's) ideas on the sublime in a current project titled *Kant and the Visual Arts*, of which this article forms a part.

3. Jean-François Lyotard, "After the Sublime: The State of Aesthetics" in David Carroll, ed., *The State of "Theory"* (New York: Columbia University Press, 1990), 297.

4. Lyotard, "A Response to Philippe Lacoue-Labarthe," in *ICA Documents 4: Postmodernism* (London: ICA,1986), 8.

5. Thomas Weiskel, *The Romantic Sublime: Studies in the Structure and Psychology of Transcendence* (Baltimore: Johns Hopkins University Press, 1976), 5, 36.

6. Frances Reynolds, *An Enquiry Concerning the Principles of Taste, and the Origins of our Ideas of Beauty &c.* (London: Baker and Galabin, 1785), 29.

7. Patricia Yaeger, "Toward a Female Sublime," in Linda Kauffmann, ed., *Gender and Theory: Dialogues on Feminist Criticism* (Oxford: Basil Blackwell, 1989), 192.

8. Jacques Derrida, *The Truth in Painting*, trans. Geoff Bennington and Ian McLeod (Chicago: University of Chicago Press, 1987), 2. Subsequent references appear in my text.

9. My references to Kant's *Critique of Judgment* are to the Werner S. Pluhar translation (Indianapolis: Hackett, 1987; this reference is to section 14, page 72) while Derrida's are to the earlier Meredith translation. Pluhar's translation is thought by many Kant scholars to be more accurate. To minimize the possible confusions of having two translations in play, I have in my references to Kant included the section number from Kant's text as well as the page number of the Pluhar version. All bracketed interpolations within the Kant quotations are Pluhar's.

10. On the distinctions between the mathematically and dynamically sublime, see Mark A. Cheetham, "The Nationality of Sublimity: Kant and Burke on the Intuition and Representation of Infinity," *Journal of Comparative Literature and Aesthetics* 10, nos. 1–2 (1987): 71–88.

11. It would be worth investigating the connections between this indication about the sublime and the final chapter of *The Truth in Painting*, which Derrida titles "Restitutions of the Truth in Pointing."

12. Richard Rorty, "From Ironist Theory to Private Allusions: Derrida," in *Contingency, Irony, and Solidarity* (Cambridge: Cambridge University Press, 1989), 128.

13. On travel literature and the sublime, see Cloë Chard, "Rising and Sinking on the Alps and Mount Etna: The Topography of the Sublime in Eighteenth-Century England," *Journal of Philosophy and the Visual Arts* (London) 1 (1989): 61–69. An especially rich discussion of the many contexts for the sublime in the eighteenth and early nineteenth centuries is found in Peter de Bolla, *The Discourse of the Sublime: History, Aesthetics and the Subject* (Oxford: Basil Blackwell, 1989).

14. A fuller discussion of this issue would need to take account of Derrida's remarks on "friendship," particularly his argument against the supposed presence and potency of the "essentially sublime figure of virile homosexuality" ("The Politics of Friendship," *Philosophical Forum* 85 [1988]: 642). Derrida certainly does not want to obviate historical specificity or materiality, as exemplified in the history of art, for example. But we need to ask the extent to which his discourse on the sublime in *The Truth in Painting* does just this precisely because it engages primarily with the tradition of philosophical aesthetics.

15. I investigate these and other examples in *Kant and the Visual Arts*.

16. Naomi Schor, *Reading in Detail: Aesthetics and the Feminine* (London and New York: Methuen, 1987).

17. Barnett Newman, "The Sublime is Now," in Herschel B. Chipp, ed., *Theories of Modern Art* (Berkeley: University of California Press, 1968), 552–53.

18. Jacques Derrida, "Fifty-Two Aphorisms for a Foreword," in A. Papadakis,

C. Cooke, and A. Benjamin, eds., *Deconstruction: Omnibus Volume* (London: Academy Editions, 1989), 67–69, Aphorism # 19.

19. For a detailed examination of the etymology of the word *sublime*, see Jan Cohm and Thomas H. Miles, "The Sublime: In Alchemy, Aesthetics and Psychoanalysis," *Modern Philology* 74 (Feb. 1977): 289–304.

20. Jacques Derrida, "Jacques Derrida in Discussion with Christopher Norris," in Papadakis, Cooke, and Benjamin, *Deconstruction: Omnibus Volume*, 75, 71.

21. Hugh J. Silverman and Gary E. Aylesworth, eds. *The Textual Sublime: Deconstruction and Its Differences* (Albany: State University of New York Press, 1990), xii; my emphasis.

On Death and the Contingency of Criticism: Schopenhauer and de Man

Stanley Corngold

> I live so resolutely apart from physical contingencies that my senses
> no longer trouble to inform me of them.
>
> —M. Bloch, in *Remembrance of Things Past*

The reflection on death, at a certain moment in de Man's critical theory, leads to his stressing the contingent character of the act of criticism, but only after it has been singled out for the intensity of its ascetic attitude. Criticism originates from "an asceticism of the mind rather than a plenitude or harmony," writes de Man[1]—hence, from a "strict self-discipline or self-control"[2] that aims to keep the mind "rigorously confined to the disinterestedness of nonempirical thought" (*BI,* 49). To stress, on the other hand, the "contingent" character of criticism is to underscore its dependency "for existence, occurrence, character, etc. on something [else] not yet certain."[3] It takes its course without foundation even in the work with which it is concerned—hence, it is transitory, intermittent, and forever subject to a kind of death. Each of these tendencies is bound up with the other. At the same time that criticism acknowledges its own fragility, it does so with the rigor and completeness of the ascetic attitude.

Within the framework of this book on the crossings of nineteenth-century thought and recent critical theory, the constellation of the terms death, contingency, asceticism, and the aesthetic inevitably leads back to Schopenhauer. "Death" is a key term in Schopenhauer's *Die Welt als*

363

Wille und Vorstellung (The World as Will and Representation); indeed, his whole philosophical enterprise can be seen as a prolonged meditation on death.[4] The truth, for example, that "human desires must be originally and in their essence sinful and reprehensible, and the entire will to live itself reprehensible" is a consequence of "the fact of death."[5] To the fatal contingency of things moved by the will, Schopenhauer opposes the aesthetic attitude—an ataraxy or ascetic calm and undisturbedness of the mortified body. Note that though the terms "aesthetic" and "ascetic" in his case are regularly opposed as distinct forms of escape from the will, this distinction cannot be strictly maintained. Artistic genius, writes Schopenhauer, "is the power of leaving one's own interests, wishes, and aims entirely out of sight, thus of entirely renouncing one's own personality."[6] One cannot imagine a higher degree of self-discipline.

In this essay, I want to explore the modern consciousness of death and the contingency of criticism through the coincidence of features of Schopenhauer's aesthetic and de Man's, especially in early chapters of *Blindness and Insight.* These pages stress the incomplete, because temporally fragile, trajectory of literary interpretation, though not before they make strong claims on behalf of "a transcendental type of self" that speaks from the work to the correlative transcendental self of the interpreter (*BI,* 49). If these selves are "exemplary," it is because they have an ascetic character. De Man, it should be noted, writes about this improved self with remarkable indirectness, as if attempting to avoid, especially in a discussion of contingency, the supposition of essential statement, preferring, instead, to work around the formulations of other writers (chiefly Lukács, Ludwig Binswanger, and Oskar Becker). In this respect too, however, Schopenhauer is the appropriate reference, for even his own dogmatic, "metaphysical" mode of statement aims to restrict the validity of judgments, their own fragility notwithstanding, to actual and hence contingent experience. In this sense, as Charles Larmore observes, Schopenhauer "has a right to be called one of the first 'anti-foundationalists'."[7] What connects Schopenhauer and de Man, therefore, is the consciousness of contingency that informs even their mode of argument; it makes even more radical their conclusion, in which the aesthetic observer is shown outfacing the contingent by an exceptional act of ascetic reflection.

At the same time what *disconnects* Schopenhauer and de Man—I want to state this right away, for it is also the point of my essay—is the different degree of rigor and constancy of the ascetic attitude they hold to be possible within aesthetic experience and hence the degree to which the experience of art might defend against contingency and death. This comparison means specifying the different type of intellectual activity within aesthetics that the obligatory ascesis concentrates. Briefly: for Schopenhauer, the ascesis of aesthetic contemplation issues into an attitude of will-less contemplation of an environing world of will hastening toward death. The exemplary aesthetic observer, the artist himself, abandons his personality "for a time, so as to remain *pure knowing subject,* clear vision of the world; and this not merely at moments, but for a sufficient length of time, and with sufficient consciousness, to enable one to reproduce by deliberate art what has thus been apprehended, and 'to fix in lasting thoughts the wavering images that float before the mind'" (H, 240). For de Man, it is true, poetic activity also figures as a type of immanent, concentrated, stripped-down consciousness pursued as a defense against the empirical human subject, against a death in life. (The empirical subject is already dead in the sense that it exists as the project of "inauthentic" desire, as objectified structures of false consciousness.) The attitude discussed by de Man, however, is not adequately described as "will-less" contemplation. Simply as a kind of theorizing it is active in the spirit of Heidegger's emphasis on the activity of *theoría* that "lets" the poetic object "come towards us in a *tranquil* tarrying alongside."[8] In de Man, in other words, we have to do with a phenomenologically conceived temporality of the act of interpretation and not the ideal time of Platonic contemplation.

Indeed, for the *later* de Man, poetry itself begins to figure forth not the resistance to death but death itself. *"The Triumph of Life,"* for example, "warns us that nothing, whether deed, word, thought, or *text,* ever happens in relation, positive or negative, to anything that precedes, follows, or exists elsewhere, but only as a random event whose power, like the power of *death,* is due to the randomness of its occurrence [emphasis added]."[9] Poetry works a blank nihilistic effect, eliciting this sort of quarrel from Richard Rorty and Harold Bloom. "Bloom is right," says Rorty, "in rejecting de Man's claim that 'every authentic poetic or critical act rehearses the random, meaningless act of death, for which another term is the problematic of language'."[10] I cite this misology to point out that de Man's early representation of poetic ascesis changes. In *The Rhetoric of Romanticism* and in an essay like "Phenomenality and Materiality in Kant,"[11] it undergoes a shift of distinctiveness and privilege, reappearing as the "aesthetic vision" from which even "the phenomenality of the aesthetic" has been subtracted and whatever sweetness or anchorage might be implied there.[12] This ascetic moment in the blank vision itself is won from an art indifferent to any of the effects (cognitive uptake, bliss, *Bildung*, estrangement) that normally warrant its authority. The basic connection, therefore, remains that between Schopenhauer and the earlier de Man. But here, too, I stress the more nearly invariant, essential, completed character of the aesthetic attitude in Schopenhauer; and the more nearly incomplete, contingent, temporal character of de Man's account of poetic reflection, even when the distinction is one of degree only. There are idealizing moments in de Man's first version of the hermeneutic circle of criticism that could occasion some wonder in readers used to his claim for the defectiveness of all such models. Finally, there is this general point connecting de Man and Schopenhauer. In Rorty's words, as he reflects on the history of philosophy peaking in Bloom and de Man, "De Man thought philosophy had given him a sense of the necessary condition of all possible poetry—past, present, and future."[13] (The more accurate word for "philosophy" here is "reflection" on the act of criticism or contemplation). The shared corollary of this view is a depreciation of the unfolding history of the empirical subject as a source of value and meaning, which is radical in Schopenhauer and de Man. In both writers, aesthetics converges on an ethics of renunciation.

The first part of this comparison requires detailed attention to Schopenhauer's aims in inducing an ascesis. I begin by taking up the main directions of his thought—easy to find in a system that undergoes very little development (Thomas Mann noted Schopenhauer's "rigidity, always expanding and buttressing the single notion without a trace of development").[14] The fate of the individual human will apart from the aesthetic demand for contemplation or the ethical demand for renunciation is throughout a negative one, to say the least.

At the end of the second book of *The World as Will and Representation*, entitled "The Objectification of the Will," Schopenhauer writes,

> Eternal becoming, endless flux, characterizes the revelation of the inner nature of will. The same thing shows itself in human endeavors and desires, which always delude us by presenting their satisfaction as the final end of will. As soon as we attain to them they no longer appear the

same, and therefore they soon grow stale, are forgotten, and though not openly disowned, are yet always thrown aside as vanished illusions. We are fortunate enough if there still remains something to wish for and to strive after, that the game may be kept up of constant transition from desire to satisfaction, and from satisfaction to a new desire, the rapid course of which is called happiness, and the slow course sorrow, and does not sink into that stagnation that shows itself in fearful ennui that paralyses life, vain yearning without a definite object, deadening languor. (H, 214-15, sec. 29)

The career of the individual human will is suffering; indeed, "all life is essentially suffering"—this is Schopenhauer writing in (section 57 of) his fourth book, entitled "The Assertion and Denial of the Will to Live, when Self-Consciousness Has Been Attained." Suffering is the product of being in time. The finite life is perishable, and we feel or ought to feel this perishing as a foreboding of death.

The human individual finds himself as finite in infinite space and time, and consequently as a vanishing quantity compared with them. He is projected into them, and, on account of their unlimited nature, he has always a merely relative, never absolute *when* and *where* of his existence; for his place and duration are finite parts of what is infinite and boundless. His real existence is only in the present, whose unchecked flight into the past is a constant transition into death, a constant dying.

No digression from this "flight" is possible at the order of lived experience.

The present is always passing through his hands into the past; the future is quite uncertain and always short. Thus his existence, even when we consider only its formal side, is a constant hurrying of the present into the dead past, a constant dying. . . . This life of our body is only a constantly prevented dying, an ever-postponed death: finally, in the same way, the activity of our mind is a constantly deferred ennui.
. . . In the end, death must conquer, for we become subject to him through birth, and he only plays for a little while with his prey before he swallows it up. We pursue our life, however, with great interest and much solicitude as long as possible, as we blow out a soap-bubble as long and as large as possible, although we know perfectly well that it will burst. (H, 401–2)

All work, all desire, is an unconscious delaying tactic. Yet there remains another, more resolute attitude toward the will available to us as "subjects of knowledge"—a comportment more nearly ethical, for it sees the stakes involved. This is the attitude achieved by the creator of works of art and made available to the contemplator of these works by virtue of a sort of separation that takes place in the artist between his empirical subject and his "pure will-less subject of knowledge."

The work of art, for Schopenhauer, produces a suspension of desire: it invites, indeed it "compels" (H, 272) the desiring mind to lose itself and its anchorage in the will in contemplation of aesthetic objects.[15] These objects, it turns out, for Schopenhauer as for Plato, are the Ideas "behind" the phenomena and the true content of perception. The aesthetic attitude mobilizes a type of perception leading to knowledge of the *forms* of empirical experience over and against an awareness of the blindness of the will.

"The pleasure we receive from all beauty," continues Schopenhauer,

> the consolation which art affords, the enthusiasm of the artist, which enables him to forget the cares of life,—the latter an advantage of the man of genius over other men, which alone repays him for the suffering that increases in proportion to the clearness of consciousness, and for the desert loneliness among men of a different race,—all this rests on the fact that the in-itself of life, the will, existence itself, is . . . a constant sorrow, partly miserable, partly terrible; while, on the contrary, as idea alone, purely contemplated, or copied by art, free from pain, it presents to us a drama full of significance. This purely knowable side of the world and the copy of it in any art, is the element of the artist. He is chained [note change of tone!] to the contemplation of the play, the objectification of will; he remains beside it, does not get tired of contemplating it and representing it in copies; and meanwhile he bears himself the cost of the production of that play, i.e. he himself is the will which objectifies itself, and remains in constant suffering.[16] That pure, true, and deep knowledge of the inner nature of the world becomes now for him an end in itself: he stops there. (H, 345-46)

It might be supposed, from rumors about Schopenhauer spread, for one, by Nietzsche's mistaken polemic, that he gives a radical sort of security to the ascesis of aesthetic contemplation, but this is manifestly not the case. He says it plainly enough:

> Therefore it does not become to him a quieter of the will as . . . it does in the case of the saint who has attained to resignation; it does not deliver him forever from life, but only at moments, and is therefore not for him a path out of life, but only an occasional consolation in it . . .

[till his power, increased by this contemplation and at last tired of the play, lays hold on the real]. (H, 345–46)

The option of genuine quietude is reserved for the saint. Only in him do we encounter the full ascesis of which the artist has glimmerings—a fullness that our own limited space constrains us to pass over in respectful silence.

Ten years ago I wrote about de Man: "He reads all local instances of indetermination only to point to a universal void of indetermination. The audacious surmise arises that de Manian rigor is not at all proof against (metaphysical) pathos—a pathos that appears to owe more to Schopenhauer (at least in Nietzsche's polemical assault on him) than it does to the historical, social, rhetorical tradition of Aristotle, Hegel, and Nietzsche."[17] I think this is right.

Here is de Man's ascetic poetic, which amounts to a practice of concentration on a moment of disparity or divergence as between the empirical person defined by desires and intentions and the so-called pure aesthetic intentionality. In the chapter in *Blindness and Insight* chiefly dealing with the psychiatrist Ludwig Binswanger (both Binswanger and de Man gain leverage from Lukács's early essay "The Subject-Object Relation in Aesthetics" of 1917), de Man writes, paraphrasing Lukács,

> But this totality of the [artistic] form by no means implies a corre-sponding totality of the constitutive self. Neither in its origin, nor in its later development does the completeness of the form proceed from a fulfilment of the person who constitutes this form. [Recall Schopen-hauer: the artist continues to suffer—at least intermittently.] The dis-tinction between the personal form of the author and the self that reaches a measure of totality in the work becomes concretely manifest in these divergent destinies. The divergence is not a contingent acci-dent but is constitutive of the work of art as such. Art originates in and by means of the *divergence* [emphasis added]. (*BI*, 41)

This passage is very interesting. The divergence is constitutive of art— it is not itself contingent. It is a principle; and because it is a principle, it has the power, necessarily, to repeat its action in the reader. Something of this principled power that, following Lukács, de Man attributes to the text, he will go on attributing to texts, witness the comment in his preface to Carol

Jacobs's book *The Dissimulating Harmony* (in 1978): "The text imposes its own understanding and shapes the reader's evasions."[18] The remark is most interesting when the "evasion" it identifies in the reader is grasped as his resistance to self-consciousness, as a movement antithetical to the exemplary divergence by means of which the work of art originates. In imposing its own understanding, the text imposes a general truth, something that it "knows" qua text. This is, precisely, the knowledge of the futility of associating desires and intentions with fulfilled ends, including the cognitive ends of science.

This argument about divergence fits well with other things de Man published at the beginning of *Blindness and Insight*. There, glancing at Homer, he writes,

> [The beauty of Helen] prefigures the beauty of all future narratives as entities that point to their own fictional nature. The self-reflecting mirror-effect by means of which a work of fiction asserts, by its very existence, its separation from empirical reality, its divergence, as a sign, from a meaning that depends for its existence on the constitutive activity of this sign, characterizes the work of literature in its essence [emphasis added]. . . . [The assertion of the priority of fiction over reality] transcends the notion of a nostalgia or a desire, since it discovers desire as a fundamental pattern of being that discards any possibility of satisfaction. (*BI*, 17)

Thus, literary language—as we read now in another essay in *Blindness and Insight*, "Form and Intent in the American New Criticism,"

> does not fulfil a plenitude but originates in the void that separates intent from reality. The imagination takes its flight only after the void, the inauthenticity of the existential project[,] has been revealed; literature begins where the existential demystification ends and the critic has no need to linger over this preliminary stage. Considerations of the actual and historical existence of writers are a waste of time from a critical viewpoint. These regressive stages can only reveal an emptiness of which the writer himself is well aware when he begins to write. Many great writers have described the loss of reality that marks the beginning of poetic states of mind. (*BI*, 34–35)

De Man instances Baudelaire: "[T]out pour moi devient allégorie." The condition of grasping allegory, i.e. literature, is the obliteration of the empirical personality.

"Considerations of the actual and historical existence of writers are a waste of time from a critical viewpoint." At the same time, the purging of aesthetic consciousness does not drive out one distinctive cognition: the paradoxical knowledge of the irreducibly fictional and hence noncognitive character of literature, the insight into its quasi-Platonic form as fiction. Fitted into a Schopenhauerian frame, this translates as: "Considerations of artists as contingent personalities are a waste of time from the aesthetic standpoint." The fit is perfect; it is the heart of what Schopenhauer gives to de Man. What de Man does not take, however, is Schopenhauer's view of art's contemplative benefit: art gives knowledge of the Ideas of the objects constituting worldly experience. De Man's more radical asceticism drives off knowledge, in the sense of a science of the given, from the stage of the aesthetic performance. He performs this ascesis in the moment in which he calls art a *fiction*. "Considerations of . . . actual and historical existence," not only of writers, "are a waste of time from a critical viewpoint."

A crucial concluding question that should engage us is: how rigorously in de Man is this ascetic claim asserted? In other words, What performative power has the pure aesthetic intentionality in the work of art? The jolt out of the stupefaction of contingent desires and interests is produced by a certain understanding conveyed to us through the work of art. What is the fate of this understanding? Does it not itself have a temporal, a contingent character?

It is precisely de Man, in the earlier essay, who forces this doubt on us. In "Form and Intent in the American New Criticism" he writes,

> The hermeneutic understanding is always, by its very nature, lagging behind: to understand something is to realize that one had always known it, but, at the same time, to face the mystery of this hidden knowledge. Understanding can be called complete only when it becomes aware of its own temporal predicament and realizes that the horizon within which the totalization can take place is time itself. The act of understanding is a temporal act that has its own history, but this history forever eludes totalization. (*BI*, 32)

This history forever eludes totalization. The act of understanding cannot be contemplated from the standpoint of complete divergence as a complete divergence, because the moment of divergence is itself essentially incomplete, essentially contingent. It too has its own career in time—necessarily, of dispersion and loss. This can be summed up in the words of David L. Clark: "De Man's sense of the temporal flux of understanding itself implicates and disrupts his early Schopenhauerism."[19]

One continues to find in the later de Man a Schopenhauerian near-equivalence of the aesthetic and the ascetic with its bordering claim on the autonomy or steadfastness of the contemplator. Here de Man does not so much extirpate the Schopenhauerian root of *Blindness and Insight* as displace its mode and aim. "De Man continues to have a certain Schopenhauerian stake or faith in the notion of aesthetic contemplation," continues Clark, "but both the mode and the object of this ascesis change: *from* resistance to death thought of as contingency (sheer flux) *to* identification with death thought of as materiality (sheer stasis)." This is quite true.

De Man's reflections on poetry at the end of his life think death differently; they think it "materially." Quite another concept of death is in play in the aesthetic.[20] Death means, at the beginning, a kind of entropy, a maximum of contingency and dispersion; ascetic concentration, exacted by the poem, defends against it. Now another kind of death is figured through the hardness and materiality of the letter, a state resistant to reflexive consciousness: this kind of death compels, in turn, the reader's stony gaze. De Man writes, apropos of Kant's text on the sublime, of "the *pure materiality* of *Augenschein*, of aesthetic vision [emphasis added]." But this only leaves open another question: whether the gaze of the interpreter can in any sense be stony, whether the interpreter can himself be as steadfast as stone, and whether the letter does not read him differently.

Indeed, readers of *The Resistance to Theory* (1986) should be puzzled to learn that deconstructive, "technically correct rhetorical readings" could nonetheless be "totalizing" and even "potentially totalitarian."[21] To achieve such readings, readers would have to arrest the essential instability and elusiveness of acts of understanding. It is suggestive that de Man at this late stage conveys an image of death in the hardening of matter: the rigorous, technically correct reading could then be grounded on the rigor mortis of the literary object. The factor of hardening in the work serves as the metaphor of that divergence that steadily maintains the knowledge of divergence. It provokes in the reader the equivalence of its own already-deadness in a *Verfestigung*— "a hardening, solidifying, strengthening, stabilizing, consolidating"—of the gap by means of which the technically proficient self diverges from its empirical counterpart. That this gap might produce an assured technical competence, however, is an error, for the gap could never be sustained.

Certainly de Man is not unaware of this difficulty and proceeds to retract it through a logical move that, incidentally, seems incredible. Technically correct rhetorical readings, he writes, "are also totalizing (and potentially totalitarian),

> for since the structures and functions they expose do not lead to the knowledge of an entity (such as language) but are an unreliable process of knowledge production that prevents all entities, including linguistic entities, from coming into discourse as such, they are indeed universals, consistently defective models of language's impossibility to be a model language. (*RT*, 19)

This provision means to ward off a falling-back that would indeed be Schopenhauerian: for even if the "technically correct reading" does not give reliably complete knowledge of contingent entities (the materials of perception), it is nonetheless in danger of so doing at one remove—namely, of giving reliable knowledge of the workings of figures, the principles that regulate the rhetoric by which the illusion of a world of natural objects is produced.[22]

De Man withdraws from this danger on the edge of the thinnest of logical razors. He wants to keep for "reading," for his tense version of "aesthetic contemplation," a moment of knowledge. He wants to keep an epistemological privilege for the reading of texts that are rhetorically complex enough—for "literature." The insight uniquely granted by reading must be nonsubstantive, not a knowledge of entities; it could not be more than the bare aura of knowledge. So the saving formulation fuses total reliability (the totalizing reading) with total contingency ("unreliability," "consistent defectiveness") in a kind of negative knowledge. It is bemusing to consider how well the formulation I shall now cite fits de Man's conclusion:

> All that can be left behind when the [perspective of the subject] has been surmounted is a kind of nothing. . . . Even this nothing turns out to be a kind of something, a negative form of knowledge; but at least one has now shed the illusion of a positive mode of transcendence.

The words are Terry Eagleton's to describe Schopenhauer's aesthetic. But in leaving out of Schopenhauer's moment of knowledge the element of Platonic science, Eagleton makes Schopenhauer more of a late de Manian than he is and early de Man less nearly a Schopenhauerian than he is.[23]

A scholar of Schopenhauer, William Desmond, puts this conjuncture as the following predicament:

> Art itself has become so "aestheticized" that it is a genuine question as to how seriously we can take it anymore. Even were one to accept the Schopenhauerian assumption, we are still left, however, with having to swallow the notion of an unintelligible rupture [N.B. what we have been calling "divergence"] between the dark origin and the saving reversal that art is said to effect. If the dark origin is the whole, then the reversal, while seeming to free us from the origin's irrationality, takes place within its embrace, and will inevitably be swallowed by the absurdity that supports and surrounds it. If this is the truth of being, then art as a meaningful consolation is in the end just metaphysical whistling in the dark, no matter how elegant, plaintive or intense its song.[24]

"Intense," for my purposes, is the important word here: it means "concentrated," hence informed by an ascetic suspension of will.

The essential constitutive principle of a rupture or divergence from contingency remains a feint only. Desmond's excavation of the great contradiction in Schopenhauer disqualifies de Man's late claims to the authority of technically correct readings. We could indeed linger at the point where de Man, both early and late, does often stop, in a heightened contemplation, not void of pathos, of the only fragile though repetitive character of the feint.

Or we could ask further: if only a feint, and not a principle, then the factor of "divergence" is not essential. It, too, is without foundation—unsteady, feigned. A host of different questions then becomes inevitable: What are the conditions of possibility (historical, political—circumstantial) under which the feint that generates the illusion of art can take place? How much (political) alienation, how much depression or despair, must be overcome to enable such a feigned thing as this "divergence" enabling "technically correct rhetorical readings" to occur?

Schopenhauer, it seems, had to be corrected by Marx; de Man is being corrected—has already been corrected to death—by types of historicism, and also psychoanalysis, feminism, and breeds of postmodernism at once more lurid and more egalitarian. The tendency of all these modes is to demythologize the moment of aesthetic rapture. This has happened with blinding speed, some of it to the good. Adorno, for one, excoriated the myopia of "the belief in a culture of spirit *[Geist]* which, for its ideal of self-sufficient purity, renounces the realization of its content and abandons reality to power and its blindness."[25] But as it proved needful, in turn, to correct Marx by means of an existential phenomenology of the human subject, I believe it is urgent now to reacquaint ourselves, with due intensity, with the human subject at a level powerful enough to engender its refusal to be subjected to contingent powers—to society, language, the unconscious. Thus we need to reacquaint ourselves with the attitude of ascetic concentration on texts, which, whether acknowledged or not, was Schopenhauer's legacy to de Man[26]—study to know the thing itself before we are satisfied to do its history.

POSTSCRIPT

Baudelaire wrote: "Modernity is the transient, the fleeting, the contingent; it is the one half of art, the other being the eternal and the immutable."

Commentary. When everywhere we are surrounded by inhuman simulacra in slack play with the journalistically "real"—a hypertext without perceptible grammar—the moment of ascetic aversion may be the last, the only resource of the human. Just say "No" to contingency.

Notes

1. Paul de Man, *Blindness and Insight: Essays in the Rhetoric of Contemporary Criticism*, 2d ed. rev. (Minneapolis: University of Minnesota Press, 1983), 49. Citations from this work henceforth appear in text as *BI* with appropriate page number.

2. *Random House Dictionary of the English Language*, 2d edition, unabridged (1987), s.v. "askesis."

3. Ibid., s.v. "contingency."

4. "It would not be an exaggeration to say that death is the phenomenon which ultimately preoccupied Schopenhauer, the hub of the wheel from which all his various doctrines radiate like spokes." Michael Fox, "Schopenhauer on Death, Suicide, and Self-Renunciation," in *Schopenhauer: His Philosophical Achievement*, ed. Michael Fox (Totowa, N.J.: Barnes & Noble, 1980), 147–48. Cited (and interestingly resisted) in David Cartwright, "Schopenhauer on Suffering, Death, Guilt, and the Consolation of Metaphysics," in *Schopenhauer: New Essays in Honor of his 200th Birthday*, vol. 10 of *Studies in German Thought and History*, ed. Eric von der Luft (Lewiston, N.Y.: Edwin Mellen, 1988), 55.

5. *Arthur Schopenhauer: Essays and Aphorisms*, ed. R. J. Hollingdale (Harmondsworth: Penguin, 1970), 63.

6. *The World as Will and Idea by Arthur Schopenhauer*, vol. 1, trans. R. B. Haldane and J. Kemp (London: Kegan Paul, Trench & Trübner, 1907), 240. Citations from this edition, much more readable than the allegedly more accurate translation by E. F. J. Payne (New York: Dover, 1966), henceforth figure in the text of this essay in parentheses: thus the citation above would appear as (H, 240). I have checked the Haldane and Kemp translation and made adjustments when necessary.

7. Charles Larmore, "Where There's a Will," review of *Schopenhauer and the Wild Years of Philosophy*, by Rüdiger Safranski, *The New Republic*, 4 March 1991, 39.

8. Martin Heidegger, *Being and Time*, trans. John Macquarrie and Edward Robinson (New York: Harper and Row, 1962), 177.

9. De Man, *The Rhetoric of Romanticism* (New York: Columbia University Press, 1984), 122.

10. The fuller citation reads: "The most important difference between Bloom and Paul de Man . . . is that de Man thought philosophy had given him a sense of the necessary condition of all possible poetry—past, present, and future. I think that Bloom is right in rejecting de Man's claim that 'every authentic poetic or critical act rehearses the random, meaningless act of death, for which another term is the problematic of language' (Bloom, *Agon* [Oxford University Press, 1982], 29)." Richard Rorty, *Contingency, Irony, and Solidarity* (Cambridge: Cambridge University Press, 1989), 25.

11. In Gary Shapiro and Anthony Sica, eds., *Hermeneutics: Questions and Prospects* (Amherst: University of Massachusetts Press, 1984).

12. This reduction occurs apropos of de Man's reading of Kant's sublime in the *Critique of Aesthetic Judgment*, in "Phenomenality and Materiality in Kant," 143.

13. Ibid.

14. The full entry in Thomas Mann's diary for 31 January 1938, reads: "Talked to Golo about Schopenhauer, his beleaguered position vis-à-vis professional philosophers, his being essentially a European man of letters, his friends Jewish, his character only half German, his rigidity, always expanding and buttressing the single notion without a trace of development" (Thomas Mann, *Diaries 1918–1939*, selection and foreword by Hermann Kesten, trans. Richard Winston and Clara Winston [New York: Harry N. Abrams, 1982], 293. Mann's comment on Schopenhauer could remind us of de Man's invariant view of all literature and every "critic's task"—"a task which we can only do empirically, by exercising it upon particular forms among different authors, knowing that they are 'windowless monads' and that basically they are all saying the same thing" *(Les chemins actuels de la critique* [Paris: UGE, 1968], 86; my translation).

15. The question arises: How could the work of art, which floats constitutively above the world of will, keep this distinction and yet "compel" the desiring mind? I owe this perception of contradiction, as well as that in note 16 infra, to Catherine Perry.

16. Schopenhauer's ascription here of constant suffering to the artist contradicts his earlier statement (H, 240, cited earlier) that the artist "abandons" the sufferings of his personality "not merely at moments, but for a sufficient length of time."

17. "Error in Paul de Man," in *The Yale Critics: Deconstruction in America*, ed. Jonathan Arac, Wlad Godzich, and Wallace Martin (Minneapolis: University of Minneapolis Press, 1983), 102.

18. De Man, introduction to Carol Jacobs, *The Dissimulating Harmony: The Image of Interpretation in Nietzsche, Rilke, Artaud, and Benjamin* (Baltimore: Johns Hopkins University Press, 1978), 5.

19. David L. Clark, letter to the author, 8 August 1992.

20. This will remind us—as David Clark also suggests—"that 'death' itself is an eminently contingent trope in de Man's texts, . . . constructed and reconstructed from moment to moment in his critical itinerary." I am saying, of course, that this itinerary is willy-nilly informed by the figure of Schopenhauer.

21. De Man, *The Resistance to Theory* (Minneapolis: University of Minnesota Press, 1986), 19.

22. De Man's account in "Phenomenality and Materiality in Kant" of a passage from Kant testifies to such a science: "Such personified scenes of consciousness are . . . not actually descriptions of mental functions but descriptions of tropological transformations. They are not governed by the laws of the mind but by the *laws of figural language*" (emphasis added) (141).

23. Terry Eagleton, *The Ideology of the Aesthetic* (Oxford: Basil Blackwell, 1990), 170.

24. William Desmond, "Schopenhauer, Art, and the Dark Origin," in Luft, *Schopenhauer: New Essays*, 122.

25. Theodor Adorno, "On the Question: 'What Is German?'" trans. Thomas Y. Levin, *New German Critique* 36 (Fall 1985): 127.

26. The metaphor of the "legacy" tells only a small part of the story. Another metaphor is also necessary to suggest how de Man—or more precisely the reading of de Man—is changed by this gift. De Man does not only consume his legacy; he is himself consumed by it, in the sense that as its recipient his thought is de-idealized and is then situated otherwise in history. The reverse is also true. The very existence of this paper proves that *de Man's legacy to Schopenhauer* is also in circulation—one specific enough to provoke a renewed sense of the centrality of Schopenhauer's thesis on asceticism to modern critical theory.

Notes on Contributors

ANDREW BOWIE is Professor of European Philosophy at Anglia Polytechnic University, Cambridge, England. He is the author of *Aesthetics and Subjectivity: From Kant to Nietzsche* (Manchester University Press, 1990), *Schelling and Modern European Philosophy: An Introduction* (Routledge, 1993), and has translated and edited Schelling's *On the History of Modern Philosophy* (Cambridge University Press, 1994).

JUDITH BUTLER is Professor of Rhetoric and Comparative Literature at the University of California, Berkeley. She is the author of *Subjects of Desire: Hegelian Reflections in Twentieth-Century France* (Columbia University Press, 1987), *Gender Trouble: Feminism and the Subversion of Identity* (Routledge, 1990), and *Bodies that Matter: On the Discursive Limits of "Sex"* (Routledge, 1993). She is coeditor of *Feminists Theorize the Political* (Routledge, 1992), and of *Erotic Welfare: Sexual Theory and Politics in the Age of Epidemic* (Routledge, 1993).

MARK A. CHEETHAM is the author of *Alex Colville: The Observer Observed* (Essays in Canadian Writing Press, 1994), *The Rhetoric of Purity: Essentialist Theory and the Advent of Abstract Painting* (Cambridge University Press, 1991), and *Remembering Postmodernism: Trends in Recent Canadian Art* (Oxford University Press, 1991; French edition, 1992), and coeditor of *Meanings and Methods: Art History from the 1990s* (Cambridge University Press, forthcoming) and *Theory Between the Disciplines: Authority/Vision/Politics* (University of Michigan Press, 1990). He has also published numerous articles in the fields of Canadian and European art and art theory of the eighteenth, nineteenth, and twentieth centuries. He is Professor in the Visual Arts Department at the University of Western Ontario.

DAVID L. CLARK is Associate Professor of English at McMaster University. He is the author of essays in *Studies in Romanticism*, *The Wordsworth Circle*, and

Recherches Sémiotiques/Semiotic Inquiry. He is contributor to and coeditor of *New Romanticisms: Theory and Critical Practice* (University of Toronto Press, 1994), and has contributed essays to *The Mind in Creation: Essays on English Romantic Literature in Honour of Ross G. Woodman* (McGill-Queen's University Press, 1992) and *Negation, Critical Theory, and Postmodern Textuality* (Kluwer, 1994).

STANLEY CORNGOLD is Professor of German and Comparative Literature at Princeton University. He is the author of *The Fate of the Self: German Writers and French Theory* (Columbia University Press, 1986; revised paperback edition, Duke University Press, 1994), *Franz Kafka: The Necessity of Form* (Cornell University Press, 1988), *Borrowed Lives* (with Irene Giersing) (State University of New York Press, 1991), and a volume provisionally entitled *Forms of Feeling: Tensions in German Literature* (University of Nebraska Press, forthcoming).

PAUL HAMILTON was a fellow of Exeter College, Oxford, and is now Professor and Head of the Department of English at the University of Southampton. He is the author of *Coleridge's Poetics* (Blackwell, 1983), *Wordsworth* (Harvester, 1986) and has contributed to *Rethinking Historicism: Critical Readings in Romantic History* (Oxford, 1989).

NED LUKACHER is Professor of English at the University of Illinois, Chicago. He is the author of *Primal Scenes: Literature, Philosophy, Psychoanalysis* (Cornell University Press, 1986), and *Daemonic Figures: Shakespeare and the Question of Conscience* (Cornell University Press, 1994). He is editor and translator of Jacques Derrida's *Cinders* (University of Nebraska Press, 1991), for which he also provides a critical introduction, called "Mourning Becomes Telepathy."

ERIC MEYER is Assistant Professor of English at the University of Louisville. His articles have appeared in *Criticism, ELH*, and elsewhere. He is currently working on a study of romantic poetry and nineteenth-century historiography.

JEAN-PIERRE MILEUR is Professor of English at the University of California, Riverside. He is the author of *Vision and Revision: Coleridge's Art of Immanence* (University of California Press, 1982), *Literary Revisionism and the Burden of Modernity* (University of California Press, 1985), *The Critical Romance* (University of Wisconsin Press, 1990), and coauthor of *Nietzsche's Case: Philosophy as/ and Literature* (Routledge, 1992).

CHRISTOPHER NORRIS is Professor of Philosophy at the University of Wales in Cardiff. His books include *The Deconstructive Turn: Essays in the Rhetoric of*

Philosophy (Methuen, 1983), *The Contest of Faculties: Philosophy and Theory after Deconstruction* (Methuen, 1985), *Derrida* (Harvard University Press, 1987), *Paul de Man: Deconstruction and the Critique of Aesthetic Ideology* (Routledge, 1988), and *What's Wrong with Postmodernism? Critical Theory and the Ends of Philosophy* (Johns Hopkins University Press, 1990).

THOMAS PFAU is Assistant Professor in the Department of English at Duke University. He is translator and editor of *Idealism and the Endgame of Theory: Three Essays by F. W. J. Schelling* (State University of New York Press, 1993), and *Friedrich Hölderlin: Essays and Letters on Theory* (State University of New York Press, 1987). He is currently at work on *Immediacy and Cultural Dissolution: Poetic Style and Cultural Motives in Wordsworth.*

ARKADY PLOTNITSKY teaches in the departments of English and Comparative Literature at the University of Pennsylvania. He is the author of *In the Shadow of Hegel: Complementarity, History and the Unconscious* (University Press of Florida, 1993), *Reconfigurations: Constraints and Possibilities in Interpretation and Theory* (University Press of Florida, 1993), and *Complementarity: Anti-Epistemology After Bohr and Derrida* (Duke University Press, 1994).

TILOTTAMA RAJAN has taught at Queen's University and the University of Wisconsin-Madison, and is currently Professor of English at the University of Western Ontario, where she also teaches in the Centre for the Study of Theory and Criticism. She is the author of *Dark Interpreter: The Discourse of Romanticism* (Cornell University Press, 1980) and *The Supplement of Reading: Figures of Understanding in Romantic Theory and Practice* (Cornell University Press, 1990). She is currently working on two books: *Romantic Narrative* and *Deconstruction Before and After Post-Structuralism* (of which the present essay forms a part).

JOHN SALLIS is W. Alton Jones Professor of Philosophy at Vanderbilt University. He is the author of numerous books, including *Delimitations—Phenomenology and the End of Metaphysics* (Indiana University Press, 1986), *Spacings of Reason and Imagination in Texts of Kant, Fichte, Hegel* (University of Chicago Press, 1987), *Echoes: after Heidegger* (Indiana University Press, 1990), *Crossings: Nietzsche and the Space of Tragedy* (University of Chicago Press, 1990), and *Stone* (Indiana University Press, 1994).

Index

abjection, the abject, 110, 187–88, 194–95

Abrams, M.H., 336, 338

absolute, the, 28–30, 128, 132, 247, 250, 294, 305, 338; absolute identity, 127, 248, 250; absolute knowledge, 24, 113, 272–73, 294; absolute origin, 276; absolute subject, 289, 292–93, 295; aesthetic or literary absolute, 23, 27–28, 30, 269, 304, 326–35; linguistic absolute, 16, 166; philosophical absolute, 27–28

Adorno, Theodor W., 23, 32, 161, 210–11, 243–46, 249–59, 287, 290, 296, 303, 308, 311, 319, 375

aesthetic, the, 363–64, 368, 371–73; aesthetic education (aesthetic rationality), 295–96, 298–300

Agamben, Giorgio, 35n

allegory, 249–50, 346, 370

alterity, otherness (the Other), 12, 19–20, 86, 89, 98, 102, 111, 118, 125–26, 133, 136, 176, 180–82, 184, 186, 208, 249, 278–79, 281, 292; as interiorized outside, 92

Altieri, Charles, 242

Althusser, Louis, 3, 26, 159, 165, 295, 304–5, 311, 316

Aristotle, 62, 64–67, 71, 94, 103, 227, 369

art, 10–11, 15, 25, 30–31, 60–61, 243–44, 249–50, 259, 296, 330, 363, 365, 368–69, 371–72, 374; Hegel on, 3, 61–62, 68–77; Heidegger on,

62, 77; Kristeva on, 158, 163–65; Nietzsche on, 77, 151–53, 163–65, 167n; Schopenhauer on, 61. *See also* literature, music, visual arts

Artaud, Antonin, 163

asceticism, mortification, 18, 31–32, 148, 130, 167, 174–75, 185–87, 189, 191, 330, 344, 363–66, 368–69, 374–75. *See also* sadism/masochism

Austin, J. L., 21–22, 34n, 226–27, 233–36, 238–39

Baader, Frantz von, 128

Babbitt, Irving, 303

Baillie, Sir James, 17

Barnard, Philip and Cheryl Lester, 327, 330, 332–37

Barthes, Roland, 166, 311, 319

Bataille, Georges, 24, 26, 30, 160, 271, 273, 278–79, 281, 306–7, 310

Baudelaire, Charles, 317, 370, 375

Baudrillard, Jean, 165, 287, 298

Becker, Oskar, 364

Behler, Ernst, 167n

Benjamin, Jessica, 195n

Benjamin, Walter, 6, 246, 249, 294

Bennington, Geoffrey, 123

Berlin, Isaiah, 308

Binswanger, Ludwig, 364, 369

Blair, Hugh, 150

Blake, William, 85, 269, 355

Blanchot, Maurice, 23, 30, 79, 108, 155

Bloch, Ernst, 165

Blondel, Eric, 153